Educating the Retarded Child

SAMUEL A. KIRK , *1904 =*
Professor of Special Education, University of Illinois

G. ORVILLE JOHNSON
Professor of Special Education, Syracuse University

HOUGHTON MIFFLIN COMPANY

The Riverside Press Cambridge

TO Frank E. Baker, *leader, educator, courageous innovator, and friend, whose vision, sympathy, and faith in human beings find ever-new expression in the work of those who have come within the wide circle of his influence*

Preface

Early in our history the education of the retarded child was the function of the home or of an institution. Today it is commonly accepted as being a function of the school.

After the compulsory education laws were passed in the latter part of the nineteenth century the schools found more and more mentally retarded children in attendance. Since many of these children were so retarded that they could receive little benefit from the regular school curriculum, teachers, administrators, and others associated with public-school education realized that some type of special facilities would have to be provided to meet this problem. It was recognized that educating these children who could not learn as fast as the average child was the responsibility of the community and the state. Since the mentally retarded could not benefit sufficiently from the instruction they received in the regular classes, some type of adapted instruction became a necessity. As a result, the first special classes were organized for retarded children at the turn of the century. Marked growth of public-school special classes has followed their initial organization. Only fifty years later, almost one hundred thousand retarded children were in attendance, and there is no reason to suspect that this growth has ceased.

The legislatures of many states are now appropriating large sums of money for the organization of classes for retarded children in the public schools. The number of states having legislation designed to aid this group is steadily increasing.

Educating retarded children by appropriate procedures has been shown to be of value to the individual and to society. Through an educational program adapted to their needs and capacities, they are able (1) to lead fuller and personally more satisfying lives, (2) to develop a better understanding of their own problems and make a better adjustment to them, (3) to become more socially adequate, and (4) to achieve greater economic independence. From the point of view of the state and society it is economically sound to educate the retarded child. It is less costly to provide a special education program that will enable these persons to care for themselves either partially or totally than it is to support them on public relief or in institutions for the feeble-minded or the delinquent.

Efforts have been made to educate retarded children for the past century and a half. There is, however, a great paucity of organized, educational literature on the subject. The available material on retarded children is widely scattered among numerous journals from different disciplines, since the retarded child has been of interest to doctors, educators, psychologists, sociologists, and others in related fields.

The purpose of *Educating the Retarded Child* is to (1) present the information from various sources, (2) synthesize the materials into a meaningful sequence, (3) develop programs of rehabilitation and instruction for these children, and (4) describe the teaching procedures used with them. It has been written for students, teachers, supervisors, administrators, psychologists, and others interested in the problems of children who are retarded in intelligence. It is designed to present a comprehensive description of the problem with suggested methods for its solution.

Throughout the book an effort has been made to include both theory and practice. It is hoped that the approach will give some perspective and lessen the tendency to consider mental deficit as a static problem which can be solved only by institutionalization. For the teacher we have tried to present a theoretical basis as a matrix integrated with the principles and techniques for teaching the mentally retarded. For the psychologist an effort has been made to relate the aims and facilities for teaching these children to the psychological problems faced in their diagnosis. For the pediatrician we have hoped to give a picture of social and educational potentialities so that he may direct the parent to existing facilities.

For the social worker we have tried to delineate the contribution of education toward the life adjustment of these children. The vocational guidance expert may find help in interpreting and organizing the abilities and disabilities of these children in the direction of better training and better placement.

Acknowledgements are made to authors, publishers, and journals who have been very generous in granting permission to use quoted materials from books, pamphlets, and periodicals.

The authors wish to express their indebtedness to Robert L. Erdman for his help in revising and adding recent publications to the "Selected Annotated Bibliography"; to Ivan Garrison for many of the examples used in the "Secondary-School Program" in Chapter 10 and the "Sociodrama" in Chapter 15; and to Dr. Robert H. Haskell for his review and criticism of the "Wayne County Training School Experiment in Self-Determination" also used in Chapter 15.

Special appreciation is expressed to the authors' wives, Winifred Day Kirk and Margarete Gesch Johnson, for their critical evaluation and editorial assistance in the preparation of the manuscript.

SAMUEL A. KIRK
G. ORVILLE JOHNSON

Contents

PART THREE

Special-Class Programs

PART FOUR

Special Teaching Procedures

PART ONE

❧

Classification, Etiology, and Diagnosis

Chapter 1

Children With Low Intelligence

CHILDREN WITH LOW INTELLIGENCE have been of interest to numerous workers — physicians, psychologists, educators, sociologists, geneticists, and others — and each has evolved his own classification, concepts, and terminology. As a result, the beginning student becomes quite confused with such different terms as feebleminded, mentally deficient, amentia, dementia, slow learner, mentally handicapped, idiot, imbecile, moron, oligophrenia, exogenous, endogenous, and many other terms designed to denote children with low intelligence.

This chapter will review briefly the different classifications of children with low intelligence and discuss a unified classification designed for educational purposes rather than for clinical diagnosis.

CLASSIFICATION ACCORDING TO DEGREE

Children with low intelligence differ in degree of mental deficit. Consequently, one of the common classifications of such children is based upon the degree of the defect. This classification emphasizes quantitative rather than qualitative differences; it differentiates children according to degree of deficit rather than kind. For this purpose the following subdivisions have been used:

3

IDIOT

The category indicating the greatest degree of defect is that of idiocy. A child who is an idiot is so low intellectually that he does not learn to talk and usually does not learn to take care of his bodily needs. These children require complete custodial care and supervision, since they cannot be trained even in the simple routines of daily life and do not possess the ability to learn to survive without external support. Idiots have been generally classified as those persons having I.Q.'s of 0 to 20 or 25 on psychometric tests.

IMBECILE

An imbecile represents the next level in the intelligence scale. An imbecile will probably develop some language, be trained to care for his bodily needs, and have trainability as far as daily habits and routines are concerned. He will, however, require supervision and care in his home or in institutions throughout his life. In terms of I.Q. the imbecile rates between 20 or 25 and 40 or 50 on intelligence tests. The criteria upon which an individual is classified as an imbecile also include whether he is uneducable in social and occupational areas. He requires or will require care and supervision as an adult as the result of a marked intellectual defect. A classification of imbecile means that the individual must remain dependent upon others for support and supervision throughout his life.

MORON

The term moron was used by Goddard to denote the child of low intelligence who is above the imbecile level, who has some degree of educability in terms of reading, writing, and arithmetic, considerable trainability in habits, and some degree of educability in the area of social and occupational competence. The moron is found in considerable numbers in institutions for the mentally deficient. A substantial number of such children, however, are also found in special classes for the mentally handicapped, and in some communities are admitted into the classes of the regular school even though their educability is quite low compared to that of normal children. As measured by the conventional intelligence test, such as the Binet, the moron obtains an I.Q. ranging roughly between 50 and 70. The moron can usually learn to adjust socially outside of an institution and can become partially or totally self-supporting, providing adequate education has been acquired and some supervision provided.

BORDERLINE CHILD

The next category in this intelligence classification consists of the borderline child, or the child whom it is difficult to classify as either moronic or normal. Some are placed in special classes, while others remain in the regular classes of the public schools. Such children are usually retarded educationally to a degree which causes difficulty in school adjustment. According to Terman's earlier classification, such children have I.Q.'s between 70 and 80 or 85.

DULL-NORMAL CHILD

The category of "dull-normal" has been used to describe the child at the lower end of the average range. Such a child is capable of competing with the majority of children in most activities except the strictly academic subjects of the school. In the latter he is slightly below average and in general retarded a year or two in the elementary grades when compared with children of similar ages. He sometimes completes high school with difficulty but in many cases drops out of school before completion.

Although the foregoing categories serve their purpose, many children cannot be neatly pigeonholed into a specific category. Since each child is a unique individual, these classifications have caused considerable difficulty. Between each group are borderline cases. For example, it is difficult to distinguish a low-grade imbecile from a high-grade idiot; it is difficult to distinguish a high-grade imbecile from a low-grade moron. Each category merges into the other when one uses quantitative terms. Since the categories are sometimes unsatisfactory in dealing with a particular child, workers in the field of mental deficiency have not been totally satisfied with the classification according to degree.

CLASSIFICATION ACCORDING TO CAUSE (ETIOLOGY)

The inadequacies in a classification according to degree of defect have led to an attempt to classify children with low intelligence according to cause. Hence we find such classifications as hereditary mental deficiency, mental deficiency caused by physiological disturbances, mental deficiency caused by brain damage, or such classifications as exogenous (acquired mental deficiency due to brain damage) or endogenous (mental deficiency resulting from familial and sometimes congenital factors).

This topic will be discussed in more detail in the next chapter. At this point, it is sufficient to say that this classification, although of great value for many purposes, does not assist significantly in educational organization. Although a child may be mentally defective because of a brain injury, the mental defect may be severe, marked, or only slight. A child with a brain injury who is an idiot differs significantly from a brain-injured child who is a moron or only dull-normal. For instructional purposes it is sometimes important to know the cause or etiology of the intellectual defect. The classification of these children according to cause alone is not sufficient for the organization of educational programs for them.

CLASSIFICATION ACCORDING TO CLINICAL TYPES

The term "clinical types" refers to mentally deficient persons who possess "... certain anatomical, physiognomical, or pathological features which are sufficiently pronounced to enable them to be placed in special categories." [1] The medical profession has emphasized classification according to clinical diagnosis, and many of the medical books devote a major proportion of their space to a description of clinical types. Such clinical types are cretins, mongols, microcephalics, hydrocephalics, cerebral palsied, and others. Diagnoses of these clinical types are made on the basis of the physical anomalies or syndromes found in the children.

[1] Tredgold, A. F., *A Textbook of Mental Deficiency*, 6th Ed. Baltimore: William Wood and Co., 1937, p. 207.

Clinical types are found more frequently among the idiots and imbeciles than among the more educable moron or borderline group. The emphasis on such a classification is made more for medical reasons than for educational or sociological ones. A cerebral palsied child may be an idiot or a child of normal intelligence, even though the physical manifestations are the same for both children. From the point of view of diagnosis and educational prognosis, classification according to clinical types is very important. From the point of view of educational procedures, it is of less importance, since few clinical types are found in school, and since the criterion of educability is of paramount importance.

CLASSIFICATION FOR EDUCATIONAL PURPOSES

The public schools, the welfare departments, and society in general have the responsibility of providing for children with low intelligence. Making provisions for such children requires some sort of organization. It requires administrative procedures as well as educational techniques. For that reason it is necessary that we classify children for educational purposes rather than only for medical, psychological, or sociological ones. The following classification is an attempt to simplify the classification of children with low intelligence in terms of school and welfare provisions for them. It is to some extent a classification according to degree, rather than according to cause.

The educational classifications will be discussed under three headings: namely, (1) the feeble-minded or mentally deficient, (2) the mentally handicapped, and (3) the slow learner.

THE MENTALLY DEFICIENT OR FEEBLE-MINDED CHILD

For the purpose of care and education society would like to know what groups of children require custodial care, either by parents or by social agencies and institutions. It is proposed that the terms "feeble-minded" and "mentally deficient" be used synonymously for the group of children who require care and supervision by their families or by the state. The question then arises "Who is mentally deficient or feeble-minded?" This problem has attracted the attention of many persons, and some of their views and definitions will be given here.

Tredgold [2] defines mental deficiency from a biological point of view as follows, "a state of incomplete mental development of such a kind and degree that the individual is incapable of adapting himself to the normal environment of his fellows in such a way as to maintain existence independently of supervision, control, or external support."

Edgar Doll [3] has elaborated on Tredgold's definition by asserting that in order to be diagnosed as mentally deficient a person must be (1) socially incompetent, that is, socially inadequate and occupationally incompetent and unable to manage his own affairs, (2) mentally subnormal, (3) retarded intellectually from birth or early age, (4) retarded at maturity, (5) mentally deficient as a result of constitutional origin, through heredity or disease, and (6) essentially incurable. Doll considers these six factors an essential comprehensive concept of mental deficiency.

According to Doll's definition, the child who is diagnosed as mentally deficient is irremediable and uneducable. The difficulty of determining whether this mental deficiency is likely to obtain at maturity makes the diagnosis of mental deficiency at an earlier age a little precarious. Writers in the field of mental deficiency have tended to presume that if a child so diagnosed is ultimately trained or educated to become socially competent and is able to manage his affairs in life, then the earlier diagnosis was wrong. Such terms as "pseudo-feeble-mindedness" or "errors in diagnosis" have been applied to cases of children who were once diagnosed as mentally deficient and who later became socially competent, either partially or totally.

Kanner [4] has used the term "absolute feeble-mindedness" to describe the child who is so deficient in his "cognitive, affective,

[2] *Ibid.*, p. 4.
[3] Doll, Edgar A., "The Essentials of an Inclusive Concept of Mental Deficiency," *American Journal of Mental Deficiency*, 46, No. 2 (October, 1941), pp. 214–219.
[4] Kanner, Leo A., "Miniature Textbook of Feeblemindedness," *Child Care Monographs*, No. 1. New York: Child Care Publications, 1949.

and conative potentialities" that he is considered defective in any society. This category corresponds to the idiots and imbeciles described earlier. These children do not respond, according to Kanner, to any known educational or therapeutic treatment. Kanner also agrees with Doll that these children are irremediable.

From an educational point of view, a child who is diagnosed as feeble-minded or mentally deficient must be cared for by his parent or by society, because he is unable to manage his own affairs. From a public school point of view, this child would be excluded from both regular and special classes. Society must therefore provide care for this child in one of the following ways:

(1) The child may be legally committed to an institution for mental defectives, to be taken care of as long as he lives in a supervised and controlled environment. Such a child usually becomes a charge of the state.[1]

(2) Some parents prefer to care for the child themselves. In such a case the family takes on the responsibility of custodial care in their own home. Social agencies can assist such a family through consultative service. A little pamphlet entitled *Teach Me* [5] gives to parents some suggestions concerning the care of their young mentally defective child.

(3) Public schools can organize custodial classes within the public school system for the care, training, and supervision of the trainable mentally deficient child (imbecile). Such an organization would attempt to assist parents in caring for the child at home and would supervise the child for several hours during the day in a public school class. It would not be expected that such children could be educated to care for themselves at the adult level, but through training (not education as we usually conceive it) could be taught to function socially at a higher level around the home and neighborhood. This is a method sometimes preferred to commitment to a state institution since it assists those parents who wish to maintain responsibility for the child at home. The child's care and supervision in the home assisted by a public school class is not at present an established procedure. However, such a com-

[5] *Teach Me.* Published by Mental Health Unit, Division of Public Institutions, Department of Social Security, St. Paul, Minnesota, 1945.

munity organization will lessen the burden on those parents who wish to provide for their own children. The group that must be excluded from such classes consists of those children, such as idiots, who cannot be trained in the simplest routines of life.

For practical educational purposes a child who is diagnosed as mentally deficient would be considered by the community as a custodial case and one who would not profit from educational procedures in either the regular classes or in special classes for the mentally handicapped. In most school systems such children are excluded from the public schools unless special custodial classes have been provided for them. Such classes are today very rare in school systems but may increase as society organizes for them in communities, rather than only in institutions.

THE MENTALLY HANDICAPPED CHILD

The term "mentally handicapped" is the term used for children who can be educated in special classes in the public schools. How to differentiate the mentally handicapped from the mentally deficient is a problem for psychological diagnosis. This problem of differentiating those who can be educated in special classes from those who will remain custodial cases has been a problem of major proportions. Because of its complexity, great confusion has arisen concerning the diagnosis of such children and their educability.

Mentally handicapped children differ primarily from the mentally deficient or feeble-minded in some of the following characteristics:

(1) The mentally handicapped child is one who has some degree of educability in the social area. Special-class training should be so designed as to assist this child in ultimately managing his own affairs with ordinary prudence. The prognosis of social competency under favorable circumstances would differentiate the mentally handicapped child from the feeble-minded child who cannot be educated to become socially competent.

(2) The mentally handicapped child should have some degree of educability in the occupational areas. To be occupationally competent, the child must develop to a point where he can earn a living, partially or totally. Occupational adequacy, or the prognosis of

ultimate occupational adequacy, is another criterion which differentiates the mentally handicapped child from the feeble-minded child.

(3) Like the mentally deficient, using Doll's criterion, the mentally handicapped child is thought to have developmental retardation. This factor is not an important one since all that is known in most cases is that the child is retarded at school age. Whether the retardation existed at birth is in many situations impossible to determine. The major criterion is: does intellectual retardation exist to such a degree that the child is unable to profit sufficiently from the instruction in the regular classroom and requires special education for his maximum growth and development?

(4) Retardation obtaining at maturity is likewise characteristic of the mentally handicapped. This criterion of Doll's is too rigid since it does not account for changes in growth as a result of more adequate medical, social, or educational training. It appears somewhat fatalistic. Since we cannot wait until maturity to diagnose the mentally handicapped, the psychologist is called upon to predict the condition likely to obtain in the future. Should new discoveries or developments alter the condition, it should not be considered a case of "pseudo-feeble-mindedness" but rather one of temporarily arrested mental retardation. This problem will be discussed in later sections.

(5) The criterion of constitutional origin is one which in practice often becomes theoretical. There are many cases of mental handicap whose constitutional origin or etiological factors cannot be determined with present techniques. This criterion is not an important one for the diagnosis of mentally handicapped children for special classes.

(6) As measured by intelligence tests, and by educability, the degree of deficit is not as great in the mentally handicapped as it is in the mentally deficient. The major consideration with the mentally handicapped is that they cannot profit sufficiently from the curriculum of the regular schools and require a special curriculum for their social and occupational growth. This is one of the major criteria in determining whether a child, because of an intellectual defect, should be placed in a special class for the mentally handicapped. Children with I.Q.'s of 50, 60, or 70, as determined by a

battery of individual intelligence tests, are usually likely candidates for special classes for the mentally handicapped.

THE SLOW-LEARNING CHILD

The term "slow learner" has been loosely applied to all grades of children with low intelligence. In dealing with parents, the term is sometimes used because it is a kinder term than "mentally deficient," not because it has greater scientific meaning. The slow learner does not have the six characteristics described earlier by Doll. He tests slightly below average in learning ability, but should not be considered mentally handicapped. A slight intellectual retardation does not necessarily result in social incompetence. There may be constitutional or environmental causes for retardation, and the slow-learning ability probably obtains at maturity because of inadequate cultural and educational environments. This, however, assumes a constant school environment rather than an adaptation of school to the abilities and disabilities of such a child. From the point of view of educational organization, the term "slow learner" should be applied to the child who seems to have some difficulty in adjusting to the curriculum of the academic school because of slightly inferior intelligence or learning ability. He will require some modification of school offerings within the regular classroom for his maximum growth and development.

Not too much is known about the constitutional origin of the slight deficiency in learning ability except that it may represent the ordinary variation found in all biological organisms. These slow learners happen to be at the lower end of the average range in learning the academic subjects and can acquire the subject matter but not to the same exent or with the same facility as the normal child. For educational purposes the slow learner does not belong in the special class for the mentally handicapped. He is the child for whom the regular class should so differentiate its instruction as to adjust to the wider concept of the average. Slow learners should remain in the regular classes of the public schools, and teachers should adapt instruction to fit the wide variation which will include the slow learner, the average, and the superior. In every school system and nearly every class there is found this variation. The reason for the organization of a special class for the mentally handicapped is that the mentally handicapped child presents too marked a deviation from the broad average. His retardation in school is so significant that he requires a different curriculum from that presented to the slow learner or the average child.

Summary

The foregoing discussion of classification of children with low intelligence has attempted to indicate that there are various methods of classification. These classifications are of varying value to psychologists, geneticists, etiologists, sociologists, and educators.

For educational purposes within a school system it is necessary, however, to differentiate children with low intelligence according to an educational criterion. Rather than categorize children according to degree of defect (such as idiot, imbecile, moron, dull-normal, borderline, etc.) or according to causes, or clinical types, it is important that school systems classify these children in such a way that school administrators will know whether the child should be excluded from school and given custodial care, whether he will profit most from a special class for the mentally handicapped, or whether the regular grade should be adapted to his slow-learning ability. Although differing from the concepts of other authors, this concept will use the classification of feeble-minded or mentally deficient to indicate to the school administrator that the child is a custodial case and that he cannot be educated to be socially competent or occupationally adequate in the community. Provisions of institutionalization, home training, or custodial classes within a public school are indicated.

The mentally handicapped child is one who is diagnosed as having low intelligence, who is unable to profit sufficiently from the curriculum of the public schools, but who can be educated to become socially adequate and occupationally competent, provided special educational facilities are furnished. The school administrator then knows that this child belongs in a special class for the mentally handicapped. Thus public school organization differentiates the mentally handicapped from the mentally deficient.

The slow-learning child is one who requires some adaptation of instruction in the regular grades because of his slow-learning ability.

He is not mentally handicapped in the sense that he requires a special class and a different curriculum. He is the child that requires special organization within a class. To the school administrator, the slow learner, constituting a larger proportion than the mentally handicapped, becomes a problem of adapting instruction within the regular classroom rather than a special organizational program, such as a special class for the mentally handicapped.

The determination of a diagnosis within the educational classification here proposed is usually the responsibility of a competent school psychologist. Whenever there is doubt concerning the classification of the child as mentally deficient, a trial period in a special class is indicated. Likewise, if there is doubt concerning a child of slow-learning ability, it is advisable to retain the child in the regular grades and to try adaptations of the regular curriculum before assignment to a special class for the mentally handicapped is made. A thorough study of a child should, in most cases, place the child in the most profitable situation for both the child and society.

REFERENCES

Davies, S. P. *Social Control of the Mentally Deficient.* New York: Thomas Y. Crowell Company, 1930.

Doll, Edgar A. "The Essentials of an Inclusive Concept of Mental Deficiency," *American Journal of Mental Deficiency,* 46, No. 2 (October, 1941), pp. 214–219.

Kanner, Leo A. "Miniature Textbook of Feeblemindedness," *Child Care Monographs,* No. 1. New York: Child Care Publications, 1949.

Sarason, Seymour B. *Psychological Problems in Mental Deficiency.* New York: Harper and Brothers, 1949.

Teach Me. Published by Mental Health Unit, Division of Public Institutions, Department of Social Security, St. Paul, Minnesota, 1945.

Tredgold, A. F. *A Textbook of Mental Deficiency,* 6th Edition. Baltimore: William Wood and Company, 1937.

Wallin, J. E. W. *The Education of Handicapped Children.* Boston: Houghton Mifflin Company, 1924.

Wallin, J. E. W. *Children With Mental and Physical Handicaps.* New York: Prentice-Hall, Inc., 1949.

White House Conference in Child Health and Protection: *Report of the Committee on Physically and Mentally Handicapped.* New York: Appleton-Century-Crofts, Inc., 1933.

Chapter 2

Etiology of Mental Retardation

WHEN STUDYING and teaching children with low intelligence, it is important for both clinicians and teachers to determine as far as is possible the cause of the intellectual defect in each child. The etiological factors involved sometimes determine the prognosis and educability of the child. Although at present we do not have much evidence concerning differential procedures in educating children whose intellectual defects arise from different causes, it is possible that in the future many educational techniques will be based, at least in part, on the etiological factor. Already Strauss and Lehtinen [1] have presented differential techniques for some children diagnosed as brain-injured. An understanding of the child for educational purposes requires a complete study of the child and his environment including, wherever possible, the cause of his intellectual retardation. With such information at hand, a teacher may develop educational procedures and techniques of social rehabilitation which might not otherwise be evolved.

As with all other classifications, causes of mental retardation are classified differently by different authors. Tredgold,[2] a modern

[1] Strauss, Alfred A., and Laura E. Lehtinen, *Psychopathology and Education of the Brain-Injured Child*. New York: Grune and Stratton, 1947.

[2] Tredgold, A. F., *A Textbook of Mental Deficiency*, 6th Ed. New York: William Wood and Company, 1937.

15

British authority, originated the classification of primary and secondary amentia. By primary amentia, Tredgold referred to that group of individuals whose mental defect was caused by inheritance. Secondary amentia was defined as mental defect caused by external factors — acquired through disease or other "adverse environment." In some cases both causes operated to produce mental defect.

Variations of these classifications are used by other authors. Doll,[3] for example, accepts the classification of endogenous and exogenous types of mental deficiency, which signifies a differentiation in terms of cause. The endogenous type constitutes the group diagnosed as mentally deficient because of "hereditary transmission of psychobiological insufficiency." These individuals are organically and physically adequate, but mentally inadequate. The exogenous type, on the other hand, constitutes that group resulting from ". . . pathological alterations of normal development as well as some relatively rare hereditary types of pathological morphology represented by the clinical varieties of mental deficiency." [4] Strauss and Lehtinen [5] classify the endogenous type as a group of children who are mentally deficient as a result of familial factors. The exogenous types include children with brain injuries from any cause and Strauss asserts that among the idiots and imbeciles many such exogenous types are found. He further states that approximately 15 to 20 per cent of the total population of the higher-grade mentally defective show exogenous characteristics.

Davenport [6] discusses the causes of mental retardation under seven categories; namely, (1) defects arising in the germ plasma, (2) defects resulting during fertilization of the egg, (3) defects connected with implantation, (4) defects arising in the embryo, (5) defects arising in the fetus, (6) defects arising from birth injuries, and (7) defects arising in infancy and later childhood.

[3] Doll, Edgar A., "The Essentials of an Inclusive Concept of Mental Deficiency," *American Journal of Mental Deficiency*, 46, No. 2 (October, 1941), pp. 214–219.
[4] *Ibid.*, p. 217.
[5] Strauss and Lehtinen, *op. cit.*, p. 16.
[6] Davenport, Charles B., "Causes of Retarded and Incomplete Development," *American Association on Mental Deficiency*, 41 (May, 1936), pp. 208–214.

Another method of classifying mental retardation in children is to categorize them according to (1) hereditary, (2) congenital, and (3) post-natal causes. Although this classification has some merit, it has been difficult to separate the congenital from the hereditary factors.

In a recent publication Kanner [7] discusses "determinants" of mental retardation. He lists these as:

(1) Genetic determinants: hereditary or genetic variants with due reference to social or emotional implications.
(2) Cultural determinants: factors in the culture affecting mental development.
(3) Material determinants: economic condition of the family.
(4) Physical determinants: physical defects associated with mental deficit.
(5) Educational determinants: education and training in a broad sense.
(6) Emotional determinants: emotional impacts resulting from impaired functioning and masking endowment.

In the following discussion etiological factors will be considered under four major headings, namely, (1) brain injuries, (2) physiological disturbances, (3) hereditary factors, and (4) cultural influences.

BRAIN INJURIES

One type of mentally defective child has been diagnosed as brain-injured. In these cases the mental defect is ascribed directly to the organic pathology. The prevention or alleviation of this kind of mental defectiveness is dependent upon a knowledge and understanding of the causes of brain injury which result in mental retardation. The following section will summarize briefly some of them.

BIRTH INJURIES

Birth injuries refer to destruction of some area of the brain during

[7] Kanner, Leo, "A Miniature Textbook of Feeblemindedness," *Child Care Monographs*, No. 1. New York: Child Care Publications. 1949

the process of birth.   It appears to be most common among first-
born children and in difficult labors, but it occurs at other times also.
According to Tredgold [8] the lesion in the brain is the result of
intracranial hemorrhage.   The hemorrhage during birth is the
result of rupture of some meningeal blood vessels.   Although intracranial hemorrhage is found to be rather common at birth, in many
cases the hemorrhage is not great and the blood is absorbed without
any damage to the brain.   In more extreme cases the hemorrhage
results in lesions causing mental and/or motor disabilities.   When
the hemorrhage is great at birth, the child is sometimes cyanotic,
or in more popular terms "a blue baby."   As indicated earlier, the
hemorrhage may not affect the child later, may result in death to
the baby, or may result in mental retardation or cerebral palsy, or
both.   The cause of the intracranial hemorrhage is not adequately
known.

HYDROCEPHALUS

The condition of hydrocephalus also causes brain damage.   This
condition, whose clinical sign is an enlarged cranium, is sometimes
commonly referred to as "water on the brain" and involves an
accumulation of cerebro-spinal fluid, within the ventricles of the
brain, which is not normally absorbed.   The pressure on the cere-
brum causes deterioration of the brain and a reduction of mental
function.

In general, hydrocephalus results in varying degrees of mental
retardation.   In one type of case the condition is progressive and
the child continues to deteriorate mentally and physically until
its condition usually results in death.   In the second type of case,
the condition progresses very slowly or becomes arrested for some
unknown reason.   Even after the progress of the disease has been
arrested, the damage to the brain already acquired leaves the patient
mentally defective and sometimes cerebral palsied.   The degree
of the defect depends on the degree of cortical destruction and not
necessarily on the size of the skull.

CEREBRAL ANOXIA

Another form of injury is caused by the lack of oxygen to the
[8] Tredgold, *op. cit*

brain during the period of birth. Frederick Schreiber [9] studied this problem extensively and has presented evidence that mental defects in children are sometimes the result of what he terms "cerebral anoxia" or "paranatal asphyxia." According to Schreiber the brain cannot function without an adequate supply of oxygen. When the oxygen supply to the brain is blocked for more than a few minutes, irreparable damage to the brain cells results. During pregnancy or birth there are a number of conditions which may cause oxygen deprivation and result in irreparable cell destruction and consequent mental deficiency.

Schreiber has differentiated four conditions which produce anoxia in children; namely, (1) anoxic anoxia, (2) anemic anoxia, (3) stagnant anoxia, and (4) histotoxic anoxia.

(1) In "anoxic anoxia" the blood is not sufficiently saturated with oxygen. This may be the result of strangulation from a number of causes or intense suffocation of the mother during pregnancy, resulting in lack of oxygen supply to the fetus.

(2) In "anemic anoxia" the blood is abnormally low in oxygen due sometimes to fewer red blood cells in circulation. Anemia in the mother during pregnancy has been cited as one cause.

(3) In "stagnant anoxia" the quantity of the blood is below normal. This is caused by a failure of the heart to adequately maintain circulation, low blood pressure in the mother, pressure on the fetal head by forceps, hemorrhage, and so forth.

(4) "Histotoxic anoxia" results when the tissue cells of the brain are poisoned and cannot absorb the normal oxygen supply. "Doses of scopolamine, morphine, or any of the barbiturates influence the degree of asphyxia in the newborn babies." [10]

---

[9] Schreiber, Frederick, "Mental Deficiency from Paranatal Asphyxia," *Proceedings and Addresses of the Sixty-Third Annual Session of the American Association on Mental Deficiency*, 44, No. 1 (1939), pp. 95–106.
   [10] *Ibid.*, p. 103.

INFECTIOUS DISEASES

There are a number of infectious diseases which in a few cases result in brain damage and in mental retardation. Such childhood diseases as whooping cough,[11] measles, scarlet fever, meningitis, and encephalitis have been known to produce brain injury. Although evidence in these areas is somewhat meager, it is possible that the brains of many mentally handicapped and slow-learning children have been partially affected by such diseases.

PHYSIOLOGICAL DISTURBANCES

This category is listed here to differentiate direct causes of brain injury from lack of mental development as a result of physiological conditions, although many of the physiological disturbances cause brain damage or lack of cortical development. The following conditions have been known to produce mental deficiency.

RUBELLA — GERMAN MEASLES

In recent years it has been discovered [12] that German measles (rubella), contracted by the mother during pregnancy, may result in congenital defects in the child, including mental deficiency. Such defects as cataracts, deafness, heart disease, microcephalis, as well as mental deficiency have been associated with this disease. It appears that when rubella is contracted during the trimester of pregnancy, the offspring is apt to suffer from one or more of the defects noted above.

THE Rh FACTOR

In 1940, Landsteiner and Wiener [13] reported a study of a condition involving the presence of agglutinen in the blood of rabbits,

[11] Levy, Sol, and H. A. Perry, "Pertussis as a Cause of Mental Deficiency," *American Journal of Mental Deficiency*, 52 (October, 1948), pp. 217–226.

[12] Swann, Charles, A. L. Fostevin, and G. H. Barhamblock, "Final Observations on Congenital Defects in Infants Following Infectious Diseases During Pregnancy with Special Reference to Rubella," *Medical Journal of Australia*, 2 (December, 1946), pp. 889–908.

[13] Reported by Gates, R. R., *Human Genetics*, Vol. I. New York: The Macmillan Company, 1946, pp. 700–709.

which was produced experimentally by injecting blood from the rhesus monkey. The Rh positive factor, which in the experiment was taken from the rhesus monkey, is found in about 86 per cent of human beings. Fourteen per cent of human bloods do not contain the Rh factor. They are said to be Rh negative. The incompatibility of Rh positive and Rh negative, resulting in agglutinen, produces immature blood cells due to their failure of maturation in the bone marrow.

Yannet and Lieberman [14] and Snyder [15] have shown a relationship of Rh factors to mental deficiency. The writers indicate that when there is a mother-child incompatibility in the Rh blood factor, the child is apt to be mentally defective. Statistics indicate that this incompatibility is greater among the feeble-minded than among the normal population.

Although there is some evidence of the Rh factor causing mental deficiency, much further work must be carried on in this area to determine how this occurs, and why the child should be mentally defective if he lives.

Associated with the Rh factor are other blood conditions involving factors A and B. Yannet and Lieberman [16] reported a study of the distribution of incompatible A and B mother-child blood groups in 280 middle and low grade mental defectives. They found seventy cases of A and B incompatibility in this group but only in ten of these was the specific substance absent in both the saliva and gastric juice of the child. Yannet and Lieberman conclude: "This strongly suggests the possibility that A and B iso-immunization is of definite etiological importance in an appreciable number of mental defectives at present considered in the undifferentiated or undiagnosable group." [17]

[14] Yannet, Herman, and Rose Lieberman, "The Rh Factor in the Etiology of Mental Deficiency," *American Journal of Mental Deficiency*, 49 (October, 1944), pp. 133–137.

[15] Snyder, Lawrence, M.D. Schonfeld, and Edith M. Offerman, "The Rh Factor and Feeblemindedness," *Journal of Heredity*, 36 (1945), pp. 9–10.

[16] Yannet, Herman, and Rose Lieberman, "A and B Iso-Immunization as a Possible Factor in the Etiology of Mental Deficiency," *American Journal of Mental Deficiency*, 50 (October, 1945), pp. 242–244.

[17] *Ibid.*, p. 244.

MONGOLISM

The term "mongolism" was applied to a certain type of mental defect by J. Langdon Down in 1866 since the slanting eyes of children suffering from this mental defect are suggestive of Mongolian peoples. Dr. Down felt that it was an example of retrogession to an earlier Mongolian race.

The mongoloid child is physically and mentally defective from birth. The eyes are obliquely placed and usually more than a normal distance from one another. The face is flat and broad, the cheeks are roundish, lips are usually large and thick, and the tongue is long and apparently too large for the mouth, causing habitual protrusion. The nose is usually small, the skull from the front to the occiput area is short, and the epicanthic fold in the eyes is obvious.

The condition of mongolism has been studied for a great many years. Of all the clinical types, the mongoloid has been one of the most perplexing. The cause of mongolism has not yet been established although a number of hypotheses have been postulated. At birth the mongoloid baby shows the characteristic syndrome. The deficiency, therefore, exists during intra-uterine life. Benda [18] has made the most recent study and summary of literature pertaining to factors and causes of mongolism and states that there are three main theories which have been advanced to explain such a condition. These are heredity, damage to germ plasm, and other factors originating in the mother during gestation.

In discussing these theories Benda, like most other recent authorities, feels there is little or no evidence to support the theory that mongolism arises through hereditary causes. There is some scattered and inconclusive evidence, however, which suggests the possibility of damage to the germ plasm giving rise to the defect, but most of the cases cited could be explained by other factors.

The third possibility for the occurrence of mongolism, according to Benda, is a pathologic condition of the mother during the beginning of pregnancy. Many of the studies have pointed toward this theory. Some of the factors under this condition are listed as follows:

[18] Benda, Clemens E., *Mongolism and Cretinism*. New York: Grune and Stratton, 1946.

(1) Mongoloid children seem to be more prevalent in older mothers than in younger mothers, although mongolism occurs in both. More than 50 per cent of the mothers Benda studied were beyond the age of thirty-five when their mongoloid child was born.

(2) Birth order is one factor that also has been investigated. No evidence was found that the first child, last child, or middle child is more apt to be defective.

(3) High-strung, nervous, easily-upset mothers were found more frequently among those having mongoloid children. Benda explained this by indicating that the high-strung type of woman shows a psychosomatic reaction characterized by instability of circulatory and autonomic functions.

(4) Because "The frequency of abortions is one of the most striking features in case histories of mongolism," [19] threatened abortion has also been ascribed as a cause or related factor.

(5) Benda also states that bleeding or a continuation of regular menstruation during the second and third months of pregnancy sometimes terminated in a mongoloid child.

(6) The condition of partial sterility has been cited as a possible factor. In this condition the mother has been apparently sterile for a period of time but finally conceives, giving birth to an "ill-finished child."

There are considerable discrepancies between the observations of different investigators, but also considerable agreement regarding the nocuous factor originating in the mother during gestation. In conclusion, Benda states:

The material indicates that potentially, under certain conditions, every mother can give birth to a mongoloid child. . . . The factors which condition the development of a mongoloid child, although varying to some degree, seem to be uniform in the one result that they interfere with the endocrine environment of the fetus. The inadequacy of hormonal environment of the fetus is borne out by many indications.

. . . Fertilization puts a heavy tax upon the maternal organism which is met through a number of quick adjustments and changes in the endocrine environment.[20]

According to Benda, the chief demands of pregnancy upon endo-

[19] *Ibid.*, p. 264.   [20] *Ibid.*, pp. 276–277.

crine environment of the maternal organism are those of the pituitary, thyroid, ovary, corpus luteum, uterus, and placenta. He concludes:

We have seen that mongolism occurs under the same conditions as abortion, threatened abortion, prematurity and hormonal sterility. We have
further seen that there are indications of thyroid and pituitary deficiency.
Although the exact mechanism of the deficiency resulting in congenital
acromicria of the baby is still a matter of speculation, the facts at hand are
sufficient to narrow the possible causes to a small number of factors and to
proceed with a constructive program of preventive obstetrics.[21]

CRETINISM

Benda describes cretins at the adult level as dwarfs. They walk
with a shuffling, waddling gait. The head is large in circumference
and its increased size is emphasized by the dwarfishness of the body.
The head is dolichocephalic, the skull is heavy, and the bones are
thick. The cretin has abundant black wiry hair (no true cretins
have blond hair). The eyes of the cretin are set in horizontal position, the nose is broad and flat, and the ears are large and flappy.
The skin is dry, pale, and wrinkled. The neck is broad and short,
and the trunk, though also short, seems long in comparison to the
extremities. The abdomen is round and protruding and umbilical
hernia is quite common. The nails of the hand are short, brittle,
and thick. The pulse is slow and the temperature is about a degree
lower than normal, the heart usually enlarged.

The cause of cretinism has been known for some time. There is
a definite thyroid pathology. Benda [22] mentions three patterns of
thyroid pathology in cretins, namely, (1) thyroid aplasia, a congenital defect, (2) athyroidism, a loss of thyroid functioning, and
(3) thyroid disfunction. The thyroid gland secretes a hormone
known as thyroxin. A deficiency in the thyroid gland produces
lack of thyroxin in the child and a consequent deficiency of physical
and mental growth.

[21] *Ibid.*, p. 279.   [22] *Ibid.*, p. 115.

HEREDITARY FACTORS

Inherited mental deficiency means that the child is mentally deficient or mentally handicapped because the mental characteristics indicative of mental defect have been transmitted through the germ plasm. When one surveys the literature in this field, one is impressed by the tremendous discrepancies in results and in points of view. Writers' opinions varied from a disbelief in inherited mental retardation to estimates of 80 to 90 per cent of mental deficiency as being inherited. The controversy has existed for many years, and it appears that the viewpoint expressed by one author depends largely on whether he bases his opinion on one group of studies or another.

Kanner has summarized the authorities' estimates on the percentage of the hereditary origin of "feeble-mindedness." The following table shows the discrepancies in estimates by various authors:

Table I [23]

Year	Author	Percentage
1914	Goddard	77
1920	Hollingsworth	90
1929	Tredgold	80
1931	Larson	76
1934	Doll	30
1934	Penrose	29

Geneticists have established adequate evidence to prove that the eye color or hair color of individuals is determined by heredity, but they have not been able to isolate or to determine the inheritance of mental deficiency. One can ask, What specific characteristics are inherited and to what extent are they inherited?

In a recent volume, Gates [24] presented much evidence from a bio-

[23] Kanner, *op. cit.*, p. 5.
[24] Gates, R. R., *Human Genetics*, Vol. II. New York: The Macmillan Co.; 1946, pp. 1087–1149.

logical point of view indicating that mental defects are inherited. Gates, however, concludes:

> From the evidence in this chapter it will be seen that, from a genetical standpoint, widely different views have been expressed regarding the method of inheritance of some types of mental defect, and it is not yet possible to decide between them. Yet practically all are agreed that heredity is mainly concerned in their production.[25]

In 1913 Goddard [26] published his famous study of the Kallikak family. The study compared the descendants of Martin Kallikak (Kallikak meaning "good-bad") by his illicit union with a barmaid with those by a more intelligent, lawful wife. Goddard traced the descendants of Martin Kallikak and the feeble-minded barmaid for a number of generations, beginning with one of the patients at the Vineland Training School. He found many more social degenerates and feeble-minded individuals among the descendants of Martin Kallikak and the feeble-minded barmaid than he did among the descendants of Martin Kallikak and his intelligent mate. Goddard concluded from this study that feeble-mindedness is inherited. He proceeded to study a number of families at the Vineland Training School and in 1914 published his results, proving to his satisfaction the inheritance of mental deficiency.[27] In this latter study Goddard indicated that 54 per cent of the histories of these children showed inheritance as a cause, that 12 per cent of them showed questionable ancestry, and that 11 per cent showed probable hereditary causes. In all, Goddard estimated that 77 per cent of the patients who were feeble-minded showed some feeble-mindedness in their ancestry.

It should be remembered that in this study estimates of social degeneracy and feeble-mindedness were made by social workers. No tests indicating that the barmaid was feeble-minded are presented. Furthermore, the two groups of families were raised in different parts of the country and under different social standards.

---

[25] *Ibid.*, p. 1139.

[26] Goddard, H. H., *The Kallikak Family.* New York: The Macmillan Co., 1913.

[27] Goddard, H. H., *Feeble-mindedness: Its Causes and Consequences.* New York: The Macmillan Co., 1914.

Goddard did not take into consideration that culture may have something to do with social degeneracy, which was considered synonymous with mental defect.

Doll,[28] who has also studied the ancestry of patients at the same school, wrote in 1946 as follows: "Few authorities in the field of etiology question the likelihood that at least one-third of all cases are due to familial transmissions, and few modern authorities doubt that less than one-third are nonhereditary." [29]

In a Swedish study by Sjogren in 1935 the author concluded that feeble-mindedness was inherited as a recessive trait. He found one hundred and twenty mental defectives in ninety families. Feeble-mindedness in these cases was very extreme ranging in I.Q. from 0 to 35. The histories of these families went back approximately nine generations.

It will be noted that most of the evidence for the inheritance of mental deficiency has been secured primarily from family histories. Adolph Myerson has pointed out the dilemma concerning the inheritance of mental deficiency:

The study of feeble-mindedness has suffered from the overemphasis laid upon certain exceptional sociological situations, namely, the occurrence of so-called families who really represented ecological groups and who have come down in history as the great paradigms of the sociological and biological threat and danger to the race by the feeble-minded. The Nams, the Kallikaks, the Tribes of Ishmael, the Virginians, and others of the royal families of the feeble-minded became the basis of generalizations which were, as a matter of fact, based on flimsy evidence, on what may really be called statisticalized gossip. . . .

It may be stated that in those groups of the feeble-minded concerning which we have some definite knowledge, heredity does not appear to be a factor of any real importance; that in those groups where we have little real understanding, and where the appearance of the individual corresponds more to that of the so-called normal, heredity appears to be of great importance. It may safely be stated that there is some correspond-

[28] Doll, Edgar A., "The Feebleminded Child," *Manual of Child Psychology,* Leonard Carmichael, Editor. New York: John Wiley and Sons, Inc., 1946, pp. 845–885.
[29] *Ibid.,* p. 876. Reprinted by permission from *Manual of Child Psychology* by Carmichael, published by John Wiley & Sons, Inc., 1946.

ence, on the whole, between diffuse bodily defect and inferiority, on the one hand, and mental inferiority, on the other. It also appears quite certain that we are not yet at the point in understanding where we can speak of feeble-mindedness as anything like a biological unit for which we may expect Mendelian ratios.[30]

Studies of environmental influences by Skeels [31] showed that when children of mentally retarded mothers were placed in adequate foster homes before the age of six months they showed average or superior I.Q.'s three to five years later. The I.Q.'s of these children, whose true mothers were below 80 I.Q., were found to be on the average over 112. These figures were similar to I.Q.'s of children from true mothers whose I.Q.'s were above 100. In another study Skeels showed that when preschool age children in an orphanage were given preschool experiences, the I.Q. tended to rise slightly. Similar children who were not given such experiences and who remained in the routinized institutional environment tended to drop in I.Q.

Such studies as those of Skeels and others question the inheritance of mental defect when the environment of the child is changed in early childhood. Until we have more extensive studies of children of feeble-minded parents who are placed in early infancy in a good environment and who, in spite of environment, remain feeble-minded, it will be hazardous to be dogmatic about the inheritance of mental deficiency.

Again the question which may be raised regarding the inheritance of mental defect is, Specifically, what is inherited? Shall we accept the statement of Goddard and others that feeble-mindedness is a Mendelian recessive trait? Recent evidence presented by Jervis [32] showed there is a type of mental deficiency which is accompanied by a lack of amino acid metabolism. This he called phenylpyruvic amentia. It is suggested by this study that the biochemical

[30] Meyerson, A., "Medical Psychiatry." From *The Problem of Mental Disorder*, Edited by M. Bentley & E. V. Cowdry. Copyright, 1934. Courtesy of McGraw-Hill Book Co.

[31] Skeels, Harold M., "Mental Development of Children in Foster Homes," *Journal of Consulting Psychology*, 2, No. 2 (March–April, 1938), pp. 33–43.

[32] Jervis, George A., "Phenylpyruvic Oligophrenia," *Archives of Neurology and Psychiatry*, 38 (November, 1937), pp. 944–963.

deficiency is what is inherited and that this may be the cause of the mental deficiency. Then, too, the Rh factor may also run through whole families and thus seem to indicate an apparent inheritance of mental deficiency, actually it may be nothing more than Rh positive or Rh negative in other family groups. When we arrive at conclusive evidence for such inherited conditions (in the study of the biochemistry of the mentally deficient) we will then be able to interpret more intelligently the causative factors which are inherited.

Cultural Factors

The effect of nurture on intelligence and of lack of nurture on mental deficiency have been controversial problems for many centuries. In the earlier days philosophers were engaged in a battle between the so-called "nativists" and the "sensationalists." The nativists believed that intelligence was innate and that what was produced in the form of behavior was the result of the workings of the mind without the influence of outside factors. The sensationalists, or empiricists, alleged that our intelligence was derived through sense impressions and implied that lack of adequate sense impressions or experiences resulted in mental retardation.

It is not surprising that Itard attempted to train the idiot found in the forest of Aveyron. He launched a training program because he was imbued with the philosophy of sensationalism. He believed that his educational procedures would develop the mind through the training of the senses. The fact that Itard was unable to cure Victor's idiocy neither proves his theory nor disproves it.

The literature bearing on the effect of cultural factors on mental retardation is obscure. Evidence for or against such effects is inferred from some case studies and a few experiments.

Typical of the case study approach is that found in the reports on the wild children in India. Arnold Gesell [33] described the development of one of these children found among wolves in India and later brought to an orphanage. This child did not become normal with extreme change in environment, but the description does not

[33] Gesell, Arnold, *Wolf Child and Human Child*. New York: Harper and Brothers, 1941.

indicate that social deprivation was the sole cause of mental retardation.

Kingsley Davis [34] described the case of Anna, who was found at the age of five after having spent all her life in an attic. She had been isolated in an attic because she was an illegitimate child and because her grandfather did not allow her mother to keep her in the house. Removal to a favorable environment and better nourishment and care increased her physical size so that she became overweight. At the age of seven and one-half, however, she was still an idiot. Davis states that five years of social and physical neglect in early life is sufficient to make it impossible for any child to learn to speak, think, and act like a normal child. Anyone reading the history would ask whether this child was defective from the beginning or became defective because of lack of social and physical stimulation.

In addition to the case studies, there is some experimental data available. Of the earlier experimental studies, that of Freeman [35] is the most extensive. By placing children in foster homes of different cultural and educational levels, Freeman demonstrated that intelligence, as measured by the Binet Intelligence Tests, tended to show an increase in higher cultural homes. This study indicated that there was a slight rise in I.Q. when the children were placed at a young age and that the better the home, the higher the I.Q. later. The difference between the initial I.Q. and the final I.Q., however, was approximately seven points, which in itself does not change the child from being mentally deficient to normal. While this study did not deal primarily with mental defectives, the data showed that even though twenty-six of the children had feeble-minded parents, most of the children rated higher than that usually considered mentally defective. The average I.Q. of the twenty-six children after placement in foster

[34] Davis, Kingsley, "Extreme Social Isolation of a Child," *American Journal of Sociology*, 45 (January, 1940), pp. 554–565.

[35] Freeman, Frank N., Karl J. Holzenger, and B. C. Mitchell, "The Influences of Environment on the Intelligence, School Achievement, and Conduct of Foster Children," *The Twenty-Seventh Yearbook of the National Society for the Study of Education*: Nature and Nurture, Part I. Bloomington, Illinois: Public School Publishing Company, 1928, pp. 103–218.

homes was 81. This study suggests that cultural factors have something to do with intelligence-test ratings but does not really point out the effect of social deprivation on mental deficiency.

There are actually few studies dealing with the effects of environment on mentally defective children. Kephardt [36] reports a study of changing I.Q.'s on fifty children admitted to the Wayne County Training School. This study showed a tendency for the I.Q.'s of the children to decline while they remained in their subcultural homes. After the children were admitted to the institution, there was a tendency for the I.Q.'s to increase. This institution, it should be noted, is an educational institution designed primarily for the education of borderline and high-grade mentally defective children.

Skeels [37] reports a much more dramatic study. He took thirteen children from an orphanage and placed them in an institution for the feeble-minded. These children were under three years of age and had an average I.Q. of 64, their initial I.Q.'s ranging from 35 to 89. They were placed on different wards of the institution so that they would receive a great deal of individual attention from older girls and attendants. One year and a half later their I.Q.'s had increased on the average 27.5 points as measured by the Kuhlmann Test of Mental Development. Skeels used a contrast group of twelve babies who were retained in the orphanage. These twelve children had an initial average I.Q. of 87.6, ranging from 50 to 103. After thirty months this group, who remained in the orphanage under a nonstimulating environment, dropped in I.Q. on the average 26.2 points. If Skeels' study is correct, it means that cultural influences at a very young age may have something to do with intelligence-test results. This study is subject to criticism from a number of angles, including such criticisms as the unreliability of

[36] Kephart, N. C., "Influencing the Rate of Mental Growth in Retarded Children Through Environmental Stimulation," *The Thirty-Ninth Yearbook of the National Society for the Study of Education: Intelligence: Its Nature and Nurture*, Part II. Bloomington, Illinois: Public School Publishing Company, 1940, pp. 223–236.

[37] Skeels, Harold M., and H. B. Dye, "A Study of the Effects of Differential Stimulation on Mentally Retarded Children," *Proceedings and Addresses of the Sixty-Third Annual Session of the American Association on Mental Deficiency*, 44, No. 1 (1939), pp. 114–1136.

the Kuhlmann-Binet test at that age level. Nevertheless, the study should not be regarded as insignificant without further work in this area.

The most sensational results yet published are those reported by Schmidt.[38] In this study of 254 children attending special classes in the public schools of Chicago, it is reported that the I.Q.'s increased from an average of 52.1 to 71.6 in a period of three years. Moreover, after five years of post-school experience the I.Q.'s again increased to an average of 89.3. Progress reported for social adjustment and personality was similar to that found for the factor of intelligence. In an investigation of this study, Kirk [39] found numerous discrepancies in the data. Among some of the discrepancies, he found that the initial mean I.Q.'s of three of the classes were closer to 70 than to the mean I.Q. of 50, as reported by Miss Schmidt. Kirk's study throws serious doubt on the authenticity of both the initial diagnosis of feeble-mindedness and on the original data. Until Schmidt's study is verified, little stock can be placed in the results.

Town [40] presented evidence in support of the theory of inheritance of mental deficiency by studying 141 mentally defective families. The data presented showed that these families were far below average in the cultural scale. Her data showed that among these families there were (1) a very high mortality rate among the children, (2) a high incidence of broken homes, malnutrition, illegitimacy, and severe neglect of children, and (3) flagrantly bad housekeeping conditions. Town interpreted this data as being indicative of the hereditary nature of mental deficiency. Since Town has shown that these mentally defective children were reared in culturally inferior homes, it is plausible to believe that

[38] Schmidt, Bernardine G., "Changes in Personal, Social, and Intellectual Behavior of Children Originally Classified as Feebleminded," *Psychological Monographs*, 60, No. 5 (1945).
[39] Kirk, Samuel A., "An Evaluation of the Study of Bernardine G. Schmidt Entitled: Changes in Personal, Social, and Intellectual Behavior of Children Originally Classified as Feebleminded," *Psychological Bulletin*, 45 (1948), pp. 321–333.
[40] Town, Clara H., *Familial Feeblemindedness*. Buffalo: Foster and Stewart Publishing Corp., 1939.

the mental defect could be ascribed as much to social heredity as to biological heredity.

The studies on both the hereditary characteristics of mentally retarded children and the cultural factors in intelligence are not conclusive. The term "cultural factors" is itself vague since it refers to numerous situations in the home, the community, and the school. The studies on heredity, on the other hand, do not control the variables of culture.

In the light of studies and experiments relating to the possible effect of culture on mental retardation, the following observations are made:

(1) Idiots and imbeciles are found about as frequently in families of high intellectual ability as in families of low intellectual ability. It is doubtful that cultural factors can account for idiots or imbeciles.

(2) The high-grade mental defective, the mentally handicapped, and the borderline defective child seem to be found more frequently in families of low socio-economic, intellectual, and educational level. The question here is whether the low mental functioning ability of these children is due to inheritance or to the cultural environment in which they find themselves. It is possible that the answer will involve both factors.

(3) The studies on preschool children, such as those reported by Freeman and by Skeels, indicate that favorable changes in intellectual growth may be accomplished more readily with younger children than with older children. It is possible that rigid and stereotyped behavior developed during the preschool years may be too difficult to change by cultural and educational advantages at a later age.

(4) Anthropologists and psychologists have stressed the importance of child-rearing practices on the personality of children and societies. There is some sporadic evidence that the parent-child relationship is an important one in the development of intelligence or in its effect on mental retardation. Future studies on this problem may throw some light on mental retardation in children.

(5) There are environmental deprivations in "good" or higher socio-economic homes which may affect intellectual growth. Prolonged sickness, repressive and overinhibiting measures, and

lack of warmth and affection could possibly explain some cases of mental retardation.

REFERENCES

Benda, Clemens E. *Mongolism and Cretinism.* New York: Grune and Stratton, 1946.

Davenport, Charles B. "Causes of Retarded and Incomplete Development," *American Association on Mental Deficiency*, 41, 1936, pp. 208–214.

Davis, Kingsley. "Extreme Social Isolation of a Child," *American Journal of Sociology*, 45 (January, 1940), pp. 554–565.

Doll, Edgar A. "The Essentials of an Inclusive Concept of Mental Deficiency," *American Journal of Mental Deficiency*, 46 (October, 1941), pp. 214–219.

Doll, Edgar A. "The Feeble Minded Child," *Manual of Child Psychology*, Leonard Carmichael, Editor. New York: John Wiley and Sons, Inc., 1946.

Freeman, Frank N., Karl J. Holzenger, and B. C. Mitchell, "The Influences of Environment on the Intelligence, School Achievement, and Conduct of Foster Children," *The Twenty-Seventh Yearbook of the National Society for the Study of Education:* Nature and Nurture, Part I. Bloomington, Illinois: Public School Publishing Company, 1928.

Gates, R. R., *Human Genetics*, Vols. I and II. New York: The Macmillan Company, 1946.

Gesell, Arnold. *Wolf Child and Human Child.* New York: Harper and Brothers, 1941.

Goddard, H. H. *Feeble-mindedness: Its Causes and Consequences.* New York: The Macmillan Company, 1914.

Goddard, H. H. *The Kallikak Family.* New York: The Macmillan Company, 1913.

Jervis, George A. "Phenylpyruvic Oligophrenia," *Archives of Neurology and Psychiatry*, 38 (November, 1937), pp .944–963.

Kanner, Leo. "A Miniature Textbook of Feeblemindedness," *Child Care Monographs*, No. 1. New York: Child Care Publications, 1949.

Kephart, N. C. "Influencing the Rate of Mental Growth in Retarded Children Through Environmental Stimulation," *The Thirty-Ninth Yearbook of the National Society for the Study of Education:* Intelligence: Its Nature and Nurture, Part II. Bloomington, Illinois: Public School Publishing Company, 1940.

Kirk, Samuel A. "An Evaluation of the Study of Bernardine G. Schmidt Entitled: Changes in Personal, Social, and Intellectual Behavior of Children Originally Classified as Feebleminded," *Psychological Bulletin*, 45, 1948, pp. 321–333.

Levy, Sol, and H. A. Perry. "Pertussis as a Cause of Mental Deficiency," *American Journal of Mental Deficiency*, 52 (October, 1948), pp. 217–226.

Myerson, A. "Medical Psychiatry," *The Problem of Mental Disorder*, Madison Bentley, Editor. New York: McGraw-Hill Book Company, Inc., 1934.

Schmidt, Bernardine G. "Changes in Personal, Social, and Intellectual Behavior of Children Originally Classified as Feebleminded," *Psychological Monographs*, 60, No. 5, 1945.

Scholl, Mary Louis, Warren E. Wheeler, and Lawrence Snyder. "Rh Antibodies in Mothers of Feebleminded Children," *Journal of Heredity*, 38, 1947, pp. 253–256.

Schreiber, Frederick. "Mental Deficiency from Paranatal Asphyxia," *American Association on Mental Deficiency*, 44, No. 1, 1939, pp. 95–106.

Skeels, Harold M., and H. B. Dye. "A Study of the Effects of Differential Stimulation on Mentally Retarded Children," *American Association on Mental Deficiency*, 44, No. 1, 1939, pp. 114–1136.

Skeels, Harold M. *et al*. "A Study of Environmental Stimulation," *University of Iowa Studies*, 15, No. 4 (December, 1938). Iowa City: University of Iowa, 1938.

Skeels, Harold M. "Mental Development of Children in Foster Homes," *Journal of Consulting Psychology*, 2, No. 2 (March–April, 1938), pp. 33–34.

Snyder, Lawrence, M. D. Schonfeld, and Edith M. Offerman. "The Rh Factor and Feeblemindedness," *Journal of Heredity*, 36, 1945, pp. 9–10.

Strauss, Alfred A., and Laura E. Lehtinen. *Psychopathology and Education of the Brain-Injured Child*. New York: Grune and Stratton, 1947.

Swann, Charles, A. L. Fostevin, and G. H. Barhamblock. "Final Observations on Congenital Defects in Infants Following Infectious Diseases During Pregnancy with Special Reference to Rubella," *Medical Journal of Australia*, 2 (December, 1946), pp. 889–908.

Town, Clara H. *Familial Feeblemindedness*. Buffalo: Foster and Stewart Publishing Corporation, 1939.

Tredgold, A. F. *A Textbook of Mental Deficiency*, 6th Ed. New York: William Wood and Company, 1937.

Yannet, Herman, and Rose Lieberman. "A and B Iso-Immunization as a Possible Factor in the Etiology of Mental Deficiency," *American Journal of Mental Deficiency*, 50 (October, 1945), pp. 242–244.

Yannet, Herman, and Rose Lieberman. "The Rh Factor in the Etiology of Mental Deficiency," *American Journal of Mental Deficiency*, 49 (October, 1944), pp. 133–137.

Chapter 3

Identification and Diagnosis

THE PURPOSE of this chapter is to familiarize the teacher of the mentally handicapped with the psychological, educational, and personality tests and methods utilized in the evaluation of children. Equipped with this understanding, he can more adequately interpret psychological reports and diagnoses by specialists or request a more adequate evaluation of a child in the event that it has not been made.

NEED FOR DIAGNOSIS

Parents, teachers, and school administrators are interested in knowing the abilities, disabilities, and personality structure of mentally handicapped children so that more adequate social and educational provisions can be made for them. In Chapter 1, children with low intelligence were classified for educational purposes into three major groups, namely, (1) the mentally deficient or feeble-minded, (2) the mentally handicapped, and (3) the slow learners. It was pointed out that the mentally deficient are custodial cases, requiring care and supervision throughout their lives. The mentally handicapped, however, are educable to some degree and should be placed in special classes. It was advocated that the slow learner should remain in the regular classes of the public school, but that some adaptations of instruction be made for him within that organization.

To differentiate these groups, and to determine the specific psychological, educational, and social needs of a child, it is necessary that an adequate diagnosis be made. Only in this way will each child be placed in the situation of most value to him.

The development and organization of a comprehensive educational program for the mentally handicapped is also dependent upon adequate diagnoses of the children to be placed in the special classes. *First*, it is essential that only those children for whom these classes are organized shall be placed in them. These classes lose their value when they become a "dumping ground" for the mentally handicapped, the slow learner, the educationally retarded or handicapped, and the socially maladjusted. No adequate program can be organized within one classroom to care for all who are retarded for other reasons than low mental ability. *Second*, it is essential that the teachers of the mentally handicapped know as much as possible about the children before developing a program to meet their needs.

A Diagnosis Requires a Study of the Whole Child

An adequate diagnosis of a child for the purpose of determining his abilities, disabilities, and needs requires a study of the whole child. This study will include:

(1) A psychological or psychometric examination to determine the level of mental ability of the child.

(2) A medical examination for the purpose of determining possible etiology and need for medical treatment.

(3) A social and personality study for the purpose of determining personality and social needs and possible etiological factors in these areas.

(4) An educational evaluation to determine the degree of retardation and possible educational disabilities.

SCREENING AND EXAMINING SCHOOL CHILDREN

Children with mental handicaps of various degrees are referred for individual examination by parents, teachers, and physicians. This referral is usually the result of the child's lack of progress (or markedly retarded progress) in mental, social, or educational growth. The usual procedure of identifying the child in school is through a teacher's referral based on (1) the child's failure to make normal progress in school, (2) low test performance on group intelligence tests, and (3) low test scores on group achievement tests.

In such cases the children are found to be mentally deficient, mentally handicapped, slow learners, or normal in intelligence. Some children with normal intelligence may have a specific educational disability. Others may perform at a low level because of emotional disturbances rather than low mental ability. In some cases the child is found to be average in intellectual abilities but is achieving in school at a low level because of marked physical disability such as cerebral palsy, extremely poor vision, or poor hearing. For these reasons children cannot be considered as mentally deficient, mentally handicapped, or slow learners until an adequate evaluation has been made by a competent diagnostic specialist.

Following the referral, a psychologist evaluates the child by means of a case study and the results he obtains on psychological, educational achievement, and personality tests. When indicated, a medical examination is also obtained.

The medical and social history of the child is used primarily to determine the prognosis of the case and to plan a program to meet the needs of the child. If it can be determined that the retardation is due to some medical cause which is becoming progressively more severe, the chances of helping the child to become a socially adequate and economically self-supporting adult are relatively poor. In such cases, the examiner may hesitate to place the child in a class for the mentally handicapped. The social history is primarily of value in planning a program for the child. In attempting to teach the child to adjust to the community, to the neighborhood, and to his family it is necessary to be familiar with the group with whom he associates.

In addition to the social history and a medical examination, it is necessary that a child suspected of having low intelligence be diagnosed by means of a battery of standardized examinations. This chapter is devoted primarily to a discussion of (1) intelligence tests, (2) achievement tests, (3) personality and social maturity tests, and (4) other types of diagnostic tests.

INTELLIGENCE TESTS

Most psychologists agree that intelligence is extremely complex and cannot be measured by a single, simple instrument or test. Consequently, it is not only advisable but usually necessary to make use of both a verbal and a performance, individual intelligence test when attempting to establish the intellectual capacity of a suspected mentally handicapped child. These two types of scales apparently test somewhat different factors or phases of intelligence. This is shown by the fact that results obtained by testing the same person often differ rather widely. The reasons for these differences in results may be the complex character of intelligence, the language development and ability of the child, the child's ability to read and understand written language, the child's general background including the home, community, playmates, sensory deviations or defects, and the child's perceptual difficulties.

After a verbal and a performance intelligence test have been administered to a child, the examiner may feel that he still does not have enough information to make a complete diagnosis. In such cases it is sometimes advisable to peruse the performance of the child obtained on other intelligence tests. An examination of the results of all these tests will enable the examiner to establish the mental level at which the child is performing.

A description of the more commonly used intelligence tests is given below.

INDIVIDUAL INTELLIGENCE TESTS

The development of mental tests, as we know them today, originated through the efforts of Alfred Binet and his interest in diagnosing mentally retarded children. Binet had been making measurements of children's abilities over a period of years. It was not until the schools of Paris asked him for a method of separating the educable from the hopelessly uneducable children that he made an effort to develop a scale. The first scale of intelligence was published by Binet and Simon in 1905. Revisions of the original scale were made in 1908 and in 1911. These tests are similar to the forms used today, being composed of a large number of items or tasks that children should be able to do at specified age levels.

The original test developed by Binet and Simon was rather widely accepted and translated into other languages with relatively minor changes. Goddard published a revision in this country in 1910. In the same year Lewis M. Terman began experimenting with the Binet scale and, as a result, published the most popular and widely accepted early revision in 1916. This was the most commonly used intelligence test until replaced by an expanded and better standardized revision by Terman and Merrill in 1937.[1]

Verbal intelligence tests. The 1937 revision of the *Stanford-Binet* is the most commonly used of the verbal, individual intelligence tests. It is actually composed of a large number of test items. The individual test items are made up of tasks of varying difficulty, the difficulty depending upon the age placement of the item. Some of them are easy enough for the average two-year-old. They then become progressively more difficult through the succeeding age levels. At the year II level the child is expected to be able to combine words, identify a number of common objects, identify parts of the body, and identify pictures; at the year V level he is expected to be able to define common objects according to their use, count four objects, and remember a sentence containing ten words; and at the year VIII level he is expected to be able to remember the essential parts of a story, recognize simple verbal absurdities, distinguish similarities and differences, and remember a thirteen- and fourteen-word sentence.

The majority of the items in the Binet can be classified into a number of larger categories. These general categories are vocabulary, memory, recognition of absurdities, language development,

[1] Terman, Lewis M., and Maude A. Merrill, *Measuring Intelligence*. Boston: Houghton Mifflin Co., 1937.

understanding of number concepts, understanding of similarities and differences, and a combination of motor co-ordination and visual perception.

To calculate the mental age (M.A.) of a child on the Binet, it is necessary first to determine his basal age. (The basal age is the highest age level at which the child can pass all the items.) To this are added the months of credit he receives for each test item he passes beyond the basal age. The credit on the various test items varies; that is, he is given one month credit for each item passed through the year V level and two months credit for each item passed from year VI through year XIV.

After the M.A. has been determined, the intelligence quotient (I.Q.) can be found by referring to a table in the back of Terman and Merrill's book *Measuring Intelligence* (which is also the manual for administering the Binet), or it can be calculated for those children under thirteen years of age by dividing the derived M.A. by the chronological age (C.A.) and multiplying the result by 100.

For example: A child has a chronological age of 9 years — 7 months. He passes all items at the IV year — 6 month level, four items at the V year level, three items at the VI year level, one item at the VII year level, and fails all items at the VIII year level. His basal age is 4 years — 6 months. To this age is added the credit he receives for items passed at succeeding age levels (12 months), M.A. of 5 years — 6 months. By dividing the M.A. (5 years — 6 months, or 66 months) by the C.A. (9 years — 7 months, or 115 months) and multiplying the result by 100, an I.Q. of 57 is derived.

Basal age 4 years	— 6 months	
plus V	4	"
VI	6	"
VII	2	"
VIII	0	"

Total	4 years — 18 months
M.A.	= 5 years — 6 months
C.A.	= 9 years — 7 months

$$\text{I.Q.} = \frac{\text{M.A.}}{\text{C.A.}} \times 100$$

$$= \frac{66 \text{ mo.}}{115 \text{ mo.}} \times 100$$

$$= 57$$

In the past the I.Q. was used for general diagnosis. Children with a valid Binet I.Q. of less than 50 were usually considered to be mentally deficient or feeble-minded. The group with I.Q.'s of 50 to 70 or 80 composed the mentally handicapped, and the slow learners consisted of those with I.Q.'s between 80 and 90. The psychologist of today still utilizes the Binet I.Q. but recognizes it as only one factor in the total diagnosis of a child.

The teacher of the mentally handicapped will find the M.A. of more value than the I.Q. in planning a program for the child. Since the I.Q. is a ratio between the M.A. and the C.A., it gives no indication concerning the child's mental level. On the other hand, the M.A. will tell the teacher at approximately what academic level the child should be achieving. That is, a child with a M.A. of 7 should be achieving academically at about the same level as a normal child of 7 although his chronological age may be 9 or 10. It must be remembered that the expected grade level cannot be predicted perfectly from the M.A. since the correlation between mental age and academic achievement is far from perfect. It does, however, give a basis upon which to make an estimate.

Another commonly used verbal intelligence scale is the *Kuhlmann Tests of Mental Development*. This test consists of a large number of individual test items grouped together into a single battery. Many of the items are very similar to those found in the Binet, but it has the advantage of having items at a lower age level.

The individual test items are standardized at specific age levels in months rather than grouped into age levels in years or six-month periods as are the Binet. A basal age is determined by the level at which the child passes a number of consecutive test items. To the basal age, a month's credit is added for each succeeding item correctly answered. When the basal age and the additional months' credit are added together, the mental age of the subject is determined. The I.Q. of a child can then be calculated by dividing the mental age by the chronological age and multiplying the results by 100, a procedure similar to that used with the *Stanford-Binet*.

Performance intelligence tests. A number of individual performance intelligence tests have been developed which attempt to measure intellectual ability by using a minimum of verbal directions and responses. The purpose of developing this type of intelligence test was to avoid penalizing subjects with deficiencies in language ability resulting from hearing defects, foreign background, or other causes.

Among the more commonly used performance tests are the

Arthur Point Scale of Performance Tests and the *Cornell-Coxe Perform- ance Ability Scale*. These tests require the subject to perform a series of intellectual tasks which do not demand the use of verbal- ization. The directions for the various test items are usually given by the examiner either in pantomime or with a minimum use of words.

All performance tests are composed of somewhat similar types of items, although those included in a specific battery may differ in some respects. The most commonly used items are: the Koh's Blocks (which consist of a number of cubes painted with different colors on the various sides, with which the subject is required to construct a pattern corresponding to a given model); the mannequin or object-assembly type test (in which the subject is given a number of pieces of an object and is required to construct the object with them); various types of form boards (on which the subject is required to place the correct object or figure in the proper position); a number of pictures which form a sequential story; and mazes of various types.

In addition to the *Arthur Point Scale* and the *Cornell-Coxe* there are other specialized performance tests. For example, two such tests have been developed for the deaf. These are the *Ontario School Ability Test* and the *Nebraska Test of Learning Aptitude for Young Deaf Children*. Such tests depend entirely upon demonstration and pantomime to inform the subject what is required of him. Hayes has also made an adaptation of the *Binet* to be used with the blind. Since mentally handicapped children may have an additional audi- tory, visual, or physical handicap, it is necessary for the psycholo- gist to be familiar with these specialized tests and also to know the problems encountered when testing a child with cerebral palsy.

Combined verbal and performance intelligence tests. The best example of this type of test is the *Wechsler-Bellevue Intelligence Scale*. This test has come into very common usage for older chil- dren and adults. More recently, a second form has been published which enables psychologists to examine most children of school age. Unlike the *Binet*, no mental age is derived on the *Wechsler*. An I.Q., however, is determined from a table.

The *Wechsler Scale* has many of the diagnostic features of the

Binet, plus some additional ones. An examination of specific items passed and failed by the subject and of the general pattern of successes on the various subtests often aids the examiner in obtaining an insight into the subject's difficulties. Its primary shortcoming for use in the schools is the lack of a derived mental age for use in determining tentative grade-level achievement to be expected from the child. Its main advantage is that comparable verbal and performance ratings may be obtained from the same instrument.

GROUP INTELLIGENCE TESTS [2]

Group intelligence tests may be divided into two relatively large subgroups, power tests and speed tests. A speed test is a test in which each of the sections of the test has a restrictive time limit. Stress is placed upon the speed with which an individual can perform a given task. A power test, on the other hand, usually has no rigid time limits on the various sections of the test. When the majority of the children have completed that section of the test the examiner may go on to the next section. Thus, the emphasis of the power test is placed upon the individual's ability to perform, not upon the speed with which he performs. Since in testing and diagnosing a mentally handicapped child, the primary interest is in his ability to do a task rather than the speed with which he does it, the power test is the one more commonly used in examining such children.

Group intelligence tests are designed primarily as a screening device to be used by examiners in choosing the children who should be given individual intelligence tests at a later date. These tests

[2] In addition to the group intelligence tests briefly described in this section, the following tests are also used: *Cole-Vincent Group Intelligence Tests for School Entrants*, Grades: kindergarten to 1 (Bureau of Educational Measurements, Kansas State Teachers College of Emporia, Emporia, Kansas); *Group Test of Learning Capacity: The Dominion Tests*, Primary for grades kindergarten to 1 and Junior for grades 4 to 6 (Department of Educational Research, Ontario, College of Education, University of Toronto, Toronto, Ontario, Canada); *Pintner General Ability Tests: Verbal Series*, Pintner-Cunningham Primary Test for grades kindergarten to 2, Pintner-Durost Elementary Test for grades 2.5 to 4.5, and Pintner Intermediate Test for grades 4.5 to 9.5 (World Book Company, Yonkers-on-the-Hudson, New York); and *Pintner Non-language Primary Mental Test*, Grades: kindergarten to 2 (Bureau of Publications, Teachers College, Columbia University, New York, New York).

attempt to measure the same mental functions as those measured by individual intelligence tests, but in a group situation. The questions are given to the subject either in written or in pictorial form, and he is then required to choose the correct answer from among a number of items. Since the correct answer is one of three or four items, the subject may accidentally choose the right one although he does not know it. When a group of children are being examined, it is impossible for the examiner to observe each child closely and to determine whether or not he is actually answering the questions from his knowledge or making some excellent guesses. It is also impossible for the examiner to observe the attitudes and methods of attack used by the children. As a result, a diagnosis of mental retardation should never be made on the basis of a group intelligence test alone since a number of intangibles, such as method of attack, real knowledge, ability to follow directions, and so forth may influence the child's score. At times, however, group tests do provide additional valuable information that may be used to supplement the information already obtained on an individual intelligence test.

The following are some of the commonly found test items used in group intelligence tests:

Similarities. The subject is given a picture of an object or form and is required to find another one that is identical to it from among a number of pictures or drawings.

Vocabulary. The vocabulary of a child may be tested by having him either check a word that is synonymous with a given word or mark the picture which correctly represents an object named.

Following directions. The examiner reads a set of directions which the subject must follow. These may involve picking out the correct drawing according to size, shape, or description, making the correct mark in the proper place, or they may be combined with one of the other types of tests.

Comprehension. This may be measured by testing the subject's ability to distinguish between opposites and similarities, his understanding of analogies, or his comprehension of a story as indicated by his selection of the correct answer to the story from among a series of pictures.

Number concept. This is measured in a number of different ways. The subject may be asked to find the wrong number from among a series of numbers; to choose the largest object, smallest object, first object, fourth object from the end, and so forth; to make quantity comparisons; or to solve an arithmetical problem.

The following tests are some representative and commonly used group intelligence examinations.

California Tests of Mental Maturity.[3] These tests are primarily power tests with ample time limits. They consist of five batteries with a range of mental ability from kindergarten through college. Each battery covers a mental range of several years so that only two, at the most, would be needed to test the children of any class.

The main advantages of these tests are: (1) Clear directions for administration and scoring, (2) well-standardized age norms, (3) accompanying studies of the relation of the tests to school progress, and (4) subscores of the child's language and nonlanguage abilities, as well as a total score.

Kuhlmann-Anderson Intelligence Tests.[4] While these tests are timed, the time limits are usually ample for most normal children. This may not hold true, however, for the mentally handicapped. The tests consist of nine batteries for grades one through twelve. Since the subdivisions are so numerous, a teacher may find it necessary to use several different batteries to test adequately the children of one class.

The main advantages of the *Kuhlmann-Anderson Intelligence Tests* are (1) relatively little time (less than one hour) is required for their administration, (2) clear directions for administration and scoring are provided, and (3) little dependence on reading skills is demanded.

Otis Quick-Scoring Mental Ability Tests.[5] The tests are composed of three batteries for grades 1.5–4, 4–9, and 9–16. With these

[3] May be obtained from the California Test Bureau, Los Angeles, California.
[4] May be obtained from the Educational Test Bureau, Educational Publishers, Inc., Minneapolis, Minnesota.
[5] May be obtained from the World Book Company, Yonkers, New York.

ranges, the teacher is usually able to test all the children in one class with a single battery. The tests at the lowest level may be given either nonverbally or verbally. The verbal test requires the teacher or examiner to recite the items. In this way the amount or quality of reading skill of the child does not affect his test scores. The test score may be influenced by the child's visual acuity, however.

The intermediate tests (grades 4–9) are designed for either hand or machine scoring. Since the number of children in a special class is small, machine scoring is of little advantage. The tests are easy to administer and score, but since some children may have difficulty in using the answer sheets, which may result in lowering the scores, it is necessary for the examiner to check carefully the accuracy of the sample responses to make certain that all children understand the method of response.

ACHIEVEMENT TESTS [6]

A typical characteristic of a mentally handicapped child is his retardation in academic achievement when compared to "normal" children of the same chronological age. It is consequently necessary for diagnosis to administer an achievement test to determine the child's academic level. If there is little or no academic retardation relative to chronological age, the child cannot be legitimately diagnosed as mentally handicapped and the examiner must look for some other cause for the low intelligence test results. If,

[6] In addition to the achievement tests described briefly in this section the following tests are also used: *American School Achievement Test*, Primary Battery I for grade 1, Primary Battery II for grades 2 and 3, and Intermediate Battery for grades 4–6 (Public School Publishing Company, Bloomington, Illinois); *Coordinate Scales of Attainment*, Grades 1, 2, 3, 4, 5, 6, 7, and 8 (Educational Test Publishers, Inc., 720 Washington Ave., S. E., Minneapolis, Minnesota); *Every Pupil Primary Achievement Test*, Grades 1 to 3, (Bureau of Educational Measurements, Kansas State Teachers College of Emporia, Emporia, Kansas); *Gray Votaw General Achievement Test*, Revised Edition for grades 1–3, 4–6, and 7–9 (Steck Company, Austin, Texas); *Iowa Every-Pupil Tests of Basic Skills*, New Edition for grades 3–5 and 5–9 (Houghton Mifflin Co., Boston, Massachusetts); and *Wide Range Achievement Test*: Reading, Spelling, Arithmetic, from Kindergarten to College, ages 5 years and over (Psychological Corporation, 522 Fifth Avenue, New York, New York).

however, the achievement is low, the results of the achievement test tend to supplement the results of the intelligence tests. The scores of the tests, however, are not used solely for the purpose of diagnosing mental retardation. An examination of the achievement tests is often of invaluable assistance to the teacher of the special class in determining the specific academic areas in which the child needs additional help, thus adding to the information required in planning a curriculum to be followed by the child.

Achievement tests also may be divided into two relatively large subgroups, power tests and speed tests. Again, the primary interest is the mentally handicapped child's ability to do a task rather than the speed with which he accomplishes it. Consequently, the power test is much more commonly used.

In construction and content, the various group achievement tests are very similar. At the primary level they commonly test word recognition, sentence comprehension, paragraph comprehension, number concepts, and some facility in the manipulation of fundamental number combinations. At the more advanced levels some additional skills are tested, such as reading comprehension, reading speed, spelling, history, geography, punctuation, language usage, and any of the other common subject matter areas found in the elementary grades.

The following tests are representative and commonly used for measuring achievement.

Progressive Achievement Tests.[7] These tests, which are primarily power tests, stressing level of achievement rather than speed, consist of four batteries — Primary (grades 1–3), Elementary (grades 4–6), Intermediate (grades 7–9), and Advanced (grades 9–13).

The directions for administration and scoring are clear and concise, and the results can be easily interpreted and applied. In addition, diagnostic suggestions that are helpful to the classroom teacher are included. As an aid in diagnosis, the reading vocabulary, reading comprehension, arithmetic reasoning, arithmetic fundamentals, and language areas are each divided into a number of subtests.

[7] May be obtained from the California Test Bureau, Los Angeles, California.

Metropolitan Achievement Tests.[8]   Separate batteries of these tests may be obtained for grades 1, 2, 3–4, 5–6, and 7–9.5.   In addition, two forms are available at each level so that the same test will not have to be repeated or a completely different test used in the event a retest is required.

The batteries consist of two or three types of tests for each of the two major areas (reading and arithmetic).   This aids the teacher in interpreting the results and making diagnoses of difficulties.

A spelling test is introduced at the grade 2 level, language at the grade 3 level, and literature, history and civics, geography, and punctuation at the grade 4–6 level.

Stanford Achievement Test.[9]   These tests are published in three batteries, Primary (grades 2–3), Intermediate (grades 4–6), and Advanced (grades 7–9).   They are well constructed and the instructions are short, simple, and clear so that there should be little chance of children failing to understand what they are to do.   The section of the manual dealing with interpretation of test scores should aid the teacher in making use of scores in diagnosing specific problems.

Gates Primary Reading Tests.[10] These tests consist of three types, each in a separate booklet — Type I, Word Recognition (15 minutes); Type 2, Sentence Reading (15 minutes); Type 3, Paragraph Reading (20 minutes).   These tests are applicable for measuring the reading ability of mentally handicapped children at the primary level.   The advantages of these tests with mentally handicapped children are their simplicity of administration and the long time limit given for each type.   They are primarily power rather than speed tests.

[8] May be obtained from the World Book Company, Yonkers, New York.
[9] May be obtained from the World Book Company, Yonkers, New York.
[10] May be obtained from the Bureau of Publications, Teachers College, Columbia University, New York.

PERSONALITY AND SOCIAL MATURITY TESTS

There are no group tests that have much validity for the diagnosis of the personality of mentally handicapped children. Personality and social maturity have been evaluated, however, by a number of different methods including case study, observation, projective techniques, and social maturity scales. The projective tests and social maturity scale will be described in this section.

The two most commonly used projective tests are the *Rorschach* and the *Thematic Apperception Tests*. While these tests are given individually and are rather time-consuming, they can give the competent examiner some insight into the personality structure of the subject, which otherwise could only be attained by an exceedingly arduous study of the child and his background, and a number of psychiatric interviews.

Since intelligence tests are inadequate for explaining all variations in behavior, projective tests act as an excellent supplement. The Binet and other intelligence tests indicate the intellectual behavior level of the individual. The Rorschach purports not only to indicate the intelligence level but also to reveal whether the tested intellectual level is being depressed by some personality problem. It also indicates the extent to which an individual has a drive to succeed. A number of psychologists allege that it is possible to estimate the person's intelligence on the basis of both the Thematic Apperception Test and the Rorschach.

Personality tests perform a very definite function in the diagnoses of mentally handicapped children. With the results of a personality test available, the psychologist can determine whether or not special class placement is most efficacious for the particular child. In addition, he will be able to suggest methods of helping the child to adjust to other children, to the community, and to the family.

Sarason summarizes the use of projective tests in making a study of the relationship between capacity and functioning as follows:

... one of the most significant contributions which projective techniques have made to the field of mental deficiency is that some people have been awakened to the fact that the behavior of the defective individual is not explained by pointing to an intelligence test score and that whatever is subsumed under intellectual processes is inextricably related to and affected by attitudinal or subjective factors which have been acquired as a result of earlier life experiences.[11]

The Rorschach Test. This test is composed of a series of ten unstructured ink blots. Some of them are shades of black and white while others contain chromatic colors. The subject is given a plate containing one ink blot at a time and asked to state what he sees in the ink blot or what it makes him think of. As a result of the subject's responses to the ink blots, the types of objects he sees, the amount of the ink blot he uses, the method in which he sees them (whether it may be form or shading), his use of color, the length of time before responding, and so forth, the examiner can make a diagnosis of the individual's personality. In relation to the use and interpretation of the Rorschach, Sarason has made the following evaluation:

It is interesting to note that the psychological pendulum seems to have swung markedly. Whereas formerly the I.Q. was the sole basis for a diagnosis of mental deficiency, the Rorschach seems now to have been given this Herculean task. It may be anticipated that just as the uncritical acceptance of the I.Q. proved embarrassing to the psychologist, so will the Rorschach be shown to have limitations. It is indeed surprising how in the clinical literature little can be found about the limitations of the Rorschach. It cannot be denied that the problems to which the Rorschach has been applied are extremely important from a theoretical and practical point of view; the relation between "personality and intelligence" remains a central problem in clinical psychology. The Rorschach *may* give a better picture of this relationship than any other single technique. But until this has been demonstrated by scientific procedure and control, the value of the Rorschach remains an open question.[12]

The Thematic Apperception Test (TAT). The TAT is much more structured than the Rorschach. It is composed of a series of pictures that are given to the subject in two successive sittings one day apart. Ten pictures are given to the subject one day and ten the following day. When a picture is given to the subject, he is

[11] Sarason, Seymour B., *Psychological Problems in Mental Deficiency.* New York: Harper and Brothers, 1949, p. 261.
[12] *Ibid.*, p. 248.

told to look at the picture and make up a short story about it. He is to tell what happened before, what is happening now, and what the conclusion of the story is. The stories must be short as the subject is limited to a five-minute period with each picture. The ten pictures that are given on the second day are more vague and less structured than the ten pictures that are given the first day. An examination of the stories told by the subject, especially their content and the behavior of the central character, reveals much concerning the thoughts, feelings, and attitudes of the subject. A consequent diagnosis of his personality problems and the problems he is encountering in school, in the community, with his family, or with his associates can often be determined.

The Vineland Social Maturity Scale. This scale is rather widely used to measure the social maturity of a specific child as compared to the corresponding maturity of children of the same age. It is composed of a large number of items which children of various age levels are expected to be able to do. For example, at age level one, such items as balancing one's head, rolling over, sitting up, pulling oneself up, standing up, not drooling, and so forth are included. The items then follow the child's development from year to year, until at the seven- to eight-year level he is expected to use a table knife, comb his hair, and participate in preadolescent play. At the fifteen-year level such items as communicating by letter, following current events, going out unsupervised, using spending money, and so forth appear. The scale starts from the zero- to one-year level and continues through the twenty-five-year-plus level. With this scale it is possible to make a comparison of the social maturity of any child with that of children at any specified age level and to determine whether or not the child has the social maturity of children of his own age level or of a younger or older age level.

OTHER TESTS

Other types of tests that have not been discussed under the previous headings but that do need at least mention are (1) readiness tests, (2) tests of primary mental ability, (3) motor ability tests, and (4) vision and hearing tests. While a good deal of work has been done on aptitude testing, the norms that have been established are for "normal" or non-mentally-handicapped children and, consequently, are even less reliable and useful for the mentally handicapped group.

Readiness Tests. Some of the readiness tests used to determine whether a child is ready to begin to learn to read are the *Gates Reading Readiness Test*,[13] the *Metropolitan Readiness Tests*,[14] and the *Monroe Reading Aptitude Tests*.[15] These tests are designed to measure the abilities a child needs in learning to read. They are usually divided into a number of areas, and a comparison of the child's abilities with the abilities of the population in general can be made in each of the areas. The subtests usually measure visual, auditory, and motor abilities as well as articulation, language, vocabulary, and perception. Ordinarily, if a child scores relatively high in all these areas, he is expected to be able to learn to read within the next year.

With the results of this type of test a teacher is able to determine the children's strengths and weaknesses and the areas on which the emphasis must be placed in preparing them to learn to read or in helping them in their beginning reading. Again it must be emphasized that these tests are not infallible. If they are used as a diagnostic tool, they are of invaluable assistance to the teacher and it is in this connection that they prove to be of most worth.

Tests of primary mental abilities. The tests composing the battery of *Primary Mental Abilities* [16] for ages five to seven years consist of items found in most readiness tests. However, this test is primarily an intelligence test which attempts to measure discreet mental abilities. Thus, in addition to furnishing a mental age and an I.Q., this test also purports to measure abilities and disabilities of perceptual speed, verbal meaning, quantitative thinking, motor ability, and space.

[13] May be obtained from the Bureau of Publications, Teachers College, Columbia University, New York City, New York.
[14] May be obtained from the World Book Company, Yonkers, New York.
[15] May be obtained from Houghton Mifflin Company, Boston, Massachusetts.
[16] May be obtained from Science Research Associates, 228 S. Wabash Ave. Chicago, Illinois.

Primary mental ability tests are speed rather than power tests. The directions for administering and scoring the tests are clear, and tables and a discussion concerning interpretation are included. It is recommended, when testing the younger or more retarded children, that they be tested in groups of five or six.

Motor proficiency tests. The *Oseretsky Test* is an example of an age scale designed to measure the genetic level of motor proficiency. The scale is divided into six groups of tests at each age level, from four years to fifteen or sixteen years. These tests purport to measure (1) static co-ordination, (2) dynamic co-ordination of the hands, (3) general dynamic co-ordination, (4) motor speed, (5) simultaneous voluntary movements, and (6) synkinesia (ability to perform without superfluous movements).

The original scale was developed in Europe and has recently been translated into English.[17] At present, however, there are no American norms or standards.

Clinicians, educators, and psychologists working in the field of child development have long recognized the need for a test of motor ability. In the field of mental retardation additional information concerning the relationship of intelligence and motor ability is especially desired. Some attempt has been made to adapt the *Oseretsky Tests*.[18] This adaptation may be used to some advantage until a more comprehensive scale has been developed and standardized.

Visual tests. The examination for visual defects in children is the responsibility of the medical profession. However, it is necessary that psychologists and teachers find children who may be functioning at a lower level because of a visual handicap. For these purposes, initial screening tests have been constructed to aid the teacher, psychologist, or school nurse in identifying those that should be referred to an ophthalmologist for diagnosis and treatment.

The more commonly used visual screening tests are the *Snellen*

[17] *The Oseretsky Tests of Motor Proficiency*, Edgar A. Doll, ed. Minneapolis: Educational Test Bureau, Educational Publishers, Inc., 1946.

[18] Cassel, Robert H., "The Vineland Adaptation of the Oseretsky Tests," *The Vineland Training School Bulletin*, Supplement to 46, Nos. 3–4, Monograph Supplement Series, No. 1, 1949.

Chart,[19] the *Betts Telebinocular*,[20] and the *Massachusetts Vision Test*.[21]

Hearing tests. Group and individual audiometers are used to test the hearing of children. Starting at about the third-grade level, the group audiometer is used as a screening test, whole classes being tested at one time. The child who shows a significant hearing loss on the group test is given an individual test to determine more accurately the amount of loss and at what specific areas or frequencies it occurs. If the child also shows a significant loss on the individual test, he should be referred to an otologist for a thorough examination to determine the cause and then receive the medical treatment needed.

INTERPRETATION OF TEST RESULTS

The purpose of administering tests to a mentally handicapped child is to determine objectively (1) his levels of achievement and intelligence and (2) his abilities, disabilities, and behavior reactions or personal adjustment. The test results should assist the examiner in (1) determining the most advantageous placement of the child and (2) recommending an educational and social program to meet the needs of the child.

The behavior, physical characteristics, and background of the mentally handicapped, the mentally deficient or feeble-minded, or the slow learners are by no means homogeneous. Consequently, attempts to classify the mentally retarded on the basis of any one characteristic or on the results of any one test are extremely futile.

In the past many clinicians attempted to diagnose children with low intelligence almost entirely on the basis of an I.Q. obtained on one intelligence test. They immediately encountered many problems in diagnosing the borderline cases. Those who believed any person with an I.Q. below 70 was mentally handicapped or below 50 was mentally deficient found cases that tested slightly above

---

[19] May be obtained from any local health department.

[20] May be obtained from Keystone View Company, Meadville, Pennsylvania.

[21] May be obtained from Massachusetts Department of Public Health, Division of Mental Hygiene, Boston, Massachusetts.

and below these limits on successive tests. At one time they might be placed in one classification, and the next time in another.

To make matters more complicated, the results of various intelligence tests are not equivalent. These variations are found from verbal test to verbal test and are even more marked from verbal test to performance test. It is relatively common to find an individual who tests fairly high on a performance test while testing low on a verbal test, or vice versa. Since the two tests apparently measure different functions of intelligence, it is essential that the examiner have the results of both in order to diagnose correctly the level of the individual's intelligence and to make the consequent diagnosis of mental retardation.

The variations in test results and behavior have turned out to be of great advantage to teachers and psychologists. Discrepancies in these results indicate that mentally handicapped children not only differ among themselves but also show different abilities and disabilities within the individual. Studies on the interpretation of test results and behavior patterns have revealed certain significant diagnostic signs. The discrepancies will be discussed under four major headings; namely, (1) intelligence test patterns, (2) test patterns and etiology, (3) discrepancies between educational achievement and tested intelligence, and (4) discrepancies between tested intelligence and personal and social adjustment.

INTELLIGENCE TEST PATTERNS

Studies have been made on the social adjustment of children obtaining different results on performance and verbal tests. Bijou [22] studied the behavior and educational achievement of mentally handicapped children whose performance quotients were significantly higher than their Binet intelligence quotients, and mentally handicapped children whose performance quotients were significantly lower than their Binet intelligence quotients. He found that (1) boys with a high performance quotient rated higher on personal-social adjustment than boys with low performance quotients, (2) boys with high performance quotients rated high on arithmetic

[22] Bijou, S. W., "An Experimental Analysis of Arthur Performance Quotients," *Journal of Consulting Psychology*, 6, 1942, pp. 247–252.

as compared to reading, (3) there is a relationship between differences of performance and intelligence quotients and reading and arithmetic achievement, and that (4) proficiency in nonacademic subjects is directly related to performance rating, providing the Binet I.Q. is above the middle moron level. Hamlin,[23] in a study of parolees from an institution for mental defectives, found that there was a greater percentage of parolees among the children whose performance quotient was significantly higher than their Binet I.Q.

The following cases illustrate the differences in adjustment of children who had discrepancies between verbal and performance test scores.

Two boys of about the same age, Richard and Jack, had been attending the special class for a number of years. On the Binet, their I.Q.'s were almost identical, but there was a great deal of difference between them in their abilities to take responsibility and "see a job through." As a result, the teacher requested a thorough psychological examination for each of them.

The Binet I.Q.'s were again almost identical; Richard had an I.Q. of 61 and Jack had an I.Q. of 60. The examiner next gave each boy a Wechsler-Bellevue and again found the I.Q.'s similar; Richard had an I.Q. of 66 and Jack had an I.Q. of 65. The difference between the boys was not noticeable until the Verbal and Performance sections of the Wechsler-Bellevue were analyzed. Richard's Verbal I.Q. was 75 compared to a Verbal I.Q. of 64 for Jack. On the other hand, Jack's Performance I.Q. was 74 as compared to a Performance I.Q. of 64 for Richard. It was found that Richard outscored Jack on the Information, Comprehension, Arithmetic, and Vocabulary subtests of the Verbal section of the Wechsler-Bellevue. They scored the same on Similarities and Jack outscored Richard on the Digit Span. This was in keeping with their academic achievement records. Richard found his sole enjoyment in achieving academically and was two or three years in advance of Jack.

Quite the opposite picture was apparent when the Performance section of the Wechsler-Bellevue was examined. Jack outscored Richard on the Picture Completion, Block Design, and Digit Symbol subtests; they scored the same on the Object Assembly Test, and Richard outscored Jack on the

[23] Hamlin, Roy, "Test Patterns of High Grade Mentally Defective Girls," *American Journal of Mental Deficiency*, 43, 1938, pp. 161–165.

Picture Arrangement subtest. While Jack did poorly in his academic work and expressed himself verbally as seldom as possible, he was a reliable, conscientious worker. He found and held after school jobs for long periods of time, was well liked by his employers and fellow employees, and did not have to be told what to do next each time he finished one job. Richard had worked very little, had difficulty holding a job, and was tolerated (at best) by his employers and fellow workmen.

The completed case studies involved a number of additional tests and supplementary information, as well as a study of the attitudes of the boys. An analysis of this information was also included in making the final diagnosis.

TEST PATTERNS AND ETIOLOGY

A number of studies have been made showing that the cause of mental retardation affects both the type of performance given and the results obtained on mental tests. Strauss [24] found in a series of studies that the scores of the exogenous (brain-injured) group were consistently low on performance when compared to their Binet M.A., while the endogenous (non-brain-injured) group scores were consistently high on performance when compared to their Binet M.A. He also found that the I.Q.'s of brain-injured children tend to decrease as they grow older as compared to the I.Q.'s of a non-brain-injured group under the same educational program.[25] The brain-injured children tended to be less socially adjusted than the non-brain-injured in the same environment. Other investigators [26] have found differences in perception and motor co-ordination between the brain-injured and non-brain-injured children.

In regard to a brain-injured case, Strauss reports:

One psychological tester remarks after a test given when this boy had been two and a half years in the training school: "Judging from his remarks it would appear that he has more mental ability than is actually brought out during the test situation. Any flow of thought is continually

[24] Strauss, Alfred A., and Laura E. Lehtinen, *Psychopathology and Education of the Brain-Injured Child.* New York: Grune and Stratton, 1947.

[25] Strauss, Alfred A., "Typology in Mental Deficiency," *American Journal of Mental Deficiency*, 44, 1939, pp. 85–90.

[26] Werner, H., "Abnormal and Subnormal Rigidity," *Journal of Abnormal and Social Psychology*, 41, 1946, pp. 15–24; and Heath, S. R., "Rail-Walking Performance as Related to Mental Age and Etiological Type Among the Mentally Retarded," *American Journal of Psychology*, 55, 1942, pp. 240–247.

interrupted by a *flight of ideas*. In the middle of test questions he would suddenly interrupt with such remarks as 'Does God like to see lions eat people? My family has hardly died yet? Has Jesus died yet? Do you think that Lincoln could do that when he was this young?' It will be seen that his range of ideas is quite widespread with remarks like these continually throughout the examination. It would seem, therefore, that he is actually handicapped by this, as at no time does he apparently integrate his mental capacity toward a definite goal or continue with one constructive line of thought without interruption. He is a loquacious child, full of observations concerning his environment and he has an unusually good speaking vocabulary. He referred to his 'mentality' and wondered how well it rated. He does try to cooperate and is extremely responsive to praise."

On special qualitative performance tests, developed for brain-injured children, the examination revealed a severe handicap of form perception, form retention, and form abstraction, and a severe defect in visuomotor organization. This result explains his arithmetic retardation, his low manual performance age, his inability in handwork and justifies the vocational supervisor's report about the boy when leaving the Training School: "He proved to be totally incapable of even the simplest tasks, after several years of vocational placement on simple jobs." [27]

DISCREPANCIES BETWEEN EDUCATIONAL ACHIEVEMENT AND TESTED INTELLIGENCE

Teachers and psychologists are familiar with the fact that discrepancies often exist between a child's achievement and his tested intelligence. It is because of this that a child cannot be diagnosed as mentally handicapped on the basis of his academic ability or achievement alone.

By the time a child reaches the middle elementary grades, all academic work except mechanical arithmetic computation is based upon his ability to read. If a child has a severe reading disability, he is unable to do the required work and may be suspected of being mentally handicapped. Actually, there may be no mental retardation present, even though on the basis of his achievement he is working at the level of a mentally handicapped child. A thorough diagnosis, as advocated in the earlier part of this chapter, will

[27] Strauss and Lehtinen, *op. cit.*, p. 68.

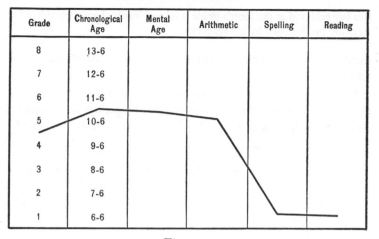

Grade	Chronological Age	Mental Age	Arithmetic	Spelling	Reading
8	13-6				
7	12-6				
6	11-6				
5	10-6				
4	9-6				
3	8-6				
2	7-6				
1	6-6				

Figure 1

Educational Profile – The Case of Bill

eliminate any possibility of the child being placed in a class for the mentally handicapped.

The case of Bill illustrates the need for this type of an analysis:

Bill was a fourth-grade boy — ten years and eight months old. He had an I.Q. of 100 and a mental age of 10–8 on the Binet test. In arithmetic computation he had fifth grade ability. In reading and spelling he was in high first grade.

The average child with an I.Q. of 100 and a mental age over 10 is usually in the fifth grade in all or most of his academic work. On the basis of scores on arithmetic reasoning, spelling, and reading, Bill's achievement is at the level of a mentally handicapped child. He might be diagnosed as such if the diagnosis were based on his achievement alone. His I.Q., mental age, and arithmetic computation indicate that he is not mentally handicapped. This boy's reading ability was three years below his mental capacity, and he was therefore considered a severe case of reading disability. This diagnosis was supported by the fact that the arithmetic computation grade indicated that in a subject unrelated to reading he had made considerable progress. It appeared from the educational profile that his disability was specific to reading. After one year of remedial reading this boy achieved at the fourth-grade level and was no longer considered as mentally handicapped by his teacher.

DISCREPANCIES BETWEEN TESTED INTELLIGENCE AND PERSONAL AND SOCIAL ADJUSTMENT

Certain children test in the mentally handicapped range, achieve academically in the mentally handicapped range, but their personal and social adjustment is relatively normal. Thus, if diagnosis

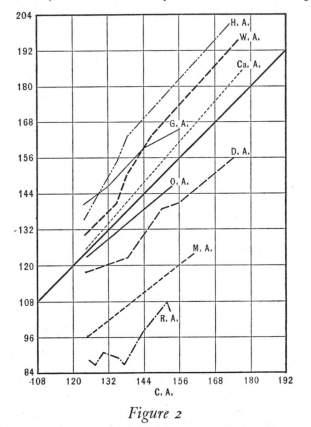

Figure 2

Pattern of Growth for a Socially Competent,
Mentally Retarded Girl

were made on the basis of tested intelligence or academic achievement, the child would be classified as mentally handicapped. If the diagnosis were made on the basis of personal and social adjustment, however, the child would be classified as normal.

Olson and Hughes cite a case of this type: Figure 2 gives a

. . . dramatic illustration of variations in pattern and the significance of these variations for education. The attributes of growth for this girl are somewhat more scattered than for most children. The physical assets are particularly high with height, weight, carpal development and strength above the line of average growth and with intellectual factors such as mental age and reading age several years below. If attention is focused on the mental age and reading, it would appear that this child has borderline intelligence. No observer is likely to reach this conclusion if the behavior as a whole is viewed. This child in the elementary period was one of the best baseball players and runners in the room, could sing well, and had artistic talents beyond the average. As she went on into high school she did well in these areas. Her organismic age is not markedly retarded and a measure of social age, not shown in the figure, is slightly above the average. She is very good at taking care of young children. She does not do well at abstract intellectual tasks. "Capitalize on strength" is an essential aspect of the philosophy and practice of a growth point of view in a classroom.[28]

SUMMARY

The diagnosis of the mentally handicapped and the curriculum planning for them requires a thorough study of the children. This study should include medical and social history, school history, and the results of a number of tests — verbal and performance intelligence tests, achievement tests, social and personality tests, and any of the other tests needed for an adequate diagnosis. With this data, the necessary information is available for the psychologist to make a diagnosis and the educator to formulate a school program to meet the needs of mentally handicapped children.

[28] Olson, Willard C., and Byron O. Hughes, "Concepts of Growth — Their Significance to Teachers," *Childhood Education*, 21 (October, 1944), pp. 55–56.

REFERENCES

Bijou, S. W. "An Experimental Analysis of Arthur Performance Quotients," *Journal of Consulting Psychology*, 6, 1942, pp. 247–252.

Buros, Oscar K. (Editor). *The Third Mental Measurements Yearbook.* New Brunswick: Rutgers University Press, 1948.

Cassel, Robert H. "The Vineland Adaptation of the Oseretsky Tests," *The Vineland Training School Bulletin*, Supplement to Vol. 46, Nos. 3–4, Monograph Supplement Series, No. 1, 1949.

Cronbach, Lee J. *Essentials of Psychological Testing.* New York: Harper and Brothers, 1949.

Doll, Edgar A. (Editor). *The Oseretsky Tests of Motor Proficiency.* Minneapolis: Educational Test Bureau, Educational Publishers, Inc., 1946.

Durrell, Donald D. "The Influence of Reading Ability in Group Intelligence Measures," *Journal of Educational Psychology*, 24, 1933, pp. 412–416.

Frank, Lawrence K. *Projective Methods.* Springfield, Illinois: Charles C. Thomas, 1948.

Freeman, Frank N. *Mental Tests*, Rev. Ed. Boston: Houghton Mifflin Co., 1939.

Hamlin, Roy. "Test Pattern of High Grade Mental Defective Girls," *American Journal of Mental Deficiency*, 43, 1938, pp. 161–165.

Heath, S. R. "Rail-Walking Performance as Related to Mental Age and Etiological Type Among the Mentally Retarded," *American Journal of Psychology*, 55, 1942, pp. 240–247.

Henry, Nelson B. (Editor). *The Forty-Fifth Yearbook of the National Society for the Study of Education:* The Measurement of Understanding, Part I. Chicago: University of Chicago Press, 1946.

Klopfer, Bruno, and Douglas M. Kelley. *The Rorschach Technique.* Yonkers: World Book Co., 1942.

Olson, Willard C., and Byron O. Hughes. "Concepts of Growth — Their Significance to Teachers," *Childhood Education*, 21 (October, 1944), pp. 53–63.

Sarason, Seymour B. *Psychological Problems in Mental Deficiency.* New York: Harper and Brothers, 1949.

Strauss, A. A., and L. E. Lehtinen. *Psychopathology and Education of the Brain-Injured Child.* New York: Grune and Stratton, Inc., 1947.

Strauss, Alfred A. "Typology in Mental Deficiency," *American Journal of Mental Deficiency*, 44, 1939, pp. 85–90.

Terman, Lewis M., and Maude A. Merrill. *Measuring Intelligence.* Boston: Houghton Mifflin Co., 1937.

Thurstone, L. L. *The Vectors of Mind.* Chicago: University of Chicago Press, 1935.

Wechsler, David. *The Measurement of Adult Intelligence*, 3rd Ed. Baltimore: Williams and Wilkins, 1944.

Werner, H. "Abnormal and Subnormal Rigidity," *Journal of Abnormal and Social Psychology*, 41, 1946, pp. 15–24.

PART TWO

❧

The Development of
Educational Programs

Chapter 4

Early Educational Procedures

Introduction

It is important for teachers to obtain a perspective. They need to know what methods people have used in the education of the mentally defective, why they used these methods, how to get the best results from known methods, and how to develop new ones. It is possible that in the past some techniques have been evolved that were successful even though one may not agree with the explanations or reasons given for their use. For that reason, this section has been included to give teachers and students of the mentally handicapped a condensed review of the teaching methods and theories evolved during the nineteenth century and the beginning of the twentieth century — a period of about a hundred years.

Throughout the centuries — ever since the advent of man — the human race has had the problem of dealing with those among them who, through disease, accident, or inheritance, were not endowed with the ability to learn and to function in society as well as the great majority of people. In ancient times the feeble-minded were persecuted, mistreated, and neglected. The term "idiot" is derived from the Greek "idiotas," or "idios," which implied a "peculiar individual," hence one to neglect or "get rid of." With the rise of Christianity certain religious groups began to apply the philosophy of the brotherhood of man, and attempted to house, clothe, and feed those among them who were feeble-minded. It was not until the seventeenth century that society began to organize institutions for them. Very little attempt at educating the feeble-minded, however, was introduced at that time.

It can rightly be said that the education of the mentally defective began about 1800. During the nineteenth century and the beginning of the twentieth we find that the educators of the mentally defective, and those contributing most of their diagnosis and education, were practically all medical men. Itard, Seguin, Montessori, and Decroly were all physicians, yet their major contributions were in the fields of psychological diagnosis and the education of the mentally defective child. This chapter will review the attempts of these persons in the education of retarded children.

The Contribution of Itard [1]

During the later part of the eighteenth century, special education methods were being successfully applied to the deaf. It was at about this time that Jean Marc Itard, a French philosopher and physician working in an institution for the deaf, decided that similar methods of training may have some effect on the education of the feeble-minded. He was inspired by the philosophy of sensationalism and the French post-revolutionary belief that man had unlimited possibilities, and that education and environment were the determining factors in mental development.

In 1799 a boy about twelve years of age was captured in the forest of Aveyron. This boy resembled a wild animal more than a human being, since he was unable to speak, selected his food by smell, attempted to escape, and in general did not respond like a human being. He did not respond to the sound of a pistol fired

---

[1] Itard, Jean Marc Gaspard, *The Wild Boy of Aveyron*, trans. by George and Muriel Humphrey. New York: Appleton-Century-Crofts, Inc., 1932.

behind him, but did respond to the fall of a nut from a tree. His sense of smell did not appear to discriminate between foul or pleasant odors, nor did he seem to notice any difference between hot and cold. His mood was uncontrollable — he was sometimes in a state of depression, and at other times in a state of hilarious excitement. He reacted in general as an animal did and was consequently called "The Wild Boy of Aveyron."

The philosophical controversies of that age, not too much unlike those of our own, were between the nativists and the sensationalists or empiricists. The nativists, like those of today who have a hereditarian bias, believed that intellectual functions and knowledge were innate and could not be developed. The empiricists, epistemologists, or sensationalists, on the other hand, asserted that knowledge or intelligence was obtained through the senses and was therefore contingent upon education.

Itard, agreeing with the sensationalists, felt that the wild boy of Aveyron was a good example of a human being who was completely untutored, and that with proper educational procedures applied to the training of the senses this untutored boy could be made human. Pinel, a French psychiatrist, diagnosed the boy as an idiot, and, leaning toward the nativist point of view, asserted that the boy could not be educated and that it was useless to try.

Itard, however, initiated an extensive training program for the boy to demonstrate to the world the educability of an idiot through the training of the senses. For five years he tried to educate Victor (the boy) and then gave up, declaring the experiment a failure. Later the French Academy of Science, investigating the case, decided that Itard had made a significant contribution and requested him to publish a report of his efforts. The book which resulted, *The Wild Boy of Aveyron*, has become a classic in the history of the education of the mentally deficient.

Itard's objectives, together with some of the methods of instruction, may be summarized as follows:

SOCIALIZATION

Itard wished to socialize the boy by giving him instruction based on the established patterns of the boy at that time. He wanted to give as much latitude to his primitive and untrained impulses as possible, since Victor appeared more content when he was sleeping or eating or just running unrestrained through the fields. At the end of the experiment, through the gradual giving up of long-established habits, the boy Victor settled down to a somewhat more restrained life.

MENTAL TRAINING THROUGH SENSORY STIMULATION

A major objective of Itard was to activate the nervous system by a carefully developed program of sensory stimulation, and to develop sensory discrimination through the education of each sense separately. This objective determined much of Itard's training methods.

(1) By special exercises for the senses of taste, touch, temperature, and smell, Itard was able to demonstrate some improvement. The exercises consisted of paired sensory stimulations with great contrasts such as hot and cold, and then a gradual decrease in the difference between the two extremes until some improvement in discrimination was effected. In training for temperature discrimination the boy was immersed in hot baths. This procedure was instituted because Victor appeared to have no temperature discrimination. He was indifferent to cold winds when he was naked; he could handle hot coals with ease.

(2) Much effort was made in developing the sense of touch, since his sense of smell had already been developed and the sense of taste was to be used only to appreciate new and better foods. In the tactual field Itard was able to train him to distinguish between a key and coin money, and to differentiate metal letters such as a B and an R by feeling them.

(3) The sense of hearing appeared to give much more difficulty than the sense of touch. In training hearing Itard blindfolded the boy to decrease visual sensations. He sounded a bell and then a drum and the boy was required to make the sounds himself to indicate that he heard and could discriminate between them. Progressively these sharply different sounds were made more similar with the expectation that as hearing discrimination became more acute and precise the boy could then be trained to distinguish

the various sounds of the human voice. Auditory training at the primitive level was successful, and Itard succeeded in producing some results in the training of attention to different auditory stimuli. He then proceeded to teach the boy to discriminate between vowels. After much training, Victor learned to discriminate between the sounds of A and O. Frustration upon failure and extreme joy, even hilarious excitement, when success was achieved, prevented further learning. As a result Itard dropped auditory training and proceeded with the other senses, such as vision.

(4) Visual training followed the same principles of education as were used with hearing. Large visual objects were contrasted with small ones because of their ease of discrimination. Then finer visual discriminations were introduced. Itard succeeded in conditioning the boy to certain words, such as "milk" (lait), and produced an association between the printed word and the milk. The boy learned a number of words and could read them and write some of them before the experiment was terminated.

CREATING HUMAN WANTS AND DESIRES

A third objective of Itard was to create in the boy some human wants and desires — stated in other words, to decrease his animal-like impulses and to replace them with human, social characteristics. Little success was attained in this area, with the exception of a developed fondness for the woman who cared for him. He also had some affection for Itard who played with him and tried to teach him. Beyond these attachments he paid little attention to other people, played with no toys, and was difficult to engage in a game, except when it came to finding hidden nuts, or substitutes for nuts.

SPEECH

Another of Itard's aims was to teach him to speak. He tried auditory training, then the association of words with objects. He also tried imitation of speech as practiced with deaf mutes, but all to no avail. Victor remained mute until the end.

INTELLIGENCE

The last and final objective of training was to develop the

intelligence. This aspect of mind, according to Itard and the sensationalists, was not separate but a part of the ideas implanted in the mind through sense training. This aspect of training, however, was related to speech and reading. To teach Victor reading Itard associated objects, such as a knife, with the printed word "knife." After the boy had learned these, objects were placed in one corner. The boy was then given a card with the name of an object printed on it and learned to bring the correct article. When Itard changed the objects, and substituted a larger knife for the smaller one used, the boy was confused. Itard discovered that Victor had no ability to generalize and was unable to develop this aspect of intelligence.

Itard felt that with the onset of puberty the boy might flower out and respond more intelligently. The opposite occurred. The boy became unmanageable and was finally sent to an institution in Bizerte. Later he was returned to the woman who originally cared for him; he remained with her without improvement until his death in 1828. Itard subsequently dropped the work with the feeble-minded but continued his experiments with the deaf.

ITARD'S INFLUENCE

The contribution of Itard to present-day education of the mentally handicapped is difficult to appraise. He demonstrated that even idiots can be improved to some degree, since this boy had learned to read a few words and had developed some control of the emotions through the training received. It was the first extensive record of training an idiot and providing objective reports of the progress. Certainly he gave impetus to the work with the mentally defective. The work of Seguin, Montessori, Decroly, and others followed his lead.

In addition to giving impetus to the work with the mentally deficient, Itard demonstrated the application of psychological principles to problems of learning. Even today there is much similar sensory training and readiness education at preschool levels. Many activities of the nursery schools and kindergartens today are similar to those used by Itard, with the exception that today they are not strictly sense training, but sense training through natural and life activities, now called "experiences."

THE CONTRIBUTION OF SEGUIN

Edward Seguin was first a teacher, and later a medical and surgical student under Itard. Through the influence and teaching of Itard, Seguin became inspired with the potentialities of mentally defective children, and devoted his whole life to their training and treatment.

Seguin's contribution to the education of mental defectives is called the "physiological method." In 1846 he published a book, *The Moral Treatment, Hygiene, and Education of Idiots, and Other Backward Children.* For this contribution he was not only crowned by the French Academy but also commended in a letter by Pope Pius IX for the contribution which he had made to humanity.[2]

Following the revolution of 1848 in France, which interfered with the functioning of his school in Paris, Seguin emigrated to the United States to continue his work with the feeble-minded. He became the superintendent of the Pennsylvania Training School for Idiots. Because of his lack of knowledge of English and his dislike for administrative work, he retired from institutional life and devoted the next twenty years to the private tutoring of mental defectives in New York City.

In 1866 Seguin wrote his second book. This book elucidated in great detail his philosophy of education and his reasons for advocating the physiological method.

Seguin's theory of education was based on a neurophysiological hypothesis. Since neurologists had divided the nervous system into two major categories, the peripheral nervous system and the central nervous system, Seguin likewise differentiated between two types of feeble-mindedness, the superficial and the profound. The superficial type of feeble-mindedness, according to Seguin, was that in which the peripheral nervous system was believed to be damaged or weakened. The profound type of feeble-mindedness resulted from defects in the central nervous system.

The educational methods for these two types of feeble-minded-

[2] Seguin, Edward, *Idiocy: And Its Treatment by the Physiological Method.* Albany: Brandow Printing Company, 1866. Reprinted. New York: Teachers College, Columbia University, 1907.

ness were the same. In the peripheral nervous system defect, or superficial feeble-mindedness, it was believed that the central nervous system was intact, but that the sense impressions did not reach the central nervous system due to weakened or damaged receptors. To educate this type of feeble-minded person Seguin believed that specific training of the peripheral nervous system through muscle and sense training would strengthen the receptors, thereby allowing impulses to reach the central nervous system more readily. In the profound type of feeble-mindedness, where the central nervous system was thought to be damaged, the same treatment prevailed since Seguin believed that the bombardment of the central nervous system through the receptors would stimulate the nerve cells of the cortex to greater mental functioning.

Seguin explained the physiological method of education as consisting of ". . . adaptations of the principles of physiology, through the development of the dynamic, receptive, reflexive, and spontaneous functions of youth." [3]

In accordance with these theories, Seguin's first task was to educate the muscular system. He believed that activities must be those which satisfy the child's own needs, desires, and capacities — a very modern approach to education. The exercises must come from the daily activities and games common to all children. The schoolroom, he believed, must be in the open air; the exercises must be simple and designed to harmonize all motor and vocal functions and to develop any part of the body which is weak or ill-nourished. Materials required are nothing beyond a table, a ladder, a balancing pole, and a springboard. Using the whole-part method he felt that all movements should be learned as total movements first and then followed by learning partial movements. His system of gymnastics taught first the use of the feet, then the legs, the body, the shoulders, the arms, wrists, hands, and finally the fingers.

To Seguin no muscular training was more important than that of the hands since hand work incorporates many associated skills, both physical and mental. Closely associated with hand training is the education of the sense of touch. He felt that parents and

[3] *Ibid.*, p. 57.

teachers should not inhibit or discourage children's handling of objects and stated that one of the earliest and most fatal antagonisms taught to a child is the forbidding of their using the hands to ascertain the qualities of surrounding objects. He believed that it is the teacher's duty to foster and direct tactual curiosity, and that touch is the first and perhaps the most important sense to be trained. Touch is trained by presenting the child with stimuli of varying shapes, sizes, textures, temperatures, and weights. The training of taste and of smell are introduced shortly after that of touch and are treated together, usually through the medium of food.

In the education of the auditory sense, Seguin recognized three training areas. The first related to sound in general, the second to the recognition of the musical scales, and the third to vocal expression. Seguin used music to set the tempo and spirit of the task at hand; he used gay, bright music for the morning hours, shading off to more reflective types favorable to study as the day advanced. Lively music preceded physical exercises and long prolonged tones accompanied speech exercises. From music training the activities merged into speech training.

Seguin recognized that the speech of the mentally defective was the most difficult skill for them to acquire. He attempted to teach speech, then writing, and lastly reading. Speech was treated as a combination of voice and articulation forced by wants: cries of the children were converted into voices; articulation was derived from imitation. Writing was introduced as imitative exercise, and reading was later introduced as a result of the combination of both speech and writing. Words such as "apple," "book," or "bread" were spoken, the names were then written, and the objects were then placed in the child's hands. In like manner, verbs were presented through demonstration and use. Seguin believed that there was merit in both individual and group reading, the former for cool mild weather and the latter during stormy gales and dull afternoons.

The education of visual abilities involved the use of colors, forms and combinations of forms, dimensions, distances, and planes. These were taught through the use of objects which the child actually handled and manipulated. In conjunction with this work, Seguin took the opportunity to again stress the importance of the hand as a helper to the eye.

Seguin's philosophy of education, with the exception of its mechanistic approach through the senses, is not too different from many of the principles advocated today. He emphasized the education of the whole child, the individualization of instruction, the importance of rapport between the teacher and the pupil, the physical comfort of the child during the learning period, and the importance of beginning with what the child needs, wants, and desires before progressing to areas that are unknown.

For many years following Seguin, teachers of the mentally handicapped used a great deal of hand work in an attempt to educate the child through eye-hand co-ordination. Many of the ideas and techniques advocated by Seguin are still sound today. Even though one may not agree with Seguin's concept of superficial and profound idiocy, some of the techniques and ideas which he used in teaching are still worth-while.

The Contribution of Montessori

About 1897 Dr. Deteressa Maria Montessori became interested in mental defectives. At that time she was an assistant at a psychiatric clinic in Rome where she found a number of mentally deficient children housed in insane asylums. Society in general believed that paralysis, idiocy, and other diseases of that nature were primarily medical. After studying the work of Itard and particularly the work of Seguin, Montessori concluded that the problem of mental deficiency was primarily a pedagogical one rather than a problem for medicine. Advocating this view, she organized the Orthophrenic School for the Cure of the Feeble-minded. In this school, which she conducted personally, she not only educated the feeble-minded, but also conducted a training center for teachers of mentally defective children. Enrolled among her students were visiting personages from London and Paris.

Through the construction and use of her own didactic materials, she taught a number of retarded pupils to read and write so well that they were able to be presented for examination at a school on a level with normal children. The results, according to the reports, were miraculous. This made her wonder why the normal pupils should not do as well. Her explanation of this difference was that the feeble-minded were well educated, while other children were being presented with poor educational opportunities.

In 1907 [4] Montessori was given an opportunity to open a school, the purpose of which was to educate the young normal children of working mothers. This school, the Case Dei Bambina, was opened in a tenement house improvement project in Rome, and later became internationally famous in the educational field.

Montessori [5] described her system as an attempt to combine home and school by introducing this new idea into education. Activities in the school were designed to duplicate some of the home activities. She agreed with Seguin in ascribing great importance to sense and muscle training as part of the early education of children. Although Seguin believed that bodily movement is a psychological activity, Montessori did not emphasize this factor. She regarded muscular activity as merely physiological.

"Auto-education," or self-teaching, was the keynote of the Montessori system. Activities and materials were so organized and designed that the children taught themselves while the teacher withdrew into the background, merely supervising the activities. This self-teaching method was carried out by means of didactic materials.

The didactic materials consisted of twenty-six different items, which made provision for training all of the senses except those of taste and smell. To educate visual abilities the child was given wooden cylinders to fit into holes in a solid block of wood. In the perception of dimensions, the training was continued with larger objects which required more difficult movements and greater muscular efforts. The materials used in this were cubes, big stairs, long stairs, and other such objects. For the training of the temperature sense, the hands were put in cold water, in lukewarm water,

[4] Boyd, William, *From Locke to Montessori*. London: George G. Harrap and Company, 1914.
[5] Montessori, Maria, *Montessori Method*, trans. by Anne E. George. New York: Frederick A. Stokes Company, 1912.

and in hot water so that the child would learn to discriminate between differences in temperature. The tactile experiences consisted of touching alternating strips of smooth paper and sandpaper. For the chromatic sense, fine distinctions of color were learned by means of colored tablets consisting of a set of sixty-four spools of eight colors in eight shades. For the sense of hearing, small boxes filled with sand and pebbles were employed to help distinguish gradation of noises. She also used a number of games of silence. A deep silence was gradually produced in the classroom, and the children were invited to listen to the buzzing of flies or the rustling of trees. Then a succession of different sounds and noises were introduced, beginning with strong contrasts and gradually becoming more alike. According to Boyd,[6] so far as hearing goes, the didactic method was not carried out by Montessori because it is not possible for the child to exercise himself through his own activity in hearing as he does for the other senses.

The material for the training of the baric sense consisted of little wooden tablets of the same size, made of different kinds of wood, hence of different weights. The stereognostic sense, in which the tactual and the muscular sense are simultaneously brought into play, was trained by distinguishing objects of different shapes.

In addition to exercises with apparatus — swings, wooden staircases, a wooden platform adapted for the broad jump, and a rope ladder — Montessori also made use of gymnastics through directed exercises and free games without apparatus. For free games she furnished the children with balls, hoops, and kites, while for direct exercises she used marching and other similar formal activities.

The work of Montessori aroused interest in the education of preschool children throughout the world. She was brought to the United States for a series of lectures, and was quoted widely in circles interested in the education of both the mentally defective and the preschool normal child.

William H. Kilpatrick, [7] one of America's foremost interpreters of the Dewey philosophy of activity and interest, was not im-

---

[6] *Ibid.*, p. 154.
[7] Kilpatrick, William H., *The Montessori System Examined.* Boston: Houghton Mifflin Company, 1914.

pressed with Montessori's method. He commended Montessori's
alliance with the scientific aim and attitude as the only rule of
educational faith and practice. He believed, however, that in
actual practice she had only the spirit of modern science.

The system, according to Kilpatrick, is quite restrictive due to
the use of the didactic materials. While the practical life activities
afforded excellent opportunities for self expression, imaginative or
constructive play had no place in the use of the didactic materials.
Games and the fine arts were inadequately utilized. Her method is
too simple because transfer of training does not take place. The
best sort of self education takes place where real problems present
themselves naturally to children. Her system of auto-education is
too restrictive.

In addition, Kilpatrick maintained that no sense can be improved by training. Experiments on the improvements of sense
training have not supported Montessori's view.

According to Kilpatrick, the success of the Montessori system
in the field of reading was due essentially to the phonetic character
of the Italian language. He admitted that she may have a contribution in the teaching of writing with her advanced preparation
in the use of tools and her combination of reading and writing at
the same time, but that her teaching of arithmetic seems to be no
better than that found in America.

Kilpatrick concludes that the Montessori method falls essentially
below the best American methods. Her greatest contribution is
the Case Dei Bambina as a social institution, and her greatest
service is in her emphasis upon scientific education and practical
utilization of liberty. The greatest defect in her theory is the
assumption that there is a transfer of training from didactic materials to life situations.

OTHER EARLY CONTRIBUTIONS

Although there are many other contributors to the study of the
mentally defective child only two of the followers of Seguin and
Montessori will be mentioned here. They both worked in the
early part of the twentieth century.

Dr. O. Decroly, working in Brussels, Belgium, was another

physician faced with the treatment of the mentally defective. Like others in the field, he concluded that the best treatment must be an educational program. Decroly also began his educational ventures with mentally defective children. He found that the methods used successfully with these children apply equally well to average children and later devoted most of his time to the education of normal children.

It is reported by his student, Descœudres,[8] that Dr. Decroly believed the education of the mentally defective child must center around the child and his needs. He and his fellow workers developed many educational games and activities designed to correct the defects observed in the mentally defective child by cultivating spontaneous attention and leading the child on to working by himself. Many of the games attempted to develop sensory discriminations, as Itard and others had done, and to train the observations of likenesses and differences.

It will be seen from the brief description of some of the activities that Decroly emphasized learning on the part of the mentally defective in terms of the child. The program was based upon the child's physical and mental constitution, his needs in terms of food, clothing, vocational training and so forth, and his environment — i.e., the relation of the child to his family, to his school, and to the society in which he lives. Decroly, like Montessori, attempted to construct curricula based on games in which children were engaged. The difference between Montessori and Decroly lies primarily in the fact that Decroly emphasized educational games in a natural setting whereas Montessori used didactic materials of a much more formal nature. Thus Decroly can be considered one of the more modern educators of mentally defective children.

Another worker in the field of the mentally deficient is the well-known Alfred Binet. Binet, an experimental psychologist, obtained his doctor's degree in science, rather than in medicine. He was one of the few earlier contributors in the field who was not himself a physician.

[8] Descœudres, Alice, *The Education of Mentally Defective Children*, trans. from the Second French Edition by Ernest F. Row. Boston: D. C. Heath & Co., 1928; London: George G. Harrap & Co., Ltd., pp. 59–62.

Alfred Binet is known for constructing the age scale for test-ing intelligence. It should be remembered that Binet became interested in the measurement of intelligence, not because of his interest in the average child, but because of his interest in the diagnosis of mentally defective children in the public schools. To use Binet's own words,

. . . the main purpose of the authors (Binet and Simon) in the devisal of these tests is to furnish to the teacher a *first* means by which he may single out mentally backward children, who, upon further examination, may also be found to have some mental defect or peculiarity which prevents them from fully profiting by the education of the ordinary school, and who probably would benefit more by being educated in a special school or in a special class.[9]

Binet did not organize an extensive and unique educational program for the mentally defective. His major task was to diag-nose public school children, to differentiate the higher-grade mentally defective from the average child, and to assist in the or-ganization of special classes within the public schools in France. His identification of these children was accomplished through diagnoses consisting of psychological and pedagogical examina-tions of the children, assignment to institutions or special classes, and some ingenious observations on their education. Binet demon-strated original thinking in diagnosis as well as in educational procedures.

He was not a follower of either Seguin or Itard. As a matter of fact he states:

The essential thing is for all the world to understand that empiricism has had its day, and that method of scientific precision must be introduced into all educational work, to carry everywhere good sense and light.[10]

About Seguin, Binet states in a footnote:

. . . Seguin's work must not be examined too closely; those who praise it have certainly not read it. Seguin impresses us as an empiric, endowed with great personal talent, which he has not succeeded in embodying

[9] Binet, Alfred, and T. Simon, *Mentally Defective Children*, trans. by W. B. Drummond. New York: Longmans, Green and Co., 1914, pp. v–vi.
[10] *Ibid.*, p. 146.

clearly in his works. These contain some pages of good sense, with many obscurities, and many absurdities. . . . One might make many criticisms on the writings of alienists; but not to what end? We prefer to say of such predecessors what Ingres said to his pupils in the Rubens Gallery at the Louvre, "Salute them, but pay no attention to them!" [11]

The quotations given above represent, to some extent, Binet's philosophy of education. He did not accept the work of his predecessors. Instead he was desirous of finding out the mental workings of the mentally defective child, his learning ability, his assets, and his liabilities. He was interested in organizing an educational program for the higher-grade mental defectives in the public school which would make them socially and vocationally adequate, rather than public charges in institutions. His concentration on the measurement of intelligence, the identification of such children, and the organization of educational provisions, did not leave him much time for actual instructional procedures. His contribution therefore was mostly in diagnosis, rather than in educational methodology.

SUMMARY

During the nineteenth century we find the beginnings of the education of mentally defective children. Most of the major contributors, with the exception of Binet, were physicians. Educators were willing to delegate the responsibility for the development of methods and techniques in the education of mental defectives to doctors and psychologists.

It is interesting to note also that most of the work in the education of the mentally defective was carried on in France, Italy, and Belgium. The social philosophy of the times, following the French Revolution, and the consequent virility of ideas and faith in the potentialities of the human personality drove many to new achievements. Scientists were willing to delve into the realms of the unknown to discover methods of educating those who previously could not be educated.

Another element bearing upon the education of the mental

[11] *Ibid.*, pp. 3–4.

defective during the nineteenth century was the dominant philosophy of sensationalism and its influence on educational techniques. It was believed that man, including the mentally defective, obtained his knowledge and his mental ability through sensory processes. Education, therefore, was aimed primarily at sense and muscle training, often by means of didactic or self-teaching materials. During the earlier part of the twentieth century Decroly and Binet were the first to break away from this type of education, to implement the philosophy of learning through experiences, and to approach education from a more modern point of view.

REFERENCES

Binet, Alfred, and T. Simon. *Mentally Defective Children*, trans. by W. B. Drummond. New York: Longmans, Green and Company, 1914.

Boyd, William. *From Locke to Montessori*. London: George G. Harrap and Company, 1914.

Descœudres, Alice. *The Education of Mentally Defective Children*, trans. from the Second French Edition by Ernest F. Row. Boston: D. C. Heath & Company, 1928.

Itard, Jean Marc Gaspard. *The Wild Boy of Aveyron*, trans. by George and Muriel Humphrey. New York: Appleton-Century-Crofts, Inc., 1932.

Kilpatrick, William H. *The Montessori System Examined*. Boston: Houghton Mifflin Company, 1914.

Montessori, Maria. *Montessori Method*, trans. by Anne E. George. New York: Frederick A. Stokes Company, 1912.

Seguin, Edward. *Idiocy: and Its Treatment by the Physiological Method*. Albany, N.Y.: Brandow Printing Company, 1866. Reprinted. New York: Teachers College, Columbia University, 1907.

Wallin, J. E. Wallace. *The Education of Handicapped Children*. Boston: Houghton Mifflin Company, 1924.

Chapter 5

Modern Educational Procedures

MANY OF THE ATTEMPTS to educate mentally handicapped children in institutions and in public schools have not been published. There have, however, been a few publications dealing with educational procedures and courses of study developed by individuals and by curriculum committees in local school systems. This chapter will review some of these philosophies and educational procedures developed since the first World War.

THE EDUCATIONAL SYSTEM OF DESCŒUDRES [1]

Descœudres' book, *The Education of Mentally Defective Children*, has had very little recognition in the United States, yet the book is one of the few accounts of a comprehensive educational system for mental defectives. It was translated from French for English consumption and only a limited number of copies sold in this country. The book has been out of print for a number of years.

Descœudres obtained her education and interest in the field of

[1] Descœudres, Alice, *The Education of Mentally Defective Children*, trans. from the Second French Edition by Ernest F. Row. New York: D. C. Heath & Company., 1928, and London: George G. Harrap & Company, Limited.

mental retardation by working as an apprentice to Dr. Decroly in his school for mental defectives in Brussels. Her philosophy of education of the mentally handicapped and her techniques of education are therefore an extension and implementation of Decroly's work.

Descœudres believed in a thorough diagnosis of mentally defective children and felt that *idiots and low-grade imbeciles were not educable in the public schools,* but that the higher-grade mental defectives (which we have called the mentally handicapped) could be educated in the special classes of the public schools. She enunciated the following principles of education, many of which are very representative of modern philosophical trends in education:

(1) Education of the mentally defective must utilize the *natural activity* of the pupil. Here she accepts Dewey's philosophy of "learning by doing." She deplored the fact that although this philosophy was prevalent in writings and teachings, schools did not follow it in practice.

(2) A second principle of education is that it is necessary to emphasize *perceptual knowledge* and *sense training.* The objective was to add precision to knowledge already acquired, to create new knowledge, and to improve and enrich verbal expression through social activities.

(3) A third principle advocated by Descœudres was *correlation* or *concentration.* By this she meant that different subjects have a way of grouping themselves around a central theme. She felt that although correlation is an important educational method for normal children it is much more important for the mentally defective, since the correlation of subjects into natural groups makes content more understandable to children. She believed that correlation strengthens and improves associations of ideas.

(4) The fourth principle was *individualization of instruction.* This does not necessarily mean teaching children individually, but rather the adaptation of instruction to the individual needs of each particular child, whether the instruction is in groups or with individuals.

(5) The fifth principle was the emphasis on the *utilitarian character of teaching.* She insisted that the learned activity should be

immediately used in actual life if the learning is to take place and become functionally effective.

Descœudres' objectives for the education of the mentally handicapped and the techniques of teaching them represent, to some extent, a transitional period between the sensory and physiological approach of Itard and Seguin and the more modern progressive methods of teaching mentally handicapped children according to their needs in our society. The reader is referred to her book which explains in great detail her philosophy and procedure. Although a brief description of her curriculum and her teaching techniques will not do her justice, a brief summary of her method and point of view is nevertheless of value.

TRAINING THE SENSES AND THE ATTENTION

Descœudres, like Binet and his predecessors, emphasized the training of the attention and of the sense processes of the mentally handicapped child. Many authors have stated that the attention span of the mentally defective is very short. In order to learn, therefore, they must pay attention particularly to sensory cues. To train the senses and attention, Descœudres, taking her cue from Decroly, organized a series of games and exercises to develop those senses relating to sight, hearing, muscular sense, touch, taste, and smell.

In visual training, for example, she tried to develop the ability to make careful discriminations of color, form, size, orientation, and shade by presenting the child with games such as color lotto. This game required the child to put shapes of different colors on pictures that had the same shape and color. It was a type of form and color discrimination. Her method of instruction in this area was to teach children to discriminate shapes and colors, sizes, direction, or position of objects. She carried these discriminations and generalizations a step further by observing objects and events in their natural environment. This was carried out by groups on excursions and trips in which the children were asked to distinguish different shades of color in the sky, and to compare different clouds, trees, and other objects in their environment. Matching exercises were used such as finding a leaf of a particular shape and asking the children to find other leaves of the same shape.

The sense of hearing was given particular attention by Descœudres. Her approach was similar to what is known as "auditory training" today. Her exercises were to a large extent of a formal nature. However, many games cited are of interest to children: blindfolding a child and having other children call out his name to see if the child could guess who called; sounding different objects such as a bell, whistle, watch, key ring, glass, money, to see if the child can distinguish between these sounds. Many other games were used in developing attention and the sense of hearing.

The sense of touch and the muscular sense were emphasized by Descœudres because she felt that the younger children learn more through the sense of touch than through vision.

Sense training through games, exercises (formal and otherwise), and natural activities constituted the program for the young mentally defective child, who is, according to Descœudres, deficient in sense perception and in attention.

PHYSICAL TRAINING

Physical training for mentally handicapped children was also emphasized in the Descœudres curriculum. She stated that physical exercise is very important for mental defectives because such children are not only mentally defective but also physically defective. She believed that physical education was very important for the following reasons:

(1) Physical training "directs the harmonious development of the body." It is important for the mental defective to develop adequate physique which can only be developed through physical exercise.

(2) Movement of the body is an important factor in the development of the mind. This idea is very similar to Seguin's approach to the training of the mentally defective.

(3) Motor co-ordination or motor capacity can be developed through exercise.

(4) Moral training is assisted by physical training exercises, since physical training develops the power of "decision and of will." It also develops endurance and the ability to communicate with others as well as its part in sociability and self-confidence.

(5) Physical training assists the child in self-confidence since he

usually comes to school with many fears of climbing stairs, running, or other physical activities.

(6) Physical training assists the child in everyday activities such as washing, eating, and dressing.

(7) School work later is assisted through physical training since some school work involves handwork, drawing, and writing.

In Descœudres' exposition of physical training activities there is a short section on natural training, which includes recreation, games, walks, excursions, and practical tasks involving physical activity around the school. Gardening and other physical activities are included. The large part of physical training for mental defectives advocated by Descœudres is of a formal gymnastic type, including training in rhythms, marching with halts or handclaps at given signals, and so forth. Even the use of the dynamometer was used by Descœudres for physical training.

HANDWORK

Handwork, to Descœudres, had aims similar to those of physical training and included the training of attention, interest, will power, self-confidence, visualizing ability, ability to express thoughts, and the ability of the child to see a completed task.

Handwork ranged from modeling, common everyday tasks, and threading beads, to the use of Froebelian materials of blocks, laths, sticks, counters, and so forth. Folding paper into a variety of shapes, pleating, cutting and making of various articles with paper, cardboard, matchboxes, and other available material are described in detail. For older children embroidery, sewing, crocheting, knitting, basket-making, cardboard work, woodworking, carpentry, and metal working are advocated.

ART

Descœudres presented a modern note in her exposition of drawing. She considered drawing as a form of speech and says ". . . drawing is sometimes the first method by which the child succeeds in expressing or projecting his thoughts." [2] She felt that drawing was a means of self-expression and a method of training

[2] *Ibid.*, p. 136.

eye-hand co-ordination. Considerable psychological insight was shown by Desœcudres in explaining the drawing of young mentally defective children. She developed a correlation between drawing, writing, number concepts, and the development of space perception and orientation.

THE OBJECT LESSON

Descœudres explained that many activities in the classroom should remain concrete and within the child's level of comprehension. Like the modern educator, she stated that activities should be drawn from *the child's own experience*. She stated further that the education of the mentally handicapped must meet the practical needs of children, since these are the most profitable. She agreed with Seguin when he said "to teach nothing indoors that can be learned outdoors," or "to teach nothing with dead things that you can make observations on living ones." The object lesson, to Descœudres, included the utilization of objects and activities within the child's experience and the incorporation of these activities into projects that would include handwriting, numbers, reading, and so forth. Her object lessons sound like a forerunner of the "units of experience" used later by Ingram and others.

SPEECH

Descœudres included speech development for the mentally retarded as part of the educational program. She recognized that the mentally handicapped are defective in speech, sometimes because of poor hearing, sometimes because of lack of understanding, sometimes because of poor habits, or sometimes because of pathological defects in the speech organs. For that reason speech training for the mentally defective was advocated, first as a specific element of the curriculum, and second in connection with the teaching of other subjects.

READING, SPELLING, AND ARITHMETIC

Descœudres advocated the teaching of reading, spelling, and arithmetic for all who could learn. Like many modern educators she advocated that reading must not be started too soon. She stated for example:

Yet there are cases in which to lose time is to gain time, and by training the child in attention, in observation, the use of the senses, progress is far more surely made than by cramming him prematurely with food that he cannot assimilate — a process painful alike to teacher and pupil.[3]

She taught primarily by means of games and activities. An analysis was made of the psychological functions involved in reading, spelling, and arithmetic, and a systematic method of developing these educational skills is presented. The method follows Decroly's synthetic method. This approach is the natural method in which the child learns the word or sentence first, since it is the simplest, and then proceeds later to learn by the phonetic method, or part method (analytic method).

Arithmetic was developed systematically by Descœudres. Games and activities utilizing concrete objects were first used to develop the concept of numbers through the various senses, after which the number symbols and names of numbers were taught. Arithmetic followed the training of attention and sense perception since many of the concepts involve shape, size, color, and so forth. The series of arithmetic games devised by Decroly was extended and added to by Descœudres. Arithmetic was correlated with handwork, drawing, rhythm, and physical training whenever possible.

It will be noted from this brief description of Descœudres' teaching methodology and objectives, that she borrowed considerably from Seguin, Binet, and particularly Decroly; she did, at the same time, however, enunciate and practice many modern theories of education. Her distinct contribution for modern teaching involves rather ingenious psychological explanations of difficulties which mentally handicapped children encounter in learning, and games and activities which she devised to utilize the child's desires and experiences in developing the educative process. In Descœudres' system we find a combination of formal exercises and modern philosophy of teaching through experiences.

[3] *Ibid.*, p. 214.

The Unit of Experience

During the 1920's and the 1930's education in general was developing the activity method of teaching. Numerous names have been given to this movement by progressive educators and others advocating the Dewey philosophy. The method has been spoken of as the project, unit, correlation, or experience method. Educators believed that children "learn by doing" and that the subject matter of the school could be taught more effectively if it were related to areas of interest or units of work interesting to children at appropriate age levels. Reading, writing, arithmetic, geography, history, civics, and other school subjects were correlated in some one activity in which the children participated.

In 1924 Wallin [4] recommended that "Extensive use should be made of the method of 'concentration' or 'correlation' or of the problem, or the project methods." He felt that the project method had many advantages over formal drill in specific areas, and should be utilized, at least to some extent, in the special classes.

The foremost advocate of the unit plan of teaching in the special class is Ingram,[5] who devotes five out of eighteen chapters to the exposition of units of work, methods of choosing them, and procedures for carrying them out. Descriptions of suggested units of work for different age levels are presented in detail.

To make educational enterprises vital and closely related to life's needs, it is necessary, says Ingram, to organize a classroom in such a way that units of work or centers of interest dominate the activities of the children in the classroom. Ingram lists a number of criteria for effective units of work. These are:

(1) The units of work should evolve from real life situations of the children and grow out of the direct interest of the children.

(2) The choice of the unit should depend on the child's level of development in mental, social, and physical activities. Children of different ages are interested in different activities.

[4] Wallin, J. E. Wallace, *The Education of Handicapped Children.* Boston: Houghton Mifflin Co., 1924.
[5] Ingram, Christine P., *Education of the Slow-Learning Child.* Yonkers: World Book Company, 1935.

(3) The unit should develop the individual as an individual and should further group activities in participation and co-operation. In most units, every child can profit from some aspect of the unit depending on his interests and abilities.

(4) The unit should offer opportunity for the development of basic habits and attitudes. These should include knowledges and skills necessary in social participation.

(5) The unit selected should be one that develops interest in out-of-school activities. A unit that goes beyond the classroom participation into the home and the community would be superior to a unit that exists only in the classroom.

(6) The unit selected should include activities which utilize the tool subjects. Teaching of reading, writing, and arithmetic should be correlated with the unit whenever possible.

(7) The unit should be of such a nature that it provides children with a variety of experiences.

Ingram presents detailed descriptions of units of various kinds which can be used in special classes for mentally handicapped children and indicates how these units can be carried out. Units for different age levels are outlined as suggestions to teachers.

Ingram does not feel that all skills, attitudes, and tool subjects can be developed through units of experiences. Although five chapters were devoted to the unit and only one to the acquisition of the tool subjects, Ingram states:

The experiences of a unit may often be so planned as to develop knowledge and skill in the tool subjects, as has already been suggested. The idea too has been expressed that if pupils are to attain a satisfactory degree of mastery of these subjects, definite periods must be set aside for their development and practice. The importance of this second fact must be thoroughly sensed by teachers of slow-learning groups.[6]

Because of the emphasis on the unit plan of teaching, the United States Office of Education under the leadership of Elise Martens,[7] compiled a series of units that had proved to be successful in

---

[6] *Ibid.*, p. 334.

[7] Martens, Elise H., *Group Activities for Mentally Retarded Children.* A Symposium, Bulletin No. 7, 1933. Washington, D.C.: United States Government Printing Office.

various parts of the country as suggestions for teachers of the mentally handicapped. The description of units in this bulletin consists of units on the home, our city, the food market, pay telephones, books and book making, foods for boys, child care, manicuring, beautifying the school room, the toy orchestra, how we send messages, U.S. money, a nature history museum, a study of cotton, and a study of trees.

Subject Matter Curricula for the Mentally Handicapped

In practice, most classes for the mentally handicapped throughout the country have not followed the unit plan of education. Classes for the mentally handicapped have been organized by school systems and have usually been assigned to teachers trained in elementary education. For that reason the elementary curriculum at a reduced level has been applied to the organization and teaching methodology of the class for the mentally handicapped. This has been known as a "watered-down curriculum," and has been frowned upon by most specialists in the field of the education of the mentally handicapped.

Inskeep [8] presented such a curriculum in the twenties in which she described a modified traditional curriculum for the education of mentally handicapped and slow-learning children. The book is divided into chapters on reading, language, spelling, arithmetic, and other subjects of the elementary school curriculum. Several chapters, however, are devoted to games and recreational activities for the mentally handicapped which are not necessarily emphasized in a curriculum in elementary education.

Not all present-day educators of the mentally handicapped agree that either the unit plan as described by Ingram or the "watered-down" elementary curriculum is the most effective method of teaching the mentally handicapped. Duncan [9] has recently formulated a program or curriculum for the education of the mentally

---

[8] Inskeep, Annie D., *Teaching Dull and Retarded Children*. New York: The Macmillan Co., 1926.

[9] Duncan, John, *The Education of the Ordinary Child*. New York: The Ronald Press Co., 1943.

handicapped in England which differs markedly from any of the plans that have been presented. He states that the unit plan, or project plan as described by Ingram or Descœudres, has major defects. He asserts:

The Project Method has two weaknesses which do not exist in the Subjects Methods:

(i) It offers great difficulties in the planning of exercises that will enable all the children in a class to work at their highest possible intellectual lev‧ els. Much of the work is apt to be repetitive and much may be merely of manipulative type calling for little or no intellectual effort. If the exercises for children are planned to suit their abilities, they have often an artificial and unreal connection with the project. Projects must tend to impose limitations.

(ii) Education in the form of a series of Projects tends to lack continuity. There is for the child no steady progress.[10]

Duncan felt that the success ascribed to the project plan as such does not indicate a superiority of projects over subjects. He believes that the features embodied in the project plan "... can be embodied in a Subjects Method to obtain, not just as good, but better results." [11]

To understand Duncan's hypothesis and his curriculum one has to understand the theory upon which the curriculum is structured. Duncan obtained his theory from Professor Spearman of the University of London who stated that intelligence consisted of a "g" factor of general intelligence, and an "s" factor, or many "s" factors (meaning specific intelligence). Alexander, a follower of Spearman, continued the studies and concluded that there is a concrete intelligence, defined as the ability to deal with materials intelligently, and an abstract intelligence, usually measured by verbal intelligence tests. Duncan felt that the general intelligence, or "g," of mentally handicapped children was measured by the Stanford-Binet Test, which measured the "v" factor or the abstract factor in intelligence. The "f" factor of concrete intelligence was usually measured with a performance type examination.

---

[10] John Duncan, *The Education of the Ordinary Child.* Copyright 1943, by The Ronald Press Co.

[11] *Ibid.*, p. 30.

The group of children with whom Duncan worked (at the Lankhills school of Hampshire County, England) tested in the range of 54 to 76 I.Q., with a mean I.Q. of 66 on the Stanford Revision of the Binet Scale. When the Alexander Performance tests, which measured concrete intelligence, were administered, the range was 67 to 119 with a mean performance quotient of 96. Duncan concluded, therefore, that all mentally handicapped children seem to have better intelligence in the concrete field — that is, in dealing with things — than in the abstract field which deals primarily with verbal intelligence. Consequently, the curriculum for the mentally handicapped should be taught primarily through a medium of exercises with things that can be handled, seen, touched, or heard, rather than through a medium of words, i.e., the verbal and the abstract. Working with the hands alone would not be satisfactory. The activities of the children should be planned in such a way that the children will observe relationships and should consist of systematically planned provisions for working with things which should stimulate thinking in series and sequences.

Duncan describes the series of subjects which the children are taught at the Lankhills School. These subjects consist of handwork and crafts, paper and cardboard work, woodwork, needlework, the domestic subjects, housewifery, cookery, laundry work, art, country dancing, physical education, school gardening and rural science, English, numbers and mathematics, and history and geography. This array of subject matter seems to be an adaptation of the curriculum of the regular school with greater emphasis on activities in the manual and occupational field.

To illustrate Duncan's point of view several of the subjects which he describes will be explained briefly. Duncan agreed that while a subject in itself is not important, the child is. Children are studied and subjects are assigned according to the children's abilities. In considering handwork and crafts, for example, Duncan stated that handwork and crafts must be so developed as to be an educational subject, rather than limited to the development of the object or product itself. To Duncan, handwork is a means of education. Handwork and crafts are used as a means for ". . . the stimulation of thought, the intellectual activity in solving visual and concrete problems — that came first, followed by the arrangement of exercises into steps and stages to form a graded scheme." [12] Duncan discarded such works as plastic, raffiawork, and cane work, because many of these are simply manipulative and repetitive.

The first step in studying handwork and crafts was through paper and cardboard work. Here he planned a series of graded exercises of increasing intellectual difficulty, whose purpose was to give the children an opportunity to plan, to think in sequence, and to grasp relationships. After some handwork and craft work of this sort, the educational tasks merged into woodwork, book crafts, and needlework.

As an example of Duncan's procedure, successive steps of paper and cardboard work are given here:

(1) Initially the children were supplied with cardboard rulers having simple measurements, such as an inch, and given exercises in marking off the paper in inch squares and coloring the squares. The work then developed into making different patterns with adjacent squares, or making diagonals and making and cutting out triangles.

(2) In stage two actual objects, such as furniture, were made from paper and cardboard. Children measured and systematically followed a drawing so that they could learn to visualize the complete object as they worked.

(3) In the third stage they made three-view drawings and translated them into developments. They then made models to scale of the actual furniture in the room.

(4) During the fourth stage a three-view drawing of an unknown object was given to the children and they were required to visualize the object. This required abstract thought, but if the previous steps had been developed accurately, the children, according to Duncan, could construct these objects.

(5) During the fifth stage an oral description of a model, such as a match box, was given and the children were required to understand the directions, to draw a rough sketch of the match box in three views, and to record measurements of the object. His

[12] *Ibid.*, p. 67.

instruction for concrete mental activity was presented verbally (abstractly).

(6) During the sixth stage the children used a written description of the object, and from this description drew the box, using the actual measurements to complete the job.

It will be seen from the description above that the task is systematically developed from simple operations to much more complex operations with an increase in the mental process involved in each step. Woodworking and needlework are similarly developed through a series of systematic, step-by-step, developmental projects.

Duncan feels that modern teaching of art by means of free expression is of little value to mentally handicapped children. He says:

Children must have freedom to express their ideas, but they must learn to use their tools correctly and to plan their work to obtain the best and (to them) the most satisfying results with the minimum expenditure of effort and time. Our view, then, is that Art Work in a third phase, in which both technique and freedom of expression have a place, will be on sound educational lines.[13]

Art to Duncan means free expression up to a certain point, then a systematic development of art techniques. He feels that the teaching of colors, designs, fabric-printing, pictorial composition, object drawing, and plant drawing, should be developed step by step.

The descriptions of the activities in school gardening and rural science are very similar to the traditional "project methods" in their exposition and accomplishment.

Duncan states, without comparative evidence, that the attainments of the children in English and in mathematics is superior to other children of the same Binet mental age. He explains this superiority of learning, not on the basis of the methods of teaching reading and English, but on the transfer of the training from the systematic activities developed in the other subjects. He feels that there are common usable elements in the other subjects which

[13] *Ibid.*, p. 125.

are transferred to the academic area. Motivation for reading, for example, is aroused in other activities such as handwork and cookery.

In teaching reading Duncan feels that the children make progress because phonics is emphasized. Some sentence form and word study is included, but in general the system starts with phonics supplemented by other methods — rather than by other methods supplemented by phonics. The New Beacon Readers (Ginn) are used to teach reading. In addition, oral work, silent work, written work, and individual work, with exercises in word discrimination and word recognition, are included in the instructional program.

By way of comment one can say that:

(1) Duncan's subject matter curriculum is not the subject matter curriculum usually recognized in this country. The subjects which he uses are actually practical subjects of woodwork, needlework, housewifery, and so forth. The academic curriculum of the regular school is included in Duncan's curriculum but is not given prominence.

(2) It is possible that the curriculum which Duncan has devised is applicable to the type of mentally handicapped child which he described. Although the mean I.Q. on the Stanford-Binet was 66, the mean Performance Quotient on Alexander's Performance Test was 96. This group seems to represent a particular kind of mentally handicapped child whose performance with concrete material is normal, even though his verbal test performance is subnormal. It is doubtful that all children referred to special classes for the mentally handicapped have such wide discrepancies in verbal and performance intelligence. Some individual children may have higher performance quotients than verbal intelligence quotients, but this usually does not hold for classes as a whole. Duncan explains this discrepancy by the fact that many of his clients came from the country and may differ from children in urban communities.

(3) The systematic step-by-step plan and the instruction of the children in the various subjects has definite merit with mentally handicapped children. Whether these exercises actually accomplish the objectives of "finding relationships" and "developing intellec-

tual abilities" has not been demonstrated by Duncan. Whether the development of the eduction of relations in one particular task has any transfer to other tasks, as Duncan seems to think, is another problem that should be investigated. Certainly the experience with objects, terms, and concepts before the verbal aspect is emphasized, gives the child a familiarity with the subject matter which makes reading and understanding easier.

Occupational Education

There has been considerable interest in recent years concerning the occupational adjustment of mentally handicapped children. The term "occupational education" has been used differently to mean different programs, but all of the programs have been aimed at the adjustment of the mentally handicapped child on some sort of a job.

It was believed by many that since mentally handicapped children do not excel or achieve to any appreciable degree in the academic subjects, such as reading, writing, arithmetic, geography, history, etc., that the best program of education for them should be their assignment to some sort of occupational or trade training class. In certain parts of the country these children were sent to vocational schools for the purpose of having them develop a vocation. It was soon discovered, however, that mentally handicapped children in such schools were assigned to general shops, i.e., wood-working, home economics, or other educational activities requiring a certain degree of academic training, rather than to a specific trade class.

Surveys of the occupational status of mentally handicapped children, such as that of Channing,[14] indicated that the occupations which mentally retarded boys and girls obtained and held at the adult level were mostly of the unskilled and semiskilled types requiring little academic or vocational training. Channing's study, together with other similar studies, tended to indicate that rather

[14] Channing, Alice, *Employment of Mentally Deficient Boys and Girls.* United States Department of Labor. Children's Bureau Publication M, No. 210, 1932. Washington, D.C.: United States Government Printing Office.

than attempting specific vocational training, they should be taught the habits and attitudes of work that would be helpful to them in unskilled and semiskilled positions in after-school life. For these reasons schools attempted to emphasize occupational training or occupational education rather than vocational training, especially at the adolescent level.

Industrialization caused teachers of the mentally handicapped, in such cities as Detroit, to begin to think of occupational education for mentally retarded children. In 1940 a group of teachers compiled a list of occupations suitable for mentally handicapped boys and girls. These occupations were to be the basis upon which teachers were to develop projects and activities.[15]

Douglas defines occupational education as that education which ". . . deals with the common elements in obtaining, maintaining and advancing in a job." [16] She states that the objectives of occupational education can be accomplished through:

1. Presenting those materials emphasizing wage earning as a privilege which demands certain responsibilities (such as careful, steady performance). We must strive to have the girl or boy accept and be conscious of the individual's importance in a job and to take pride in doing his part to the best of his ability.
2. Pointing out that there is a bond between employer and employee with rights and privileges for each; that the obligations in any job are usually well founded and are not based upon personal whims.
3. Bringing in those items which stress financial management and independence, such as personal expenditures, savings, insurance, money to be sent home, and community charity, etc.[17]

Douglas feels that the emphasis in occupational education for the adolescent child who is now becoming interested in jobs should be placed on those aspects of jobs that are common to all occupations. She feels that occupational education fits into a school program most effectively when the members of the class have at least some proficiency in academic tool subjects. She also feels that giving

[15] Douglas, Marcella E., "Some Concrete Contributions to Occupational Education in the Academic Classroom," *American Journal of Mental Deficiency,* 48, No. 3 (January, 1944), pp. 288–291.
[16] *Ibid.,* p. 288.   [17] *Ibid.,* p. 289.

information about specific jobs which these children can handle is not as important a part of occupational education as is the familiarity with obligations and circumstances common to all wage earners.

Richard Hungerford, director of the Bureau for Children with Retarded Mental Development in New York City, broadened the concept of occupational education for mentally retarded children to include the total educational process. The objectives and techniques of implementation have been published in numerous articles in *Occupational Education*,[18] a magazine for those interested in the guidance of the non-academic pupils.

The concept of occupational education according to Hungerford is that:

The whole program for the mentally retarded must be built around the achieving of vocational and social competence, for here, if anywhere, the retarded will most nearly approach normalcy. This *different developmental program* is called Occupational Education.[19]

The essentials of an effective program of occupational education are to give the retarded child an opportunity to develop his abilities for self-support and at the same time to protect him from becoming hopelessly discouraged as he competes with others in his task. Occupational education provides occupational and social skills which lead to social and occupational adjustment in society. This program is developed in five major areas as follows:

(1) Occupational information. Occupational information consists of giving the pupils information about jobs and job analysis of the work which is available to them. This information helps them see the importance of these jobs to themselves and to the world.

(2) Vocational guidance. In vocational guidance the child is

[18] *Occupational Education.* A Magazine for Those Interested in the Guidance of the Non-Academic. 224 East 28th Street, New York: The Association for the New York City Teachers of Special Education. Published monthly October–May.

[19] Hungerford, Richard H., Chris J. De Prospo, and Louis E. Rosenzweig, "The Non-Academic Pupil," *Philosophy of Occupational Education.* 224 East 28th Street, New York: The Association for the New York City Teachers of Special Education, 1948.

assisted in meshing his abilities with the jobs which interest him to discover the ones for which he is best fitted. It assists the child in finding out about other jobs in the same area.

(3) Vocational training. In vocational training the pupil is given training in the manual skills found in the work area, training in many non-manual skills necessary in work, together with training in general habits, attitudes, and skills necessary for good workmanship and citizenship.

(4) Vocational placement. In this area the child or individual is helped in finding a job.

(5) Social placement. In this area the individual is helped in adjusting to the job and to society for as long as such assistance is necessary.

According to Hungerford, the teachers are responsible for the first three areas. The last two can be carried out by placement personnel, United States Employment Service, and by other social agencies.

To achieve the aims of occupational education the New York group has designed a curriculum around cores of interest. These cores are listed as follows:

Core 1	The Home, applicable to children of	ages 7–9
Core 2	The Neighborhood, applicable to children of	age 10
Core 3	The Borough, applicable to children of	age 11
Core 4	The City, applicable to children of	age 12
Core 5	Study of Job Areas, applicable to children of	age 13
Core 6	Ways of choosing, getting, and holding a job, applicable to children of	age 14
Core 7	Ways of spending one's income, applicable to children of	age 15
Core 8	Worker as a citizen and a social being, applicable to children of	ages 16–17 [20]

Studies of New York workers show that 60 to 80 per cent of them lose their jobs for non-manual reasons, rather than for poor vocational skills. The program of occupational education therefore includes areas of study which would lessen lay-offs. These include personal health and appearance, manners, means of getting em-

[20] *Ibid.*, p. 17.

ployment, means of keeping a job, means of adjusting to accidents and unemployment, ways to get along with the "boss," ways to get along with fellow workers, budgets and banking, ways to travel in the city, suggestions for living at home, suggestions for living away from home, recreation, personal relationships, group relationships, and citizenship.

Committees of teachers in New York have been structuring the implementation of these cores. Whatever the dominant interest of the child is at the time, the specific teaching sequences developed by these committees include and correlate with the dominant interest such skills as reading, writing, arithmetic, language, and other aspects of the curriculum of the elementary school. The curriculum for each core is planned for a whole year. Specific attainments are broken down for each month, week, and day. These guides assist the teacher in focusing attention on specific goals to be attained and allow the teacher to develop instructional materials to attain these goals.

The New York plan is an attempt to organize a special program for mentally handicapped children which will mesh with their abilities and interests, and which emphasizes the goals of occupational adequacy and social competency. It correlates the learning activities of the children at each age-level with a center of interest such as the core curriculum. Although the plan does not differ from most programs for children at the younger age level, it does emphasize, for the adolescent, a more realistic program of vocational information, vocational guidance, and vocational training than is usually offered these children.

EDUCATING SPECIAL GROUPS

There has been very little study of the differential education of the different types of mentally handicapped children, i.e., the brain-injured, the Mongolian, or other types. In 1947, however, Strauss and Lehtinen [21] published a book on the education of a particular type of mentally handicapped child, the brain-injured.

[21] Strauss, Alfred, and Laura E. Lehtinen, *Psychopathology and Education of the Brain-Injured Child.* New York: Grune and Stratton, 1947.

Dr. Strauss conceives of a brain-injured child as one

. . . who before, during, or after birth has received an injury to or suffered an infection of the brain. As a result of such organic impairment, defects of the neuromotor system may be present or absent; however, such a child may show disturbances in perception, thinking, and emotional behavior, either separately or in combination. These disturbances can be demonstrated by specific tests. These disturbances prevent or impede a normal learning process. Special educational methods have been devised to remedy these specific handicaps.[22]

Dr. Strauss has attempted to relate three different disciplines in his education of the brain-injured child. First, he has attempted to determine the neurological, or brain pathology involved in children who have brain injuries. He believes that destruction of the forebrain, including the telencephalon, or cortex, and the diencephalon, or thalamus, results in disturbances in psychological functions. The non-volitional, expressive movements, such as facial expressions, are regulated primarily by the diencephalon, sometimes called the extrapyramidal system. Our emotions, gestures, and expressive movements are regulated to some extent by the thalamus. The latter is responsible for anger, fear, aggressiveness, and withdrawal. The mental processes of perception have some matrix of dynamic forces. In this way the thalamus continually influences the processes of the cortex. During the process of growth the child develops inhibiting power which is, according to Strauss, a function of the cortex. A lesion in the cortex therefore reduces the inhibition, and the thalamus reacts in an uncontrolled manner with more primitive impulses. Strauss accepts Kahn's concept of "driveness" to explain the hyper-excitability of the thalamus when it is not inhibited by the cortex. Thus brain damage to either the thalamus or the cortex, or both, may not produce motor disabilities but may produce a disrupting effect on the behavior of the organism as a whole in its emotional, perceptual, and thinking processes.

The next discipline which Strauss has used to explain the effects of brain lesion is the study of psychological reactions of brain-

[22] *Ibid.*, p. 4.

injured children. From first-hand experience and numerous studies which he cites in his book, he has noted certain disturbances which seem to characterize brain-injured children. Some of the psychological and behavioral disturbances noted are as follows:

PERCEPTUAL DISTURBANCES

Brain-injured children seem to be attracted to the *details* of an object, rather than to its *wholeness*. In practice the children note a button on one's clothing, a buckle, or small details of pictures rather than the concept of the picture as a whole. This is also represented in writing and in arithmetic problems in which they seem to be lost in details rather than acquiring concepts of the perceptual object as a whole.

By means of specially constructed tests, Strauss was able to demonstrate that brain-injured children show some ". . . disintegration in the visual-perceptual field, whereas non-brain-injured children follow global procedures, conforming to a known developmental sequence." [23] The same disturbance as in visual-motor perception was found also in the tactual field and in the auditory field.

The second perceptual disturbance which was found more frequently with brain-injured children is *perseveration*. This is represented when a child continually repeats what he has done. In writing, the child repeats the same letter or word when he is unable to continue. In arithmetic he repeats certain numbers over and over again when he is blocked.

The perceptual disturbances produce *distractibility* in children. The tests on perception showed that they did not follow a logical sequence on the marble board but jumped from place to place even though their end result was adequate. Distractibility suggests a hypersensitivity to chance stimuli and seems to be characteristic of brain-injured children.

THINKING DISORDERS

Thinking disorders seemed to be more frequent in brain-injured children than in non-brain-injured children. The ability of the

[23] *Ibid.*, p. 41.

brain-injured child to reason and to form concepts seemed to deviate from the normal. With a series of tests Strauss demonstrated that the following reactions indicated a disorganization of the thinking process which were more severe and more commonly found in the brain-injured child than in the non-brain-injured child:

1. The child sorted the objects according to form or color.
2. The child sorted according to an unessential detail.
3. The child saw a relationship between the objects in regard to their function, but the relationship was vague or far-fetched.
4. The child placed objects together on the basis of their relationship in a hypothetical or imaginary situation.[24]

In the qualitative analysis of the responses of brain-injured children, Strauss found several factors characteristic of these disorganized relationships. These children tend to place objects in a formalistic arrangement, such as a semicircle, rather than according to some concept or image of relationship. The other reaction of brain-injured children was the ease and frequency with which they stepped off from a certain line of thinking to something else. Strauss summarizes as follows:

To summarize the findings of these tests of conceptual relationships, we found that brain-injured children, as compared with non-brain-injured normal and mentally deficient children, selected more objects, made more uncommon choices, "went off" easily to elaborate on conceptual units only loosely connected with the task at hand, and exhibited pedantic and formalistic behavior in arrangement of objects. Some of the peculiar behavior of brain-injured children can be compared with the findings of Goldstein and others concerning brain-injured adults who also showed pathological meticulosity, formalistic behavior, attraction by unessential details and so on. The results of our investigations with brain-injured children have their parallel in studies of brain-injured adults.[25]

BEHAVIOR DISORDERS

Brain-injured children show behavior disorders peculiar to their disability. Studies of case histories and observations of the behavior of brain-injured children have shown certain kinds of

[24] *Ibid.*, p. 56.   [25] *Ibid.*, p. 64.

impulsive behavior peculiar to them. The description of psychopathic personalities seems to fit these ·children. They seem ". . . to lack fear or prudence, rushing heedlessly before automobiles, jumping from high places, climbing trees, etc." [26] Hurting other children and then repenting about their behavior is sometimes common. Inhibitions are trained, and sometimes these children can be educated to inhibit certain impulsive behaviors.

The purpose of any diagnosis, or the determination of etiology, is to assist in structuring the most adequate rehabilitation procedures. Therefore the third discipline which Strauss and Lehtinen utilized in their work was that of the education of brain-injured children — actually the most important since it involves treatment. Strauss and Lehtinen describe in detail their educational process, some of the highlights of which are as follows:

(1) It is believed ". . . that the undamaged portions of the brain hold resources from which the organism may substitute, compensate for, or restitute the disabilities resulting from injury." [27] Strauss and Lehtinen believe that they are using the individual's reserve of the intact portion of the brain to reorganize his mental functions so that he can learn like a non-brain-injured child.

(2) Distractibility on the part of brain-injured children reveals an organism which responds abnormally to the stimulations of a school environment. The child reacts "unselectively, passively, and without conscious intent." The child either is distracted by the external stimulus of the environment of a classroom or may sit quietly at his desk noting a detail of the task at hand but not completing the task. This hypersensitive behavior on the part of the child, resulting from his lack of inhibition, indicates lack of effective cortical control. If there is a noise outside he runs to the window to find it; the classmates distract him by movement and by other activities. Attempts on the part of the teacher to motivate and stimulate such children result in boisterousness, uncontrolled laughter, and in running around the room.

The treatment for such a child is to decrease environmental stimulations. It is advisable, then, to have him in a small group, to seat him at a considerable distance from the other children so

[26] *Ibid.*, p. 97.   [27] *Ibid.*, p. 129.

that they will not distract him, or to place him in an isolated part of the room where he is not distracted by moving stimuli, noise, visual objects from the window, or the other children. In some cases they have faced the child's desk against the wall and have separated him from the others in order to assist him in paying attention to tasks at hand. Ornamental dresses worn by the teacher, jewelry, excessive make-up, buttons, pictures, and other distractions seem to attract the child's attention away from a given task. For that reason the teacher dresses plainly and simply so as not to produce a distracting influence on the child. After the child has learned to complete a task, to concentrate, and to pay less attention to environmental stimulation other than the task at hand, he is gradually returned to the group and later to his regular classroom or special class.

(3) Since brain-injured children are attracted to moving stimuli, the lessons and activities should include motor activity, such as cutting, sorting, and manipulating objects or gadgets. This helps direct the child's attention toward the task at hand.

(4) Because of the tendency for such children to have disturbances in perception, remedial perceptual training is given so that perception will be better structured and organized. The particular teaching device should depend on the child's perceptual disturbance. If the child has a disturbance in figure-ground relationship, if he is unable to work at a given task because of the confusion of figure and background, then the teaching methods and materials should be so adapted that this confusion does not exist. Strauss states:

Thus if the picture a child is to color is outlined with a heavy black crayon, the heavy line is a cue which enables the child to keep constant the relationship between the foreground of the picture and the background of the paper and to color successfully within the lines.[28]

In other words, certain teaching cues and crutches are exaggerated to keep the child at the task at hand. Sometimes letters are delineated with color cues so that the child can recognize the letters. Certain devices and techniques have been developed by Miss

[28] *Ibid.*, p. 136.

Lehtinen to exaggerate cues and to restructure the perceptual organization. In one case, a deaf child who was unable to read lips was taught lip-reading when the teacher exaggerated her lips with excessive use of lipstick so that the child would pay more attention to that cue in lip-reading.

(5) The materials and methods used are to some extent self-tutoring. It is the objective of the teacher to assist the child in working by himself and educating himself rather than requiring complete individual instruction from the teacher. Although Strauss and Lehtinen recognize the disadvantages of crutches and devices, they state that these cues must be used and that the child discards them as soon as he is able to function without them.

(6) The project method is not used in the education of brain-injured children because it is felt that the project or unit plan produces great distractibility for this type of child, and does not assist in the reorganization of the perceptual process. It is believed that learning by doing is actually achieved through methods which are concrete and manipulative, and which fit the child's mode of learning. When the child is able to function in a regular group using the project method, he is transferred to that type of activity.

(7) It was noted earlier that perseveration is one of the defects of brain-injured children. Teaching materials, as well as teaching methods, should be of such a nature that a child is not encouraged in his use of perseveration. Drill, therefore, is the last step in educating a brain-injured child. Repetition is used when insight is a part of the task. Repeating the writing of words and letters over and over again or rote serial counting is discouraged.

(8) In addition to these specific techniques the authors suggest that the child return to his regular class whenever sufficient correction of his psychological disturbances has been achieved. Teaching of rhythms, speech, and manual training should all be included in the curriculum for the child after he returns to his class. All of these can be designed to decrease the recurrence of distractibility, perseveration, hyperactivity, and perceptual disturbances.

(9) The authors give in detail their methods of teaching arith-

metic, reading, and writing. Writing, for example, is taught by starting with single letters. The authors feel that the brain-injured child cannot perceive or structuralize a whole word. The first letter taught, for example, is "m." Strauss states that this letter is taught first because the ". . . abductor movements of the arm (those which proceed outward from the body) develop earlier and are executed with greater strength than adductor movements (those moving inward, across the body)." [29]

The work of Strauss and Lehtinen indicates a special type of education for a special type of mentally handicapped child. It does not apply to all mentally handicapped children. Maybe this explains why some teachers feel children can learn by the whole and the experience method, while others feel children can learn best by a more detailed method. In nearly every class for the mentally handicapped there will be both brain-injured and non-brain-injured children. These children will probably learn differently even though their mental ages are the same. The educational procedures used by Strauss and Lehtinen are the application and elaboration of special educational techniques that have been used for many years. The contribution these authors have made is to relate these specialized teaching techniques to the disturbances in psychological functions and neurological deficit. The teaching technique of Strauss and Lehtinen is based not on a trial and error procedure used by many teachers, but on definite reasons. Some may not agree with the theoretical reasons or with some of the experimental results. Nevertheless, it should be said that if a teacher knows what she is doing, and knows why she is doing it, she will do a much better job than just knowing that what she is doing *seems* to be producing some progress.

SUMMARY

Methods of educating mentally handicapped children have been developed by numerous individuals. The common elements in these methods include an attempt (1) to adapt the instruction to the slow learning ability of the children, and (2) to make the program

[29] *Ibid.*, p. 187.

practical and less academic. Examples of the different emphasis in the various programs include:

(1) Emphasis on sense training with an attempt to develop these and the tool subjects through concrete, doing activities (Descœudres).
(2) Emphasis on "watering down" the elementary curriculum by including the subjects of the elementary school but at a lower level of required achievement (Inskeep).
(3) Emphasizing the practical subjects in a school such as home economics, gardening, woodworking, and so forth, correlated with the tool subjects through a very systematic, step-by-step method of presentation (Duncan).
(4) Emphasizing occupational information, guidance and training, and social competence through core programs (Hungerford).
(5) Emphasizing education through units of experience, as the method of educating the mentally handicapped (Ingram).
(6) Developing special clinical educational procedures for special mental disabilities found in brain-injured children (Strauss).

REFERENCES

Channing, Alice. *Employment of Mentally Deficient Boys and Girls*, United States Department of Labor, Children's Bureau Publication No. 210, 1932. Washington, D.C.: United States Government Printing Office.

Descœudres, Alice. *The Education of Mentally Defective Children*, trans. from the Second French Edition by Ernest F. Row. New York: D. C. Heath & Co., 1928.

Douglas, Marcella E. "Some Concrete Contributions to Occupational Education in the Academic Classroom," *American Journal of Mental Deficiency*, 48, No. 3 (January, 1944), pp. 288–291.

Duncan, John. *The Education of the Ordinary Child*. New York: The Ronald Press Company, 1943.

Hungerford, Richard H., Chris J. De Prospo, and Louis E. Rosenzweig. "The Non-Academic Pupil," *Philosophy of Occupational Education*. 224 East 28th Street, New York: The Association for the New York City Teachers of Special Education, 1948.

Ingram, Christine P. *Education of the Slow-Learning Child.* Yonkers: World Book Company, 1935.

Inskeep, Annie D. *Teaching Dull and Retarded Children.* New York: The Macmillan Company, 1926.

Martens, Elise H. *Group Activities for Mentally Retarded Children.* A Symposium, Bulletin No. 7, 1933. Washington, D.C.: United States Government Printing Office.

Occupational Education. A Magazine for Those Interested in the Guidance of the Non-Academic. 224 East 28th Street, New York: The Association for the New York City Teachers of Special Education. Published monthly October–May.

Strauss, Alfred, and Laura E. Lehtinen. *Psychopathology and Education of the Brain-Injured Child.* New York: Grune and Stratton, 1947.

Wallin, J. E. Wallace. *The Education of Handicapped Children.* Boston: Houghton Mifflin Company, 1924.

Chapter 6

Aims, Purposes, and Organization

PRINCIPAL AIMS

A CLASSIFICATION of children with low intelligence for educational purposes was presented in Chapter 1. Three groups of children were differentiated as the mentally deficient, the mentally handicapped, and the slow learner. It was stated that the mentally deficient or feeble-minded child is one who needs custodial care since he will be unable to get along in society or support himself economically without the help of others and supervision by his family or by an institution. This book does not elaborate on the methods of custodial care for such children. It is concerned rather with the educable child of low intelligence who does not profit sufficiently from the program of the regular school, but who requires a modified or differentiated curriculum for his maximum growth and development.

The mentally handicapped child, though handicapped by mental deficit, is sufficiently educable to be able to learn to conduct his daily affairs without undue supervision. He can profit from a particular type of educational procedure or educational organization. He can become socially competent — that is, he can get along in our society — hold a job, and become totally or partially economically sufficient. Without this specialized training he and many like him may, instead, become custodial cases. It should be noted that the definition of mentally handicapped children includes the characteristics of both the children and the situation in which they are placed. This is predicated on the belief that many mentally handicapped children *without* the proper environment and the proper educational opportunity may become mentally deficient custodial cases.

The point of view underlying the education of the mentally handicapped assumes that inherent in the philosophy of democracy is the doctrine that all children are entitled to education according to the limit of their capacities. "All men are created equal" has been interpreted to mean that all are equal before the law and have equal rights to an education even though they do not have equal abilities to learn. In American democracy we are committed to the principle that all who can profit from education are entitled to that education, regardless of ability, race, or creed. Our task then is to determine how best to educate the mentally handicapped child.

The educational organization and procedures described here are primarily for the child who has been diagnosed as mentally handicapped. It is questionable whether the slow-learning child requires a different kind of educational organization from that given the average child except for certain adaptations and modifications. The mentally deficient as defined, however, will not profit from an educational program but might respond to certain forms of training.

OBJECTIVES AND PURPOSES

The education of the mentally handicapped differs from the education of the average child in the lack of emphasis placed upon academic achievement, and the emphasis placed upon the development of personality and adequacy in the occupational and social areas. Mentally handicapped children cannot achieve the skills and degrees of knowledge in the academic areas of reading, writing, arithmetic, science, or social studies attained by the average child. They can, however, learn to adjust to society and to show accomplishment in an unskilled or semiskilled job.

The Education Policies Commission has listed four major objectives of education, namely:

(1) The objectives of self-realization.
(2) The objectives of human relationship.
(3) The objectives of economic efficiency.
(4) The objectives of civic responsibility.[1]

In general these objectives are applicable to mentally handicapped children as well as to average or superior children. It is necessary, however, that we list the purposes of education of the mentally handicapped in more specific terms in order to differentiate them from the specific objectives of children with average intelligence.

Ingram [2] states that the differences between the mentally handicapped and the average occur primarily in the following ways:

(1) The mentally handicapped child's mental development will be slower than the average.
(2) The mentally handicapped child will attain standards in the physical and social field to approximate that of the average, more than in the field of mental and educational development.
(3) The home backgrounds of mentally handicapped children are usually more inadequate and the experiences are narrower.
(4) Mentally handicapped children will attain hand skills closer to that of the normal and will find greater success in these areas.
(5) Their adaptation to the vocational field will be more in the unskilled and semiskilled trades.

Ingram lists the following questions which should be asked regarding the activities of mentally handicapped children in a classroom:

Does it promote health, both mental and physical?
Does it promote a practical application of the tool subjects?
Does it promote better home membership?
Does it promote better group and community living?
Does it promote a better use of leisure time?
Does it promote desirable working habits and attitudes? [3]

[1] Educational Policies Commission, *Policies for Education in American Democracy.* Washington, D.C.: National Education Association, 1946, p. 47.
[2] Ingram, Christine P., *Education of the Slow-Learning Child.* Yonkers. World Book Company, 1935.
[3] *Ibid.*, p. 73.

Objectives can be stated in a number of ways and in different terms. In general, however, all specialists agree that the more specific aims for the mentally handicapped include the following:

(1) They should be educated to get along with their fellow men; i.e., they should develop social competency through numerous social experiences.

(2) They should learn to participate in work for the purpose of earning their own living; i.e., they should develop occupational competence through efficient vocational guidance and training as a part of their school experience.

(3) They should develop emotional security and independence in the school and in the home through a good mental hygiene program.

(4) They should develop habits of health and sanitation through a good program of health education.

(5) They should learn the minimum essentials of the tool subjects, even though their academic limits are third to fifth grade.

(6) They should learn to occupy themselves in wholesome leisure time activities through an educational program that teaches them to enjoy recreational and leisure time activities.

(7) They should learn to become adequate members of a family and a home through an educational program that emphasizes home membership as a function of the curriculum.

(8) They should learn to become adequate members of a community through a school program that emphasizes community participation.

The program for the mentally handicapped stresses (1) occupational adequacy, (2) social competence, and (3) personal adequacy.

Occupational adequacy. A mentally handicapped child should be trained in such a way that he will be able to support himself partially or totally in some productive activity. Occupational training, therefore, should begin when the child enters school and end when the child has been successfully placed on a job and is supporting himself partially or totally.

Occupational training should not be thought of as specific vocational training. The positions in which the mentally handicapped will be successful later in life are in the unskilled and semiskilled activities. Success on the job is going to depend on getting to the job on time, personal appearance, manners, getting along with other employees and the employer, personal health, ability to handle money wisely, safety on the job, responsibility in following directions and carrying the task through to completion, and many other personal characteristics which are developed from early childhood. The school should attempt from the beginning of the child's school career to establish those habits and attitudes which will develop a responsible, efficient worker, regardless of how unskilled the job is. Even reading, writing, and arithmetic are parts of occupational education since a child will require a minimum of the academic skills in order to read signs, simple directions, and possibly to communicate by means of writing even at a simple level.

Social adequacy. Social adequacy refers to the individual's ability to get along with his fellow men in some sort of a co-operative relationship. The mentally handicapped child will, in most cases, become responsible for, or belong to, a family. Personal habits which make possible getting along in a home, raising children, getting along with the neighbors, and becoming an acceptable member of a community are the major goals. The educational program for the mentally handicapped child should emphasize social relationships, working with others, getting along with people, and having a certain degree of consideration for rights and desires of others. This program should start when the child enters school and should continue until, as an adult, the individual is a stable member of the community in which he lives.

Personal adequacy. In addition to getting along with the neighbors and holding a job, the individual must live within himself. Physical and mental health are important factors in the educational process. Mentally handicapped children have many frustrations in their home and school environment which interfere with their normal emotional development. Failure to cope with the regular school curriculum has been one obvious frustration. This failure does not give them personal adequacy but rather it results in feelings of inferiority followed by unwholesome compensatory behavior.

It has been said that the major motives of all human beings consist primarily of two aspects: (1) a desire for security, and (2) a desire for adequacy. Every child and even every adult must have a feeling of security or belongingness. This means that the child must feel he is a desired member of the family, the school, and the community. The child develops security if he is wanted by his own peer group in addition to being wanted by his parents and teachers. That means that the activities and experiences in a classroom should be directed so that each child in a class becomes recognized as an individual, has a "feeling of belongingness" to that class, and recognizes that he has been accepted by the group in which he finds himself. Security for a child means that he must belong and feel that he belongs to his parents, to his teachers, and to his peer group. It is doubtful whether a mentally handicapped child in a regular grade establishes this security. On the contrary, the curriculum of the school which is too difficult for him, the reactions of average and superior children to his lack of academic ability, and the frustration of the teacher because he is not able to keep up to grade are apt to shatter the child's security rather than develop it.

Everyone must gain his own self-respect — he must feel he has a certain degree of adequacy or an ability to accomplish something. Mentally handicapped children should have a curriculum in which they develop this feeling of adequacy and accomplishment. That is one reason for introducing much handwork into the curriculum for the mentally handicapped; in this particular area they can accomplish something at a certain level and know by seeing the product of their accomplishment that they are worth-while.

This suggests how necessary it is that the curriculum for the education of mentally handicapped children should stress mental health. It should stress an environment in which the child feels secure with his teacher, with his peer group, and at home with his family. The curriculum must be of such a nature that he accomplishes something at his level of abilities. Frustrations due to inability to achieve according to the arbitrary standard of average children should be avoided at all times. Some emphasis should be placed on the significance and worth-whileness of lowly activities — the benefit the group receives from monotonous jobs that must be done by someone.

The curriculum of the special class at all levels should be so designed that it assists in the development of a sense of security and adequacy and thereby contributes to the personal happiness and social adjustment of the child. These factors of personal security should permeate all activities in the classroom, should extend to the home through parent understandings, and should assist the child in becoming a member of the community by means of participation in out-of-school activities with other children in playgrounds, clubs, Boy Scout and Girl Scout organizations, and so forth. These children should not be placed in situations in which the feeling of security or the feeling of adequacy is thwarted.

ORGANIZATION OF EDUCATIONAL PROGRAMS

REGULAR GRADES OR SPECIAL CLASSES

There has been considerable controversy concerning the organization of classes for the education of mentally handicapped children. Many school administrators have confused the slow-learning child with the mentally handicapped child. It is common to hear school superintendents say, "We do not have children in the school system with I.Q.'s below 75; those are sent to institutions." For that reason many have been opposed to the organization of special classes for mentally handicapped children within a public school organization because they do not differentiate the mentally handicapped child from the slow-learning child who can be educated in the regular grades or the mentally deficient child who is usually excluded from the public school classes.

Can mentally handicapped children adjust to the traditional public school grade? This problem has been argued for many years, yet we have very little experimental evidence to support one or another point of view. Many mentally handicapped children are allowed to sit in the grades. If they are docile and obedient, they are tolerated. If they become aggressive because of continual failure, they are given some attention, are excluded as incorrigibles or as mental deficients, or are sent to special classes or special schools.

It has been stated that it is educationally unsound to "segregate" mentally handicapped children into special classes. All educable children according to this view should be in the regular classes. The term "segregation" has been greatly abused. Actually in a public school system children are segregated according to ages. Thus most six-year-old children are placed in the first grade whereas most ten-year-old children are placed in the fifth grade. To some extent, therefore, we have segregated children according to chronological ages. Six-year-olds, or first-grade children, do not necessarily participate in school activities with second-graders, third-graders, fourth-graders, fifth-graders, or those of other grades. Assemblies may include the whole school, but as far as participation of children with one another in a school system is concerned, our grading system is a form of segregation. Few however, object to "grades" as a form of segregation. Yet many object to placing children according to abilities in grades.

Johnson [4] has presented experimental evidence concerning the adjustment of mentally handicapped children in the regular grades. By means of sociometric techniques in regular grades, one through five, that contained one or more mentally handicapped children, he found that mentally handicapped children were, in general, isolated, rejected, or isolated and rejected by their peer group in the regular grades. Average children felt that the mentally handicapped exhibited annoying traits such as bullying and fighting. This experiment indicated that physical integration of the mentally handicapped in the regular grades did not mean social integration, and that in practice it may mean isolation, rejection, and insecurity for the mentally handicapped. If this is the case, in general, what is happening to the security and adequacy of these children, and how does it reflect on their future social competence, or occupational adequacy?

It is admittedly difficult for a teacher to assist the adequate adjustment of the mentally handicapped children in the regular grades. A teacher of the regular grades does not usually understand the differential curriculum or the characteristics of the children; nor can she organize her regular grades to take care of the one or two

---

[4] Johnson, G. Orville, "A Study of the Social Position of Mentally-Handicapped Children in the Regular Grades," *American Journal of Mental Deficiency,* 55 (July, 1950), pp. 60–89.

mentally handicapped children who have been placed in her class. Adaptation of instruction in the regular grades can be accomplished to some degree if the teacher is highly trained, has had work and experience in the field of the mentally handicapped, and has her regular class reduced to about half the size now found in most public schools in the United States. It is easy to assert that classes should adapt instruction to all individual differences, but it is difficult to accomplish this task when classes, especially in the elementary school, have many emergency teachers and classes with thirty to forty children or more.

Classes for mentally handicapped children, as separate classes within a public school system, are common organizational procedures. It is the aim of the special class organization to educate children with markedly low intelligence to become socially adequate and occupationally competent so that they will not be classified as, or perform like, mentally deficient individuals. The remainder of this chapter will be devoted to a description of special class organization.

SPECIAL EDUCATIONAL PROVISIONS

The regular school is organized according to grades. This seems to be a relatively universal procedure since most school systems start with the first grade and continue through the high-school level. In general, normal children are classified according to chronological age. With mentally handicapped children it is difficult to organize according to definite ages except in very large schools and in very large cities. Thus in New York City is found a special organization for mentally handicapped children according to chronological ages. In most school systems, however, there is not a sufficient number of mentally handicapped children within one elementary school to organize classes according to chronological age. As a consequence various kinds of organizations have evolved. The following will give a description of the various types of organizations for mentally handicapped children within public school systems.

The segregated departmentalized special school. In a few school systems special schools have been organized to house all mentally handicapped children in that city or school system. Whenever a mentally handicapped child is found, he is transferred to this special school which may contain fifty or more children of varying levels of mental abilities and chronological ages. In these schools there is often found a departmentalized organization in which the children go to certain teachers for certain subjects — shop, home economics, physical education, arithmetic, social studies, arts and crafts, and so forth at different periods of the day.

The special school for mentally handicapped children in the United States is on its way out. Such schools have usually been stigmatized as "dummy schools." Departmentalization for these children by sending them to three or four teachers a day takes away both the personal element and the mental-hygiene approach to the total rehabilitation program for the child. The teachers have a great number of children each day and tend to emphasize the education of the subject rather than the education of the child. The work of the various teachers is usually not integrated and correlated and the school operates in a way similar to that of a departmentalized elementary or high school. The only advantage of having such a school is that special teachers of special subjects can be employed, such as industrial arts teachers, arts and crafts teachers, and so forth. Furthermore the equipment in such a school is usually more adequate than can be provided for smaller units within an elementary school. It is believed, however, that such a school organization is not a suitable one for mentally handicapped children, since it tends to become institutionalized and takes the children away from opportunities to associate with average children in an elementary or high school.

The homogeneous special class. The homogeneous special class is one which is organized according to a small range of chronological and mental age abilities. Most special classes are to some extent relatively homogeneous if they enroll children who are eight, nine, or ten years of age or at the high-school level of fourteen, fifteen, or sixteen. Such a class with a certain degree of homogeneity is usually organized in an elementary or high school according to age groupings of primary, preadolescent, or adolescent. This organization has been considered superior to a departmentalized special school since one teacher is in charge of from twelve to eighteen children and is able to correlate activities, establish a mental-hygiene program, and educate children rather than emphasize subjects. This type of organization is probably the most adequate one in school systems in which a sufficient number of children are found for two or three special classes within a school system.

The ungraded special class. The ungraded special class is one in which all mentally handicapped children from six to sixteen years of age are enrolled. Here the teacher has a very heterogeneous group of children with a wide range of chronological and mental age abilities. Such classes are usually smaller than the homogeneous ones and much smaller than those found in departmentalized special schools. A teacher of an ungraded class must be more broadly trained and experienced than one who teaches at a single level, or one who teaches a subject in a departmentalized school. The ungraded class is not the ideal type of organization, but it is the only practical solution for a small school system which has within the school only twelve to eighteen children who require assignment to a special class.

The modified special class. Many school systems are so small that they do not have a sufficient number of children for either a homogeneous special class or for an ungraded class. The modified special class organization is most commonly found in small school systems in which there are only a few mentally handicapped children. In practice it takes a number of forms, some of which are: (1) The mentally handicapped children are assigned to a teacher for part of the day and placed in the regular grades the rest of the day. The teacher, in this instance, may tutor educationally retarded children while the mentally handicapped children are in the regular grade. (2) The mentally handicapped children are assigned to a teacher of a regular class who is interested in their problems. Usually the size of the regular class is reduced so that she may give the necessary individual attention to the mentally handicapped children. In determining class load, it is suggested that one mentally handicapped child be counted as two normal children. (3) The mentally handicapped children are assigned to a regular grade but a special itinerant teacher is provided for tutoring purposes. This procedure is based on the false premise that tutoring in an academic subject, such as reading or arithmetic, will alleviate their mental retardation. Although this premise is sound for educationally retarded children, it does not apply to the mentally handicapped. (4) The mentally handicapped children are sometimes placed in a special class with educationally retarded children, behavior-problem children, or other kinds of children who are not adjusting to the program of the regular grade. This procedure usually does not provide for a class that meets the specific needs of the mentally handicapped — or any of the other groups enrolled.

PRINCIPLES OF ORGANIZING SPECIAL CLASSES

Some principles which should be applied to the organization of special classes are listed here:

1. *The younger the children, the smaller the class.* A preschool class should not have more than a ratio of five or six children to one teacher, whereas a class of adolescent children in the secondary school, where many of them are sent to other classes, could probably have a ratio of fifteen to twenty children per teacher. State regulations which set a lower and upper limit should differentiate between the younger and the older children.

2. *The more homogeneous the class the larger it can be, and vice versa, the more heterogeneous the class, the smaller it should be.* When a heterogeneous class of children from eight to sixteen years of age is organized into one special class for the mentally handicapped, the class should be relatively small. It is more difficult for a teacher to organize for such a class than for a class of children ranging in age from eight to ten. Class size, therefore, should be determined by heterogeneity and age, rather than by a set standard.

3. *Special classes for mentally handicapped children should be organized within the elementary and secondary schools.* A centralized elementary school is usually selected for a class for the mentally handicapped, serving the mentally handicapped children from the schools in the surrounding area. Since the enrollment of the secondary schools is usually much greater than the enrollment of the elementary schools, it is often feasible to organize one or more classes in each.

The purpose of placing the special classes in the regular schools is to provide the mentally handicapped children with opportunities for wider experiences through contacts with normal children, to make available additional supplies and special facilities, and to make it possible to hold classes with other teachers in such areas as physical education, art, music, manual arts, home economics, and so forth. The teacher of the special class should recognize, however, that the supplying of facilities and services should be reciprocal. While the mentally handicapped children are with another teacher, the special-class teacher should be doing some remedial instruction with normal children who are in need of it. His training is such that he is well qualified to supply this type of instruction and there is no reason why, given the time and opportunity, his efforts should be confined to work with mentally handicapped children only. In addition, this "trading" of services has proved to be an excellent method of installing the special-class teacher as a contributing member of the faculty and aiding the children and class in being accepted as integral parts of the school.

4. *The teacher selected for the organization and education of these children should be thoroughly trained in the education of the mentally handicapped.* Regular elementary school teachers without special training tend to pattern the special class after the curriculum of the elementary grades. A teacher of the mentally handicapped must obtain supplementary specialized training to understand the children, their needs, and the curriculum of the special class.

5. *Adequate diagnosis of these children should be made before they are referred to the special class.* The teacher should know the assets and liabilities of the child from the beginning, rather than find them out gradually during the year. Prior knowledge is apt to save a great deal of later difficulty.

6. *Cooperation of the parents should be solicited before assignment to a special class.* Although it may take time for the parents to accept the retardation of their child, it is more profitable for all concerned to obtain the cooperation of the parent before the child is assigned to the special class. This procedure is a part of a parent-education program.

7. *The initial organization of a class should be accomplished gradu- ally.* When a new teacher is placed in a new class with fifteen or

eighteen children, most of whom come from different schools, imposes a problem of adjustment of the children to each other and to the teacher. It is better to activate such a class with five or six children at first, then gradually enroll a new pupil each week until the desired class size is reached. Such a procedure will allow for a smoother functioning classroom, and will prevent the problems which arise when fifteen children who have failed in school have been placed in one class at the same time.

8. *The teacher of the special class should be given freedom in organizing the curriculum according to the needs and abilities of the children assigned to his class.* Since special classes do not follow the regular curriculum of the school the teacher should be accorded the freedom of organizing the curriculum for the class. This does not mean that the teacher should have no program. On the contrary, the teacher should be required to outline the objectives to be attained during the year. A program is required, but the program should be determined by a specially trained teacher.

GROUPING OF CHILDREN

School systems group children according to age, mental level, educational achievement, social maturity, and other factors. Mentally handicapped children should also be grouped for efficient instruction in some way. Since they require a special class organization, the grouping will depend upon the number of children found in each school.

If, for example, twelve mentally handicapped children, ranging in age from seven to fourteen, are assigned to one special class, the teacher will find it advisable to group the children into three or more small groups within the class. If there are a larger number of children in one school, two classes could be organized with children of seven to ten, and eleven to fourteen. In very large school systems they can be grouped generally according to chronological ages.

In general, and for most school systems, a complete program for the mentally handicapped should begin before the child starts the formal school at the age of six, and continue after the formal school period into social and vocational placement and follow up.

1. *The preschool class.* The preschool class of mentally handicapped children should consist of children whose chronological

ages are below the age of six. When such classes are organized — and very few exist today — children with chronological ages of three, four, and five, and mental ages of two to four, will be included in this group. The purpose of such a class is to develop the mental and social abilities of the children during the formative years.

2. *The primary class.* The primary class should consist of children whose ages are six, seven, eight, nine, and possibly ten. Mental ages for this group of children will be three to about six and a half. Since this class continues to be a preparatory class it is designated as "the primary class." The purpose of such a grouping is to continue the social and mental development of the children, and to provide them with readiness activities, so that failure at the next level will be minimized.

3. *The intermediate class.* Children in this group will consist of boys and girls of ten, eleven, twelve, and possibly thirteen years of age, depending on their mental and social abilities. This class has sometimes been called "the preadolescent class" since children have not yet arrived at the stage of puberty. Such a class is organized in an elementary school and is possibly the most common type of class for the mentally handicapped.

4. *The secondary class.* The secondary-school class is an organization of children of ages thirteen to sixteen, sometimes including seventeen- and eighteen-year-olds. It should be organized in the junior or senior high school of the city. The mental ages of these children range from about eight to twelve.

5. *The postschool period.* Like the preschool class, postschool education and adjustment of mentally handicapped individuals have not found extensive support. It has been assumed that mentally handicapped children are mentally handicapped until they leave school (which in most cases is at the age of sixteen) then become relatively fast learners in the world outside. In practice they are expected to adjust to the social and occupational competition of the average individual, even though they were unable to do so in school. A total program for mentally handicapped youth will include a program sponsored by the school system in cooperation with social agencies and the vocational rehabilitation division.

The chapters which follow in Part Three will describe the objectives and activities of the five groupings listed above. It is recognized that few classes will consist of children of only one grouping and that a teacher may have one or more groupings within a single classroom. In either case mentally handicapped children should be grouped for instructional and administrative purposes according to their needs and levels of performance.

The curricula described in the next five chapters have been organized according to the nature and needs of children at each age level. Unlike other curricula the approach has been one of adapting instruction to the growth levels of the children, rather than stressing one procedure or one curriculum for all levels.

(1) The preschool class is designed as an environment which allows the child to react according to the structured and adapted attractions of the moment. Permissiveness of activity is emphasized. The teachers utilize the child's reaction to the environment to elevate his play level or to increase his ability.

(2) The primary class is more structured than the preschool class. Children learn by means of games and activities of short duration. These games and activities are structured for a particular goal, but the games and activities are selected from those naturally played by the children.

(3) The intermediate class emphasizes the learning of the tool subjects and experiences in areas of living. These activities are planned by the children, because at this level they can plan and accomplish larger units than short duration games and activities, typical of the primary class.

(4) The secondary class emphasizes areas of experience in harmony with major areas of living. At this level the children are preparing themselves for life outside of the school environment.

(5) The post-school period is one of assisting the young mentally handicapped adult in social and occupational adjustment in the community. It is organized to fill the gap between school life and life in the community.

References

Ade, Lester K. *Meeting the Needs of the Mentally Retarded,* Bulletin No. 420, Harrisburg, Pennsylvania: Pennsylvania State Department of Public Instruction, 1939.

Berry, Charles Scott. "Helping the Mentally Retarded Child," *Nation's Schools,* 13 (May, 1934), pp. 27–32.

Educational Policies Commission, *Policies for Education in American Democracy.* Washington, D.C.: National Education Association, 1946.

Featherstone, William B. *Teaching the Slow Learner.* New York: Bureau of Publications, Teachers College, Columbia University, 1941.

Ingram, Christine P. *Education of the Slow-Learning Child,* Yonkers: World Book Company, 1935.

Johnson, G. Orville. "A Study of the Social Position of Mentally-Handicapped Children in the Regular Grades," *American Journal of Mental Deficiency,* 55 (July, 1950), pp. 60–89.

Martens, Elise H. *A Guide to Curriculum Adjustment for Mentally Retarded Children.* Bulletin 1936, No. 11. Washington, D.C.: Government Printing Office, 1936.

Williams, H. A. and H. A. Stevens. *A Public School Program for Retarded Children.* Madison, Wisconsin: Department of Public Instruction, 1947.

PART THREE

❧

Special-Class Programs

Chapter 7

A Preschool Program

In most school systems children enter school at the approximate age of six. Like most children, the mentally handicapped are sent to school and placed in the first grade at that age. In many instances their slow mental development is not recognized or accepted until they fail. They usually remain under failure conditions until they create enough difficulty to require special attention by the school officials.

In general, mentally handicapped children are placed in the regular grades until they have demonstrated failure for two or three years. The practices have been to: (1) retain them in the first or second grades for two or three years since they have not learned to read; (2) exclude them from school; (3) institutionalize them if the parents and the institution accept that procedure; or (4) admit them to special classes for mentally handicapped children when such an organization exists in a school system.

In school systems that have established kindergartens, mentally handicapped children are usually admitted with children of normal intelligence. When they are observed and examined in the kindergarten, one of two procedures is usually followed. One practice is to exclude the mentally handicapped from the kindergarten. In these cases the parents are usually informed that their children have not matured sufficiently to profit from kindergarten, and that they should retain their child at home for a year or two until the child has matured sufficiently to warrant his admission. This practice assumes that kindergartens do not aid the mental and social maturation of mentally handicapped children and that the cultural influences of the home are not important factors in mental development. A second procedure is to retain the mentally handicapped child in the kindergarten for two years, since it is unlikely that he will be able to cope with the first-grade curriculum.

One state introduced into the regulations for special classes the statement that no mentally handicapped child can be referred to a special class until he is eight years of age. The makers of the regulation felt that all children should be given a chance in the regular schools. It was believed that after a trial period and failure on the part of the child for several years, one could be more certain of the mental retardation. In another state, mentally handicapped children are required to have a mental age of at least five before being admitted into a class for the mentally handicapped. This means that a child must be seven, eight, nine, or ten years of age before he is admitted to a special class suited to his needs and abilities. In the meantime the child remains at home until he matures sufficiently to be admitted to school.

In addition to the frustrations of such children due to failure in school, there have usually been frustrations at home. Parents have often compared their retarded child with children of normal intelligence. In many cases, due to parents' frustrations, unfavorable parent-child relationships have developed. The children in the neighborhood have also rejected the mentally handicapped child because of his inability to participate adequately in neighborhood play with other children of his own age.

Scattered evidence (see Chapter 2) indicates that these children might have made a better psychological and social adjustment if a preschool program had been instituted before the children were permitted to face failure during their initial school career. But schools have been reluctant to organize programs for the preschool mentally handicapped because of the difficulty involved in organization, the cost, and the identification of mental defect in children at a young age.

Some attempts have been made to devise a program for young mentally handicapped children.[1] These programs, called "delayed academic training programs," or "preacademic curricula," have been devised primarily for children who are eight, nine, and ten years of age but whose mental ages are below six. The activities are very similar to the kindergarten or primary readiness programs but do not constitute a preschool program for the mentally handicapped whose chronological ages are three, four, or five.

There have been no published attempts to organize a preschool program for mentally handicapped children in the public school systems. The only attempt that has been made so far is an experimental school for preschool mentally handicapped children in the Champaign Public Schools in co-operation with the University of Illinois.[2] The program discussed in this section is the result of experience derived from this organization.

SELECTION OF CHILDREN

One of the major problems facing schools is to discover children at the ages of three, four, and five, who are mentally handicapped. It is relatively easy to discover these children after they have been admitted to school and after they have failed. The great problem, however, at the preschool level, is to find these children in the community before they have come to the attention of school authorities. Here are some suggestions for locating such children:

Referrals by pediatricians. One of the sources for locating children is through referrals by pediatricians in the community. Pediatricians, therefore, should be appraised of the proposed organization

[1] Curtis, Ethel Louise, "Building Toward Readiness in Mentally Deficient Children," *American Journal of Mental Deficiency*, 48 (October, 1943), pp. 183–187. Kirk, Samuel A. and Irene Stevens, "A Pre-Academic Curriculum for Slow-Learning Children," *American Journal of Mental Deficiency*, 47 (April, 1943), pp. 396–405. Patterson, R. Melcher, "Organization of a Residence Unit for Pre-Academic Training of Mentally Deficient Children," *American Journal of Mental Deficiency*, 48 (October, 1943), pp. 174–178.

[2] Kirk, Samuel A., "A Project for Pre-School Mentally Handicapped Children," *American Journal of Mental Deficiency*, 54 (January, 1950), pp. 305–310.

of such a preschool. It is relatively easy for a doctor to diagnose an idiot, a Mongolian, or a cerebral palsied child during early infancy. It is much more difficult to diagnose a child as mentally retarded whose difficulty is not of a clinical nature. In many instances mentally handicapped children are not discovered by pediatricians because mothers are apt to bring a child to a doctor only for inoculation or for diagnosing physical ailments. The doctor often treats the specific ailment and does not usually make an evaluation of mental development. Unless pediatricians are specifically requested to look for such children, many will be overlooked.

Referrals by public health organizations. The health department, well baby clinics, and other health organizations are in touch with many families in a community. Visiting nurses frequently find children who show signs of slow mental development at an early age; hence the health departments are another source which can aid immeasurably in the identification of such children.

Referrals by social agencies. Numerous social agencies in the community are in constant touch with families. Social workers who have had some training in the detection of slow mental development in children are apt to find such children in families among their case load.

Publicity. It is important that the school be given fairly wide publicity so that relatives and friends may refer children, whom they believe are slow in mental development, to the school authorities for diagnosis and admission.

Siblings of special class children. If there are classes for the mentally handicapped in the school system, it is possible that the younger siblings of the children in the school classes may also be mentally handicapped. This is another source through which young children may be discovered.

Diagnosis of the Children

The adequate diagnosis of mental handicaps in children of ages three, four, and five is more difficult than in older children. Young children are often bashful, shy, and may not respond at their maximum ability to a psychological examination. It is important that these children be brought to the psychological clinic several times before an examination is given, or be brought to the preschool to play for a day or two before a diagnosis is made. After the workers become acquainted with the child, rapport is more easily established and a more adequate mental rating can be obtained.

Since admission to the school is determined by the rate of mental development, the logical examinations to use would be psychological mental tests. Instruments such as the *Stanford-Binet* examinations (the norms of which go down to two years) and the *Kuhlmann Tests of Mental Development* (the norms of which go down to four months) are suitable verbal tests for this type of examination. The *Minnesota Pre-school Test* which gives both a verbal and a nonverbal score is also one that can be used at that age level. Together with Doll's *Vineland Social Maturity Test* and the clinical observations on the part of the examiner, mentally handicapped children can often be detected at that age level.

A thorough case study of the child should be made. This would include a medical examination, a social history, a history of the development and problems of the child, the attitudes of the parents and siblings toward the child, his eating and play habits, and a diagnosis of special disabilities in intellectual or emotional traits. This data should (1) aid in the diagnosis of mental retardation, and (2) aid in determining the kind of educational program the child needs.

THE PROGRAM OF THE PRESCHOOL CLASS

The education of young mentally handicapped children at the preschool level is basically similar to the education of preschool children of average intelligence. Methods and procedures, equipment, personnel, and organization of such a preschool follow the pattern of nursery schools in general. These procedures have been adequately described by Landreth [3] and others.[4] The majority

[3] Landreth, C., *Education of the Young Child.* New York: John Wiley and Sons, Inc., 1942.
[4] Updegraff, Ruth, *et al.*, *Practice in Pre-School Education.* New York: McGraw-Hill Book Co., 1938. *Childhood Education.* Published monthly

of the suggestions made by the authors cited can apply to a preschool for young mentally handicapped children.

Because of the lower mental and generally lower cultural levels of these mentally handicapped children, it is inevitable that some differences will be found. In general, the preschool program herein described follows three major principles: (1) educating the children according to good child development principles and good nursery school educational techniques; (2) using special clinical educational procedures with some of the children that show special disabilities over and above their lower mental ability; and (3) supplying additional provisions which must be adapted to the lower cultural and mental abilities of most of these children. This chapter will describe these approaches.

The major goals and objectives of the preschool will be described here, together with examples and with observed adaptations of instruction. These major objectives may be listed as follows: [5]

(1) The preschool should provide an environment for each child which will foster emotional health through providing a feeling of security and belongingness, and a feeling of accomplishment.

(2) The preschool should foster good physical health.

(3) The preschool should provide opportunities for maturation through self-help throughout the day.

(4) The preschool should offer opportunities for the development of imagination and the expression of ideas and feelings.

(5) The preschool should offer opportunities for social development.

(6) The preschool should offer opportunities for the development of motor skills.

(7) The preschool should offer ample opportunities to develop intellectual abilities.

September through May by the Association for Childhood Education International, 1200 15th Street, N.W., Washington 5, D.C., to stimulate thinking by those concerned with children rather than to advocate fixed practice.

[5] This material is based on the experiences of the teachers in a preschool for mentally handicapped children. The authors are indebted to Miss Evelyn Peters, Mrs. Helen Kramer, and Miss Hannah Ikeda of the Child Development Project, Champaign, Illinois.

(8) The preschool should offer opportunities for parent education.

(9) The preschool should provide for special clinical education for special disabilities found in the children.

The following sections will include a description of how the objectives can be achieved through: (1) examples of activities for each objective; (2) observed differences between normal and mentally handicapped children in the activities; and (3) adaptations of instruction because of these differences.

EMOTIONAL HEALTH

Creating an emotional atmosphere of acceptance in the preschool is essential for the development of the child as well as for the fulfillment of all other objectives. This feeling of security is established by somewhat intangible means when:

(1) Each child, regardless of his lack of abilities, his awkwardness, or his behaviorisms, is accepted as he is.

(2) Teachers can appreciate and become sincerely enthusiastic over the slightest sign of achievement on the part of the child in any activity.

(3) Teachers enjoy their work with children of this type.

(4) Teachers in the school are able to work co-operatively and harmoniously with one another.

(5) Teachers have a sense of humor.

(6) Teachers can give considerable attention on an individual basis to each child when he needs adult attention. Additional attention may also be necessary because of specific disabilities in the child.

(7) The school has a permissive atmosphere and a permissive attitude on the part of the teachers. It is only in this sort of environment that these children, who come generally from restricted homes (physically and mentally), can develop their more latent possibilities.

The basic emotional needs of mentally handicapped children do not differ from the emotional needs of children with normal intelligence. There are, however, some differences which should be noted and provided for. These are:

(1) Mentally handicapped children from subcultural environments are often starved for adult attention. The bid for adult attention in this type of preschool is greater than that usually found in regular nursery schools and kindergartens. Provision for this difference is made through a smaller ratio of children to teachers, usually one teacher to four or five children.

(2) Many more physical disabilities are found among preschool mentally handicapped children. It is necessary, therefore, to provide assistance for these children in motor activities and self-help so that frustrations do not occur.

(3) Much more parent education and more parent-teacher interaction must be provided to help parents accept and understand their mentally handicapped children.

PHYSICAL HEALTH

The physical health and care of such children should be a part of the school program. The major provisions are:

(1) Maintaining an adequate balance between play and rest as part of the school program.

(2) Maintaining a proper balance of nutrition through the noon lunch and suggestions to parents.

(3) Soliciting the co-operation of doctors and other health and community agencies for the purpose of removing handicaps and preventing illness.

(4) Assisting children in learning about health habits and sanitation at the noon lunch, bathroom, and sleeping and rest periods.

(5) Providing for medical treatment and correction in community centers dealing with physical problems.

(6) Providing for daily inspection in the morning by the teachers and the school nurse.

There are a few differences between health care of mentally handicapped children and normal children. Some that have been noted are:

(1) Mentally handicapped children come more frequently from subcultural homes. This may require more attention to cleanliness and physical care on the part of the teachers.

(2) There appear to be more physical handicaps among mentally

handicapped children, such as cases of malnutrition, cerebral palsy, the results of rubella, and so forth. These are either the cause of the mental defect or concomitants of it. Provisions for medical care and physiotherapy are needed more frequently in preschools of this sort.

SELF-HELP

The children should be given opportunities throughout the day for growth in self-help. Some of the activities which are incorporated into the daily routine of the school are:

(1) Taking off and putting on clothes is a common activity in the preschool. This activity occurs many times during the day — when the children arrive in the morning, when they go out to the playground, before and after rest periods, and before going home. They need to learn to take care of clothes, to hang them up, and so forth. In this situation self-help is encouraged and assistance is given only when the task is too great for the child.

(2) The care of self in the bathroom — washing their hands, going to the toilet, combing their hair, and promoting general appearance and cleanliness — is part of the daily program.

(3) Housekeeping activities are an integrated part of the daily program of the preschool. Examples of these activities are putting toys away, opening and shutting doors, dressing and undressing dolls, and helping with clean-up activities.

(4) Self-help activities during eating periods consists of setting the tables, pouring their own milk, passing around crackers, helping themselves to more food, and stacking dishes.

To adapt instruction to children of low mental and cultural levels it is necessary that differences between subnormal and average children be determined.[6] The following differences have been noted by teachers after careful observation:

(1) The children seem to take a longer time to learn to dress

[6] It should be pointed out that the organization of activities in a preschool differs from similar activities at home in a number of respects. The preschool proper and its equipment are designed for children, whereas homes are basically designed for adults. Small pitchers to pour milk, small tables and chairs, and low lockers for clothing all facilitate self-help. In addition, the teachers are constantly on the alert to prevent frustration in self-help activities. This

and feed themselves than do normal children. This means that preschool teachers of young mentally handicapped children must have patience and must repeat activities over and over again in a variety of situations.

(2) The children do not seem to follow directions in logical order, as do normal children. For example, they may attempt to take off their T-shirts before loosening the straps on their overalls; they sometimes put on their caps before putting on their sweaters; or they may put on their mittens before their coat. They sometimes put on their boots before their snowpants, and in a few instances attempt to take off their socks before their shoes. Although some of these may occur in regular nursery schools, the difference here is that they do not occur in nursery schools for normal children as often as they do in the preschool for mentally handicapped children. The examples cited seem to occur over and over again, without noticeable learning from experience, whereas normal children learn after a few such attempts.

(3) Mentally handicapped children seem to be more distracted by extraneous stimuli. This appears to occur with the non-brain-injured as well as with the brain-injured children. While playing, eating, or in other activities they become distracted or attracted to other things in the environment, causing them to drop the first interest and go to the second attraction. Teacher attention and suggestions are needed to counteract distractibility and aid the children in completing a task.

(4) The children seem to repeat errors over and over again in the preschool. This tendency appears more prominent than is found with normal children in a nursery school. Constant guidance on the part of the teacher in a variety of activities tends to assist learning and counteract repetition of errors.

---

teaching approach toward children means that procedures differ considerably from the approach of many mothers who, for example, dress the child completely so that he will not be late, or help serve his food so he will not spill it. Small portions are given to the children in the preschool so that they will have the satisfaction of completing their meal. They serve themselves with other portions as they desire. The social factor in self-help in the school is a much more prominent one than is usually found in the home since in the school they can imitate other children of their own age.

IMAGINATION AND CREATIVE EXPRESSION

Children in the preschool should be offered opportunities to develop their imagination and to express their ideas and feelings through free play and the use of a variety of constructive materials. Since mentally handicapped children are deficient in creative and imaginative expression, the preschool is designed to exaggerate this phase. Some of the activities which are designed to accomplish this objective are as follows:

(1) The preschool program is organized around free play, which may include opportunities for house play, sand play, water play, block play, and the use of various art media.

(2) The teachers attempt to stimulate creative activities by telling stories and having children relate incidents of daily happenings.

(3) Creative rhythms are used to stimulate imagination. An example of the latter is to present a rhythm activity and have the children clap to it. Later they may suggest stamping their feet to the music, rolling or nodding their heads. Through a variety of suggestions the children may evolve some creative activity relating to the rhythm.

(4) The physical placement of materials in the school and the playground tends to suggest new relations and new ideas to the children.

Some of the differences between the children in the preschool for mentally handicapped and regular nursery schools which have been observed by the teachers are:

(1) The scope of imagination of these children seems to be confined to everyday things which happen in the home or in the school. There is less originality in imaginative and expressive or creative activities. When evidence of continued repetition of home and school activities occurs in any of the imaginative and creative projects the teachers attempt to stimulate new activities and encourage originality at the children's level. This means that the mentally handicapped child needs more adult guidance than is needed by the average nursery school child of that age. For example, a child may be pushing a train aimlessly. By the addition of materials or questions and suggestions by the teacher, there are added other experiences with a track, a bridge, and so forth. This is necessary to

avoid the child's becoming stereotyped and rigid in his constructive ability.

(2) Mentally handicapped children tend to repeat the pattern of activities over and over again. More materials to work with in their play are needed for them to see, to feel, and to touch because of their lack of imagination and abstraction. For example, two children were shoveling gravel. The teacher noted that this shoveling and piling gravel became repetitive. She pushed a wagon close to them which suggested that they fill the wagon with gravel which they called coal. Through questions by the teacher and through the addition of such material as the wagon and even by the entering of the teacher into their play they tend to go on and on carrying play further into imaginative activities. When the gravel was called coal by one child they decided that coal goes down the chute as it does in their homes. So they set up a board which they called the slide and let the coal (gravel) slide down the chute. Later when coal trucks passed the street they recognized these as something related to their activities and talked about the coal going to someone's house and going down the chute.

(3) Mentally handicapped children tend to experiment less with new things. They do not test new possibilities, but require questions and suggestions by the teachers and suggestions through the addition of materials to assist them in experimenting and exploring new situations.

(4) Mentally handicapped children appear to be more imitative of the activities of other children. In rhythms, for example, the teacher asked "What song shall we play?," and one child answered, "Pop Goes the Weasel." Then all the children repeated the request. Through questions and suggestions the teacher attempts to stimulate individuality. This is done through teacher suggestions when she reminds them of several other songs they have learned or when she introduces a new song.

(5) The children do not seem to recognize and become enthusiastic over accidental creations such as those that occur in mixing paint colors. The reason for this is probably because they do not experiment or explore a great deal and consequently do not notice deviations when they occur. The enthusiasm of the teacher here

attempts to stimulate recognition of new experiences when the occurrence is accidental.

(6) These children tend not to carry projects through to their completion. Many of the activities are short-lived, especially when the teacher leaves the scene. It is important that the teacher begin the activity, leave for short periods of time, and then return; in this way the project will be completed but some independence of activity may be attained.

(7) The children do not seem to put their feelings into art activities as do normal children. It is difficult to analyze projection in art because of the meagre imagination expressed through art media.

(8) The best dramatic play that is carried out by the children appears to be related to home activities like cooking, doll playing, and various household activities. This may be the result of their limited experiences at home. With normal children, dramatic play tends to extend beyond the home to "doctor," "grocery store," and so forth. Through excursions with the children and introduction to various activities in the school, the teachers attempt to widen the range of interests of the children.

SOCIAL DEVELOPMENT

Children in the preschool are given a great number of opportunities for social development. These are, in general, implemented through learning to live together in a co-operative fashion. All of the activities of the preschool are pointed toward this important objective.

(1) The free-play period may be utilized for the development of social interaction. For example, one child may be building with blocks. Another child may be encouraged to build blocks in close proximity to the first child. As they build, they get closer to each other. Through questions and suggestions by the teacher they are soon working together on the same project.

(2) The noon lunch period is also designed to facilitate social interaction. In the school one teacher sits at each table with four or five children and guides the conversation, allowing and encouraging the children to pass the milk and bring things for each other.

(3) Playing with trains, having tea parties, and going on trips

or excursions contribute to social interaction and social development of the children. Learning to take turns, helping to prepare dinner, assisting other children with their wraps, and participating in various group games are other activities which further this goal.

There appear to be some differences between normal children and mentally handicapped preschool children in this area. These differences are:

(1) The teacher has to initiate many activities. The lack of imagination of these children, as indicated earlier, makes it necessary for the teacher to stimulate activities for them. In addition teachers must repeat and initiate some type of play over and over again. In regular nursery schools the teachers use less repetition of their initiated activities since the children learn faster and continue by themselves more than do these children.

(2) The tendency of these children for isolated or parallel play appears to continue longer than it does for normal children. It should be pointed out that with normal children, it is at this period of life that the beginnings of group participation emerge. It is important that this emergence be facilitated with mentally handicapped children through stimulation by the preschool activities.

MOTOR DEVELOPMENT

The preschool should offer opportunities for the development of motor skills which may lead to more effective use of one's body. This is attempted through:

(1) Providing a wide variety of equipment on the playground, such as jungle gym, swings, walking boards, slides, and so forth, for the use of gross muscles. Moveable equipment can be changed from day to day with various seasons of the year, or with the changing interests of the children.

(2) Providing equipment on the playground and in the school for finer motor co-ordinations, such as puzzles, peg boards, pounding boards, hammer and nails, and so forth.

(3) Providing activities in dressing, eating, washing, and playing, involving gross and fine motor co-ordinations.

(4) Providing rhythm activities such as dancing and singing.

There are few differences in motor skills between these children and normal children. With children inflicted with motor disabilities, such as is the case with cerebral palsied children, there is naturally a great difference. Many of the latter become inhibited in motor activities, which tends to inhibit their reactions socially and mentally, or increases their verbalizations, in lieu of physical activity.

INTELLECTUAL DEVELOPMENT

One of the major purposes of the school is to stimulate intellectual development of these children. In general this includes:

(1) Activities for the development of language.

(2) Activities to develop the ability to plan ahead and to do problem solving.

(3) Activities which will assist in increasing their perception and ability to grasp meaning and gain knowledge of the world about them. (No isolated activities are designed for them except those which occur in the natural activities of the children during their numerous experiences throughout the day.)

(4) Telling stories to children, stimulating dramatization, letting them talk about things that happen at home or in school, instigating activities through questions, and supplying materials to increase their judgment, their abilities to find solutions to problems presented, and their planning ability are emphasized.

(5) The teachers attempt to stimulate intellectual activity by adding pets, providing excursions about the neighborhood, allowing assistance in the kitchen, initiating conversation, encouraging the children to look at books, and allowing them to relate stories about pictures seen, and assisting them in planning their activities.

(6) The children are given opportunity for self-expression, verbally and otherwise, throughout the day in an attempt to increase their intellectual ability, and to correlate their feelings with intellectual activities.

Mental retardation means deficiency in psychological processes. The preschool should, in addition to its emphasizing self-help and socialization, utilize every conceivable opportunity to develop the intellectual abilities which are usually deficient in young, mentally handicapped children. In general, these intellectual activities appear to differ from those of normal children either quantitatively or qualitatively in the following ways:

(1) The language ability seems to be inadequate in most mentally handicapped children. This is the age in which language develops at an accelerated rate. For that reason every activity in which the child participates should be utilized for the development of his receptive and communicative language abilities. He should learn to understand language and should be able to use language in the expression of his ideas. The development of language at this age may stand the child in good stead throughout his life, for it is his chief means of communication with others.

(2) There appear to be many more speech defects among the mentally handicapped than among normal children of the same mental age. Emphasis on speech and speech correction is necessary for these children.

(3) The mentally handicapped children seem to be unable to look ahead in their activities, as demonstrated by poor planning ability, rigidity, or perseveration. In play, for example, a mentally handicapped child may move sand from one pile to the other and then back again. It is the aim of the teacher in this setting to elevate the play functions of these children to include more imagination and more intelligent construction.

(4) Learning seems to be at a much slower rate than that of average children. This requires continued repetition of the same experience in a variety of situations.

(5) Conceptualizations through verbal ability, art activity, and so forth seem to be inferior, as indicated earlier. Again guidance by the teachers in all activities is indicated. Analyzing an experience, discussing it, and "rehashing" it is of great value in developing a clear concept of the ideas involved as well as furthering the psychological process of memory.

(6) Young mentally handicapped children are deficient in concepts of quantity. Utilization of all activities for the development of concepts of quantity and quantitative abstractions should be developed whenever the opportunity is presented.

(7) The development of the psychological processes of perception and memory, through discrimination of objects, through dif-

ferentiation, and through classification, should be developed through materials and suggestions by the teacher during the children's play activity. Similarities and differences between comparable objects may be discussed and the child may be encouraged to think of or find objects which are alike in some way.

PARENT EDUCATION

Parent education is one of the major aims of the preschool. Parent education requires:

(1) An appreciation of the parents and of their problems with the children.

(2) Interviews with the parents concerning the problems of their children both at their request and at the school's request.

(3) Frequent visits by the parents to the preschool to discover what is being done, to learn some of the techniques from the preschool teachers, and to see their children in relation to others.

(4) Notes may be sent to the parents so that they will know what their children do.

(5) An effort should be made to reduce the anxieties of the parents in order to assist them in understanding the limitations of their children, and to have them deal with the children more intelligently as a result of the preschool experience. This is done by frequent discussion of the problems of the child with the parent at the school and at home.

The major differences in parent education with parents of mentally handicapped children relate to differences in intellectual and cultural levels, and to attitudes toward handicapped children.

(1) The intelligence and cultural level of the parents in the preschool are lower for more of the parents than is found in a regular nursery school. At times it is so low that the habits of the children have to be changed in the preschool and then transferred to the home. Discussion of the problems, or instruction to parents, is many times not sufficient to produce changes in attitudes of parents or habits of children.

(2) Parents of children who show slow mental growth, especially as a result of disease or injury, sometimes have a feeling of guilt or anxiety which may interfere with their understanding of the

child. Showing them what the child can do, discussing his limitations, and allowing the parents to work out their own problems through these discussions sometimes assists in achieving the goal.

SPECIAL CLINICAL EDUCATIONAL PROCEDURES

In addition to the careful attention given to the children in the group situation, it is sometimes necessary to offer special educational help on an individual basis to children who need clinical educational treatment. The diagnosis and observation of these children should determine their area of major weakness. Clinical education means special training in the area in which the child has potentialities and needs assistance in their development in an individual or group situation. To illustrate what is meant, brief case studies will be given to indicate how two children in the same class can differ very widely.

Case A had, in addition to mental retardation, cataracts and nystagmus and poor visual acuity. In addition to extremely poor health during the first two years of life she was deprived of normal contacts because of low vision. A few months in the preschool demonstrated that her mental abilities are not as low as the results of two mental tests (administered one year apart) had indicated. On mental tests administered at the preschool she showed good verbal ability, good judgment, organizing ability, and adequate memory. Her major deficiencies appeared to be due to sickness during the early years and her visual handicap which had deprived her of learning about her environment. In her case, the preschool environment and stimulation has given her the opportunity to grow. Since her vision was corrected as much as it could be, one of the major problems was to train her visual perception with what little vision she had. This training required special education lessons on an individual basis. Associating tactile perceptions with visual perceptions and assisting in the discrimination of visual objects, such as colors, were provided this girl as a part of her special education program. A tachistiscope was used to determine her educability in perceptual speed in spite of the marked nystagmus. As a result of the program and the special training this child's test results showed gradual progress.

Case B was five years of age and had not yet talked. On verbal intelligence tests she rated at the imbecile level. However, when given a performance test usually used with the deaf, she was of borderline intelligence.

The clinical picture was similar to "word deafness," since she was unable to *understand* language, even though she apparently had no marked hearing defect. Special education in her case involved individual instruction in language understanding. In addition, emphasis on this phase was carried out in the school whenever the occasion arose in group activities, i.e., at the noon meal and on the playground.

These two cases are cited to show that although each child is mentally handicapped, each presents a unique problem. These cases require very different kinds of special training. One was relatively advanced in language but her visual perception was the area of greatest deficit. The other child was relatively advanced in visual perception but required intensive training in language understanding and speech.

Summary [7]

The field of preschool education of the mentally handicapped within a public school system has been a much neglected field. The cost of operation, the difficulties of discovering the children, and the lack of experience of school personnel in this area of education have retarded projects of this type.

How would these children develop if preschool training were provided at the ages of three, four, and five, and they were then placed in appropriate classes instead of being allowed to fail in the public schools as has been done in the past? This question will have to be answered by means of future research. This phase of the education of mentally-handicapped children may be more important than the phases that follow, after children have faced frustration and failure in the school. It is possible that many children who are unable to adjust to our society, would have been able to make an adequate adjustment following an intensive program of preschool education. The cost of education at this level may be insignificant compared to the cost of support and care at a later age.

[7] As this manuscript is going to press, the experimental project upon which this chapter is based has been in progress for two years. The results have been encouraging. A continuation of the project and an evaluation of the results of this program, with appropriate controls, is being carried out through a research grant by the Institute of Mental Health, U.S. Public Health Service.

References

Childhood Education. Published monthly, September through May, by the Association for Childhood Education International, 1200 15th Street, N.W., Washington 5, D.C.

Curtis, Ethel Louise. "Building Toward Readiness in Mentally Deficient Children," *American Journal of Mental Deficiency*, 48 (October, 1943), pp. 183–187.

Forest, Ilse. *Early Years at School.* New York: McGraw-Hill Book Company, Inc., 1949.

Foster, Josephine C., and Marion L. Mattson. *Nursery-School Education.* New York: Appleton-Century-Crofts, Inc., 1939.

Kellogg, Rhoda. *Nursery School Guide.* Boston: Houghton Mifflin Company, 1949.

Kirk, Samuel A., and Irene Stevens. "A Pre-Academic Curriculum for Slow-Learning Children," *American Journal of Mental Deficiency*, 47 (April, 1943), pp. 396–405.

Kirk, Samuel A. "A Project for Pre-School Mentally Handicapped Children," *American Journal of Mental Deficiency*, 54 (January, 1950), pp. 305–310.

Landreth, C. *Education of the Young Child.* New York: John Wiley and Sons, Inc., 1942.

Patterson, R. Melcher. "Organization of a Residence Unit for Pre-Academic Training of Mentally Deficient Children," *American Journal of Mental Deficiency*, 48 (October, 1943), pp. 174–178.

Symonds, Percival M. *The Dynamics of Parent-Child Relationships.* New York: Bureau of Publications, Teachers College, Columbia University, 1949.

Updegraff, Ruth, *et al. Practice in Pre-School Education.* New York: McGraw-Hill Book Company, 1938.

Chapter 8

A Primary Program

THE PRIMARY CLASS

THE GENERAL school practices with mentally handicapped children were described in some detail in Chapter 7. It was indicated that in most school systems these children are allowed to fail several years in the regular grade before special provisions are made for them. In school systems where no provisions are made for mentally handicapped children, they are permitted to "sit" in classes, repeat grades at the lower elementary level, and in general are tolerated until they can be passed on to another teacher or until they quit school.

In a study by Johnson [1] concerning the social status of mentally handicapped children in the regular grades (one through five) in school systems that had no special classes, he found that (1) the mentally handicapped children were significantly older than the children with whom they had been placed; (2) the mentally handicapped children were isolated and rejected by the other children; and (3) in spite of their age, the mentally handicapped children

---

[1] Johnson, G. Orville, *A Study of the Social Position of Mentally-Handicapped Children in the Regular Grades.* Unpublished Doctor's Dissertation, University of Illinois, 1950.

were educationally retarded below the grade level in which they were placed.

The organization of a primary class for mentally handicapped children is an attempt to modify the school program for these children to such an extent that they will learn to adjust to a school situation in harmony with their low intellectual abilities. It is designed to provide adequate educational facilities for mentally handicapped children during their initial school career and for those who have already experienced failure in the regular grades.

The curriculum proposed in this chapter is designed for children having most or all of the following characteristics:

(1) The chronological ages range between 6 and 10.

(2) The mental ages on verbal intelligence tests are below 6.

(3) The children have not been ready to learn to read or do the arithmetic of a first-grade class.

(4) The children, in many cases, come from subcultural homes.

(5) They have usually experienced failure in the regular grades before admission to a special class.

(6) They usually dislike school, probably because of their lack of success.

(7) Some of them have associated physical disabilities; some of them are brain-injured children.

(8) They probably have faced isolation and rejection by children in the regular grades and have developed compensatory aggressive or withdrawn tendencies.

(9) Their physical abilities and activities, because of their age, are similar to those of second and third grade children.

(10) Their mental and social activities are similar to kindergarten and beginning first grade children.

The purpose of a primary class, therefore, is to assist the children in adjusting to a schoolroom organization in a successful way, to prepare them by means of a readiness program for the work that will follow in other classes for the mentally handicapped, and to develop their habits and attitudes to the point where they will overcome the frustrations which they have experienced.

GOALS AND OBJECTIVES OF THE PRIMARY CLASS

The general objectives listed in preceding sections are the major objectives for the primary class as well as for all classes. Many of the activities and programs which further the development of all children are applicable to mentally handicapped children. For the purpose of being more concrete, the following sections will deal with more specific goals and objectives. It should be cautioned, however, that although the objectives and goals are listed separately under different headings, the more the integration of these activities there is, the better. If, for example, an activity in a class assists the development of four objectives, it is a better activity than one which taps only one or two of the objectives. With this concept in mind, the following goals and objectives will be discussed:

(1) Mental health
(2) Physical health and safety
(3) Parent education
(4) Social participation and adjustment
(5) Language development
(6) Quantitative thinking
(7) Higher mental processes
(8) Visual abilities: discrimination and memory
(9) Auditory abilities: discrimination and memory
(10) Motor and muscular abilities
(11) Speech development
(12) Attitudes and habits

MENTAL HEALTH

The mental health aspect of the primary class is to develop in these children a regained confidence in their own abilities. In most instances these children have failed in the regular classes of the public schools; they have been isolated or rejected by the other children in the class; they have been unable to understand or to cope with the requirements of the regular class; they have become frustrated and have developed inadequate habits and attitudes of work

because of their lack of security or feeling of inadequacy in a classroom situation.

One of the first objectives of the primary class is to provide tasks
and activities for these children which will give them a sense of
security, a sense of belongingness, and a sense of adequacy in a
classroom situation.   All activities of the classroom should be
directed toward the fulfillment of that objective for each individual
child in the class.   Experiences of teachers and others [2] have noted
that children who come to such a class with histories of behavior
problems, appear to function in quite a normal fashion as soon as the
curriculum is adapted to their abilities and they have overcome the
fear and avoidance of tasks presented to them.   It has been known
from numerous studies on motivation and learning, that encouragement is more effective for learning than discouragement.   It has
also been found that encouragement is more effective with dull
children than it is with superior children.   It is, therefore, important that these children be encouraged not only by the manner and
words of the teacher, but by *knowledge of success*, which can be
achieved with these children when the curriculum is so organized
to fit their needs and is within their abilities to achieve.   Under
mental health, therefore, in addition to other principles of mental
hygiene, the feeling of security and adequacy on the part of these
children is one of the important factors the teacher must recognize
and provide for in *all* activities in the classroom.   Other factors in
the mental hygiene of school management are discussed later in a
section on social adjustment.

HEALTH HABITS AND SAFETY

In addition to mental health provisions in the curriculum, the
teacher should include provisions for habits of health and safety.
Many of these children come from home backgrounds which do not
teach or facilitate health habits.

The first task of the teacher is to survey the health and the health
habits of the children in her class.   Many will not yet have learned

    [2] Kirk, Samuel A., and Irene Stevens, "A Pre-Academic Curriculum for
Slow-Learning Children," *American Journal of Mental Deficiency*, 47 (April,
1943), pp. 396–405.

to brush their teeth. Some will not yet have learned to keep themselves clean. Many will not have learned safety rules on the streets.
Through discussion of these topics, and through actual practice in
washing themselves, brushing their teeth, and following safety
habits, these children should learn not only the elementary habits of
health and sanitation, but should be made to feel more adequate by
learning these modes of life. Daily inspection of ears, teeth, and
so forth as practiced in some classrooms, often results in a feeling
of inferiority on the part of children from substandard homes who
have not achieved cleanliness. It is, therefore, necessary for the
teacher to devise a program that will make them feel proud of their
achievement. A positive approach is more important than a negative one. Most of the time it isn't what the teacher does, but *how*
she does it that is important. Some of the more specific objectives
to be attained in the area of health and safety are discussed below:

(1) Control of communicable diseases will include discussions
with the parents and the health authorities about immunization
against those diseases which should have been taken care of
earlier. This may include "booster shots." In addition, special
emphasis should be made in the prevention of respiratory conditions such as the common cold. Teaching the children the practice
of using disposable tissue instead of "putting the cold back into the
pocket" is one example. Drawing the attention of the parents and
health department to the existence of pediculosis is another example.

(2) Attention to the nutrition of the children through noon
lunches, discussions, and parent education is an important aspect of
health education. Most children obtain an adequate supply of
milk, but do not obtain or eat a sufficient amount or variety of vegetables.

(3) Special attention should be given to cleanliness and appearance. The most important aspects should be emphasized first, and
habits firmly established before less important ones are introduced.
Washing the hands before eating as a health habit, for example, is
more important than a concern about getting hands dirty, or finding
dirt behind the ears.

(4) The care and wearing of suitable clothes should receive
some attention with these children.

(5) A balance between activity, rest, and relaxation should be maintained in the class. Continual stimulation leads to fatigue and distractibility. Rest and relaxation by quieting down before and after meals, and learning how to relax at certain periods should be included in the program.

(6) Safety education should be included as a part of the classroom instruction. The areas to emphasize at this age level are: (*a*) selecting the proper route going to and from school and some understanding of the hazards connected with this travel; (*b*) establishing proper attitudes toward fire drills; and (*c*) safety at play, such as the necessity of taking one's turn.

Suggestions for units and objectives on health education are found in State Bulletins [3] and books.[4]

PARENT EDUCATION

The parent education of children at the primary class should consist of a plan of home-school co-operation in the development of the child. Although daily contacts with the parents at this age level are not as necessary as they are at the preschool level, parent-teacher relationships are very important. Some suggestions for parent-school relationships in this area are:

(1) The teacher should remember that parents are interested in hearing good things rather than bad things about their children. A common practice is to get in touch with the parents only when the child has been misbehaving. Better results can be achieved when the teacher approaches the parents with positive contributions and positive behavior on the part of the child. In all conversations the good aspects of the child should be brought out; the misbehaviors should be discussed and analyzed but minimized. This is an important fact to be remembered by the teacher of mentally handicapped children.

(2) The parent should feel that the teacher has a genuine interest

[3] *Health and Physical Education for Elementary Schools of the State of Illinois*, Circular Series A, No. 17. Issued by Superintendent of Public Instruction, Springfield, Illinois, September, 1944.
[4] Coops, Helen, *Health Education in Elementary Schools*. New York: A. S. Barnes and Co., 1950.

in the child. When parents find that a teacher is interested in their child they tend to become more interested themselves. There is a tendency, in many instances, for the mentally handicapped child to be rejected by the parents. The parents often have nothing good to say about such a child, sometimes gain some ego satisfaction or self-justification in letting the teacher know that they recognize the child's shortcomings and are therefore exonerated. In such cases the teacher must make a special effort to emphasize the child's good qualities and strong points; she must build up the parents' respect for the child as well as their interest in him.

(3) It is wise to obtain the parents' consent to the assignment of the child to the special class. Sometimes the parents' ignorance of the problem or lack of knowledge of the facilities available makes this difficult at first. Perhaps a visit to the class or special conferences will be necessary. But the teacher can do a great deal in "selling" the class to the parents and keeping them informed of the progress and activities of their child.

(4) A parent-teacher's meeting should discuss the curriculum of the class. It would aid a great deal in parent understanding if they were allowed at least a voice in what activities are carried on in this type of classroom. They will appreciate the curriculum of the class when they understand it better. In addition, there is some benefit derived by a parent in discussing with other parents their common problems.

(5) Making things for the parents or for the home by the children is another factor that assists home-school co-operation. The child may not be able to demonstrate rapid progress in reading to the satisfaction of the parents, but he can take home articles and materials that he has completed in school. These tangible things can be seen by the parents and are appreciated by them.

SOCIAL PARTICIPATION AND ADJUSTMENT

One of the goals of the primary class is to assist the child in getting along with his peer group. The purpose here is to assist children in working together co-operatively with other individuals and in groups. There are certain attitudes and certain behavior that will aid them in being accepted by others, and conversely certain attitudes and behavior reactions which will cause them to be rejected by other children. They must learn, for instance, to share, to take turns, to utilize the suggestions of others, to co-operate in joint efforts, and to consider the wants and feelings of others. Many of these children have had their responses negatively conditioned by unfortunate contacts with others. Some have always been thrown with children of superior ability and have become so cowed and docile that they have shrunk from contacts with others, while some have compensated by an overaggressiveness and self-assertion which makes their playmates reject them all the more. They have to learn a new set of responses, be conditioned to a new type of behavior.

Activities in the classroom need not be designed specifically for socialization purposes, but this objective should be kept in mind in organizing and executing all activities of the classroom. In addition to classroom activities, the teacher should assist the child in adjusting to his brothers and sisters at home, or with the children in the neighborhood. The extension of co-operation in the classroom and its transfer to the home and the community is an objective of the primary class.

LANGUAGE DEVELOPMENT [5]

Mentally handicapped children are deficient in language abilities. This is partly because of low intelligence, and partly the result of poor environment and failure in school. For adjustment to a group and for progress in school, particularly in learning to read, language is an important function.

Developing language ability requires emphasis on (1) an ever-increasing speaking vocabulary, (2) growth in concepts and meaning of words, and (3) the ability on the part of the child to express himself in adequate sentences. Since most retarded children have meager concepts, and speak in short and inadequate phrases and sentences, the teacher must emphasize language development if the child is to make progress in school. Some successful activities used for language development are:

[5] Much of the following material was originally published by Kirk, Samuel A., and Irene Stevens, *op. cit.*

(1) Encourage free expression related to their immediate experiences, such as their home, weather, health, individual activities, and so forth. In these discussions, the teacher should aid the child in speaking in complete sentences rather than in one- or two-word responses. For example, after talking about families in general, a child is asked what his father does. The usual response is "works." After additional questions the child probably has said "in a factory" and "makes shoes." After securing this much information, the teacher should put it in a sentence herself, and then ask the child to "tell all about it." By this approach the teacher can finally elicit the complete sentence, "My father makes shoes in a factory." *It should be cautioned that sentence length can not be developed mechanically, but should be done in a natural setting.*

(2) Another procedure for language development is the following: Have the child carry out instructions in any activity, and then encourage the child to tell all about it, such as, "I went to the cupboard, found two pairs of scissors, and gave them to Mary and to Paul." This activity involves the ability to follow directions and to describe in adequate sentences what he has performed. *It should be emphasized that the activity expressed by the child should be of immediate value to him — not drilled in a formalized sentence pattern.*

(3) Books and pictures serve a useful purpose in developing language and language concepts. With the use of pictures, the teacher can aid the children in increasing their sentence length and vocabulary. For example, in one picture which included a shoe, it was discovered that the terms "heel" and "sole" were foreign to the children. The discussion which followed not only aided their vocabulary but also their meaning concepts.

(4) A common approach in kindergartens is the utilization of trips and excursions as a basis for language experiences. These activities, when properly used, aid in increasing the language abilities needed. On one occasion, a walk was taken where seventeen different kinds of stores were located. All the stores except the hardware store were more or less familiar to the children. After returning to the school, various nails, screws, and tools were borrowed from the school shop, and the children built a hardware

store of their own. When tools were needed for other activities, or when paint and brushes were required, the children went to their own hardware store to secure them. In this way they increased their meaning concepts and vocabulary in this area.

(5) Stories are a good source for language development as well as for the development of other abilities. In utilizing stories that are to be retold by the children, it was found that at first the stories should be very short and about the children themselves. Later they can be increased in length and may gradually take in a wider field of experience, such as incidents in the home, the school, or the neighborhood.

(6) Finger games, rhymes, and riddles are language aids. The latter has proved to be a favorite pastime with these children.

(7) Classification and fluency in remembering words is developed ɔy asking the children such questions as "How many tools can you name?" "How many animals do you know?" "What things do you eat?" "What can you do?" Later, in ear or auditory training, the children are asked to name as many words as they can that start with a particular sound, or words that rhyme with a certain word.

Language development is introduced in practically all of the activities of the classroom. Regardless of the activity, the teacher should keep in mind the opportunities for the development of language in the children. Hence, the teacher should utilize all opportunities to develop vocabulary, meaning concepts, and sentence length. In so doing, the teacher must aid the child in using adequate sentences, yet should not guide so much that the child becomes a parrot. Adequate questions and just sufficient aid to get the child started or corrected does a great deal in developing this important function.

QUANTITATIVE THINKING

Mentally handicapped children are deficient in quantitative thinking — the functions, abilities, and achievements which are necessary before a child is ready to learn what is commonly called arithmetic. Many such children have difficulties in learning number concepts and the meanings of the quantitative vocabulary, such as "above" and "below," or comparative terms, such as "biggest," "longer," "nearer," "far," "top," "middle," "between," and so forth. They sometimes do not know how to count, do not know the difference between one, two, and three objects, and cannot recognize written numbers. Before any arithmetic is taught, these children should have a curriculum which develops in them what the ordinary child "picks up" through life experiences and through informal presentations in the kindergarten and first grade.

For the development of quantitative thinking the teacher should keep in mind four major areas in which growth is necessary. These are (1) the ability to understand and use the language of quantitative thinking; (2) the ability to count and understand number concept; (3) the ability to recognize at a glance simple groupings such as one, two, and three; and (4) the ability to recognize and understand written numbers. For the retarded child, the following games, exercises, and activities have proven of aid in the development of the functions listed above which will later be necessary in school and in life.

(1) An interesting activity for the development of a comparative vocabulary and for number concepts has been found in building a tiered shelf of three layers. The smallest shelf was at the top, while the longest and widest was at the bottom. Utilizing a group of toys the children were directed during the "cleaning up" period, to "put the doll on the top, middle or bottom shelf"; "to put the toy car on the widest"; "to put the large ball (or small ball) on the longest or shortest shelf." From simple directions the teacher gradually increased the difficulty of the task to "put the large ball on the top shelf and the small ball on the longest shelf," or "put two cars on the top shelf and one red ball on the bottom shelf." In addition to understanding directions involving quantity, size, shape, and so forth the children also described what they had done and directed each other to perform certain tasks. This activity not only develops quantitative thinking but also language development, auditory memory, the ability to follow directions, and the ability to work together.

(2) Another classroom activity similar to the one described above is to substitute a tree for a shelf, using fruits cut out of colored

paper to be hung on the tree. The directions are: "Hang the orange on the top of the tree"; "put the apple below the orange"; "put the cherries near the apple," and so forth. Toys can be placed around the tree in like manner. Other activities throughout the day utilize quantitative concepts of "top," "bottom," "under," "over," "large," "small," "round," "square," and so forth, which can be used by the teacher to develop quantitative concepts.

(3) Another game which develops quantitative thinking consists of a series of pictures containing such objects as a plate with three apples, and a plate with one apple, a tall boy and a short boy, a large ball, a small ball, and a big balloon. The teacher asks the children to put a bead on the tallest boy, or two beads on the plate with the most apples, or to place a bead on the ball that is smaller than the balloon. In this way the child compares like and unlike objects, and also learns some differences between groups of one, two, and three.

(4) An interesting game for the purpose of teaching grouping is to make cards the size of playing cards with a different number of objects on each. Each child is dealt out four cards, and then takes his turn in drawing from the remaining pile as in "Rummy." When the child gets three pictures that are identical, or a sequence of 1, 2, 3, and 4 he puts them down on the table. He may place his fourth card on any other pile that is made up of that group of objects. This game can be played by the children unsupervised, and is a substitute for the workbook type of exercise. In this way they are playing, co-operating, sharing, and at the same time undergoing a learning experience.

(5) The game of "jacks" has been utilized in a modified form to teach grouping to children. The children throw up a ball, then pick up two jacks, three jacks, and so forth. This game is too well known to need further elucidation.

(6) The desire of children to build under direction also has been utilized for training in quantitative thinking. In one of these activities the child is given parts of a flower, and then is instructed to place four petals and three leaves on it. In another such activity pictures of houses and their parts have been used. Directions such as, "Put three windows in the house," and "Put two doors in the

house," are given the children, as they construct, build, or manipulate blocks and objects in school.

(7) Many games can be played with dice to assist children in recognizing number groups. Games such as Parchesi require the recognition of the number of spots on dice and also give practice in counting spaces on the board. Such games have the added advantage of promoting co-operation.

(8) For the development of number recognition various games can be played. This is done by associating the numbers with the groups in the various games of dice, the spinning wheel, and the "Rummy" game.

(9) A table of objects is set up in front of the children. The objects are discussed and then cards indicating price, such as 2 cents, 3 cents, 4 cents, and so forth, are placed on the objects. As the activity proceeds the children buy various objects using either pegs, play money, or real pennies. In the recitation period questions for the development of number recognition are asked such as "I have three pennies. What can I buy?" or, "I want to buy a top. How many pennies must I have?" A little store in the class provides a real experience in the use of money and number recognition.

(10) Bingo offers an interesting game for the development of number recognition. At first the game consists of numbers up to five. Later the numbers are increased. The child whose card is completely covered first wins the game and becomes next caller.

Training in number concepts and number recognition should not be confined to the games listed here. Many other games have been used. In addition, most activities in the classroom involve some quantitative thinking. The teacher should utilize all opportunities for the development of these concepts in the children, and preferably in a socializing experience type of activity.

HIGHER THOUGHT PROCESSES

One of the aims of education is to aid children to develop the ability to think. An attempt has been made to stimulate higher mental processes in these children by giving them games and activities which develop (1) induction, or the ability to generalize on the basis of a series of events; (2) deduction, or verbal reasoning or the ability to draw conclusions from a simple premise; (3) the ability to detect absurdities in pictures, stories, or real life situations; (4) the ability to detect similarities and differences; (5) the ability to plan constructively; and (6) the ability to solve problems. Since mentally handicapped children seem to be particularly deficient in these abilities, an attempt has been made to stimulate their development. Some suggested activities are:

(1) Give the children six squares, each one lettered. Three of the squares are red, and have identical letters in them. The child's attention is called to the fact that certain squares are red. Why? He must make the generalization that all red squares have the same letter in them. There are many variations of this particular device which seems to have an element of induction in it.

(2) Objects of different classifications, such as clothes, tools, furniture, and so forth, are drawn on a large tag board, and presented to the children. Lines are drawn between the coat, hat, glove, and so forth. The child is asked to tell why these articles are connected, or to connect them. Here again an attempt is made to aid the child in generalizing on the basis of past experience.

(3) Games may also be used to develop inductive ability. The teacher places colored beads in a definite pattern before the children, such as two red, two blue, two red, and then asks them to tell what comes next. This can be complicated or simplified to fit the abilities of the children.

(4) For more advanced children numbers can be used in a pattern, such as 1 2 ... 2 4 ... or 4 3 2. This activity includes quantitative thinking as well as induction.

(5) Life situations often present problems which the teacher can and should use. For example, the teacher can begin to arrange the chairs for storytelling in a certain pattern and then allow the children to complete the pattern. If they are able to follow a pattern which has been started, they will be generalizing. The teacher should watch for occasions in which children can utilize their experience and generalizations for new tasks.

(6) Auditory absurdities are presented in sentences, stories, or in stories with a number of absurdities. Examples of these are,.

"We closed our book and began to read." "When it was time to go home I took my rubbers off because it was raining outside." The children are asked to tell what is wrong with the statement and to explain their reasons.

"When Robert was walking to school he saw Lois walking a long way in front of him. He wanted her to wait for him, so he was as quiet as he could be, and called softly to her so she would be sure to hear him. Lois kept right on walking, and Robert had to walk to school alone."

"John and Charles played together yesterday. John liked Charles so much that he would not play with him. It was very cold so they went swimming. When they arrived home, they were so hungry they couldn't eat any lunch. In the afternoon they were sleepy so they went for a long walk. On their way they met a kind dog, who liked them so much that he bit Charles. When they arrived home, Charles' mother was so glad to see them she spanked them both. The sun was shining that night, so the boys sat outside in the rain until John's mother called them to come in and go to school."

(7) Understanding relationships is another factor that is emphasized with these children. An example of an activity which develops this function is to present to the children a chart with pictures of a hammer, a coat, a cow, and a knife. On separate cards there are pictures of nails, a hat, a fork, and milk. The children are required to place one of the small cards on the large chart with the picture with which it goes, i.e., the hat with the coat, the fork with the knife, and so forth.

Another example of this process presented with concrete objects is for the teacher to say during an activity, "I want to cut a board; which of these tools will I use?" The children select the saw from a number of tools.

(8) Other activities for the development of higher mental processes are found in *riddles, guessing games,* and *determining opposites,* such as: "I am a small toy. I am a red toy. I can spin. What am I?"; "Who has something that is round?" or, "Mary had twenty-five cents to spend. When she came home, she had no money, and she brought nothing with her. She was crying. What

do you think happened?"; and "If your father is not rich, he is .... , if you are not fat, then you are .... , if you are not a boy you must be a .... ."

In the classroom situation, many incidents arise which give the children a chance to do their own thinking, if the teacher will avoid providing all the answers. The teacher should be continually on the alert to take advantage of any classroom situation which will aid the children in solving their own problems in reasoning or in judgment. The activities listed here and elsewhere are activities that can be carried out individually or in small groups, and appear to be enjoyed by the children. They are presented here only as examples to illustrate what is meant by higher mental processes. A good teacher utilizes these principles in natural situations in the classroom whenever they are needed.

VISUAL ABILITIES: DISCRIMINATION AND MEMORY

In order to learn to read and to make accurate observations, a child must learn to discriminate between things seen, and to visualize and to remember things seen. Many books on reading readiness emphasize these factors. Since many of these children are mentally too immature to use workbooks, games and activities adapted to their level which use some of the same principles found in workbooks have been developed.

(1) Real balloons of different colors and sizes and shapes are used for color and size discrimination. The children are directed to pick out a large red balloon, a small blue balloon, and so forth.

(2) The teacher lays out simple patterns using colored sticks. The children are asked to "make one just like it." At first the pattern is shown to them while they make it. Later the pattern is shown, and then covered, requiring the children to reproduce from memory what they had seen. This approach includes color discrimination, ability to follow directions, and visual memory.

(3) The children are given cards having on them various geometric figures. They are given identical forms which are to be matched with the ones on the original sheet. Variations in orientation, size, and shape are also presented.

(4) The "Rummy" game offers an interesting activity for the

development of fine visual discriminations. The visual objects given should start with easy discriminations and proceed to more difficult ones.

(5) The ladder game has been popular with the children as it consists of action pictures made of stickmen in various poses of activity. The word, such as "hop," "skip," or "sing," is written below the picture. Cards with the word alone are given to the children and the children are required to match the word and carry out the direction, for example, by hopping or skipping in the room, after which they place the card on the ladder, the rungs of which are made like a chart holder. All similar words are placed on the same rung, or according to direction given, as "Put your card on the rung below the word 'hop'."

(6) Many activities involve speed of perception. One of these is to show the children a picture of a great number of objects and to ask them to find the doll, or some number (such as 2), or two dots, or some geometric design. Such an activity involves speed of perception and discrimination.

(7) One activity for the training of visual memory is to place objects, such as toys, on a table and discuss them with the children. Have one child turn around and name as many objects from memory as possible. When all have had their turn one object may be removed while the children's eyes are closed. They are to look and tell which object is missing. Another variation is to rearrange the objects while their eyes are closed. The children are then asked to place the objects in their original position.

(10) Cut out pictures of telephones for the children, and mount them along the blackboard. Each telephone has a child's name, and a telephone number. A card with either one of the numbers or a name is shown to the children for only a moment. The children must find from memory the telephone the card designated. A variation of this activity is utilizing the children's own house numbers.

AUDITORY ABILITIES: DISCRIMINATION AND MEMORY

The ability to discriminate fine auditory differences in sounds sometimes aids speech and is probably an important factor in learning to read. Besides simple discrimination of sounds this function should include auditory training, the ability to blend or synthesize sounds, and the ability to remember things heard. Some activities for the development of the functions are:

(1) A series of pictures, such as a book, bell, and bat, are shown to the children. The teacher asks them to find "boy," "bell," "boat." Such exercises assist in developing auditory discriminations.

(2) Nursery rhymes and poems of all sorts can be taught the children. The teacher gives the rhyme, stopping just before the rhyming word is given. The children finish it. In this type of activity the teacher at first aids them in finishing the rhyme, and just as soon as they can, they are allowed to fill in the missing word or phrase.

(3) Simple exercises such as "Who can think of a word that rhymes with 'cat,' 'tree,' and so forth?" aid in the development of auditory discrimination.

(4) To develop the ability to blend sounds, pictures of various objects are shown to the children. For example, if the pictures are those of a ship, a shoe, and a tree, the teacher sounds out the words "Who can find the sh-oe — ?" "Who can find the sh-i-p?" At first the teacher sounds these with very little break between the sounds, later a definite break is made. Similarly, the teacher should start out with two sound words and later increase them to three and then to four sound words.

(5) Repeating sentences told by the teacher has been used to develop sentence length and logical memory. In this type of exercise the teacher gives a short sentence and calls on a child to repeat it. The length of the sentence is increased as the children learn.

(6) To develop memory of ideas in logical sequence, short stories are told to the children. They are asked to retell the story in their own words. In the initial stages the stories should be short with only a few ideas, but as the children learn, the stories can be increased in length.

(7) Since these children have difficulty in remembering directions, activities involving the ability to follow directions are used. In the initial stages one direction is given, such as, "Put the ball on

the top shelf." Later the child is told to put the ball on the top shelf and the doll on the bottom shelf. In this way the child learns to remember one, two, three, or more directions.

(8) Learning of songs and rhymes also aids auditory memory.

(9) Dramatics and the learning of spoken parts in a play is another activity that develops auditory memory.

(10) To develop auditory memory, stories of actual experiences are given. An example is, "John went to the store to buy some bread, meat, and milk. When he returned he had bread and milk. What did he forget?" This type of story can be varied in numerous ways for the development of auditory memory.

MOTOR AND MUSCULAR ABILITIES

Motor coordination is developed in many activities. The task of the teacher is to develop fine motor coordinations that are not trained in play and in the regular course of living. Some of the activities are:

(1) Rhythms — these are too well known to require elaboration.

(2) Handwork of various kinds.

(3) Writing, drawing, coloring, and other similar activities.

(4) Cutting, pasting, and constructive activities.

(5) Finger plays and imitation games.

(6) Ocular motor coordinations. One successful game involved the following of crooked paths drawn on the board from a starting point to an unknown destination, such as to a kite, a balloon, or some such object. These can be simple or quite complex.

The playground should be equipped adequately for the kind of play that will develop gross motor activities. It should be remembered that these children must be taught how to play. Games played by children in their neighborhood should be taught in school so that they can more adequately participate in children's play in their neighborhood.

SPEECH DEVELOPMENT

Many mentally retarded children are deficient in speech and in correct enunciation and pronunciation. These defects should be corrected or improved if possible. The practice in these classes does not differ from classroom speech correction training with the exception that more individual instruction can be given. Some of the practices are:

(1) The teacher (with the assistance of a speech correctionist) checks each child when he is admitted into the class to discover what speech defect he has. Usually many sound substitutions are found in these children.

(2) Individual instruction for the correction of the defects is given by the teacher or speech correctionist when the other children are occupied with educational games.

(3) In conversation and discussions in the classroom the teacher corrects the children. An attempt is made to transfer the practice in the individual instruction to all situations. Care must be exercised that the child does not become so self-conscious that he hesitates to speak, thus retarding his language and vocabulary development.

(4) For group work in correct enunciation and pronunciation, poems and nursery rhymes are used. They are given chorally and individually. Activities such as a radio program with participation by the children are enjoyed by them.

ATTITUDES AND HABITS

Mentally handicapped children have the reputation of being easily fatigued, of having short attention spans, of being unable to pay attention, of being incapable of concentrating or cooperating with others, and in general of having poor work habits. In situations where the work is too difficult for the children and where failure is certain, the characteristics listed above do appear. They are probably the result of the situation rather than the characteristics of mental retardation.

The primary class curriculum does not include specific activities for the purpose of developing adequate attitudes and habits of work. These attitudes and habits are a part of all the activities in the curriculum. Some of the principles upon which the curriculum is based and upon which adequate attitudes and habits of work are built are:

(1) All materials and activities presented are within the capacity of the children.

(2) Functions to be developed are within their achievement level and are presented in the form of games and activities that are interesting and challenging to the children.

(3) The teacher guides the activities and games and gradually allows the children to play them with each other as soon as they can do so. Co-operation, waiting for their turn, and ability to work in a group are stressed in all activities.

(4) All children experience success in the activities. Success is a factor in self-respect and adjustment.

(5) Attention, concentration, and other factors necessary for success in school develop as a result of experiences in an adapted curriculum.

SUMMARY

The primary class for mentally handicapped children is designed to educate children of ages six to ten, whose mental level is six or below, and who are unable to cope with the curriculum of the first or second grades of the regular public school. The purposes of such a class are:

(1) To establish, or re-establish, the confidence of the child in his own abilities by giving particular attention to mental and emotional factors in development.

(2) To develop habits of physical health and safety according to the needs of such children.

(3) To provide parent education so that parents will accept the limitations of the child in academic achievement, and accept the child for his abilities and his worth-whileness.

(4) To emphasize the importance of social adjustment and social participation, and to achieve the goal of social competency.

(5) To develop language ability in these children since this is one of their major deficiencies.

(6) To develop quantitative concepts at the pre-arithmetic level.

(7) To develop better thinking ability through special guidance in that area.

(8) To develop visual perception abilities as a preparation for reading activities.

(9) To develop auditory abilities as a preparation for reading activities.

(10) To facilitate the use of their muscles for better motor coordination.

(11) To develop more adequate speech.

(12) To develop, in general, habits and attitudes of work which will permit them to obtain maximum benefit from group participation in the classroom.

REFERENCES

Coops, Helen. *Health Education in Elementary Schools*. New York: A. S. Barnes and Company, 1950.

Curtis, Ethel Louise. "Building Toward Readiness in Mentally Deficient Children," *American Journal of Mental Deficiency*, 48 (October, 1943), pp. 183–187.

Etz, Elizabeth. "Pre-Academic Activities to Challenge the Mentally Deficient Child from Five to Eight Years of Mental Age," *American Journal of Mental Deficiency*, 48 (October, 1943), pp. 179–182.

Fernald, W. E. "Sense Training for Low Grade Children," *Training School Bulletin*, (January, 1945), pp. 170–174.

Health and Physical Education for Elementary Schools of the State of Illinois, Circular Series A, No. 17. Issued by Superintendent of Public Instruction, Springfield, Illinois, September, 1944.

Johnson, G. Orville. *A Study of the Social Position of Mentally-Handicapped Children in the Regular Grades*. Unpublished Doctor's Dissertation, University of Illinois, 1950.

Kirk, Samuel A., and Irene Stevens. "A Pre-Academic Curriculum for Slow-Learning Children," *American Journal of Mental Deficiency*, 47 (April, 1943), pp. 396–405.

Melcher, Ruth T. "Developmental Progress in Young Mentally Handicapped Children Who Receive Prolonged Pre-Academic Training," *American Journal of Mental Deficiency*, 45 (October, 1940), pp. 265–273.

Patterson, R. Melcher, and Ethel Louise Curtis. "Observing the Learning Difficulties in a Pre-Reading Situation for Higher Grade Mental Defectives," *American Journal of Mental Deficiency*, 49 (October, 1944), pp. 165–170.

Patterson, R. Melcher. "Organization of a Residence Unit for Pre-Academic Training of Mentally Deficient Children," *American Journal of Mental Deficiency*, 48 (October, 1943), pp. 174–178.

Wiener, B. B. "Classroom Observations for Learning Difficulties of High-Grade Mentally Defective Children with Mental Ages Below Six Years," *American Journal of Mental Deficiency*, 50 (April, 1946), pp. 495–502.

Chapter 9

An Intermediate Program

PREADOLESCENT CHILDREN IN AN INTERMEDIATE CLASS

THE INTERMEDIATE class for mentally handicapped children is the one most commonly found in school systems, since communities large enough to require several special classes for the mentally handicapped usually establish the intermediate class first. Later, as the need becomes apparent, classes for the adolescent group and finally for the primary group are organized.

The children assigned to the intermediate class are usually ten, eleven, twelve, and thirteen years of age. They represent the age group of elementary school children who are normally in grades four to eight. Many children are older than ten years before entering the intermediate class; a few may be only nine years of age. Occasionally, a child of more than thirteen years of age will continue to attend the intermediate class because he is socially, emotionally, physically, mentally, and academically immature. Unless further provisions are made, the intermediate class may become the terminal point of formal education for some of these children.

Most mentally handicapped children enter the first grade along with normal children at the age of six. They may repeat the first grade or be promoted to second grade even though their achievements are not up to grade standards. This same process of promotion, regardless of academic achievement, or alternate retention and promotion, may continue for several years. Whether the mentally handicapped child is promoted or is retained at a grade level for varying lengths of time depends upon the philosophy of the school: (1) promotion yearly regardless of academic and social ability, thus keeping chronological age groups together; (2) social promotion, requiring occasional retention to keep social age groups together; or (3) strict academic promotion, requiring a specific proficiency in the tool subjects before permitting promotion.

Academic achievement, particularly reading ability, is of great importance by the time a child reaches the fourth grade. At this and succeeding levels much of the work is almost entirely dependent upon the child's ability to read. Since most schools follow some type of a social promotion policy, the mentally handicapped child in the fourth grade finds himself in the unenviable position of having a curriculum dependent upon a great deal of reading, a skill which he either has not learned or is only in the beginning stages of learning. As a consequence, the mental retardation and lack of academic progress become more noticeable and more serious. The activity program of the primary grades becomes less and less prominent, depriving the mentally handicapped of many areas in which he can compete on somewhat equal terms.

These, then, are the reasons most school systems first organize classes for the mentally handicapped at the intermediate or pre-adolescent age level. The farce of promotion without achievement or satisfaction to either the child or the teacher has reached its climax. The school system is literally forced to make provisions for mentally handicapped children ten, eleven, and twelve years of age.

The intermediate class for the mentally handicapped is designed for children who:

(1) Are ready to learn to read.

(2) Have mental ages of approximately six and one-half to eight and chronological ages of about ten to thirteen.

(3) Are ready to learn some of the elements of other tool subjects such as writing, spelling, and arithmetic.

(4) Need the experience of success in a class adapted to their learning ability.

(5) Need socialization experience without coping with the frustrations which they meet with brighter children.

(6) Need experiences which are adapted to their ability and capacity.

A typical intermediate class is represented in Table II. In this class the children's chronological ages range from 9 years–4 months to 13 years–6 months. Their educational achievement, as represented by the results of standardized tests, range from the beginning of the first grade to the third grade. The achievements in the tool subjects are similar to those of a primary grouping of average children ranging from six to eight years of age.

The performance quotient is a little higher than the verbal I.Q. for most of the children. The social maturity quotient is likewise a little higher than the Binet I.Q. on the average. Many of these children have been isolated and rejected in their regular classes by the normal children. They have faced failure in school ever since admission, and most of them have repeated several grades. Because of frustration and lack of success, they have developed compensatory behavior characteristics which are not accepted by the other children in the regular grades. Bullying, showing off, teasing, and stealing other children's things are some of the behavior characteristics shown.

The Curriculum

The curriculum for preadolescent children is an extension of the curriculum outlined for the primary class. The same general objectives are applicable to this age group with some change in emphasis plus the addition of experiences with which they can now cope.

The structure of a curriculum for the intermediate or preadolescent group must take into consideration two major areas; (1) the development of skills in the tool subjects, and (2) experiences in the areas of living. Different degrees of emphasis have been placed on these areas by curriculum makers.

Some curriculum makers have emphasized the development of the

Table II

A Typical Intermediate Class

	Sex	C.A.	Binet Test		Grace-Arthur Test		Reading Grade	Arithmetic Grade	Social Maturity Quotient
			M.A.	I.Q.	M.A.	I.Q.			
1	F	9–4	6–9	72	7–6	80	2.0	1.9	80
2	F	9–8	7–2	74	6–10	71	1.5	2.1	68
3	M	10–1	6–5	64	7–0	69	1.8	1.5	75
4	F	10–3	7–7	74	7–10	76	2.2	2.5	85
5	M	10–6	6–4	60	6–11	66	1.6	1.5	71
6	M	10–9	6–2	57	6–5	60	1.0	1.4	67
7	M	11–3	7–11	70	7–6	67	1.5	1.8	69
8	F	11–7	8–11	77	8–7	74	2.9	3.0	87
9	M	11–9	7–6	64	7–11	67	1.4	2.5	73
10	F	11–10	8–4	76	9–1	83	3.3	3.7	84
11	F	12–2	6–10	56	7–10	64	1.0	1.4	74
12	M	12–8	7–10	62	9–11	78	2.7	3.1	84
13	M	12–10	8–5	66	9–11	77	1.5	2.7	71
14	M	13–6	7–10	59	9–7	72	2.5	2.8	68

tool subjects; filling most of the school day with relatively formalized teaching in reading, writing, and arithmetic. Feeling that proficiency in this area will be of most value to the children in making future social and economic adjustments, the curriculum of the special class was patterned after that of the intermediate grades.[1]

Other curriculum makers have decided that the program for the intermediate mentally handicapped group should consist of only activities or units of experience. They base this decision on the fact that the mentally handicapped have difficulty in learning the tool subjects and will never become proficient beyond the third or fourth grade level. The academic subjects, in such a curriculum, do not completely vanish but become secondary to the experience units being used. Academic skills are presented as the need arises but with little or no additional practice provided to aid the child in becoming proficient in their use.

In organizing a curriculum for the intermediate class, it is necessary that a well-balanced program be developed which will include the tool subjects and the areas of experience. The inclusion of the tool subjects makes the curriculum of this class more closely resemble that of the elementary school grades than does the curriculum of the other special classes. Specific times are often set aside to insure a logical presentation and learning of the basic skills. Academic fundamentals must be learned at this time to be available for use by the child when he begins the study of (1) homebuilding, (2) occupations, (3) societal relations, and (4) physical and mental health at the secondary or adolescent level (Chapter 10). These skills, however, must be taught in a meaningful way to the child. While practice periods are often necessary for their economical use, the fundamental understandings and concepts are best taught through the use of activities and units of experience. The two major areas of emphasis thus become completely interwoven and interdependent.

THE TOOL SUBJECTS

One of the objectives of the intermediate class is to develop

[1] See Chapter 5 for a discussion of a subject matter curriculum.

skills in the tool subjects. Table II shows the different achievement levels of children in the same class, levels which range from beginning reading and arithmetic to third-grade achievement. This heterogeneity of achievement means teaching beginning reading and arithmetic to some of the children. For those who have grasped the fundamental skills, it means the further development of them.

Many mentally handicapped children entering the intermediate class at the age of ten years will be unable to read or will be reading at the beginning first-grade level. When the children leave the intermediate class at the age of thirteen or fourteen years, they should have developed sufficient skills in the basic tool subjects to adjust to the program of the secondary school special class. This will greatly aid the teacher of the secondary class in planning a program designed specifically for community, social, and occupational adjustment with a minimum of class time having to be spent on remedial work in the academic area necessary.

Reading. Mentally handicapped children never become highly proficient in reading. The extent of the reading ability for most of them ranges from third to fourth grade. The reading ability of a few mentally handicapped children never reaches the third-grade level while occasionally the ability of some exceed the fourth-grade level. It is important, however, that all mentally handicapped children learn to read to the best of their ability. There are numerous occasions when even a small amount of reading ability will be exceedingly valuable. There is also a vast difference between a complete illiterate and an individual who can read even a little. The fact that mentally handicapped children have difficulty in learning to read should not cause an elimination of reading instruction. On the contrary, reading should be emphasized and systematically developed.

The emphasis on the unit plan of instruction has given some the impression that reading can be developed through a unit plan alone. This may be true for normal children, but mentally handicapped children require systematic, step-by-step development of the reading process. It is, therefore, necessary that a special period be set aside each day for reading in order to insure the systematic development of these skills. This does not necessarily mean that the reading skills must be taught in complete isolation. They may be correlated with spelling and writing during the same period. In addition to the special period, reading activities can be correlated with many other activities of the classroom and used whenever feasible in the experience periods.

Reading instruction for the mentally handicapped is described in more detail in Chapter 12. A much more extensive treatise on the instructional procedures for the teaching of reading at the various levels is found in *Teaching Reading to Slow-Learning Children.*[2]

Arithmetic. As indicated in Table II, the preadolescent mentally handicapped children have about the same arithmetical ability as reading ability. It ranges between the first and third grade as measured by academic standards. A phenomenon that often confuses teachers is the mentally handicapped child's ability to perform arithmetic computations considerably in advance of his other academic achievement levels. When this occurs, it is usually a mechanically learned process which comes from repeated drill and practice. The mentally handicapped child learns the mechanics of certain computational exercises. He then practices them because it may be the one academic success he is experiencing. He will, however, be unable to apply them in problem situations. The arithmetic which he needs is the practical application of concepts to life situations.

Like reading, arithmetic concepts have to be developed gradually and through concrete means. They should be used in as many of the activities of the classroom as possible, both as a means of providing additional practice in their use as well as in developing understandings of basic concepts. In addition, time during the day should be allotted to their systematic development. This is especially true in the learning of various combinations that act as shortcuts in making computations. For a discussion on arithmetic principles and instructional procedures, see Chapter 13.

Writing and spelling. It is necessary for mentally handicapped children to learn the essentials of writing and spelling. These

[2] Kirk, Samuel A., *Teaching Reading to Slow-Learning Children.* Boston: Houghton Mifflin Co., 1940.

skills should be taught functionally in relation to other school experiences. The children should learn to write by writing answers, writing letters, writing stories describing the unit or an experience, writing lists of materials or supplies needed for an activity, and so forth. The spelling words to be learned should evolve from the same activities rather than from spelling lists. Supplementary time may be needed by the children to learn the essential words commonly used in written expression. Comments on the teaching of writing and spelling are found in Chapter 12.

THE EXPERIENCE AREAS

Teachers of the mentally handicapped have always noted that their children have difficulty in relating experiences taught separately. To circumvent this difficulty Descœudres advocated the project or correlation method of teaching the mentally handicapped. She states that:

The fundamental principle, on which all concerned with defective children are agreed, and which cannot be too much insisted on, is the utilization of the *natural activity* of the pupil. The child must *do* things, with his body, his hands, and his brain. This principle, however, should not be the special prerogative of the mentally defective, and it may be that the stress laid upon its importance for all children will be one among several improvements that special training will introduce into ordinary teaching.[3]

In this country various terms have been used to denote the teaching procedure which allows the children to work as a group or class on some activity over a long period of time, and in which the various "subjects" of the curriculum are related through this "center of interest." The terms, group activity, project, unit of experience, unit of work, or even "core" have been applied to the teaching procedure which attempts to relate school offerings and skills through learning experiences centered around a topic, a problem, or an interest.

The unit plan of teaching is particularly applicable and practical in a heterogenous class of children such as is found in intermediate

[3] Descœudres, Alice, *The Education of Mentally Defective Children.* Boston: D. C. Heath & Co., 1928, p. 53. London: George G. Harrap & Company, Limited.

special classes for the mentally handicapped. It provides a common experience around which children of different abilities and disabilities can contribute to the unit according to their interests and levels of development. It offers an excellent socializing experience in which each child can contribute to the project for the common good. It furnishes concrete experiences which will give meaning to some of the other learnings in the classroom.

The unit plan of teaching has had many advocates, both for the special class for mentally handicapped children and for regular school children. Some teachers use the unit plan throughout the year, attempting to correlate all subject matter in the unit. Others use the unit plan only occasionally, and especially at holiday periods such as Christmas and Easter.

No one denies the value of the unit plan in the education of the mentally handicapped. It is doubtful, however, that all needed learnings and all skills can be developed to their fullest through the unit plan. Most children can become motivated in one dominant interest for a month, a semester, or even a year. But children have minor interests at the same time. They also have special needs which the unit may not completely satisfy. The tool subjects of reading, writing, spelling, and arithmetic can be utilized in a unit. But, as stated earlier, it is also necessary to set aside some period of the day for special instruction in these skills, especially with the mentally handicapped, who need more repetition in learning such skills.

The recommended procedure in the special class is, therefore, the use of units of experience for part of the day, or at times for the whole day, but to set aside some time during the day for minor interests and for special instruction in the tool subjects and other needed learnings.

Units may be of short duration or of long duration. Some units may occur over and over again during the child's school career at different levels. There is no set pattern or set unit. It must be created by the teacher and the children, and be practical from the point of view of school facilities and community resources, children's interests and possibilities for learning experiences.

In structuring a curriculum for mentally retarded children,

Martens [4] attempted to integrate the subjects of the elementary school into broader areas of experience. Consequently she organized the curriculum into logical areas such as physical and mental health, social experiences, academic experiences, experiences in science, experiences in the arts, and manual and prevocational experiences. The purpose of this organization was to broaden the basic experiences of the children beyond that offered by the traditional elementary school curriculum which included such subjects as geography, history, science, art, music, and so forth. Units of experience are usually broader in scope than the individual subjects, in that they include a number of the subject-matter areas with the emphasis changing from one to another.

Since teachers should have some structure upon which to plan a curriculum and units within a curriculum, it might be advisable to view the curriculum from the point of view of adjustment to the environment in which the child lives rather than as experiences in the areas of the elementary school.

In selecting units in the experience areas, the teacher can view the program from the point of view of areas of adjustment. It appears logical to discuss these areas of adjustment under three major headings namely, (1) adjustment to the physical environment, (2) adjustment to the social environment, and (3) adjustment to the personal environment.

Adjustment of the child to his physical environment. The child should become familiar with his physical surroundings; he should know where his home, the school, police department, fire department, business districts, industrial areas, and so forth are located in relation to one another and to the neighborhood and community. He should become familiar with the location of various social and recreational agencies. In addition, he should know enough about transportation services to learn how to get about the community most economically, from a viewpoint of both time and money.

Most of the experiences designed to adjust the child to his physical environment should be provided through trips in connec-

[4] Martens, E. H. (Editor), *A Guide to Curriculum Adjustment for Mentally Retarded Children*, Bulletin 1936, No. 11, United States Department of the Interior, Office of Education.

tion with the study of the various units. In this way the child will learn the practical geography that will be of value to him. As already indicated, knowledge of the immediate community should be stressed most highly. Where indicated, it may be expanded to include a larger locality, the state, section of the country, and possibly the nation. While he should know that other places exist, concepts beyond this are probably beyond his ability to grasp as well as being of little or no practical value to him.

Adjustment of the child to his social environment. Martens [5] lists the following as some of the desirable social habits and attitudes that should be developed in the mentally handicapped: neatness and cleanliness, tolerance, co-operation, fair play and honesty, self-reliance and courage, and loyalty. These are developed through co-operative work and mutual constructive help in the various unit experiences.

All persons, whether normal or mentally handicapped, need to learn how to get along with their fellow man. The school must help the mentally handicapped child to form those habits or patterns of behavior that will facilitate his adjustment to his social environment. Use should be made of the many experiences common to all the children — the home, the neighborhood, the class, the school, and the community. The child should be aided in understanding his position in the home, his responsibilities to the home, and his relations with the various members of the family. He should be helped in the development of the attitudes and relationships that will make him an adjusted and contributing member of the home and family. A similar effort should be made to aid him in his social adjustment with the children and adults of the neighborhood, with the children and teachers of the class and school, and with the people with whom he comes in contact in the community.

In making a study of the community, group community recreational facilities should also be included and emphasized. Visits should be made to the Y.M.C.A., Y.W.C.A., community recreation centers, and so forth. Following the visits, discussions of their programs, how to join, who attends, and other related subjects should be taken up in some detail. The social adjustment of the

[5] *Ibid.*

children will be aided if they can learn some of the games and carry on some of the activities in the recreational periods of the class. In this way, the situations will not be completely unfamiliar to them. For example, some of the elements and courtesies of social dancing may be started for some of the older boys and girls.

Adjustment of the child to his personal environment. In addition to the child's need for adjustment to his physical and social environment, it is necessary that he learn to adjust within himself. This includes the removal of inner conflicts and the wholesome development of physical and mental health. There is little, if any, difference between mentally handicapped children and normal children in their need to achieve good physical and mental health. The difference lies in the methods of presentation in order that the mentally handicapped may grasp the necessary principles and become efficient in their application.

The health units should give the child practical experience in the care of the body and aid in the development of good health habits, and attitudes. Stress should be placed upon personal habits of cleanliness, good posture, healthful dress, care of the body, need for exercise, choice and preparation of healthful foods, observation of safety rules, healthful work habits and conditions, and so forth, depending upon the needs of the child. As stated by Martens, "There is not a field of the curriculum that does not offer an opportunity for stressing some aspects of health education." [6]

Aspects of mental health pervade the entire program. They are extremely important for a child who has failed in his efforts to compete with other children, and who as a result of these failures, develops emotional conflicts and compensatory behaviors that make his future adjustments even more difficult. While it is impossible to cure the original cause (mental retardation), the teacher must provide experiences in which the child can succeed and attain a feeling of security. The child must develop an insight into his conflicts, an understanding of his capacities, and a confidence in his abilities. If he does, competition is largely eliminated from the curriculum and comparisons are made on the basis of what he has previously accomplished. In this way the child becomes aware of

[6] *Ibid.*, p. 41.

his own growth and development and increasing capabilities.

The program of the special class is thought of as one that is designed to aid the mentally handicapped in their social and economic adjustment. As a result of the increased leisure time of workers, the special class must make definite provisions for experience in leisure time activities. It is commonly recognized that the mentally handicapped have difficulty in adjusting to social and to industrial situations without training and guidance. They have an equal amount of difficulty in adjusting to recreational activities with persons of normal intelligence.

What leisure time activities are then open to them? They commonly take spectator roles, attending movies, sporting events, or listening to the radio. This narrow use of leisure time can be considerably increased through special class activities.

The fine and applied arts (Chapter 14) play an important role in the development of leisure time activities. Enjoyment of music, both listening and singing, provides valuable experiences that should be carried over into home and community life. All skills taught in the practical arts need not be for the sole purpose of providing prevocational background. Knitting, crocheting, embroidering, leather work, metal work, wood carving, and so forth are all excellent leisure time activities and should be encouraged as such.

How to Plan a Unit

Before a teacher launches into a unit of experience with the children he must become acquainted with the children, their interests, and the resources of the school and the community. The following suggestions should help a teacher in preparing for a unit of work:

(1) Study the *interests* of the children, through a familiarity with the case history, observation of their behavior in the classroom and on the playground, home visitation, their conversation with each other, general discussion, and their accomplishments in class and at home.

(2) Study the *abilities* and *disabilities* of the children, their general educational level, their potentialities, their desires, inferiorities, compensations, and successes and failures.

(3) Study the *dominant interests and activities of the community*, and

especially those that affect the children. Familiarity with the community can be achieved through visitations to the home, discussion of local events by the children in the class, finding out about the organizations in the community for children such as the boy and girl scouts, church activities, community affairs, park programs, Y.M.C.A.'s and Y.W.C.A.'s.

(4) Study the *educational resources of the community*; libraries, audio-visual aids, social agencies, and so forth.

(5) Discover the *current centers of interests in the community*, such as a new building in the neighborhood, problems of disease and sanitation, parks, skating rinks or other seasonal activities, as well as industries and factories which may later employ the children.

(6) Study the *individual homes* of the children so as to utilize any possible contributions that the home can make to the unit, and conversely, the benefits the unit has for the home.

When a teacher has become familiar with the interest, abilities, and activities of the children and the community, a unit of work can be initiated. In choosing a unit the teacher may use the following guides:

(1) The unit should be selected by the children under the guidance and leadership of the teacher. A unit selected and organized by the teacher is rarely successful. When the children are allowed to select, plan, and think through the organization of the unit, ask questions, and look for facts, the unit remains within the interest of the children, and in harmony with their abilities. If mentally handicapped children are motivated through natural activities and appropriate questions by the teacher they can select, plan, and carry out a unit within their ability.

(2) The unit of work should be one in which all the children can participate. The interest of the most verbal or aggressive child is not necessarily the one that will appeal to all the children. It should be a unit in which all the children can participate at their levels of ability. In ungraded and heterogenous classes for the mentally handicapped, the unit should be broad enough to foster participation by young children as well as older children.

(3) In selecting a unit consider the learnings which children will experience through participation in the unit. Will the unit

foster co-operation; provide sufficient, varied, and new experiences; develop habits and attitudes needed in out-of-school activities; and provide for natural use of the tool subjects? A unit that includes many of these objectives of education is more desirable than one that includes only a few objectives.

(4) The unit selected should be of such a nature that the children will have a feeling of success when it is ended. The unit may occupy a few days, a whole semester, or a whole year. It can be continued as long as the objectives of the class are being achieved and the children are enthusiastic and interested.

AN EXAMPLE OF A UNIT

Units of work differ from school to school and from teacher to teacher. A teacher cannot read about a successful unit and carry it out in her classroom as a lesson. Each teacher and his pupils must select a unit peculiarly suitable to the particular class and carry out this unit in a unique fashion. This is necessary since composition of classes differ, and communities and neighborhoods differ. Suggestions for units may be obtained but should be adapted by the teacher at the proper time to the conditions of the class. The teacher will want to refer to a number of resource units relating to his chosen unit for ideas to assist in carrying out his objectives. An example of a unit on "The Home" is reproduced below as an illustration of selecting, planning, and building a unit of work in a class for the mentally handicapped.

THE HOME [7]

This activity on the home found its origin in the unusual amount of interest shown by the children in the construction of a house not far from the school. From day to day they noted the progress made in the building, beginning with the steam shovel digging the basement, continuing throughout the erection of the

[7] Werner, Elizabeth, "The Home," reproduced from Martens, E. H., *Group Activities for Mentally-Retarded Children*, U.S. Government Printing Office, Bulletin 1933, No. 7, pp. 5–10.

structure of the house, the addition of the walls and roof, and finally the finishing processes. Thus, for some time previous to the actual initiation of our project, the children showed great enthusiasm in this type of work. Consequent observations and comparisons with their own homes were encouraged, and finally the incident was seized upon as the crucial moment in which to develop a plan of work embodying all the various phases of our school activities under the guise of real life situations.

From the general discussion, admittedly directed, we found many things pertaining to homes which we were anxious to learn about, and these in turn became our objectives, the chief of which were the following:

(1) To have a knowledge of the different types of homes.
(2) To know the importance of cleanliness and beauty in the home.
(3) To have some appreciation of the relationships, duties, and responsibilities of persons in the home.
(4) To have some idea of the cost of construction and maintenance of a home.

The group of children participating in this activity numbered ten boys and five girls — the enrollment of a special class (preprimer through the third grade) in an elementary school. The entire group with the exception of perhaps two children came from the lower grade of middle-class homes, their fathers for the most part being laborers, many of them out of work.

These fifteen children were divided into four separate groups — preprimer, primer, second grade, and third grade — according to their abilities. While the activities of all the groups were closely interrelated, each group worked independently of the others, the only exception being in the construction of the playhouse itself, in which every member of the class had a part.

One morning some of the children talking together suggested that it would be fun to build a house of our own. This led to a spirited discussion of ways and means. Before beginning the project, however, we felt it was necessary to decide what was the best kind of a house for us to build. With this in mind we took a walk to observe different types of homes in our community, and also a walk to a nearby lumber yard to inquire about building materials. Returning to school we discussed these trips at some length and made notes. Some of the children brought pictures and posters of homes, home interiors, and family life about which we also had many interesting conversations. All of this helped to maintain to a high degree the interest in the work.

We received valuable cooperation from the parents, who allowed the children to bring to school toy furniture and many other articles; also from the local storekeepers, who were very kind in furnishing us an extensive supply of boxes which we used in making tables, chairs, cupboards, window boxes, and even the chimney on our playhouse.

All the various phases of our regular school work were carried on hand in hand with our progress in the erection of the playhouse; and while much the same in content for the whole class, the activities were, as has been indicated, divided into four groups commensurate with the different grade levels.

Reading. The reading material for the lower groups consisted almost entirely of original stories based on the actual activities of the day before, with the addition of simple stories about home, such as "The Three Pigs," "The Three Bears," "The Wee Wee Woman," etc. These stories were printed on the board and on charts, and were typewritten to be pasted in each child's "home book." The seat activities to accompany this work included making the home books, matching words and phrases, cutting pictures, cutting words such as "door," "window," etc., from magazines, and drawing pictures according to simple directions printed on the blackboard.

The reading material of the older groups included selected stories about home life taken from different readers, original accounts of our trips, notes we had taken, descriptions of various homes, language stories, and the reading of plans and blueprints. A great deal of work-type reading was introduced in the seat activities, which included informational reading, following written directions, making house plans, planning home interiors, etc. Achievement cards in reading were planned for the entire class as a check on the reading activities and these acted as a definite motivation in securing good results. Each card bore the child's name and was marked into groups of five squares representing the five school days. Every day three marks were entered in the proper square, indicating in turn the grades obtained in attention, seat activity, and the actual reading lesson. A perfect lesson merited a silver star. On Friday of each week the child having the highest average for his particular group was given a gold star.

Arithmetic. The number work for the lower group was chiefly incidental, but included an acquaintance with the ruler and tape measure. For the older groups were added problems involving concrete applications in counting and the four fundamental processes, as well as problems concerned with the costs of the construction, furnishing, and maintenance of a home. These problems were made up in groups of twenty, were typewritten and mounted on separate cards numbered consecutively. To be used with the cards, a large chart was made bearing each child's name with twenty numbered spaces after it. Whenever a child solved one of the problems correctly and unaided, he pasted a silver star in the space corresponding with the number of his card. If he had to have help with the problem, he marked the space "O.K." when his work was completed.

Language. The work in language for the lower groups was for the most part made up of dramatizations, such as playing house, and of discussions of the work being done on the house. The work for the older groups included some original poems, many oral and written discussions of experiences and observations, as well as the writing of letters, descriptions of homes and home interiors, and reports of work done.

Writing, spelling, music. The writing and spelling materials used in connection with the unit were entirely incidental. So also was the music, which consisted of singing songs pertaining to home and family life which happened to fit the particular part of the project on which we were working.

Manual activities. The art work presented an unusual opportunity for the children to display their originality. Aside from drawing, which included work at the easel and with crayon, illustrating simple stories about home life, the children contributed many original designs which were used in making wall paper, in stenciling curtains and pillows, and in producing various other decorations for the playhouse. They also planned color schemes for different rooms, designed covers for their home books, and made many freehand posters depicting furniture and various household objects. All the related handwork hinged directly upon the progress made in the construction of the playhouse, in which each child had a part. There were enough activities to permit every boy and girl to choose, after some experimentation, which phase of the work he wanted to pursue, and thus to add his contribution to the unit. The class was divided into woodworking, sewing, and painting committees. At the end of each industrial period a brief report was given of the work accomplished and plans for the next day were made. To safeguard any waste of time, the chairman of each committee was held responsible for seeing that every member of his group was kept busy at his assigned task.

Following is a list of some of the things accomplished by the committees besides the building of the playhouse itself:

Woodworking committee. Made and painted furniture for playhouse: table, armchair, straight chair, cupboard, doll bed, lamp, window boxes.

Painting committee. Made wall paper, lamp shade, awnings for windows.

Sewing committee. Made bedding for doll bed, curtains for playhouse, pillows, lunch cloths and napkins, table scarf, and clothes for baby doll.

By the time the playhouse was completed the children had gained many ideas which they were able to carry out in their own homes. This was evidenced by the instances cited in which the girls had arranged their rooms to look "prettier," and the boys had put up some handy shelf to help mother, etc.

The significant values of the project, aside from the actual knowledge obtained in fundamentals, involved (1) an appreciation of the relationships and responsibilities in the home; (2) an appreciation of the cost of constructing and maintaining a home; (3) a development of desirable habits and attitudes. The children learned to work well together and to appreciate the advantages of cooperative effort. They gained a sense of carefulness and accuracy made necessary by the nature of the work they were doing. They developed the ability to express themselves clearly and to give and take directions. They learned the value of planning their work carefully and of using books and other materials to help them in making their plans. Their initiative was constantly challenged by the need of experimentation in new fields. An ample variety of work with due progression provided for the individual differences of the children in the various groups. They found themselves very happy in being able to accomplish unexpected things in the wide field of self-expression which their chosen work and its resulting benefits presented to them.

SUMMARY

The intermediate class for the mentally handicapped is usually the first class organized in a community. It is at the preadolescent age level that mentally handicapped children in the regular grades are developing numerous antisocial behaviorisms to compensate for the failures they have been encountering. As a result, parents and teachers are conscious of the fact that the curriculum of the regular grades is not suited to these children and that some special facilities are necessary.

The range of ages in the intermediate special class is between about ten to thirteen years. At ten years of age most mentally handicapped children are at the beginning stages of reading and arithmetic. By the time they reach thirteen or fourteen years of age, they should be doing second- to fourth-grade work.

Two major areas are stressed at the intermediate level. These are (1) the development of skills in the tool subjects, and (2) experience in the areas of living. The actual teaching is done through a combination of specific periods devoted to the logical development of the academic skills and units of experience.

The units of experience are devoted to those areas which assist the child in adjusting to (1) his physical environment, (2) his social environment, and (3) his personal environment.

REFERENCES

Descœudres, Alice. *The Education of Mentally Defective Children*, trans. from the Second French Edition by Ernest F. Row. Boston: D. C. Heath & Company, 1928. London: George G. Harrap & Company, Limited.

Ingram, C. P. *Education of the Slow-Learning Child*. Yonkers: World Book Company, 1935.

Inskeep, A. D. *Teaching Dull and Retarded Children*. New York: The Macmillan Company, 1926.

Kirk, Samuel A. *Teaching Reading to Slow-Learning Children*. Boston: Houghton Mifflin Company, 1940.

Martens, E. H. (Editor). *A Guide to Curriculum Adjustment for Mentally Retarded Children*. Bulletin 1936, No. 11, United States Department of the Interior, Office of Education. Revised: Bulletin 1950, No. 2. Washington, D.C.: Government Printing Office.

Martens, E. H. *Group Activities for Mentally Retarded Children*. U.S. Office of Education, Bulletin 1933, No. 7. Washington, D.C.: Government Printing Office.

Scheidemann, N. V. *The Psychology of Exceptional Children*. Boston: Houghton Mifflin Company, 1931.

Strickland, Ruth G. *How to Build a Unit of Work*. Federal Security Agency, U.S. Office of Education, Bulletin 1946, No. 5.

Wallin, J. E. W. *The Education of Handicapped Children*. Boston: Houghton Mifflin Company, 1924.

Chapter 10

A Secondary-School Program

The Need for a Program in the High School

Although the problem created by the mentally handicapped child has for a long time been a serious one in the elementary grades, it is becoming increasingly acute at the secondary school level, where the child finds himself more and more a misfit.

Prior to the enactment of compulsory attendance laws, most of the traditional schools were interested primarily in those who were academically minded. Little interest was shown in those who could not learn the three R's readily and, as a result, children were allowed to leave school without any serious attempt being made to modify the curriculum to meet the needs of the nonacademic child.

When the legal philosophies of compulsory school attendance were introduced in the various states, the schools found the mentally handicapped and slow learners reluctantly remaining in school until they had reached the compulsory age limit. The new social pressures and responsibilities placed upon the school after World

---

* This chapter is extracted from *Educating the Mentally Handicapped in the Secondary Schools*, prepared by a committee (Samuel A. Kirk, Chairman, G. Orville Johnson, Martha E. Black, Russel M. Duffin, and Ivan K. Garrison) under the auspices of the Illinois Secondary School Curriculum Program, and published by the Superintendent of Public Instruction, Springfield, Illinois.

War I accentuated the problem. The necessity for total mobilization during World War II and the contributions made by all men and women, including the mentally handicapped and slow learners in the military services, have pointed up the needs as well as the advantages of having these children educated to their fullest capacity.

Secondary schools have made a number of attempts to adjust the program to the slow learner and the mentally handicapped. These attempts have been summarized in an extensive study made by the National Educational Research Association.[1] According to this study most high schools agreed that provisions must be made for the slow learner in the secondary school. In general the following practices and conditions were found:

(1) A few secondary schools established special classes.

(2) Some secondary schools placed the slow learner and the mentally handicapped in remedial classes.

(3) Some schools placed them as a group with a reduced curriculum in English, mathematics, and so forth.

(4) Variations of the three practices listed above existed in many schools.

CURRENT ADMINISTRATIVE PROCEDURES

The traditional high-school program consists of a multiplicity of courses primarily in the academic field. These courses are frequently grouped into five principal categories, from which major and minor subjects are selected. These are:

(1) English courses

(2) Social science courses

(3) Mathematics courses

(4) Science courses

(5) Foreign language courses

Additional courses offered as secondary-school requirements or electives are physical education, art, industrial arts, music, commer-

[1] NEA Research Division, "High School Methods With Slow Learners," *Research Bulletin of the National Education Association*, 21, No. 3. Washington, D.C.: Research Division of the National Education Association, 1943, pp. 59–88.

cial subjects, and home economics. Admission to institutions of higher learning, however, is dependent chiefly upon courses successfully completed in the academic fields of English, social science, mathematics, physical science, and foreign languages.

The attempts of the high school to adapt instruction to mentally handicapped and slow-learning pupils have consisted of various kinds of practices as reported by the National Education Association. Some of these are reviewed here.

"WATERING DOWN" THE TRADITIONAL SECONDARY SCHOOL
CURRICULUM

In some schools adaptations have been made by reducing or telescoping the content of the traditional courses in English, social science, and mathematics to meet the learning ability rather than the basic needs of mentally handicapped pupils. This practice of telescoping the content of the course and of simplifying the course in English or mathematics is commonly called "watering down the curriculum."

This practice does not meet the needs or abilities of children who are unable to succeed in science, mathematics, English, and other courses because of mental retardation. Such a program has not proven to be a satisfactory program for individuals with mental handicaps at the secondary-school level.

REMEDIAL CLASSES

In some schools, classes in remedial English, remedial mathematics, and so forth, have been organized as separate sections, and the mentally handicapped have been assigned to these rather than to the regular course. An emphasis on shop activities, to the dissatisfaction of industrial art teachers, has been made to keep the children in courses in which *failure* is less marked, but nevertheless obvious. Remedial instruction is designed for children who have potentialities for learning, but who, because of some specific condition, have not learned. The mentally handicapped do not fall into this category; hence, they are not properly served by remedial instruction.

SPECIAL CLASSES

Some secondary schools have organized special classes for the mentally handicapped but have retained the traditional curricula. The special teacher has offered these children the academic subjects of English, social science, science, and mathematics in the special class, and has assigned the children to physical education, shop, home economics, music, and art with other children. In one school the special teacher took one group for academic subjects in the morning, and assigned the pupils to nonacademic classes in the afternoon. A second group of mentally handicapped pupils, who had been attending the nonacademic classes in the morning, were taught by the special teacher in the afternoon. The organization of special classes just described is administratively feasible and does reduce the academic requirements and competition for these youngsters. But is this the type of curriculum needed by such children? Is the traditional secondary-school curriculum and organization so engrained in us that we continually adapt it, patch it up, or modify it, even though it is not the type of education most needed? Does this kind of reduced curriculum fulfill the purposes of education, or develop in these pupils the social adequacy and occupational competency needed by the mentally handicapped in adjusting to the society in which they live?

Experience has shown that the traditional curriculum, even though modified, results in frustration, failure, and discouragement for these pupils. An adequate program must decrease the area of frustration and emphasize social and occupational growth. This would necessitate breaking down the traditional grade competition and introducing and emphasizing good mental hygiene practices.

The Secondary-School Mentally Handicapped Youth

Classes and provisions for mentally handicapped youth in the secondary school are for children with low intelligence and not for all cases of educational and social maladjustments. Pupils assigned to these special facilities have most or all of the following characteristics·

(1) Chronological ages approximately thirteen to eighteen years.

(2) Mental ages on verbal intelligence tests of about eight to

twelve years, and I.Q.'s ranging from approximately 55 or 60 to 75 or 80.

(3) Retardation in achievement in the tool subjects of at least three years at the age of thirteen years.

(4) Likelihood of failure in adjustment to the curriculum of the regular secondary school.

(5) Potentialities for adequate social and occupational adjustment with a curriculum adjusted to their needs.

(6) Sufficient social maturity to adjust to the routine requirements of being in a secondary school. This would include finding their way about the school building, adjusting to several teachers, being acceptable (physically and socially) to the other high-school students, and so forth.

CURRENT PHILOSOPHIES AND PRACTICES

To present a somewhat logical arrangement of learning activities, it is necessary to group experiences in some arbitrary fashion. This may be achieved by one of two departures from the traditional high school program, i.e., either by relating the program to the existing areas of the high-school curriculum, or by grouping the activities into broader *experience* areas.

Lovell and Ingram,[2] in describing their attempts to build an integrated program of classroom and laboratory activities for mentally retarded girls, began with cores or units of experience that would aid the girls:

(1) In becoming socially integrated in the high school set-up and acceptable to teachers and pupils.

(2) In carrying out their share of responsibility in the family group and in utilizing and enjoying community facilities.

(3) In understanding and appreciating citizenship and the functions of government.

(4) In acquiring habits, skills, and attitudes needed for occupational adjustment.

[2] Lovell, Catherine and Christine P. Ingram, "A High School Program for Mentally Retarded Girls," *Journal of Educational Research*, 40, No. 8 (April, 1947), pp. 574–582.

(5) In acquiring knowledge of local occupational opportunities.

At first the girls gave little attention to the time pattern and curriculum organization existing in the high school. As they became aware of high-school schedules and subject programs, they asked for similar subject schedules.

Hill [3] lists several factors which seem to contribute to the success of special classes for the mentally handicapped in the secondary school. The first of these advocates that "the organizational and administrative pattern of the special groups must be identical with that of the regular junior high school." Early attempts to schedule pupils to one teacher for three consecutive periods were later modified to conform to the departmentalized organization of the school. Reading was called "English and Literature." Arithmetic was known as "Mathematics." In Hill's classes in the junior high school, four special teachers were assigned to a group of about seventy mentally handicapped youngsters. The pupils went from one special teacher to another.

Such an organization represents the minimum departure from the established curriculum and as such will find many advocates because of administrative feasibility. It is an approach which will allow the mentally handicapped to attend certain regular classes where it is believed they will be able to fit into the traditional program with the least difficulty. Music, physical education, home economics, industrial arts, and art are frequently cited as typical classes in which the retarded may be enrolled.

It must be conceded that in any subject where competition for grades is a factor, where the teacher works all children to the limits of their capacities, and where standardization is the criterion, the mentally handicapped will soon be in trouble. Much work in the more technical aspects of music, as it is presented by many secondary-school music departments, goes beyond the abstract abilities of mentally handicapped pupils. This is true also of home economics where teachers are accustomed to devote many periods to the scientific aspects of food composition, the use of fabrics, and the theories of home decoration and management.

[3] Hill, Arthur S., "Special Education in the Secondary Schools," *Journal of Exceptional Children*, 13, No. 7 (April, 1947), pp. 93–97.

To challenge the typical child art must be more than the simple drawings of the middle elementary grades, and physical education must be more than the recess-play activities of the elementary school child.

The marked differences between the abilities of typical and mentally handicapped pupils enrolled in the same class will soon be known to all members of the class. It is alleged that these differences will not seem so great in nonacademic subjects as in the traditional subjects. Other members of the class, however, will not overlook or understand differentiated assignments and accomplishments of the mentally handicapped pupils, especially if the typical pupils receive failing grades for the same quality of work. Teachers will be reluctant to appear unfair in grading by making allowances for substandard achievement. In fact, it would seem almost as easy, and certainly no more difficult to explain, to organize classes of youngsters who may have the combined benefits of personal guidance, specialized techniques, and specially planned subject matter under the direction of teachers whose philosophies are adjusted to the needs and abilities of the handicapped child.

Curriculum makers [4] in general have followed one of three organizations: (1) the subject-matter curriculum, (2) the activity curriculum, and (3) the core curriculum.

Although the activity curriculum has more merits than the subject-matter curriculum, it does not appear to be the complete answer. If the activity curriculum stresses the interests and needs of the children as a starting point, how are these interests and needs channeled into an adequate educational program? If there is some merit to what has been termed "the functional autonomy of motives," then most interests and needs are learned through experience, and the special class must be organized to develop those interests and needs which will harmonize with a program of education that will develop social and occupational adequacy in nonacademic pupils.

[4] Shores, J. Harlan, *A Critical Review of the Research on Elementary School Curriculum Organization*, College of Education, Bureau of Research and Service, University of Illinois Bulletin, 47, No. 8 (September, 1949). Wright, G. S., *Core Curriculum in Public High Schools*, Bulletin No. 5, Federal Security Agency, Washington, D.C.: Office of Education, 1950.

The core curriculum has been proposed by some as a suitable program for secondary-school pupils. In some instances the philosophy of the core curriculum means the organization of the educational program into areas of living. "The term 'core' as used in the secondary schools has had and still does have a variety of meanings. Traditionally it referred to those subjects which were required in the school's program. More recently the 'core' has been used to refer to a special type of course offering of a general education nature. Schools refer to these courses as General Education, Unified Studies, Common Learnings, Basic Living, Social Living, Integrated Program, or simply as Core classes." [5]

As a result of the differences in meaning attached to the term "core curriculum" and the fact that the level of "common learnings" used in secondary schools is not suitable to the mentally handicapped, it did not appear desirable to use a traditional label in describing a program for the mentally handicapped, since the training and experience of different readers would color their interpretation. For that reason the organization of the curriculum has been called *experience areas*, although the reader will note a resemblance to both the activity curriculum and the core curriculum.

The Curriculum

The program that will be described in this section has been evolved from the recognition of the needs and abilities of mentally handicapped youth. It is a continuation of the program of the intermediate class for preadolescents which emphasized (1) development of skills in the tool subjects, and (2) experiences in the areas of living.

At the secondary or adolescent level, the pupils have mastered the essentials of the tool subjects which require further development in applying them to functional situations. Hence, at this level the emphasis of the curriculum is in terms of (1) areas of experience, and (2) personal guidance. These two terms are not names of divisions but concurrent aspects. It is emphasized that in practice these two components are integral parts of the whole.

[5] Wright, *Ibid.*, p. 1.

THE EXPERIENCE AREAS

The areas of experience stressed at the intermediate or pre-adolescent level were the adjustment of the child to his physical, social, and personal environment. At the secondary or adolescent level it is necessary to emphasize more specifically the areas of living and the skills and attitudes essential to meeting the requirements of the social and occupational world. Many such areas could be listed. Most of the areas can be developed around the broad headings of (1) homebuilding, (2) occupational education, (3) societal relationships, and (4) physical and mental health.

The areas should not be thought of as cores. The emphasis may shift from one area to another, while skills or attitudes that are being developed in one area may also satisfy all of the other areas. Much of the teaching of skills and development of healthful attitudes necessary for physical and mental health may occur while learning how to clean a stove, while learning how to apply for a job, or while discussing something that will be done the next day. This is not incidental teaching but systematic instruction, and the skills developed have more meaning because they are parts related to a much larger system than "Health" as a subject.

Homebuilding. Homebuilding is emphasized because the mentally handicapped will have homes of their own, or be members of homes both as children and as adults. Just because one is physiologically ready to have a family one is not necessarily ready psychologically. But the reverse of this is also true: just because one is not psychologically ready to have a family there is no reason to believe that one will not have a family. By acquiring the skills of good homebuilding both boys and girls will be exposed to several of the occupational areas in which they eventually will find employment. For those who will some day find jobs in the personal service area there are occupational implications in learning how to keep a kitchen clean, to prepare a meal, or to do simple laundry. Household mechanics introduces the boys to some of the possibilities in the occupational area of the building trades. It also teaches them good work habits and methods of improving or maintaining their own homes.

Occupational education. The area of occupational education is not to be confused with vocational education or specific trade training.

Occupational education includes such things as manners, personal health and appearance, means of getting employment, means of adjusting to accidents and unemployment, getting along with the boss or fellow workers, following directions, discussing vocational goals and skills, traveling in the city, general job training, and acquiring vocational information. Learning how to fill out an application blank, how to apply for a job, and how to exchange common courtesies are a few of the skills that can be learned in the classroom. These are just as important in finding and keeping a job as actually being able to do the work.

Societal relationships. The area of societal relationships is intentionally broad. The other areas have been confined more or less to the individual, but this area brings in the broader aspect of orientation to society, geographical concepts, citizenship responsibilities, and understanding the culture of which they are a part and product. It is in the specifics of this area that the person of low intelligence is said to have very poor habits and general information. If this is so, and many writers bear this out, then here is an area where content and methodology must be modified to make possible a better understanding of these specifics.

The societal relationships include such topics as understanding our present culture, orientation to society, citizenship responsibilities at the pupils' level of operation, meeting and dealing with people, heterosexual relations, functioning democracy, geographical concepts, inter- and intracultural awareness, and respect for the individual.

Physical and mental health. It has been stated earlier that mentally handicapped children as a group have more minor physical handicaps than the average child. It has been also stated that because of the difficulties of meeting the environment designed for the average functioning individual, the mentally handicapped child meets more frustrations in and out of school than does the average person. It is, therefore, important that emphasis on physical and mental health for these youth be made. The specific areas under this heading may be listed as follows: awareness of bodily functions, practice and concepts in sanitation and hygiene, pride in personal appearance, understanding of health rules, use of leisure time, establishing adequate values, sense of achievement, acceptance of limitation, personal conduct, establishment of security, and pride in accomplishments.

THE AREA OF HOMEBUILDING AS AN EXAMPLE OF CURRICULUM PLANNING

Homebuilding may be approached from that which is nearest at hand — namely, the classroom. Interest in and attention to the project of "improving our classroom" will give both boys and girls the opportunity of using materials and tools and of planning wall designs and furniture arrangements. Building bulletin boards and bookcases and making curtains are similar activities. These may be followed by attention to clothing, particularly that of the pupils and the members of their families. Simple laundry work, hand and machine sewing, and the repair of clothing will furnish many learning experiences. Housekeeping offers innumerable opportunities to teach sanitation. Ordinary procedures which are established routines in the lives of normal children must be taught the mentally handicapped.

Homebuilding also will involve care of the sick, child care, and the ordinary precautions against accidents in the home or shop. When trips are made to factories and business houses one objective should be to study the safety programs of such organizations.

Housework may be made the basis of many learning activities for both boys and girls. Washing windows and woodwork, waxing floors and furniture, cleaning blinds and draperies, caring for rugs, painting and repairing screens, storm windows, and furniture may be a part of the home building project in the school or in the home. Such activities as gardening, the use of tools, and the care of lawns and shrubbery provide possibilities for many experiences.

SELECTING HOMEBUILDING ACTIVITIES

The process of curriculum building in this program becomes one of selecting activities. "Homebuilding" may be thought of as the name of the course being offered. The period or hour assigned to the subject may occur daily or less frequently. Boys and girls may meet jointly or separately. The schedule undoubtedly will change as the need for basic skills is demonstrated. Pupils who have demonstrated certain skills and abilities in homemaking may be placed in regular home economics classes, in addition to carrying on their homebuilding experiences in the special class.

The selection of learning activities in any field will require some grouping with reference to time and psychological considerations. The teacher of the mentally handicapped will ask: What home and community activities may we use today, this week, this month, this semester, or this year? Repetition and new approaches to activities formerly used will be common. It is presumed that the subject of homebuilding will not be learned by the close of school in June but that it must continue in new and more comprehensive patterns during the second, third, and fourth years, or as long as the child remains in school.

Compartmentalization of subject matter is not advocated or recommended. Learning in this field may and should be related to the work being done in occupational education, physical and mental health, and societal relationships.

One secondary school teacher of mentally handicapped youth began his work with ninth-grade youngsters in the homebuilding area by devoting approximately one hour daily during the first week to the project of "fixing up our room." The instructor's purpose was to emphasize orientation.

During the second week emphasis was placed upon "determining needs." The projects and activities carried out included setting in motion the actual work of improving the room, shopping tours to secure necessary small items and materials, and the purchases of tools and equipment. The use of the sewing machine was demonstrated, and some instruction was undertaken in the use of hand tools.

The third week was devoted to the general topic of "appearance." In this period a plan for keeping the room clean was established. Classroom duties were assigned and a routine was developed which would allow for rotation of assignments. The room-improvement project was continued.

In the fourth week the emphasis was shifted to "manners." The new topics of behavior at home and school, proper speech, and the importance of knowing how to act in a social situation were studied and discussed. At the same time the usual projects dealing with the care and improvement of the room were continued.

The implications of being a member of a home are much different for an eighteen-year-old pupil than for a thirteen- or fourteen-year-old pupil. One cannot guarantee that youth who participate in this program will not drop out of school as soon as they reach the age at which they are no longer compelled to attend. The number doing this may be reduced, but it must be assumed in the planning that some will leave school and some will continue until they have been graduated. Both groups deserve to be better prepared as the result of careful program planning.

The school personnel should begin to anticipate the time when the pupils will drop out of school. The school laws can be depended upon in most states to hold the child in school until the end of the school year following his sixteenth birthday. Consequently, when the children are approximately fourteen or fifteen years of age, emphasis should be given to the responsibilities of "family membership." Home arts and mechanics will be one approach to the duties of those who may soon be establishing their own homes. A year later the approach may involve the responsibilities of parenthood, including housing, feeding, and care of children. As the young person continues in school the scene may shift to home management, budgeting, child care, rent, planning for education of children, and more complicated and difficult functions common to parenthood.

SELECTING ACTIVITIES IN OTHER AREAS

As was noted previously in the example under discussion, the area of homebuilding was not isolated from the other experience areas. While the emphasis remained upon orientation, all areas were utilized to contribute their full share toward adapting the individual to his new surroundings.

During the daily period devoted to occupational education, the work of the first week consisted of making a list of places of employment in the community. The study of job areas was undertaken, with some attention being given to the existence of such areas in the locality and the opportunities for employment there.

The area of societal relationships was used to assist the pupil in his school adjustment by a study of the location of classrooms and school facilities. The processes of carrying out school and class routines were explained and demonstrated.

Physical and mental health activities were drawn into the orientation procedure through class discussions on "Our Room," "Our Class," and "Our School." A feeling of belonging was established. In this way a desire for self-improvement and for improvement of the appearance of the room was developed.

When the emphasis changed to determining needs in the second week, the activities chosen in all areas were in keeping with the objective. Occupational education continued by listing places in which the various members would wish to work. As a corollary to getting a job, the importance of grooming was introduced. Societal relationships were carried forward through the use of news stories and news broadcasts. Pupils were asked to report events read about or heard, and an effort was made to relate these current events to the daily lives of the youngsters. The health area was exploited to assist pupils in evaluating their appearance, to become aware of whatever assets they might have, and to plan a course of academic or physical improvement.

During the third and fourth weeks comparable choices were made in keeping with the activities selected in all areas. By this process of integration the pupil's whole learning procedure for a limited time was directed toward a real goal. The approach which he made was simple and personal, although the organization behind these daily activities was not necessarily simple. The youngsters talked of, thought of, and did something they were able to do. The instructor noted the progress made in certain attitudes and skills, and his effort was to keep the program growing from week to week. This had been planned in advance. As the youngsters became accustomed to certain activities, new ones were added. The first problem had been to obtain the participation of all pupils. The next was to allow rules for governing these activities to develop as boys and girls became aware of the need for them.

PROVIDING A DEVELOPMENTAL PROGRAM

As the program of special education at the secondary-school level goes into its second, third, fourth, or some greater number of years, the program must change in several ways. Typical of this change is the emphasis upon occupational education. For first-year students much attention is placed upon classroom study, with a considerable number of field trips to business establishments, industries, farms, employment agencies, and other places believed to be of educational value in adjusting the individual to his economic environment. Only a few can actually participate in earning projects because of age limitations, readiness for work, and the supply of suitable work. Those jobs which are being filled by members of the class are usually of the domestic service or handyman variety and are seldom on the level of long-term occupational service. Teachers of such classes help in finding part-time jobs for the older pupils in the community and excuse them from class during their period of work when necessary. These jobs may include assisting with the noon meal in a day nursery school, paper routes, and similar occupations.

As the learner matures in social skill and job ability, he must devote an increasing number of hours daily to exploration and learning in actual work experience situations. Whether this is to result in his assuming one job part-time at beginner's pay and gradually growing into it as a life work, or whether it is to entail a series of work experience situations during the process of finding out what the pupil can do best and most happily, is a guidance problem with each individual. Many factors will have a bearing upon the individualized curriculum of each person. The economic status of the family will be a factor. His progress in the tool subjects of education will influence the choice of work and further training. No standardized patterns of subject selection and programming can be offered.

INTEGRATING THE EXPERIENCE AREAS

After a certain topic has been selected for emphasis during an experience period a certain amount of teacher-pupil planning is always necessary. While hard and fast schedules are avoided, it is necessary to outline roughly what would be included during the period in the way of materials, occupational implications, activities, and visits. The following is an example:

The class decided to emphasize *foods* and *food handling* as a unit for a period of time. They examined the implications of this topic in all the experience areas. The pupils were keeping a notebook called "Occupations" as a part of their class work in occupational education; here they included related phases of this topic. As the class discussed the topic, the teacher outlined the possibilities of the unit on the blackboard and the pupils recorded the following in their notebooks.

What do foods and food handling include?
Preparation and serving
    Restaurants and cafes
    Institutions
    Hotels
    Homes
Processing
    Bakeries
    Butcher shops
    Slaughterhouses
    Canning
    Bottling
Storage
    Locker and cold storage
Production
    Truck gardening
    Farming
    Orchard
    Dairies
Transportation
    Local delivery of milk, candy, bread, and coke
    Market transports
Retailing
    Grocery stores
    Meat markets
    Fruit and vegetable markets
    Supermarkets
    Dairies
    Bake shops
    Confectioners
    Drug stores
    Candy stores

It should be noted that included in this outline was the breakdown of the processing and distribution of foods and the places in the community where such operations were occurring.

Using the outline as a basis the class then planned certain activities and studies that would be most applicable in all the areas, such as:
Physical and mental health
    Diet and eating habits

Digestion and elimination (use of colored charts in *Compton's En-cyclopedia* to explain and locate organs concerned with digestion)
Homebuilding
Cleanliness in kitchen
Menu planning and food storage
Defrosting ice box and cleaning (both electric and non-electric)
Dishwashing (use of teacher-prepared material for sequences in food preparation, kitchen duties, etc.)
Repair of kitchen appliances
Occupational education
Visit and study the jobs related to food handling (bakery, restaurant, butcher shop, packing house, dairy, market, etc.)
Use of Occupational Briefs: "Grocery Store," "Candy Store," "Gardening," etc.
Societal Relationships
Eating in public
Sanitation and sewage disposal
Zoning

The related learning experiences which the teacher wished to utilize were:

For Girls	*For Boys*
Making recipe boxes	Repairing kitchen appliances
Baking biscuits and muffins	Bench experiments in wiring conven-
Preparing salads	ience receptacles, extension cords,
Preparing a hot dish	and installation of switches
Preparing luncheons	Making decorative kitchen shelves
Cleaning kitchen and appliances	Reading directions on job sheets
Washing dishes	Interpreting diagrams
Cleaning silverware	
Ordering cooking supplies	
Reading directions on job sheets	
Repeating experience at home with mothers' comments each week	

For Both Boys and Girls
Experiments in food spoilage (i.e., tomatoes in clean and dirty jars)
Preparing the table
Eating together

Taking orders

Restaurant demonstration (pupil dramatization)

Use of sales handbills and advertisements in newspaper for the purpose of
intelligent shopping

Locating and tracing city water supply on city map

Use of state bulletins on "Water," "Sanitation," "Diet," etc.

Visits to industries

Use of related application blanks

Liquid and dry measurement

In addition to teacher-prepared material from newspapers, magazines,
and so forth, material was selected from graded readers, science readers,
Compton's Encyclopedia, Occupational Briefs, and the Sloan Foundation materials: *The Smith's New Garden, Improving the Garden, Storing Eggs and
Chickens, Planning the Farm, Ounce of Care,* and *Water.* Reference materials
were selected from *The Library of Wonder Books,* the American Education
Press, Inc., Columbus, Ohio, and the *Skilltext Workbooks,* Charles E. Merrill Co., Inc., Columbus, Ohio, and such magazines as *Woman's Day, Seventeen, Open Road, Popular Mechanics,* and *Better Homes and Gardens.*

Use was made of film strips from the series "Vocational Guidance
1–4–5–8–9–10," Des Moines, Iowa, and *Safety in the Home,* Visual Sci-
ences, Suffern, New York. Film strips and sound films on the subjects
were used such as applying for work, food, milk, water processing, manners, and shop safety

The task of curriculum planning depends upon the teacher's ability to work from generalities, objectives, and goals down to specifics. Suggestions for implementing the curriculum are:

(1) Determine the major emphasis of the period and the skills or
attitudes that you feel should be developed.

(2) Consider the resources for implementing the program both
within the school and classroom and in the surrounding community
(social, welfare, health, and employment agencies; films and film
strips; field trips; school activities; community drives and projects;
and training aids).

(3) Consider possible pupil activities that would give meaning
to any concepts that you are trying to develop.

(4) Build the program in outline form, then proceed as needed
(contacting agencies to set definite times for field trips, ordering
films and visual aids, arranging for any necessary purchases or ex-

penditures, or arranging in advance for any cooperation necessary beyond your own).

(5) Secure pupil participation in planning experiences and in gathering materials, such as newspapers, magazines, and equipment.

(6) Post on the bulletin board the plans proposed and the weekly schedule for films, trips, talks, and other activities.

(7) Post the daily activities, listing who is to do what throughout the day.

A DAILY PROGRAM

Among the difficulties in organizing special provisions for the mentally handicapped are the organization of the class and the scheduling to other classes. It has been pointed out that the duty of the teacher is to organize the program along four major areas of experience. These areas are carried out by the class and the teacher in the special class. The learning experiences of some of the children are supplemented by the assignment of these children to other classes in the high school, depending upon the interests and abilities of the pupils, and the adaptation of the other classes to these interests and abilities. Although some are assigned to home economics classes, the teacher of the special class assists the children in their work and confers with the home economics teacher concerning this work. To make this more concrete, a daily schedule is presented as an example of program making in one such special class.

(1) The first period of the day is devoted to physical and mental health and societal relations. This includes planning for the day, reading of newspapers, reporting of current events, and discussing daily routines in relation to health and social programs. For example, if *foods and food handling* is the experience area under consideration, there is a discussion on balanced diet, "quack" advertisements concerning digestion, and so forth. One boy, because of his interest and ability, takes an agricultural course at this hour.

(2) During the second period the boys go from the special room to a regular woodworking class. On Monday and Wednesday the girls stay in the special class for a program of homebuilding which includes the teaching of sewing, cooking, and correlated activities such as reading and dis-

cussing recipes. The girls take physical education during this period on Tuesday, Thursday, and Friday. During this free period the special teacher makes contacts with employers for work experience openings, does program planning, and discusses pertinent problems with regular teachers.

There is a short home-room meeting between the second and third periods. This home-room period includes planning of student activities, club meetings, a weekly all-school assembly, and group guidance.

(3) During the third period all students are in the special class on Monday and Wednesday. This time is given to remedial reading and free reading related to the area under consideration. On Tuesdays, Thursdays, and Fridays, the boys attend regular physical education classes while the girls remain in the special class for homebuilding. This scheduling of homebuilding at different times on different days is just one example of how flexible the program must be.

(4) The fourth period is devoted to occupational education and guidance in the tool subjects, especially in arithmetic. The time is frequently utilized in preparing for or making a visit to an industry. The preparation and the discussion after the trip may include filling out forms, application blanks, Social Security cards, and working related mathematical problems.

(5) During the fifth period the girls attend a regular home economics class. The special teacher works with the regular teacher to be sure that the work and projects are not beyond the girls' abilities. The boys remain with the special teacher for work in home mechanics. This includes such activities as work with tools, bench experiments in wiring, and safety education.

(6) The sixth period is devoted to language development and socialization. The students write stories relating to their daily experiences in school. They debate issues, have discussion groups, go to the youth center, participate in sociodrama, and engage in free play.

A summary of the foregoing schedule is presented in Table III as an example of the weekly schedule in a secondary school which has six periods a day.

PERSONAL GUIDANCE

The preceding section described the organization of a curriculum based on experience areas. It was stated earlier that a total program must be permeated with personal guidance. This section deals with the procedures by which guidance is accomplished in a program for the mentally handicapped.

Table III A Weekly Schedule for a Secondary-School Class for the Mentally Handicapped

Period	Monday	Tuesday	Wednesday	Thursday	Friday
1.	Boys and Girls Physical and Mental Health Societal Relations	Boys and Girls Physical and Mental Health Societal Relations	Boys and Girls Physical and Mental Health Societal Relations	Boys and Girls Physical and Mental Health Societal Relations	Boys and Girls Physical and Mental Health Societal Relations
2.	Boys Regular Woodworking Girls Homebuilding (Special)	Boys Woodworking Girls Physical Education (Special teacher free period)	Boys Woodworking Girls Homebuilding (Special)	Boys Woodworking Girls Physical Education (Special teacher free period)	Boys Woodworking Girls Physical Education (Special teacher free period)
Home Room	Group Guidance	Clubs	Group Guidance	Clubs	Assembly
3.	Boys and Girls Remedial Reading Related Reading	Boys Physical Education Girls Homebuilding (Special)	Boys and Girls Remedial Reading Related Reading	Boys Physical Education Girls Home building (Special)	Boys Physical Education Girls Homebuilding (Special)
			NOON		
4.	Boys and Girls Occupational Education, Guidance in tool subjects	Boys and Girls Occupational Education, Guidance in tool subjects	Boys and Girls Occupational Education, Guidance in tool subjects	Boys and Girls Occupational Education, Guidance in tool subjects	Boys and Girls Occupational Education, Guidance in tool subjects
5.	Girls Regular Home Economics Boys Home Mechanics (Special)	Girls Regular Home Economics Boys Home Mechanics (Special)	Girls Regular Home Economics Boys Home Mechanics (Special)	Girls Regular Home Economics Boys Home Mechanics (Special)	Girls Regular Home Economics Boys Home Mechanics (Special)
6.	Boys and Girls Language Development Socialization Free Play	Boys and Girls Language Development Socialization Free Play	Boys and Girls Language Development Socialization Free Play	Boys and Girls Language Development Socialization Free Play	Boys and Girls Youth Center

Although a special education program is in reality a guidance program, it should be emphasized that one of the basic techniques of special education is personal guidance or individualization of instruction. By personal guidance is meant the recognition of the unique problems of each individual and the formulation of a technique for assisting him in solving his problems. Some of these problems may be in the areas of (1) difficulties in mastering the elements of the tool subjects, (2) personal and social adjustment, and (3) occupational guidance, information, and training.

Guidance in the tool subjects. Reading, writing, spelling, arithmetic, and all the other tool subjects find their places in the curriculum but not after the traditional pattern. The emphasis on these subjects is not that they be taught as ends but as means to an end. It is important for a seventeen-year-old boy, who may possibly get a job as a painter, to be able to recognize "Chinese Bristles" or "Horsehair" printed on the handle of a paint brush, to know that there is a difference between the paint spreading qualities of two brushes, to recognize the number $3\frac{1}{2}$ or $2\frac{1}{2}$ printed on the handle, and to know which jobs require a $3\frac{1}{2}$, and which require a $2\frac{1}{2}$ inch brush. It is more important for the teacher to consider the functional use of facts in teaching a student than to develop a unit around "The Use of Chinese Hog Bristles in the Making of Paint Brushes."

A study of "spending the family income" and the use of a bank opens a new vista to vocabulary building and functional mathematics. The philosophy of special education does not deny the value of developing any mathematical or verbal concept of which the individual is capable and for which there is an immediate practical need. Money is as real to a mentally handicapped pupil as it is to any other student. A quarter is a fourth of a dollar; four quarters make a whole dollar; a quarter of anything is the same as $\frac{1}{4}$; four-fourths (4/4) is the same as all of anything; all of anything is 100%. A quarter may be written $.25; this is 25 hundredths (25/100) of a dollar; $\frac{1}{4}$ is the same as .25; one fourth of a whole may be written .25. If all of anything is 100% and $\frac{1}{4}$ of 100% is 25% and $\frac{1}{4}$ may be written .25, then 25% is the same as .25. We call $\frac{1}{4}$ a common fraction and .25 a decimal fraction. These concepts are not beyond the ability of many mentally handicapped students found in high schools.

Activities such as writing checks and figuring wages and bank balances develop the need for these concepts and demonstrate the practical use of such decimals and fractions. After the student understands these he may go on to study interest, loans, and so forth. A somewhat formal group approach with individual help does not hinder those who understand these principles; it reinforces their previous experiences and allows them to help those who need help.

A bank activity that includes a cashier (change-maker) and a bank clerk provides for writing and cashing checks and will allow all to participate at their own level. This activity can take them as far as they can go with deposits, withdrawals, loans, bank charges, and so forth.

Reading cuts across all the experience areas. This type of program includes remedial help. Some students may be achieving at their maximum insofar as can be determined by their tested academic aptitude. The teachers' task is to select materials and methods that are suitable for the pupils' continued progress.

Some students may be severely retarded in reading in comparison with their potentialities. For these, the teacher may use any remedial techniques that he has at hand to improve this skill. If the occupational potentialities of a pupil who is capable of improving indicate the need for a certain level of reading, then that part of the program devoted to remedial reading becomes important and deserves emphasis.

A program of personal guidance involves not only experience periods and activities as described, but in many cases individual instruction in the area needing intensive attention. Thus, when a child needs remedial reading, time should be devoted to a diagnosis of his difficulty, and special instruction offered at some period of the day. If a child needs special drill in arithmetic processes, special exercise periods are set aside for him. If a child is having difficulty in writing, special help is indicated. These needs become apparent when a pupil is unable to read the assignments, to fill the blanks, or to do simple arithmetic. Special periods for these children may be set aside when most of the other children are attending physical education, home economics, shop, or other classes.

Social guidance. In addition to guidance in the tool subjects, there are other areas of individual needs. Boys and girls have personal problems which they would like to discuss with a teacher whom they respect. Opportunities for personal conferences should be provided so that students may discuss their progress, their personal problems, their relations with their parents or siblings, their state of mind, their attitudes toward their peers, or any problem which confronts them.

The experience areas also provide many opportunities for social guidance. For example:

One teacher reports a very good social experience built around the idea of eating in public. This activity was developed in the foods period. All had had some instruction in setting the table, in manners at the table, in making change, and in conduct in public places.

A card table and chairs were set up, and dishes and silver were brought in from the home economics laboratory. The teacher prepared menus, secured real money for use in paying for the meals, and allowed different individuals to take parts as diners, waiters, waitresses, managers, cashiers, and kitchen help.

Others not participating in the activity kept checklists on errors in manners, serving, and seating. The reader can be assured that the boys and girls did not allow the activity to be dropped until all had had a chance to take part in every phase of the activity.

Social guidance can be given in many of the other areas whenever the opportunity arises. Special techniques of developing social concepts among mentally handicapped children are discussed in Chapter 15. Sociodrama and self-determined activities are especially effective with pupils of adolescent age.

Occupational guidance, information, and training. That a vocational or occupational guidance and placement program for the mentally handicapped is a necessity is beyond question. In most of our secondary schools, a guidance or counseling program of some type is already available to normal students. If this program is directed by some highly trained person, he can be of invaluable assistance to the special class teacher. Because the average counselor lacks training and background in working with the mentally handicapped he probably will be unable to carry out a complete guidance and counseling program with this group. The major job will fall on the special class teacher. The counselor, however, will have materials on jobs, job requirements, and information concerning jobs available in the community. He will have made contacts with numerous prospective employers. All this material and information can be invaluable to the teacher of the special class in planning a program consistent with the vocational interests and abilities of the children.

When such guidance counselors are available and their facilities can be used by the mentally handicapped, the task of the teacher of the special class becomes fourfold: (1) he must teach job information, especially dealing with the larger vocational areas; (2) he must bring the individuals in his group to an understanding of their abilities and limitations in relation to various job qualifications and requirements; (3) he must organize a school program that will develop the general skills needed in future occupations; and (4) he must aid the guidance counselor to understand the children, their special problems, and their abilities in relation to job placement.

Thus far it has been assumed that the school has a guidance program which may be expanded to help the mentally handicapped group. If this is not the case, the teacher of the mentally handicapped must function as the guidance counselor. This will include surveying the community for jobs available, making employer contacts, gathering job information, doing job placement, and fnally following up individuals placed. Actually, he must take over all the functions of the counselor previously mentioned. The rest of the program to be outlined will be essentially the same for either organization.

The heart of the program for the mentally handicapped in the high school is one of general information, development of skills needed in broad vocational areas, and familiarizing the pupils with vocational possibilities. The experiences in occupational education are developed around community jobs. Trips are taken, during which various jobs are observed and analyzed in relation to the pupils' abilities. Supplementary information is obtained from pamphlets and books read and discussed in class. Questions answered are: (1) What jobs are available in the community? (2) What are the requirements, physical and educational, for the job? (3) Does one possess the necessary requirements for the job? (4) How much does the job pay? (5) How does one apply for a job? (6) Where does one apply for a job?

SUMMARY

(1) The secondary schools are becoming increasingly cognizant of their responsibility in providing for the adolescent mentally handicapped pupil.

(2) Varying organizations within the secondary schools have been evolved to cope with the problem of the adolescent mentally handicapped pupil. These organizations include (*a*) "watering down" the traditional secondary school curriculum, (*b*) remedial classes, and (*c*) special classes of different types.

(3) The curriculum best suited to the adolescent mentally handicapped pupil has been presented in terms of (*a*) areas of experience and (*b*) personal guidance.

(4) The areas of experience are grouped around (*a*) home-building, (*b*) occupational education, (*c*) societal relationships, and (*d*) physical and mental health.

(5) Personal guidance includes guidance in (*a*) the tool subjects, (*b*) personal problems, and (*c*) the occupational area.

REFERENCES

Hill, Arthur S. "Special Education in the Secondary Schools," *Journal of Exceptional Children*, 13 (April, 1947), pp. 93–97.

Kirk, Samuel A., G. Orville Johnson, Martha E. Black, Russel M. Duffin, and Ivan K. Garrison. *Educating the Mentally Handicapped in the Secondary Schools*. Illinois Secondary Curriculum Program, published by the Superintendent of Public Instruction, Springfield, Illinois, 1951.

Lovell, Catherine, and Christine P. Ingram. "A High School Program for Mentally Retarded Girls," *Journal of Educational Research*, 40 (April, 1947), pp. 574–582.

NEA Research Division, "High School Methods with Slow Learners,"

Research Bulletin of the National Education Association, 21, No. 3. Washington, D.C.: Research Division of the National Education Association, 1943.

Shores, J. Harlan. *A Critical Review of the Research on Elementary School Curriculum Organization*. College of Education, Bureau of Research and Service, University of Illinois Bulletin, 47, No. 8 (September, 1949).

Spears, Harold. *The Emerging High School Curriculum*. New York: American Book Company, 1940.

The Illinois Plan for Special Education of Exceptional Children: The Educable Mentally Handicapped, Circular Series "B," No. 12. Springfield, Illinois: Superintendent of Public Instruction, Revised, 1950.

Wright, G. S. *Core Curriculum in Public High Schools*, Bulletin No. 5. Federal Security Agency, Washington, D.C.: Office of Education, 1950.

Chapter 11

A Postschool Program

Need for a Postschool Program

In most states the mentally handicapped may leave school upon reaching the age of sixteen. Present school programs assume that these children are slow learners up to this age, but upon dropping out of school, they are expected to become "average learners" in real life situations. Thus, children who need more education over extended periods are actually receiving less attention and shorter school experience than more capable students who remain in school throughout the high school years. They are expected to adjust to the community socially and economically. They are expected to behave as adults, to adjust satisfactorily to social situations and groups, and in general to be able to conduct themselves and their affairs with little or no help.

In a few more years the majority of them will be married, have homes, and be expected to care for their families. Society is expecting these persons to be responsible for not only themselves but also for their families. They are given no special aid in making these adjustments, however, but must "sink or swim" on their own merits and abilities.

The schools have recognized the mentally handicapped child's

226

inability to adjust to the curriculum of the regular classroom. As a consequence, special classes are being organized in more and more communities to provide a program that is not just slowed down but is also designed to meet the children's needs. It is unrealistic to presuppose that because a child has been a member of a special class for eight or ten years, this special program has corrected his basic difficulty — the inability to learn as much in a specified period of time as the average person. Logically, one would expect the mentally handicapped adult to continue to be slow in learning a job, slow in adjusting to social situations, slow in adjusting to change, and restricted in the type of position he can hold.

In spite of this, the mentally handicapped have usually been required to adjust in the postschool world with no special provisions being made for their limited abilities and ineptitudes. They are competing for jobs and status with persons of normal or average intelligence. Their disabilities are neither known nor recognized by their employers and the community in general. If they do not and cannot adjust and achieve at expected standards they are discharged from their positions or "made to pay for their mistakes." They must shift for themselves in an environment designed for adults with capacities far beyond their limited abilities to achieve.

Vocational Adjustment

In 1923 and 1924, Channing [1] made a study of the employment records of mentally handicapped adults who had attended special classes. She found that their unemployment was slightly greater than that of unselected groups of workers.

The majority of the boys and girls in the present study had been out of work at least 20 per cent of their possible working periods. Twenty per cent of the boys and 34 per cent of the girls from special classes had been out of work half the time compared with 8 per cent of the boys and 11 per cent of the girls of unselected mentality included in a Children's Bureau study of employed minors between 15 and 18 years of age in Mil-

[1] Channing, Alice, *Employment of Mentally Deficient Boys and Girls.* United States Department of Labor, Bureau Publication No. 210. Washington, D.C.: Government Printing Office, 1932.

waukee. Only 29 per cent of the boys and 26 per cent of the girls of subnormal mentality had been unemployed less than one-tenth of the time contrasted with 63 per cent of the Milwaukee boys and the same proportion of the Milwaukee girls. Employed children included in two other studies made by the Children's Bureau in Boston and in Connecticut likewise were unemployed a smaller proportion of the part of their industrial lives covered by these studies than the young persons of the present study.

Kennedy,[2] in a more recent study, found similar vocational adjustments among a mentally handicapped group, although her comparisons were made with a restricted group of workers chosen on the basis of similar sex, age, nativity, religion, and nationality rather than with an unselected group. She found somewhat more unemployment due to physical reasons, more unskilled laborers, and poorer work ratings among the mentally handicapped group than among the control group.

KINDS OF EMPLOYMENT

Keys and Nathan [3] made a comparative study of 610 specialclass children from the San Francisco schools. They found that only one in eight of the positions held by men and one in fourteen of the positions held by women were above the unskilled labor level. Factories employed the largest groups — 21.4 per cent of the men and 39.5 per cent of the women. From this study they concluded that the skills required and number of occupations represented were so large that it is very doubtful whether public schools should provide specific vocational training.

In re-analyzing the data of Keys and Nathan, Smith [4] concluded that there seems to be no general occupational or industrial field in which there are no jobs the mentally handicapped worker cannot perform. They can perform in occupations in which there is a well-defined routine and which require physical strength, endurance, and simple manipulation.

[2] Kennedy, Ruby Jo Reeves, *The Social Adjustment of Morons in a Connecticut City.* Hartford, Connecticut: Mansfield-Southbury Training Schools Social Service Department, State Office Building, 1948.

[3] Keys, Noel, and J. M. Nathan, "Occupations for the Mentally Handicapped," *Journal of Applied Psychology,* 16, 1932, pp. 497–511.

[4] Smith, John Allan, "Areas of Occupational Opportunity for the Mentally Handicapped." Unpublished Study, Los Angeles Harbor Junior College.

In 1943, a survey of the employment obtained by 302 former special class pupils in Detroit showed the following:

Of this group, 194 (64 per cent) were doing unskilled work; 105 (35 per cent) had semiskilled jobs; and only 5 men were engaged in what could be classified as skilled labor. Almost one-half of the group were doing some type of factory work; the next largest group helped in stores, restaurants, laundries, and gas stations; 11 worked in stock rooms and only two did clerical work. Thirteen of the women were married and 16 women worked at housework for others.[5]

Channing [6] found that the majority of the mentally handicapped started work as semiskilled factory operatives in occupations classified as manufacturing and mechanical. Other trades in which the mentally handicapped boys were commonly employed were transportation and clerical. The majority of the girls who did not enter factories were employed in personal and domestic service. Some of the girls found positions working in stores or doing errands.

The principal industries employing the mentally handicapped boys were metal, shoe, paper-box, button, candy, tobacco, furniture and woodworking, and automobile. In these they did a large variety of hand and machine jobs. The trades and transportation area provided them with such jobs as drivers, drivers' helpers, newsboys, peddlers, and helpers in stores and markets. The girls found positions in such industries as garment, food, button, chemical, metal, paper-box, shoe, furniture, and printing. The next most important area of occupations for girls was in domestic and personal service, where they obtained such positions as maids, general housework, caring for children, ironing, restaurant work, elevator operators, dishwashers, general cleaning in hospitals, and so forth.

Kennedy [7] found that the mentally handicapped boys were predominantly employed in semiskilled labor, followed by unskilled

[5] *Vocational Rehabilitation of the Mentally Retarded*, Salvatore G. DiMichael, ed. Rehabilitation Service Series No. 123. Federal Security Agency, Office of Vocational Rehabilitation. Washington, D.C.: Government Printing Office, 1950, p. 86.
[6] Channing, *op. cit.*   [7] Kennedy, *op. cit.*

labor, skilled labor, personal service, clerical-sales, and agriculture. The mentally handicapped girls were predominantly employed in semiskilled, unskilled, skilled, personal service, and domestic service.

The War Manpower Commission, in a pamphlet on the employment and placement of the handicapped, provides the following description of the occupational potentialities for the mentally retarded.

Applicants with low-grade mentalities need not be considered handicapped if they have already built up adequate qualifying experience in an occupation. Inexperienced applicants, however, will need Selective Placement in suitable, simple jobs until they have built up their work experience. Recent studies indicate that the mentally retarded need not necessarily be limited to *repetitive* tasks. Once learned, *varied*, simple tasks may prove more suitable for some persons.

Close and constant supervision may be a necessary factor in the proper adjustment of the individual on the job. In all likelihood, the lower the mental age of the applicant, the closer and more constant the supervision required. The mentally retarded apparently do their best work and remain at a more equable emotional level when working immediately under the supervision of a patient, tolerant person whom they can respect. In many instances, it may help the supervisor to know that some mentally retarded people learn better by observing a *demonstration* of the job than by following only verbal or written instructions.

Other factors which interviewers will particularly check include:
1. Working with or around others, or alone.
2. Mechanical or electrical hazards which the applicant can understand.
3. Working speed.

Some mentally retarded people verbalize easily. This facility is misleading and should not be made the basis for recommendations for continuing formal education. However, this glibness may frequently be used occupationally.

In certain municipalities throughout the country, specialized educational programs have successfully prepared the mentally retarded for employment by making them aware of their limitations so that they may make realistic job choices; equipping them with occupational skills within suitable job areas such as food preparation and serving, building maintenance, personal service (beauty parlor, barber shop, domestic service, cleaning and pressing), and the like; encouraging the development of character traits that facilitate job holding; drilling in methods of job getting and holding.[8]

The most surprising part of the studies evaluating the employment of the mentally handicapped is the relatively good adjustment made by many of them. Kennedy [9] found that in most respects, there was no statistically significant difference between the vocational characteristics of the mentally handicapped and control groups. These characteristics included the proportion of each group employed, never employed, self-supporting, and length of time on a single job.

FACTORS DETERMINING VOCATIONAL ADJUSTMENT

Studies of the economic adjustment of the mentally handicapped indicate that a large majority of them enter industry or obtain some type of a job for varying lengths of time. It is surprising that many make good adjustments in spite of the lack of occupational training, vocational guidance, and a planned postschool program. The question then arises, "Why are there many others who do not hold their jobs and maintain economic independence?"

Psychologists, educators, and others who work with the mentally handicapped agree that traits other than intelligence are influential in determining the mentally handicapped individual's success. Among these are character, personality, and type of intelligence, as indicated to some extent on differences of performance on verbal and performance types of intelligence tests.

According to Channing,

The importance of special aptitude for handwork in industrial success is indicated by the fact that boys and girls who had done well and had been in the upper grades in manual training and other kinds of handwork taught in the special classes were more likely to be successful in their jobs after they left school than those who had done poor work and had been in the lower grades. Boys and girls who had done good work in industrial subjects had had less unemployment on the whole, had held their positions

[8] *Selective Placement for the Handicapped.* War Manpower Commission. United States Employment Service, Washington, D.C. Revised February, 1945.
[9] Kennedy, *op. cit.*

longer, were earning better wages in their last jobs, and had had greater increases in pay after they entered industry than those who had done poor work in special class subjects.[10]

In cases in which the mentally handicapped either fail to obtain positions or fail to hold them, it is seldom because of their inability to perform the actual job to the satisfaction of the employer. It is usually because of lack of punctuality, absenteeism, failure to adjust to fellow employees or to the employer, inability to take responsibility, indifference, unreliability, and various types of personality handicaps.

What then are the factors enabling the mentally handicapped to make an economic adjustment and success? "The ability to get along with co-workers, job interest, desire for more than adequacy of performance, dependability, and cheerful acceptance of criticism seem to be the traits employers seek." [11] These are characteristics emphasized in the special class curriculum and if understood and practiced by the children in school should aid in their postschool adjustment.

SOCIAL ADJUSTMENT

Kennedy [12] found the marital adjustment of the mentally handicapped and the control groups very similar. They married at approximately the same ages and had the same number of children. However, there were more divorces and more step and adopted children among the mentally handicapped than among the non-mentally-handicapped. She also found that the mentally handicapped get into more trouble with the police and commit more antisocial acts than the non-mentally-handicapped. The mentally handicapped have more court records, are more often penalized by jail sentences and commitments to various types of state institutions, and commit a greater variety of crimes.

Social adjustment also includes leisure time activities and activi-

[10] Channing, *op. cit.*, p. 69.
[11] Johnson, G. O., "Guidance for the Mentally Handicapped," *Journal of Exceptional Children*, 16 (January, 1950), p. 104.
[12] Kennedy, *op. cit.*

ties in which groups participate. In this relation, Kennedy found that the mentally handicapped did not participate as much in social activities. Fewer of the mentally handicapped were members of social organizations and various civic groups, and fewer recognized or exercised the civic responsibility at the polls; relatively few of them voted in elections for public officials.

POSTSCHOOL PROVISIONS

Following the actual termination of formal schooling and during the final phases of their schooling, there are a number of methods and agencies that may be used to provide the mentally handicapped with the necessary counseling and training to aid them in their economic adjustment. This counseling and training may be provided through the public schools in an adult education program, through special sections of vocational school classes under the Smith-Hughes Act, in an adult distributive education program under the George-Dean Act, and through Public Law 113 (Borden-LaFollette Act), which extended the program of Civilian Vocational Rehabilitation.

PUBLIC SCHOOL ADULT EDUCATION PROGRAM

The need for an adult education program is being recognized in many communities. Vocational agriculture has been carrying on programs of this type in many areas. If there is a need for this kind of a program for persons of normal intelligence, it hardly needs to be said that the mentally handicapped have an even greater need for it.

The adult education program for the mentally handicapped would be an extension of the work-school-experience program recommended for the secondary schools. To such a class or group of classes the mentally handicapped could bring their problems of adjustment to the requirements of industry and society. The curriculum would consist of evolving methods (with students and teachers working together) for solving these problems. The school shops could be used to aid in finding solutions to industrial problems while the sociodrama (see Chapter 15) is a suggested technique that might be used to solve those problems in the area of social relations.

VOCATIONAL SCHOOL PROGRAM

The vocational schools often provide evening courses for adults who desire to learn a trade or to become more proficient in the trade they are practicing. Special sections could be devoted to the industrial needs of the mentally handicapped. Instead of teaching trades specifically, the mentally handicapped adult would be taught the necessary basic and fundamental skills required in his semi-skilled or unskilled occupation. The care of tools, neatness, names and use of basic tools, and so forth would be stressed.

In addition, most of the larger vocational schools have a group of vocational counselors and advisers. One of them, with an understanding of the problems of the mentally handicapped, could be assigned as a counselor for that group. He would discuss the problems with employers and teachers, in this way coordinating the school and industrial experiences.

One phase of vocational education which has received notice through separate legislation, and which may be an area in which some of the mentally handicapped will be working, is Distributive Education. The purpose of adult Distributive Education is to impart "facts and skills to distributive workers to enable them to better perform their present tasks. . . ." [13] Those eligible for the adult program must be over sixteen years of age and employed, have been employed, or have definite promise of employment in a distributive occupation. There is also a Distributive Education program for high-school students that resembles the work-school-experience program described later in this chapter, except that it is confined to distributive industries and jobs alone.

The program of instruction consists of subjects which will improve the skill, knowledge, occupational information, and judgment of workers engaged in that type of work. Any subject which can be shown to improve the distribution of goods and services, sales,

[13] *Distributive Education Cooperative Part-Time Programs.* Misc. Business No. 2. Springfield, Illinois: Business Education Service, Board for Vocational Education, August, 1949.

production, preparation, and personnel problems may be approved. The courses are not on a theoretical plane but designed to give the workers information concerning their daily jobs. The courses may be organized for any length of time depending upon the information and skills to be taught and the time necessary to teach them.

VOCATIONAL REHABILITATION PROGRAM

On July 6, 1943, Public Law 113 was passed permitting the Civilian Vocational Rehabilitation program to offer its services, which were previously confined to the physically handicapped, to the mentally handicapped. The services thus offered were slow to be accepted. On the status of vocational rehabilitation for the mentally handicapped, DiMichael stated:

The statistics on civilian rehabilitation closures during the last three years reflects a serious inattention to the rightful needs of the intellectually handicapped. This group represented only 9/10 of 1 per cent of the rehabilitated employed closures in 1948 (479 cases), only 7/10 of 1 per cent in 1947 (299 cases), only 5/10 of 1 per cent in 1946, and only 3/10 of 1 per cent in 1945. These percentages look pale when it is considered that national estimates place the seriously mentally retarded at six million as compared to the total blind population at 230,000 and the seriously deaf and hard of hearing at 1,915,800. And yet, for the year 1948, 4.8 per cent of the rehabilitation closures were blind cases, and 8.5 per cent were deaf and hard of hearing.[14]

Under Public Law 113 no specific standards of eligibility for any handicapped group have been issued. Who shall be trained or receive treatment is dependent upon the program of the State agencies.

Essentially, the criteria of eligibility are basically simple. In order for an individual to be considered eligible, (1) he should be of working age, (2) he must have a substantial disability which results in an employment handicap, and (3) a reasonable chance must be evident that the individual will become employable or be able to secure a more suitable job through the rehabilitation services.[15]

[14] DiMichael, Salvatore G. "The State-Federal Program of Vocational Rehabilitation for the Mentally Retarded," *American Journal of Mental Deficiency*, 54 (October, 1949), pp. 230–231.
[15] *Ibid.*, p. 232.

To prepare the individual for employment, the Civilian Rehabilitation Program is prepared to make the following services available to any client and at no cost if he is unable to meet the cost.

(1) Medical and psychological examination and diagnosis.

(2) Counseling and guidance.

(3) Medical, surgical, hospital, and psychiatric care and treatment.

(4) Hearing aids, glasses, artificial limbs and the like.

(5) Occupational training in schools or on-the-job.

(6) Maintenance and transportation while the individual is receiving treatment or is in training.

(7) Tools, equipment, licenses, and other items that may be needed to give the handicapped person a fair start on the job.

(8) Placement on the right job.

(9) Follow-up after job placement.

A law offering rehabilitation services to the mentally handicapped was in effect for almost a decade before it began to function. Educators, psychologists, and vocational counselors realize the need for such services. Yet there are only a few scattered communities that have attempted to make use of them. Minneapolis, Cincinnati, New York, Detroit, and the Caswell Training School at Kinston, North Carolina, are about the only ones that have made any serious effort to co-ordinate the work of the schools and of the local rehabilitation agency. In these areas the rehabilitation counselor either contacts the mentally handicapped individuals some time before they leave the special classes or the mentally handicapped are referred to the local agency upon leaving school.

The vocational rehabilitation programs as reported by the various communities, appear to differ in their implementation of the law. None seem completely satisfied with present arrangements. This may be due to lack of personnel to co-ordinate the school and rehabilitation programs. It also may be due to lack of personnel trained in vocational counseling and placement of the mentally handicapped. Whatever the reason may be, it behooves the schools to investigate the possibilities of making full use of the Civilian Vocational Rehabilitation Agency to further the postschool program for the mentally handicapped.

New York program. In New York the mentally handicapped youth are referred to the State Rehabilitation Agency by the public employment service, the schools, family agencies, hospital and health agencies, and so forth. A study was made of the services requested by the clients and their parents, by other agencies referring the cases, and the services rehabilitation counselors felt were most needed. These services and results as reported by Rockower [16] were:

(1) Vocational counseling — (given to all cases referred but proved to be of help only to those with good employment prognosis and in need of little training.)

(2) Job placement — (requested by the majority of the cases but of value to about half of them.)

(3) Vocational training — (few places were found for the type of training needed.)

(4) General academic training — (requested by about one-third of the cases and provided for a few through night school. Most of those requesting this service were actually unable to profit by additional academic work.)

(5) Sheltered workshop — (felt necessary for most of the cases but the services were not available.)

(6) Placement training — (help needed in areas of simple, routine, "helper" type jobs.)

(7) Family case work — (requested by few but needed by the majority of the cases. In many instances the family was the primary problem.)

(8) Organized recreation — (leisure time activities needed for the majority of the cases.)

(9) Psychiatric diagnosis and therapy — (needed by only a few of the cases.)

(10) Psychological evaluation — (seldom requested but needed by all cases to provide the counselors with the necessary information.)

[16] Rockower, Leonard W., "A Study of Mentally Retarded Applicants for Vocational Rehabilitation in New York City," in *Vocational Rehabilitation of the Mentally Retarded*, S. G. DiMichael, ed., *op. cit.*, pp. 108–139.

(11) Medical, surgical, and artificial appliances — (multiple handicaps not uncommon but few requiring major help.)

(12) Personal adjustment training — (requested by no cases but needed by 6.5 per cent.)

(13) Institutional or custodial care — (unable to make a community adjustment. Requested by no cases but needed by 2.5 per cent.)

Rockower summarized the study of the New York program, emphasizing a number of problems that must be solved in order to reduce the gap between present vocational resources and vocational needs of the mentally handicapped. These are:

(1) The mentally handicapped persons are referred to the Vocational Rehabilitation Agency from a large number and variety of community agencies, indicating the extent of the problem.

(2) The typical applicant has left school recently but his training has apparently been of little value to him for making an economic and social adjustment in the community.

(3) About one-half of the applicants have secondary disabilities (physical, social immaturity, and so forth) whose implications have not been fully recognized and understood by referring agencies.

(4) The services requested by clients and parents often did not coincide with the actual needs of the clients as indicated by a vocational appraisal by a trained counselor.

(5) Many mentally handicapped youth are unable to take their place in the community because of lack of adequate community agency services and vocational preparatory resources.

(6) At present, the New York City Rehabilitation Agency is the main community agency providing services to meet the vocational needs of the mentally handicapped. These services should be expanded in other community agencies.

(7) The New York City Rehabilitation Agency has increased the job stability of the mentally handicapped persons with whom they could work and provide necessary service.

(8) The Rehabilitation Agency has encouraged and stimulated the use of its services by other community agencies, employers, and parent groups.

(9) It was found that a large number of the mentally handicapped had been inadequately prepared by the school and parents to make adult adjustments.

(10) There is need for close co-operation between the school and the Rehabilitation Agency.

(11) Parents of mentally handicapped children should be referred to the family case-work agencies as early as possible because they have frequently proved to be the major problem in vocational planning with their children since they often fail to accept the child's disabilities.

(12) Sheltered workshops and other occupational training resources are acutely needed.

(13) Professional groups, the general public, and industry need to be made aware of this potential worker resource.

Michigan Program. One of the earliest programs attempted in Michigan is known as the Jackson Experiment. The work was done in connection with the Coldwater Home and Training School. The program was greatly needed because of the overcrowded conditions at the institution. The State Vocational Rehabilitation program for the mentally handicapped has been used more extensively in Detroit and Wayne County, however. Children, fifteen years ten months and over, are referred to the Rehabilitation Agency by the schools. From there on, the Rehabilitation Agency takes over the responsibility for the mentally handicapped youth's training, counseling, and placement, as in the New York program.

Potts [17] summarized the experience of the Michigan Office of Vocational Rehabilitation in serving the mentally handicapped and drew the following tentative conclusions:

(1) The program is limited because of lack of funds and personnel.

(2) Counselors with special training seem most successful in working with the mentally handicapped.

(3) The most suitable method of training the mentally handicapped youth has been found to be on-the-job training.

[17] Potts, Jane H., "Vocational Rehabilitation for the Mentally Retarded in Michigan," in *Vocational Rehabilitation of the Mentally Retarded*, S. G. DiMichael, ed., *op. cit.*, pp. 140–165.

(4) The mentally handicapped group requires more counselor's time per case than most of the other handicapped groups.

(5) The rehabilitation program is emphasizing services for the group of mentally handicapped youth during the transition period from school to initial employment.

(6) The effectiveness of the rehabilitation program is dependent upon the total community and interested agencies accepting and sharing the responsibility.

(7) Selected institutional referrals seem to make better adjustments than mass referrals from schools, employment services, and other agencies.

(8) Socialization and personal adjustment seem to be a greater determinant in predicting success on a job than an I.Q. rating.

(9) The majority of the mentally handicapped youth have been placed in unskilled and personal service jobs.

(10) Occasionally a mentally handicapped youth with high manual dexterity may be successful in a skilled occupation.

(11) Repetitive jobs seem to be best suited to the mentally handicapped.

(12) The vocational rehabilitation of the mentally retarded seems to require greater intensification of the counselor's efforts and greater skills in the following phases of rehabilitation: personal counseling, family relations, psychological evaluation, job analysis, employer education, and follow-up.[18]

Minneapolis Program. The Vocational Rehabilitation program in Minneapolis was developed as a result of the recognition of the need for a program to bridge the gap between school and the mentally handicapped person taking his place in society. The Vocational Rehabilitation Agency does not train the mentally handicapped but depends upon community facilities for this service for providing work for them.

The Vocational Rehabilitation Agency receives the names of the mentally handicapped youth as they approach the age of sixteen years. These clients are then tested and an evaluation is made of their abilities and potentialities. For those that qualify, adapted subjects and shop courses have been established in the Vocational

[18] *Ibid.*, p. 165.

High School. No student is placed in this special program without the recommendation of a vocational rehabilitation counselor. Those that are approved are placed in a specific program on the basis of interest and aptitude.

After a student has been in the program for one, two, or three years, an effort is made to secure employment for him. In some cases, the mentally handicapped youth may return to school for necessary additional training. Thus we see that the program is closely co-ordinated with the schools.

On the basis of experience with the Minneapolis program Haasarud and Moore [19] have made a number of general comments that are much broader than the specific problem of vocational rehabilitation.

Judging from the interests and aptitudes which the older mentally retarded students in the Minneapolis Public Schools were found to have, and judging also from the progress which they made when placed in a type of training which was in line with their interests and aptitudes, it would seem that a great number of them could become well-adjusted, self-supporting members of society. It must be borne in mind that they cannot be regarded as a homogeneous group, but must be treated as individuals. It must also be remembered that each individual is a complex human being possessing many potentialities, and that no person rates uniformly high or low in all of them. An intelligence quotient of 80 is used as the dividing line between the normal and the mentally retarded groups in the Minneapolis schools, but when compared on such items as personality, skill, and performance, the groups are found to divide quite differently. This indicates that the mentally retarded need not be segregated from others so far as either their educational or vocational life is concerned. They need to learn to take their places in the world with all other individuals, and in order to do this they need instruction in the same phases of life as do other persons. Since their learning ability is limited in certain areas, it means that the instruction must be adapted to their level if they are to benefit from it. It does not mean that they should remain untaught.

The general areas in which it seems necessary that all persons have an opportunity to develop to the fullest extent of their ability are in personal qualities, academic subjects, and trade knowledge and skill. Personal

[19] Haasarud, Florence I., and Sara W. Moore, "Vocational Rehabilitation and Education for the Mentally Retarded in Minneapolis," in *Vocational Rehabilitation of the Mentally Retarded*, S. G. DiMichael, ed., *op. cit.*, pp. 166–184.

qualities include such matters as management of money, use of leisure time, ability to cooperate and adjust to one's surroundings, knowledge of acceptable dress and actions, and willingness to accept criticism. A boy may be well trained in a trade and capable of holding a job, but if he is not capable of managing his personal life, he will not be a satisfactory employee or a good citizen. If his home has not provided him with this background, the school or community will have to do so. Supervision outside of working hours may be needed to help the boy do better work during working hours.

In the academic line the mentally retarded need all the basic knowledge they can acquire. Their ability is limited, it is true, but in many cases even that limit has never been reached. Since their rate of learning is slow, a great deal of special attention needs to be given to them if they are to reach their limit. Some of the material considered as basic for other students may be omitted from the program of the mentally retarded, but there is academic work connected with various jobs which these students particularly need to learn.

In vocational training there should be an opportunity for mentally retarded persons to learn some of the specific skills connected with a trade even though they are not capable of learning the entire trade. Girls who can sew a straight seam are employable even though they do not know the needlework trade. Boys who learn to bind books can earn a living without being master printers. There are some who make good routine typists and general office clerks without learning shorthand and bookkeeping.

All of these areas need to be considered in the education and rehabilitation of the mentally retarded. There is a need for a large number of specific courses at the junior and senior high school levels in all of the areas discussed above. Although the main emphasis of the program so far may seem to be trade training, this alone is not sufficient. The employee, no matter how skilled, who cannot fit into a job situation will not be employable. Plans are now under way to develop courses in some of these other areas, although specific details have not yet been worked out. [20]

The School's Responsibility

The postschool program is a natural outgrowth of the secondary program. It should be a part of, not apart from, the total educational and guidance program for mentally handicapped children and youth. The educational and guidance program described in the pre-

[20] *Ibid.*, pp. 183–184.

ceding chapters is envisioned as one that begins when the pupil walks into the special class for the first time. It does not end, however, when he walks out of the room or is graduated. It should continue for as long as the student or former student has need for it, i.e., until he has demonstrated ability to adjust socially and economically in the community. In this connection, Engel states:

> There is probably no aspect of education of mentally retarded children which is more important than that which concerns itself with the social and occupational adjustment in adult life. Every teacher in special education is concerned with the end result of his training and struggles to prepare his young people so that when they leave school, they will be able to adjust successfully to jobs, to home life, and to their own social group.
>
> Changing social conditions make it increasingly difficult to place boys and girls under sixteen years of age on jobs. This means that the school must not only have a longer program but it must have a different type of program. Not only need the schools be concerned with physical maturity but they must be concerned with social and emotional maturity.[21]

If school experiences are not carried into the mentally handicapped individual's occupational or vocational and social life, he is being expected to do the very thing in which he is known to be the weakest. Without help he is expected to transfer skills and information acquired in school to life situations. An additional complicating factor is also introduced when it is necessary for him to make this transfer and adjustment outside the protected environment of the home and school. He must adjust in competition with adults of normal intelligence, a group with whom he has never been able to compete on equal terms either in the school or in the community.

Since the school has been responsible for the training of mentally handicapped children from the time they enter (at about the age of six years) until they may leave (at about the age of sixteen years in most states), it seems only logical that the school expand its functions to include the postschool adjustment period. This period would start at the time the mentally handicapped youth may legally leave school until he has made an economic and social adjustment in the community.

[21] Engel, Anna M., "Employment of the Mentally Retarded," in *Vocational Rehabilitation of the Mentally Retarded*, S. G. DiMichael, ed., *op. cit.*, p. 80.

The school is in an ideal position to develop a postschool program for a number of reasons. (1) The school has been in contact with the children for a number of years and being responsible for their training is well acquainted with individual abilities, personalities, and specific training that has been provided. (2) The school has trained personnel (special class teachers, psychologists, and counselors) available to provide the necessary services. (3) The school has the necessary training facilities (various shops in the secondary and vocational schools to provide needed specific supplementary training).

The precedent for a postschool program has already been established. Many communities are providing adult education courses in numerous areas of interest and need. They are not, however, designed to benefit the mentally handicapped. Secondary schools and vocational schools are providing counseling and guidance and placement services. Again, they are not designed to benefit the mentally handicapped. To encourage the organization of a postschool program for mentally handicapped youth, a number of states will provide some financial support for such a program that extends beyond the compulsory school age.[22]

This section will describe a postschool program that may be adapted to most community situations. Since facilities and organizations differ from community to community, it is impossible to describe a specific program that will fit them all. The program should be adapted according to the specific community's needs, facilities, and so forth.

A postschool program should include (1) a school-work-experience program, (2) a job placement program, (3) a further training program, and (4) a follow-up program. These four areas should not be separate entities but should be integrated and available whenever the need arises. For clarity of description, however, they will be described separately.

---

[22] The Illinois law provides for education of the mentally handicapped to the age of 21 years. Graham, Ray, *The Educable Mentally Handicapped*, Circular Series "B," No. 12. Issued by Vernon L. Nickell, Superintendent of Public Instruction, Springfield, Ill., revised, 1950, p. 25.

SCHOOL-WORK-EXPERIENCE PROGRAM

As a pupil approaches the age at which he will be leaving school, the "school-work-experience" plan is probably the best method of preparing him to make the transition from a protected home and school environment to the more competitive environment of the community. This plan should include part-time employment for the pupils (similar to an on-the-job training program). The school will also find it necessary to provide guidance for both the employers and employees if the program is to be of maximum value.

The mentally handicapped youth, in a postschool program, should attend school part of the time and work on a job part of the time. For those in charge of the postschool program, the school-work-experience program should consist of three phases: (1) a survey of part-time work opportunities, (2) job placement, and (3) a co-ordinated class and work program.

A survey of part-time work opportunities. This should be made by the special-class teacher or the school vocational counselor. If the special-class teacher is to be responsible for this survey, he should be given time during the school day to carry out these duties. If a counselor is responsible for this phase, he needs to co-ordinate his efforts very closely with those of the special-class teacher.

Jobs may be available in the school, local industry, stores, restaurants, hotels, and so forth. Some examples of jobs that can be done on a part-time basis are busboys, stockboys, cleaners, cafeteria helpers, and helpers to workmen in factories and trades (wood, metal, garment, and so forth).

Job placement. The thing that should be watched in locating jobs and placing the mentally handicapped youth on them are: (1) that the employer and employees understand what the capabilities of the mentally handicapped youth are; (2) that the job is within the abilities of the mentally handicapped youth; (3) that the mentally handicapped youth is not taken advantage of (low wages, extra work, and so forth); (4) that the placement be made primarily on the basis of the educational experiences it will provide the individual; and (5) that the mentally handicapped youth realizes that this job is a training opportunity and not necessarily a final job placement.

A co-ordinated class and work program. Three types of schools have the facilities necessary for a postschool program. They are (1) a regular high school, (2) a vocational high school, and (3) a Smith-Hughes vocational school. The type of program should be essentially the same regardless of the type of school in which the postschool program is located. It is essential, however, that the teachers be trained to work with the mentally handicapped, that the counselors understand the special problems connected with the mentally handicapped youth's vocational placement and adjustment, and that the facilities of the school are available for almost unlimited use for the program.

The school program should be designed on an individual basis, taking into consideration (1) the job placement, (2) the interests, (3) the abilities (academic or vocational skills), and (4) the needs of the mentally handicapped youth. For the mentally handicapped individual who has acquired all the academic skills necessary or that he is capable of acquiring, the emphasis should be placed upon the acquisition of vocational and social skills. He should probably spend most of his school time in selected shops. For other mentally handicapped youth, the emphasis may be placed upon the application of necessary academic skills.

The school-work-experience program for the older mentally handicapped youth gives the pupil a chance to apply the skills and attitudes developed in class situations. It also provides him with a class where he may bring his vocational problems and receive aid in solving them. Relating school training and actual work experience serves to motivate the pupils to establish patterns of desirable conduct, good work habits, and desire to learn needed skills. Social security, withholding tax, union dues, work permits, applications, and so forth are no longer abstractions. These are some of the things they are experiencing and desire to know more about.

JOB PLACEMENT PROGRAM

The job placement program may be the responsibility of either the special class teacher or a school counselor who has had training to work with mentally handicapped youth. The job placement develops from the school-work-experience program. When a mentally handicapped youth displays the ability to adjust to full-time employment, he should be helped to find a job that he is interested in and is capable of doing.

Here again the community survey of job opportunities is necessary. The actual placement may be accomplished through the state vocational rehabilitation agency, state or federal employment agency, or an employment agency in conjunction with the school. The postschool program for mentally handicapped youth should co-ordinate its program with all agencies that can contribute, because individual teachers and counselors cannot possibly replace all of the other agencies' functions.

Whatever person or agency is doing actual job placement, a list of cooperative and understanding employers is required. Care must be taken to place the youth where the demands will not be too great, where he will be given an opportunity to learn necessary skills, and where he will be treated fairly.

FURTHER TRAINING PROGRAM

Because a mentally handicapped youth has been placed on a full-time job does not mean that the job of the school is finished. It only means that the teacher and counselor think he has the necessary skills and knowledge to adjust. The school should always be open for the mentally handicapped youth to return for supplementary training. Either he or the employer may feel that he would make a better employee with additional training. In those cases, he should be encouraged to return to receive it.

The initiative should not rest with the mentally handicapped youth or the employer. As part of the "follow-up program," employees and employers should be visited regularly to determine the vocational adjustment. Where further training is indicated, it may take the form of night school classes in which the mentally handicapped youth may be enrolled. In more severe cases, it may be necessary to urge the youth to return to school full time for a period of time.

The further training program should be entirely individualized. Specific "lacks" have hindered the mentally handicapped youth from making an adequate adjustment. Specific experiences need to be provided to help him.

FOLLOW-UP PROGRAM

When a mentally handicapped youth has made the transition from the school-work-experience program to full-time employment it does not mean that the job of a complete, comprehensive postschool program is finished. Engel lists four reasons why a follow-up program is essential. They are:

First, youth should know that the counselor's interest in him is continuous and genuine; that he has a sympathetic friend who understands him and believes in his ability to hold a job.

Second, the employer should know that he can expect help from the counselor if the young man or woman is unsatisfactory. Sometimes a slight change in work makes for success instead of failure.

Third, the family should be counseled if the individual is unhappy or failing on the job. Many times the family interferes in making the job a success by belittling the work or finding fault because there are objectionable features, like dirty clothes.

Fourth, the school should know wherein it can improve its training and also wherein it has done a good job.[23]

Both the mentally handicapped youth and his employer should be visited periodically by the teacher or counselor to determine whether or not he is making a satisfactory vocational and social adjustment. As a result of the information acquired from the follow-up program, job changes may be made, employer understandings developed, and future school programs improved.

SUMMARY

The special class program for mentally handicapped children is designed to aid these children to become socially and economically competent adults. Throughout their schooling, attitudes, habits, skills, and information that will accomplish these objectives are stressed. The purpose of the postschool program is to help the mentally handicapped youth (1) to transfer the skills learned in school to community situations, and (2) to provide whatever supplementary training may be needed.

A number of community agencies are now available that may

[23] *Ibid.*, pp. 104–105.

provide some postschool training and counseling for the mentally handicapped youth who has completed his formal schooling. These agencies are (1) the public schools through an adult education program, (2) the Smith-Hughes vocational school program, and (3) the vocational rehabilitation program.

A postschool program for which the school is responsible has a number of advantages over any other postschool program because (1) the schools have trained personnel familiar with the problems of the mentally handicapped, (2) the schools are familiar with the problems of specific mentally handicapped children because they have worked with the children over a period of time, (3) the schools have shops and personnel to provide additional training that may be needed, and (4) the schools often have counseling service and placement service that may be expanded to include the mentally handicapped group.

A good postschool program should include (1) a school-work-experience program, (2) a job placement program, (3) a further training program, and (4) a follow-up program. The schools, however, should not attempt to provide all the services required by the mentally handicapped youth. The total program should be the responsibility of the school but vocational rehabilitation, employment services, family agencies, and so forth should be included.

REFERENCES

Bridges, Clark D. *Job Placement of the Physically Handicapped.* New York: McGraw-Hill Book Company, Inc., 1946.

Burr, Emily. "Prime Factors in the Placement of the Below Normal," *American Journal of Mental Deficiency*, 51 (January, 1947), pp. 429–434.

Channing, Alice. *Employment of Mentally Deficient Boys and Girls.* United States Department of Labor, Bureau Publication No. 210. Washington, D.C.: Government Printing Office, 1932.

Coakley, Frances. "Study of Feeble-Minded Wards Employed in War Industries," *American Journal of Mental Deficiency*, 50 (October, 1945), pp. 301–306.

DiMichael, Salvatore G. "Employment of the Mentally Retarded," *Journal of Rehabilitation*, May, 1949, pp. 3–7.

DiMichael, Salvatore G. "The State-Federal Program of Vocational Rehabilitation for the Mentally Retarded," *American Journal of Mental Deficiency*, 54 (October, 1949), pp. 230–236.

DiMichael, Salvatore G. (Editor). *Vocational Rehabilitation of the Mentally Retarded.* Rehabilitation Service Series No. 123. Federal Security Agency, Office of Vocational Rehabilitation. Washington, D.C.: Government Printing Office, 1950.

Engel, Anna M. "A Study of 3,169 Retarded Pupils in the Detroit Public Schools," *American Journal of Mental Deficiency*, 46 (January, 1942), pp. 395–401.

Johnson, G. Orville. "Guidance for the Mentally Handicapped," *Journal of Exceptional Children*, 16 (January, 1950), pp. 102–108.

Kennedy, Ruby Jo Reeves. *The Social Adjustment of Morons in a Connecticut City.* Hartford, Connecticut: Mansfield-Southbury Training Schools Social Service Department, State Office Building, 1948.

Keys, Noel, and J. M. Nathan. "Occupations for the Mentally Handicapped," *Journal of Applied Psychology*, 16, 1932, pp. 497–511.

McIntosh, W. J. "Follow-Up Study of One Thousand Non-Academic Boys," *Journal of Exceptional Children*, 15 (March, 1949), pp. 167–169.

Murray, Evelyn, and Salvatore G. DiMichael. "Employment for the Mentally Retarded," *Employment Security Review*, 17, No. 5 (May, 1950), pp. 30–32.

Shartle, Carroll L. *Occupational Information.* New York: Prentice-Hall, Inc., 1946.

Smith, John Allan. "Areas of Occupational Opportunity for the Mentally Handicapped." Unpublished Study, Los Angeles Harbor Junior College.

Yepsen, Lloyd N. "Subnormal Minds are Abler whan You Think," *Journal of Rehabilitation*, May, 1949, pp. 8–12.

Distributive Education Cooperative Part-time Programs. Miscellaneous Business No. 2. Springfield, Illinois: Business Education Service, Board for Vocational Education, August, 1949.

Selective Placement for the Handicapped. War Manpower Commission. United States Employment Service. Washington, D.C.: Government Printing Office. Revised February, 1945.

Vocational Rehabilitation of the Epileptic and the Mentally Retarded. Rehabilitation Service Series No. 56, OVR:33:56:A:30. Federal Security Agency, Office of Vocational Rehabilitation. Washington, D.C.: Government Printing Office, March, 1948.

PART FOUR

❧

Special Teaching Procedures

Chapter 12

Teaching Reading, Spelling, and Writing

READING

ALTHOUGH a strictly academic program for mentally handicapped children is generally discouraged, reading is one of the skills most emphasized in special classes. For that reason, and because of the difficulty which mentally handicapped children encounter in learning to read, it is important that a systematic plan of instruction be followed.

THE READING CAPACITY OF THE MENTALLY HANDICAPPED

An important question is, "Can mentally handicapped children learn to read, and how much?" This question can be answered specifically for each child only after a thorough diagnosis has been made. There are, however, generalizations which can be made concerning the educability of the majority of such children in reading.

The mental age of a child on a verbal intelligence test, such as the Binet, gives some indication of the child's potentiality in reading. Studies by Merrill,[1] Bennett,[2] and others show that on the

[1] Merrill, Maud A., "On the Relation of Intelligence to Achievement in Case of Mentally Retarded Children," *Comparative Psychology Monographs*, 2, No. 10 (September, 1924), pp. 1–100.
[2] Bennett, A., *A Comparative Study of Subnormal Children in the Elementary*

whole, mentally handicapped children learn to read up to their mental age reading grade expectancy, as do children of normal or superior intelligence. Although the mental age is not a perfect indicator of reading capacity, it is probably the most important single factor. In interpreting the mental age as a measure of reading grade expectancy, one can state that: all other factors being equal, the mental age is the best known measure of reading grade expectancy. Using the I.Q. of a child alone does not indicate the child's reading capacity or expectancy. A sixteen-year-old boy with an I.Q. of 60 will be reading more efficiently than a six-year-old boy with an I.Q. of 110. Thus it is apparent that the I.Q. is not a measure of reading grade expectancy.

As a basis of reference the following general guides will aid teachers in knowing what reading ability to expect of mentally handicapped children.

(1) Children with chronological ages seven to nine and with mental ages of four to six:

    (*a*) Have not begun to read.

    (*b*) Should be showing interest in reading, in books, and in pictures, in the interpretation of pictures, labels, their own names, and so forth.

    (*c*) Should be engaging in an intensive reading readiness program.

(2) Children of chronological ages nine to eleven and with mental ages of five and one-half years to seven years:

    (*a*) Should be having an intensive reading readiness program with incidental reading of charts, signs, labels, etc., if readiness is not adequate.

    (*b*) Should begin reading stories of their own experiences from the board and from charts if readiness is established.

    (*c*) Should be interested in drawing pictures, interpreting pictures, and reading and writing stories about these pictures.

    (*d*) Should be able to make booklets of their own stories that they have told and which they have read from charts.

Grades, Contributions to Education, No. 510. New York: Bureau of Publications, Teachers College, Columbia University, 1932.

(*e*) Should begin to read pre-primers, primers, and simple books.

(3) Children of chronological ages eleven to thirteen and with mental ages of seven to eight and one-half years:

(*a*) Should be reading first- to third-grade material with adequate understanding.

(*b*) Should be grouping words and phrases into thought units, but are slow in reading.

(*c*) Should be developing a method of word recognition and should be capable of recognizing new words from context clues, phonic analysis, and so forth.

(*d*) Should be interested in reading simple books for information and pleasure, and engaging in out-of-school reading such as newspapers, directions for games, and projects.

(4) Children of chronological ages thirteen to sixteen with mental ages of eight and one-half to eleven years:

(*a*) Should be utilizing reading for many activities and using books from third- through fifth-grade level.

(*b*) Should be using dictionary, telephone directory, library, and reading newspapers and maps.

(*c*) Should have increased vocabulary and fair comprehension with independent methods of word recognition.

(*d*) Should be spontaneously reading for information and pleasure.

Remedial cases. Children who are mentally handicapped can also be retarded below their capacities, and be considered remedial cases. If, for example, a mentally handicapped child has a mental age of nine, and is a nonreader, he may be considered a remedial case, in addition to his mental handicap. Such children have been reported by Hegge [3] and Kirk.[4]

Literacy. The Army, during World War II, set a fourth-grade criterion for literacy. Most of the mentally handicapped admitted

[3] Hegge, Thorleif G., "Special Reading Disability with Particular Reference to the Mentally Deficient," *American Association on Mental Deficiency*, 39 (May, 1934), pp. 297–343.

[4] Kirk, Samuel A., "Reading Aptitudes of Mentally Retarded Children," *American Association on Mental Deficiency*, 44, No. 2 (May, 1939) pp. 156–162.

to special classes can reach a third- to fifth-grade literacy standard. This is considered an important achievement for life adjustment and is worthy of sufficient effort in a classroom.

PRINCIPLES OF TEACHING READING

If mentally handicapped children could learn to read in the same way as, or at the rate of, average children, there would be no necessity for outlining a reading program for them. Since mentally handicapped children show both obvious and subtle differences as well as many similarities to normal children, it is necessary to analyze these differences and to adapt instruction in reading for them. Some of these differences are:

Chronological age. Mentally handicapped children do not have the capacity to learn to read at the life age of six or seven. When a mentally handicapped child is admitted to school at the age of six, he usually has a mental age of from approximately three to four and a half years. We do not expect an average child to learn to read at the life age of three and four, and it should not be expected that mentally handicapped children should learn at that mental age level. Although this fact is trite and obvious to teachers of the mentally handicapped, most school systems admit mentally handicapped children to school at the age of six, and present them with reading materials which they are expected to learn.

In terms of instructional procedure these facts mean that a mentally handicapped child whose life age may be six, seven, eight, or even nine, should not be introduced to a systematic reading program. He should be introduced to a reading readiness program. Such a program has been described in Chapter 8. This program harmonizes with the child's abilities and needs to a greater extent than does the traditional reading program offered to first- and second-grade youngsters.

Rate of learning. The learning rate of a mentally handicapped child is slower than that of an average child. Although studies have shown that a mentally handicapped child learns as rapidly as an average child of the same mental age, these studies refer to short periods of learning. For example, an average child whose life age is seven and whose mental age is seven, may learn at the same rate as a mentally handicapped child whose age is ten, and whose mental age is seven. But in one year the seven-year-old average child will have a mental age of eight. The mentally handicapped child, cited above, whose I.Q. is 70, will have a mental age of seven years and eight months, provided the I.Q. remains constant. This means that the average child, because of his more rapid mental growth, will now have learned, after one year, more than the mentally handicapped child.

In addition to slower mental growth, mentally handicapped children sometimes present observed qualitative and quantitative differences in learning ability. Some of these differences, which make learning to read a little different, are a certain stereotyped response to environmental stimuli, inability to evaluate and criticize their work (lack of auto-criticism), poorer ability to adapt to changes in instruction, poorer ability to generalize, reliance on concrete rather than abstract learning, and lower psychological abilities of language and perception. All these factors tend to make the mentally handicapped child slower in learning and poorer in retention in a reading situation.

The slower rate of learning and the other mental characteristics of mentally handicapped children require that the reading program be modified to fit these characteristics. A reading program should provide for prolonging the reading stage at each period of development in harmony with the slow rate of learning, presenting the materials in a variety of settings to avoid rigidity and stereotyped responses, and developing the reading process in a systematic fashion.

Need for success. When reading materials are presented to a mentally handicapped child before he is ready to learn, he experiences continued failure in a reading situation. Such experience, resulting in frustration and avoidance reactions, is not conducive to a desire for reading. It is consequently important that the confidence of the child be established and maintained in a reading situation. This is best done by showing the child success in a systematic program of instruction at his level and rate of reading. Mentally handicapped children can learn to read with pleasure providing the experience is not frustrating to them. In most cases they have been presented with reading materials long before they were ready to read and have developed a negativistic attitude toward reading.

Environment. The language and environmental background of many mentally handicapped children has been poorer than that of the average child. Likewise the experiential background has been meagre and restricted in many cases. Since reading requires an experience and language background, these lacks should be compensated for through school instruction and school experience. Planned activities, rather than reliance on incidental learnings, are necessary to upgrade mentally handicapped children in language and language concepts.

A READING PROGRAM

In designing a reading program for the mentally handicapped child, it is necessary to determine the kind and extent of program which will be within his abilities and at his level of development. If a child is mentally deficient or feeble-minded, for example, it would not be a worth-while project to launch an extensive program for his growth and development. A mentally deficient or feeble-minded child cannot learn to read beyond a few simple words for his protection, hence the reason for lack of emphasis on a systematic reading program in the sense in which reading is ordinarily defined.

A prognosis of the child's ultimate reading level, based upon observation and mental diagnosis, is necessary for each child before a reading program can be designed for him.

The mentally handicapped child, as stated earlier, is one who has been diagnosed as being partially educable in the academic sense, and whose ultimate limits of reading ability will reach between the third and the fifth grade. It is for this child that the following program is designed.

A reading program for the typical mentally handicapped child will necessarily follow several levels of instruction. In listing these it should be remembered that they are not specific stages but a continuation of various levels of achievement. These programs are: (1) a reading readiness program to prepare children for success in reading; (2) a prolonged beginning reading period which will give them a good start in reading; (3) a program which develops methods of word recognition and efficiency in independent reading; and (4) definite guidance in the comprehension of more complex reading materials.

A READING READINESS PROGRAM

Reading readiness in mentally handicapped children is usually developed through mental maturation. If we wait long enough mentally handicapped children will be ready to learn to read at the older ages. In order to facilitate this maturation and to decrease the period of waiting for maturation, certain readiness functions should be developed through experiences and activities in the classroom.

Most of the activities described in a primary program for mentally handicapped children (Chapter 8) are reading readiness activities. In addition to these, the following may be mentioned.

(1) Excursions and field trips to increase a child's experiential background.

(2) Making and labeling collections so that the children will become familiar with and associate printed symbols with objects.

(3) Making equipment, collecting books, and setting up centers of interest with books and pictures.

(4) Story telling by the librarian, teacher, and other children.

(5) Story reading by the librarian, teacher, and other children.

(6) Informal discussions to plan, develop, appraise, and summarize an activity in the classroom.

(7) Associating words with pictures in activities.

(8) Preparing and presenting dramatizations by the children.

(9) Preparing booklets and scrapbooks.

(10) Learning about the kinds and care of books.

(11) Giving reports to the group on some activity.

(12) Construction activities such as "stop" and "go" signs for play cars, pens for pets, clay models, charts, and so forth.

(13) Playing games with language, number, and color.

(14) Preparing for birthdays and other parties in the classroom.

(15) Planning, assigning, and following up classroom housekeeping jobs.

(16) Planning and caring for a school garden or a school project.

(17) Organizing information for a bulletin board.
(18) Browsing through picture books and picture collections.
(19) Conducting telephone conversations.
(20) Working on puzzle games.
(21) Engaging in rhythm activities — games, hopping, skipping, and dancing.
(22) Illustrating and dramatizing stories.

It will be found that some children of the same mental ages will become ready to read before others. These children will begin to ask about reading materials in the pre-primers and other books in the classroom, and will appear anxious to read. In these cases the teacher should encourage them if the children are ready and can go into the initial stages of the reading process. The mental age used in placing children in certain categories is only an initial classification, and should not be adhered to when the child shows greater or lesser capabilities than indicated from his mental age.

INSTRUCTION DURING THE INITIAL STAGES OF READING

The problem of how to introduce reading to children both normal and subnormal has been a controversial one for many years. We have gone through the stages of the alphabet method, the phonic method, the sentence method, and even the paragraph method of teaching initial reading to children. An adequate method of teaching reading should be based on some sound theory of psychological function.

Studies in biology show us that the organism reacts first as a whole, and that later it becomes individuated. The Gestalt psychologists have informed us that children perceive wholes first and learn details later. From these studies and observation of the reading process it would appear that learning reading follows the stages of (1) seeing wholes first, (2) learning details later, and (3) then reading without awareness of details. Kirk [5] has described this theory as follows:

How children learn to read. When the child is first presented with

[5] Kirk, Samuel A., *Teaching of Reading to Slow-Learning Children.* Boston: Houghton Mifflin Co., 1940, pp. 74–78.

a short sentence or phrase which is based on his experience he probably learns the whole sentence, partly by memory, and partly by recognizing the configuration of the sentence. The child is capable of reading the whole paragraph through memory of what he had said, and through the recognition of the configuration of the sentences. In other words, the child's first impression is whole sentences and only vague blocks and gaps between words. He does not necessarily recognize or perceive the separate words in his story during his initial attempts at reading.

Although the method of utilizing vague impressions is valuable in beginning reading, children cannot learn to read and progress merely by seeing vague phrases and sentences and making some differentiation between them. To progress in reading they must go into a second stage in the reading process which is the learning of the details of the sentences and words. Learning to discriminate the word "dog" from the word "beautiful" is simple enough, but learning to discriminate the word "dog" from the word "boy" is more difficult. To accomplish this the child must recognize that "d" is different from "b," that the "o" in both words is similar, and that the "y" is different from the "g." In other words, learning to differentiate the word "boy" from the word "dog" requires a discrimination of the individual parts or items in the words.

It appears, then, that the child learns the sentence as a whole, and that to progress in reading he must learn the individual words in the sentence. Learning the individual words requires the learning of the different elements in each word. This does not mean that the child must be taught the various letters or different sounds in each word, but he must be able to make these discriminations perceptually even though he does not know the names of the individual letters or sounds.

A third stage in the reading process is the reading of thought units without being aware of the details. In the process of reading the child absorbs only thought units without being conscious of the details of the printed page.

Since advanced readers are unaware of details in reading there are teachers who believe it is unnecessary to teach details. Consequently they stress the "whole" method of teaching reading throughout the training period. Many children learn to read in spite of this method since they are capable of learning details without specific instruction. Other children develop reading disabilities because the teacher allows them to omit an essential process in reading. It is imperative that the teacher instruct the children in details of sentences and words and then use methods which will aid the child to read without attending to, or being aware of, the details. In this way the child will arrive at the ultimate aim of reading: reading thought units and ideas without being conscious of the process.

To summarize these three stages of reading, it may be said that the alphabet and phonic methods at the beginning of reading are psychologically unsound since the child at first is perceiving gross configurations. After he has had experience in reading short sentences and paragraphs, he should be aided in observing details through the use of word study. After he has had further experience with details, larger thought units can be introduced so that the child can read without noting the details of words and sentences, yet can fall back on them if necessary. The teacher who is able to recognize these three stages of reading can formulate his method to fit into the process of reading at each particular stage.

Since mentally handicapped children are deficient in making inferences, and in learning by themselves, they must be aided in these processes at each stage of their development. The teacher of backward children, therefore, has a more difficult task than the teacher of children who are mentally normal. He must be alert to detect the stage at which the child is reading and he must intensify the instruction to aid the retarded child in some of the steps that the average child learns without instruction.

It would necessarily follow from this theory that the initial stages of reading should be by means of a systematic but modified experience approach. It is possible, however, that some mentally handicapped children, including some brain-injured children, cannot profit from the experience chart method. In these cases the "Gestalt" process has probably been disturbed by a brain injury and the instruction must proceed from a more detailed approach.

Reading charts. In general, certain principles underlie the making and using of good reading charts: (1) each chart must fulfill the need for which it is prepared to serve or meet; (2) the chart must be within the child's ability; (3) the chart must be simple and unified with adequate word control; and (4) the sentences must be well spaced, the stories placed in regular paragraph form, and the print large and clear.

Kirk [6] points out that in using the systematic experience method with mentally handicapped children these steps are followed:

(1) The teacher must be sure the children are ready to read and have a desire to read.

(2) The children must be stimulated through experiences to tell a story.

(3) One day the story is dictated by the children and written by the teacher on the board; the next day it is written in chart form and the children read the story from the chart. After several readings the children are partly reading from memory and partly from recognizable configuration of sentences.

(4) Additional stories are made and charts are used in the same manner to fixate the same material in a different setting. At this point many devices are needed to insure adequate repetition in a variety of settings:

(*a*) The moving picture method [7] and the movie strip.[8] (Preparing this strip gives familiarity with the words by tracing them).

(*b*) Mimeographed stories for further repetitions to develop sight vocabulary through configuration of words and phrases.

(*c*) Projection lantern slides and stereopticon are motivating devices to provide for necessary repetition in different settings.

(5) After the children have acquired a sight vocabulary through this type of reading, instruction is begun on developing recognition of individual words. This is the second stage in reading. The teacher asks children to point out individual words in a story they

[6] Kirk, *op. cit.*
[7] Kirk, *op. cit.*, pp. 88–89.
[8] Betts, Emmett A., *Foundations of Reading Instruction.* New York: American Book Co., 1946.

are reading. He cuts the chart into sentences and has the children reconstruct the story by placing it in the correct order. Later, charts are cut into words and reconstructed, with and without the model sentences. Much repetition is needed to build a large enough vocabulary to be successful in initial book reading. This stage of the program may extend over a period of a year or more with the mentally handicapped child. Even after pre-primers are introduced experience charts are so worded to include the words the pupils will need in reading the pre-primer. At this point accuracy and not speed is important.

The teacher must constantly be evaluating the development of the basic sight vocabulary. One device for checking is through the use of word lists prepared by authorities in the field of reading [9]; another device is checking the lists of words in the back of the pre-primer before the child is given the book to read. The words that he cannot recognize by sight are the ones that need to be used in charts, in labels for pictures, in word games, and other activities so that he will know them when he is ready for the book reading.

One of the questions which teachers raise concerns the period at which experience charts should be introduced, or when pre-primers or teacher-made materials in reading should be given to the children. The following suggestions are indications that the child may be ready for such materials.

(1) A curiosity about books and an attempt to read them.

(2) Some ability to read some of the words in the primer.

(3) A background of information, vocabulary, and experience which exceeds the vocabulary level of the pre-primer.

(4) The ability to express ideas.

(5) Good habits of observing and listening.

(6) Some independence in work habits.

(7) Ability to listen.

(8) Ability to follow from left to right.

[9] Dolch, Edward W., "A Basic Sight Vocabulary," *The Elementary School Journal*, February, 1936, pp. 458–459; Gates, Arthur I., *Reading Vocabulary for the Primary Grades*, Rev. Ed. New York: Teachers College, Columbia University, 1935, pp. 1–29; Stone, Clarence R., *Better Primary Reading*. St. Louis, Missouri: Webster Publishing Co., 1936, pp. 50–53.

INITIAL STAGES IN BOOK READING

A modified-experience approach appears to be the most suitable for teaching mentally handicapped children. To accomplish the major goals of reading, the initial reading activities should grow out of and contribute to the everyday living both at home, at school, and in the community. The goals of initial reading are summarized as follows:

(1) Developing an interest in reading to satisfy personal needs.

(2) Developing facility in the use of books and desirable attitudes toward books.

(3) Continuing the development of oral language facility.

(4) Expanding the concept that words stand for experience.

(5) Developing basic reading skills and abilities, including a sight vocabulary.

Regardless of the approach used to teaching reading in its initial stage, certain basic principles and assumptions should be kept in mind, such as:

(1) Selection of books that have much repetition of vocabulary.

(2) Supplementing books with other materials containing the same vocabulary.

(3) Planning seatwork to meet individual needs and to promote effective work habits and success.

(4) Developing some independence and versatility in word recognition.

(5) Emphasizing accuracy rather than speed.

Traditionally, the material for initial reading instruction consists of a readiness workbook, one, two, or three levels of pre-primers, one or two primers, and a first reader, with workbooks to accompany some of them. The best use of the basal readers, however, is in connection with the experience approach, since the nature of the activities in the readiness books and the needs revealed through their use suggest repetition in a variety of situations.

It should be cautioned that mentally handicapped children have probably been exposed to primers and first readers for many years without success. It is important that the teacher prepare books for them at their interest level, cut out parts of primers and books, and even remake a book with a different cover. Any approach which will not produce a negative attitude will be beneficial.

DEVELOPING EFFICIENCY IN READING

To develop efficiency in reading, teachers should become familiar with (1) development of word recognition, (2) significance of oral reading, (3) the factor of interest, and (4) the importance of comprehension skills.

Word recognition. To differentiate words requires the ability to make associations and inferences. As pointed out earlier the mentally handicapped child is deficient in this psychological function. Consequently, the teacher must plan guided experiences and activities to develop this ability. However, since all children do not learn alike, a variety of methods will be needed to meet this lack. The mentally handicapped child does not "pick up" words incidentally unless he is exposed to them over and over in different settings and in a variety of situations.

Children use many methods in recognizing words. Some children depend on the physical characteristics or configuration of the word; others use the spelling method. Some use context clues and by reading a sentence and guessing at the unknown word derive the meaning of the sentence. The mentally handicapped child, deficient in the ability to make inferences, may guess incorrectly. Some children recognize new words by sounding out the word or by phonic analysis. The important thing for the teacher to remember is that phonic analysis is not a method of teaching reading; it is merely a tool to be used in recognizing strange words.

Gray [10] defines and delineates phonetic and structural analysis and presents a program for recognition based on this system of analysis. The important aspects of such a program are: (1) to teach for auditory memory and discrimination by means of reading, rhymes, games, and so forth; (2) to begin by teaching the sound of the consonants and one vowel sound. The mentally handicapped may have difficulty in blending the sounds into a word but if the teacher starts at a simple level of auditory discrimination, such as "ca-t,"

[10] Gray, William S., *On Their Own in Reading.* Chicago, Illinois: Scott. Foresman & Co., 1948.

or "c-at," and gradually and systematically increases the difficulty, the child will learn to blend sounds.[11]

Structural analysis, prefixes, suffixes, and syllabication should be taught in meaningful situations where emphasis is on comprehension. A casual system, however, is as useless as a casual system in teaching phonics. Neither phonics nor structural analysis alone, as a method of teaching word recognition, is sufficient for independent effective reading. They must be supplemented by context clues and other aids.

Oral reading as an aid to learning to read. Since reading begins through the use of visual-auditory symbols, it naturally follows that oral reading will be the child's first reading. Oral language is his tool of communication until he learns to read and write. Inaudible reading follows oral reading in the initial stages. This is the first step in silent reading. The child uses the same throat and vocal muscles as in oral reading, but not the voice. At this stage the children are frequently called "lip-readers." This period of inaudible reading will be longer for the mentally handicapped than for the normal child. Gradually the child uses less lip and vocal movement and finally there is little or no vocal movement. Kirk [12] presents research evidence to justify the continued oral reading with the mentally handicapped child: during the initial stages of reading there are more fixations per line in silent than in oral reading; oral reading is a logical first step in learning to read; and when children articulate they learn more rapidly. Further advantages of continued oral reading are these: (1) since accuracy rather than speed is stressed with mentally handicapped children, the teacher can check for accuracy when the child reads aloud, and (2) through oral reading the child learns pronunciation and enunciation. Oral reading, through the grouping of words and intonation, becomes a test for comprehension.

Interest as a factor in efficiency in reading. Research points out that learning takes place more rapidly and more efficiently if the materi-

---

[11] For a phonic method used with mentally handicapped children see Hegge, T. G., S. A. Kirk, and W. D. Kirk, *Remedial Reading Drills.* Ann Arbor, Michigan: George Wahr Publishing Co., 1936.

[12] Kirk, *op. cit.*, pp. 123–128.

als are meaningful and interesting. Consequently, the teacher is obliged to supply reading materials that have qualities of surprise, liveliness, animalness, conversation, humor, and plot. It cannot be overemphasized that the factor of *success* in reading is the most important factor in maintaining interest in reading for the mentally handicapped child.

Comprehension. Gray's four steps in the reading process point out that the aim of reading is to evaluate and interpret what one reads. In order to do this, the reader must be able to understand the "words he calls." The teacher must provide activities and experiences which aid comprehension and evaluation. Much independent reading of simple stories on a variety of topics and of a variety of difficulty levels must be encouraged. Free reading in itself does not produce comprehension skills; it does create interest, develop concentration, provide pleasurable experiences, and stimulates some thinking. Reading to get directions or to answer questions can be an integral part of a unit of work and can stimulate thinking and encourage comprehension and evaluation. Competition with one's self to better a previous record is recommended as one form of motivation for the mentally handicapped children. Extension of language facility and concepts can be accomplished through individual or group experiences and through relating experiences to the teacher and the group and then recording these stories. Other activities for continued language development, to be related with reading skills, are found in oral expression in dramatics, discussions, through the study of pictures, story reading and telling by the teacher, and through trips and projects.

SEATWORK

Not all reading instruction can be carried out under the direct supervision of the teacher. The child must develop independence in reading and at the same time engage in worth-while purposeful activities while the teacher is engaged in working with the other groups of children. The teacher provides *seatwork*, as these activities are called, that directs the child to read for understanding. This work may be a variety of activities. Kirk [13] suggests the following activities:

[13] Kirk, *op. cit.*, pp. 97–102.

(1) Making and tracing stories on charts for moving pictures.

(2) Using mimeographed pictures and words with instructions to draw a line from the picture to the correct word to develop word-recognition.

(3) Using short phrases and sentences under a picture and instructing the child to circle the phrase or sentence that describes the picture.

(4) Using picture cards, with sentences containing words the child will meet in his reading experiences.

(5) Pasting words, phrases, and sentences written or typed by the teacher on pictures which have been drawn by the child or cut out from magazines.

(6) Utilizing the sentence completion method by mimeographing known stories and omitting certain words.

(7) Executing written directions such as, "Color the apple red."

(8) Free reading that will enable the child to read for comprehension.

(9) Using reading books or work books with the purpose of guiding the child's reading, such as, "Tell how the story may be illustrated."

(10) Using the workbooks accompanying the basal readers with the activities based on the vocabulary in that reader.

Betts [14] has made an extensive summary of the workbook situation. His conclusions, as applied to the mentally handicapped, could be summarized as follows:

(1) Reading workbooks are *not* an essential part of a reading program.

(2) The chief use of reading workbooks should be for the purpose of assisting the child in learning to read and not for the purpose of keeping him busy.

(3) Commercial workbooks do not nurture individual differences.

(4) Workbooks provide a means of supplementing group instruction with individual instruction.

(5) Intelligent teacher guidance is essential to the successful use of workbooks.

[14] Betts, Emmett A., *Foundations of Reading Instruction.* New York: American Book Co., 1946.

MOTIVATION

One of the basic considerations in the teaching of reading is that of developing desirable attitudes toward reading and reading activities. Because the mentally handicapped child has met failure in the reading situation he already has the attitude of withdrawing. This must be replaced with the attitude of approach toward the reading situation. These poor attitudes toward reading may be the result of undesirable home conditions and parent attitudes toward reading. They are sometimes the result of frustration due to failure.

Procedures for building up attitudes of approaching the reading situation wholesomely are:

(1) Guiding the pupil into using materials that are understandable to him and in which he can succeed.

(2) Making the child aware of any small success or growth he achieves.

(3) Encouraging the child to compete with himself against his previous accomplishment.

(4) Providing easy but interesting reading material.

The wise teacher inventories the interests of her pupils, distinguishing between the transitory and permanent interests. The more immature the child, the more trivial the interest range. Their interests may lack social value for group experience. The job of the teacher becomes one of developing broad interests and then providing the reading materials that further extend and expand the range of interests as well as the depth of the interest. The following are suggestions for developing interests:

(1) Provide a large variety of books and encourage wide reading for information.

(2) Allow the children to select reading materials.

(3) Encourage the use of the library.

(4) Vitalize the reading through visual aids.

(5) Stimulate reading of the newspapers.

(6) Provide many opportunities for sharing interesting anecdotes, stories, poems, and dramatizations that pupils find worthwhile in the books they use.

(7) Prepare bulletin board exhibits of reading materials from recreational and informational type books.

(8) Prepare the children for introduction to new units of work.

(9) Make sure the pupils understand the purposes for which reading is done.

(10) At the appropriate time, subordinate the mechanics of reading to the getting of meaning from what is read.

SPELLING

The need of the mentally handicapped child in spelling is to learn the words he is using in everyday life, or those that he will need in adult life. As in reading, the mentally handicapped child will not exceed fourth- and fifth-grade ability in spelling. His education in this area, as well as in others, should be confined to the vocabulary used by the child at his level of development.

Spelling is primarily a visual-perceptual function. Learning to spell words requires that the child remember visually how the word looked. He uses phonics, spelling, and vocal abilities in attempting to recall the spelling of the word. He will not learn to spell, however, until he can visualize the correct form of the word. It is difficult to determine what type of imagery a child uses in spelling: visual, auditory, or motor. It is probable that the visual imagery, although aided by others, is predominant.

In teaching spelling to mentally handicapped children the following principles apply:

(1) The words used in spelling should be those that are familiar and used by the child in everyday life.

(2) A systematic method of learning spelling should be taught the child. Incidental methods are not effective with the mentally handicapped.

(3) Spelling should not be taught by rules, since this involves the application of generalizations. Mentally handicapped children have difficulty in applying and remembering generalizations.

(4) Spelling is facilitated when the child is able to pronounce the words accurately. When a child pronounces "run" as "wun" and is asked to spell it as "r-u-n," he becomes confused between what he hears and what he sees.

(5) Spelling in its initial stages should be closely supervised. Repetition of wrong spelling without correction tends to fix the

wrong spelling in the child's mind. It is more difficult to break a habit than to establish the correct one at the beginning.

(6) The spelling, reading, and writing materials used by the child should be the same. When a spelling list is used that has no relation to the reading vocabulary or the writing period, less learning takes place in all areas.

(7) Spelling should be taught after, not before, the child learns to write. Writing words, rather than oral spelling is the important aim. Furthermore, writing words, sentences, and stories is one of the most effective methods of learning to spell.

Since mentally handicapped children have difficulty in learning to spell, a more intensive method of teaching spelling should be used. Fernald [15] describes a method of teaching spelling to children who have difficulty in learning. Her steps in teaching spelling can be used effectively as one intensive method of teaching mentally handicapped children. Fernald's systematic method of teaching spelling is as follows:

(1) The word to be learned should be written on the blackboard or on paper by the teacher. . . .

(2) The teacher pronounces the word very clearly and distinctly. The children pronounce the word. . . .

(3) Time is allowed for each child to study the word. . . .

(4) When every child is sure of the word, the word is erased or covered and the child writes it from memory. . . .

(5) The paper should be turned over and the word written a second time. . . .

(6) Some arrangement should be made so that it is natural for the child to make frequent use, in his written expression, of the word he has learned. . . .

(7) Finally it is necessary that the child be allowed to get the correct form of the word at any time when he is doubtful of its spelling. . . .

(8) If spelling matches are desired, they should be written instead of oral.[16]

Fernald allows children to use their own imagery — visual,

[15] Fernald, G. M., *Remedial Techniques in Basic School Subjects*. New York: McGraw-Hill Book Co., Inc., 1943.

[16] By permission from *Remedial Techniques in Basic School Subjects* by G. M. Fernald. Copyright, 1943. McGraw-Hill Book Company, Inc. Pp. 199–201.

auditory, or kinesthetic. The method described is known as the kinesthetic method. Actually the child is obtaining visual perceptual learning when he uses the kinesthetic method. He looks at the word, then tries to write it from memory. If it does not look right he looks at the word again, and then writes it correctly. In this way he is visualizing the word, using the written reproduction as a check on the correctness of his visual image.

Fernald's method has the advantage of emphasizing the visualizations of words and at the same time giving the child a systematic method of learning. Fernald advocates teaching the child how he can become independent in learning words. Her directions to the child include the following:

(1) Look at the word very carefully and say it over to yourself.

(2) See if the word can be written just as you say it. . . .

(3) Shut your eyes and see if you can get a picture of the word in your mind. If you cannot get a clear picture of the word, you can remember the parts that are written the way you say them by pronouncing the word over to yourself or feeling your hand make the movements of writing the word. . . .

(4) When you are sure of every part of the word, shut your book or cover the word and write it, saying each syllable to yourself as you write it. . . .

(5) If you cannot write the word correctly after you have looked at it and said it, ask the teacher to write it for you with crayola on a strip of paper. Trace the word with your fingers. Say each part of the word as you trace it. Trace the word carefully as many times as you need to until you can write it correctly. Say each part of the word to yourself as you write it. . . .

(6) If the word is difficult, turn the paper over and write it again. . . .

(7) Later in the day try writing the word from memory.[17]

Not all spelling should be taught by systematic and intensive methods, such as those described by Fernald. Many spelling words will be learned by the children without such a method. Other words will cause difficulty for some of the children. The systematic method just described could be used for those children in

[17] *Ibid.*, pp. 201–202. From G. M. Fernald, "California State Speller," pp. 3–5, California State Printing Office, Sacramento, 1918.

the class who are having great difficulty in learning to spell, and for those words that are causing difficulty for all of the children. A combination of natural methods of teaching spelling supplemented with a systematic method is usually the best procedure.

WRITING

Teaching writing to mentally handicapped children does not differ significantly from the teaching of writing to normal children. The major differences are the discrepancies found in motor and mental abilities of young normal and older subnormal children.

When a mentally handicapped child is ready to learn to read and spell he is usually nine, ten, or eleven years of age. Since the motor and physical development of subnormal children is not usually as retarded as their mental development, the motor function of writing is superior to the intellectual requirements.

It can be assumed for the majority of mentally handicapped children that they have the motor ability to write when they are mentally ready to write. They have usually had considerable experience in drawing, sketching, and manipulation of pencils. They are less awkward than the normal six- or seven-year-old child who begins to write at that age. Consequently the emphasis on motor coordination, used with normal children, is not as necessary with mentally handicapped children at the ages of nine or ten.

The major difficulties in writing encountered with mentally handicapped children is the knowledge of what to write and how to write it. Reading must precede the ability to write, except for the elementary stages of learning to write their names and some simple words. Some factors in teaching writing to mentally handicapped children are discussed below:

(1) Emphasis on accuracy and legibility is the important factor in teaching writing to mentally handicapped children. Speed of writing should not be practiced. The child will gain speed in writing as he becomes confident of his ability and has practice in writing.

(2) Manuscript writing is believed to be preferable to cursive writing with the mentally handicapped. The letters are formed a little more easily, the letters resemble print (hence greater correlation is achieved with beginning reading), and manuscript is usually more legible than cursive writing.

(3) Strauss and Lehtinen [18] devote a chapter to the teaching of writing to brain-injured mentally handicapped children. They believe that cursive writing is preferable to manuscript writing with this type of mentally handicapped child. They feel that the perception of the whole word is facilitated when the letters are joined together in cursive writing, and that connecting the letters into a word helps the child in developing the kinesthetic perception of the whole word. Special exercises for writing readiness and a systematic method of teaching writing by starting with the letters first, then combining them gradually, are described by Strauss and Lehtinen.

(4) Practice in writing can be given as an aid to reading and spelling. Memory and perception of words is deficient in mentally handicapped children. Word recognition and recall may be aided by practice in writing from memory, similar to Fernald's Kinesthetic method.[19]

(5) Mentally handicapped children should be shown the correct procedures in writing, including posture and the relation of the paper to the body. Since more left-handed children are found in special classes than in the regular grades, the teacher should assist the child in adjusting adequately to the desk and paper. Many bizarre forms of writing are used by left-handed children when they are allowed to use an accidental method of approach in writing.

(6) Writing should have meaning for the child. Even though exercises in writing are given, the child should understand the reasons for the exercise. Correlating writing with reading, spelling, arithmetic, and other subjects or activities tends to give meaning to the exercise of writing.

REFERENCES

Adams, Fay, Lillian Gray, and Dora Reese. *Teaching Children to Read.* New York: The Ronald Press Company, 1949.

Bennett, A. *A Comparative Study of Subnormal Children in the Elementary*

[18] Strauss, A. A., and L. E. Lehtinen, *Psychopathology and Education of the Brain-Injured Child.* New York: Grune and Stratton, 1947, pp. 184–190.

[19] Kirk, S. A., "The Influence of Manual Tracing on the Learning of Simple Words in the Case of Subnormal Boys," *Journal of Educational Psychology*, 24 (October, 1933), pp. 525–535.

Grades, Contributions to Education, No. 510. New York: Bureau of Publications, Teachers College, Columbia University, 1932.

Betts, Emmett A. *Foundations of Reading Instruction*. New York: American Book Company, 1946.

Dolch, Edward W. "A Basic Sight Vocabulary," *The Elementary School Journal*, 36 (February, 1936), pp. 456–460.

Gates, Arthur I. *Reading Vocabulary for the Primary Grades*, Rev. Ed. New York: Teachers College, Columbia University, 1935.

Gray, William S. *On Their Own in Reading*. Chicago: Scott, Foresman & Company, 1948.

Hegge, Thorleif G. "Special Reading Disability with Particular Reference to the Mentally Deficient," *American Association on Mental Deficiency*, 39 (May, 1934), pp. 297–343.

Hegge, T. G., S. A. Kirk, and W. D. Kirk. *Remedial Reading Drills*. Ann Arbor, Michigan: George Wahr and Company, 1936.

Kirk, Samuel A. "Reading Aptitudes of Mentally Retarded Children," *American Association on Mental Deficiency*, 44, No. 2. (May, 1939), pp. 156–162.

Kirk, Samuel A. *Teaching of Reading to Slow-Learning Children*. Boston: Houghton Mifflin Company, 1940.

Kirk, Samuel A. "The Influence of Manual Tracing on the Learning of Simple Words in the Case of Subnormal Boys," *Journal of Educational Psychology*, 24 (October, 1933), pp. 525–535.

Lamoreau, Lillian A., and Dorris May Lee. *Learning to Read Through Experience*. New York: Appleton-Century-Crofts, Inc., 1943.

Merrill, Maud A. "On the Relation of Intelligence to Achievement in Case of Mentally Retarded Children," *Comparative Psychology Monographs*, 2, No. 10 (September, 1924).

Stone, Clarence R. *Better Primary Reading*. St. Louis: Webster Publishing Company, 1936.

Strauss, Alfred A., and Laura E. Lehtinen. *Psychopathology and Education of the Brain-Injured Child*. New York: Grune and Stratton, 1947.

Chapter 13

Teaching Arithmetical Concepts

I⊤ ɪs ᴀ commonly accepted fact that most mentally handicapped children will achieve between the third and fifth grade in their arithmetic abilities. Higher learning in this area would throw doubt on the diagnosis of mental defect. Some, on the other hand, are unable to achieve even third-grade ability.

A common philosophy among some educators is that the intelligence of the mentally handicapped differs from that of the normal only in amount, and that his arithmetical ability, therefore, differs only in his slow rate of learning the same materials offered to average children. Consequently arithmetic materials are presented to mentally handicapped children in the same order, in the same manner, and with the same emphasis as they are presented to average or normal children. The only adjustment made for the mentally handicapped is that the materials designed for eight-year-old normal children will be used for mentally handicapped children with a mental age of eight.

This philosophy makes several unfounded assumptions. It refuses to recognize that the individual needs of children differ. It assumes that the abilities of children are identical, or at least very similar, and that the mentally handicapped have no special abilities or disabilities in learning and using arithmetical concepts and skills as compared to normal children of the same mental age. It also assumes (1) that arithmetic materials designed for the use of normal children meet the needs or future needs of all the individuals (whether superior, normal, or retarded in intelligence); (2) that skills and concepts have been placed in order of difficulty; and (3) that factors essential to an individual's social and economic adjustment to the community are the easiest to learn and consequently taught first. Likewise those less essential skills and the "frills" are taught or filled in later.

In the grades, the average child is given the background needed for the later mastery of algebra, geometry, and trigonometry. Algebra, geometry, and trigonometry in turn furnish the background for such college courses as analytical geometry and calculus. In planning the curriculum for the mentally handicapped, however, the major consideration is to plan it so that by the time they leave school they will have the type of knowledge, the concepts, and the experience they will need to help them live as better citizens in their community. Most of the adult usages of arithmetic which are encountered in their everyday life are the fundamental concepts and addition, subtraction, multiplication, and division skills rather than the skills included in a typical secondary or college program.

LEARNING CHARACTERISTICS

While there are few comprehensive studies comparing the arithmetical abilities of mentally handicapped children with normal children of the same mental age, we do have enough information to know that a curriculum designed for normal children is not applicable to and will not meet the needs of the mentally handicapped.

Cruickshank conducted a study comparing the arithmetical abilities of a group of mentally handicapped children to the arithmetical abilities of a group of normal children of the same mental age. He and others state that the mentally handicapped children differ from normal children in the following ways:

(1) The mentally handicapped children do not have the mental

ability to grasp the advanced and complicated concepts usually taught to normal children in the advanced grades.[1]

(2) It is more difficult for the mentally handicapped children to "pick up" basic principles and concepts because of their poor insight and low ability to generalize.[2]

(3) Counting on the fingers and other immature habits are more frequent among mentally handicapped children.[3]

(4) There is probably less transfer among the mentally handicapped children than there is among normal children.[4]

(5) The mentally handicapped children are inferior in their ability to solve abstract and verbal problems.[5]

(6) The arithmetic vocabulary of the mentally handicapped children is retarded.[6]

(7) The mentally handicapped children have less understanding of the processes to be used in finding the solution to problems.[7]

(8) When confronted with a problem they are unable to solve, mentally handicapped children are more apt to guess or give some unsuitable response.[8]

In addition to the comparative arithmetical disabilities listed above, a number of authors have stated that mentally handicapped children have the following disabilities:

(1) The mentally handicapped children have more difficulty solving abstract and verbal problems than solving concrete problems.[9]

(2) The mentally handicapped children tend to do more poorly on multiplication and division than on addition and subtraction.[10]

[1] Baker, Harry J., *Introduction to Exceptional Children.* New York: The Macmillan Co., 1949.

[2] Ingram, Christine P., *Education of the Slow-Learning Child.* Yonkers: World Book Co., 1935.

[3] Brueckner, Leo J., and Foster E. Grossnickle, *How to Make Arithmetic Meaningful.* Philadelphia: The John C. Winston Co., 1947.

[4] Baker, *op. cit.*

[5] Cruickshank, William M., "A Comparative Study of Psychological Factors Involved in the Responses of Mentally Retarded and Normal Boys to Problems in Arithmetic," Doctor's Dissertation, University of Michigan, Ann Arbor, 1946. See also Baker, *op. cit.*

[6] Cruickshank, *op. cit.*   [7] Cruickshank, *op. cit.*   [8] Cruickshank, *op. cit.*

[9] Cruickshank, *op. cit.*; Baker, *op. cit.*; Ingram, *op. cit.*

[10] Cruickshank, *op. cit.*

(3) The mentally handicapped tend to have little conception of sequence and the relativity of time concepts.[11]

(4) The arithmetic habits of mentally handicapped children are characterized by immaturity and carelessness.[12]

Concerning studies comparing methods of teaching arithmetic to mentally handicapped children, one made by Costello[13] will be discussed. She divided the mentally handicapped children into three groups, each group being taught by a different method. The methods used were (a) socialization, defined as an active, experiencing type of activity, (b) sensorization, defined as a method in which concreteness or realism of presentation was used, and (c) verbalization, defined as the method conventionally used in the schools in which verbal description is used as a substitute experience. She found that the poorest method of instruction for the improvement of attention, association, vocabulary, comprehension, and judgment was the verbalization method. The best method of instruction was the socialization method closely followed, and in some cases exceeded, by the sensorization method.

In using the verbalization method, the child was told the relationship between various measurements. In using the concrete method, the child was told the relationship of measurements in conjunction with concrete demonstration. The child actually made the measurements, thus seeing the relationships. In using the socialization method, the child learned the concepts in relation to a need. If a group of girls were baking a cake, they learned a level teaspoonful, parts of a teaspoonful, a heaping teaspoonful, the tablespoon measures, and the cup measures in a meaningful, concrete situation and in a situation in which they were needed. As a result, there was a better grasp of the concepts in other needful situations as less dependence was placed upon transfer from theory to practice.

The arithmetic taught to mentally handicapped children should be chosen with care. Two major points should be kept in mind.

[11] Gothberg, Laura C., "The Mentally Defective Child's Understanding of Time," *American Journal of Mental Deficiency*, 53 (January, 1949), pp. 441–455.

[12] Baker, *op. cit.*; Cruickshank, *op. cit.*

[13] Costello, Helen M., "The Responses of Mentally Retarded Children to Specialized Learning Experiences in Arithmetic," Doctor's Dissertation, University of Pennsylvania, Philadelphia, 1941.

First, it must include the knowledge, skills, and concepts that will be of value to him now and in later life. Second, the methods used should take cognizance of the special disabilities or abilities found in mentally handicapped children so that proper presentations, amount of practice, and amount of emphasis will be in keeping with their abilities to learn.

NEEDS AND OBJECTIVES IN TEACHING ARITHMETIC

The futility of the traditional type program is illustrated by the studies done by Wilson and Adams. Wilson [14] made a study of the problems solved by over four thousand adults during a two-week period. He found that 83 per cent of the problems dealt with buying and selling goods, 11 per cent involved the use of money but not buying and selling, and 6 per cent dealt with quantitative measurements. Most of the processes used were multiplication, addition, use of common fractions, making out or understanding accounts, and the use of simple denominate numbers.

In another study attempting to determine the mathematical functions necessary in the life of the general public, Adams [15] examined all the pages of one issue of twenty representative newspapers and periodicals. He found that if a reader were to understand their contents he would need the following concepts:

(1) Time — the hour, day, week, month, and year.

(2) Numbers — ability to read and understand those used in house numbers, room numbers, and telephone numbers.

(3) Numbers — general use of one- and two-place numbers.

(4) Money — most frequent values used were under $100.

(5) Simple ratios.

(6) Various units of measure.

(7) Wide variety of mathematical ideas, expressions, concepts, and terms.

(8) Practical, as opposed to theoretical, problems.

[14] Wilson, G. M., "A Survey of the Social and Business Usage of Arithmetic," Teachers' College Contributions to Education, No. 100. New York: Teachers College, Columbia University, 1919.

[15] Adams, H. W., "The Mathematics Encountered in the General Reading of Newspapers and Periodicals," Unpublished Master's Thesis, Dept. of Education, University of Chicago. 1924.

It is true that many of the computations which the average adult encounters in his daily life are usually done for him. When we go to the store there is an accurate machine to calculate for us the total cost of our purchases. When we go to the bank, there is a clerk with a comptometer to check our deposits or withdrawals. In fact, there are places where the entire business of arithmetic is taken care of by machines. In such situations, the individual needs to know the function of the machine and have some concept of its use. In a grocery store, for example, the computing cash register seldom makes a mistake, but the checker using it may punch the wrong number, thus under- or over-charging the customer. With this mechanization in many areas of business, there are, nevertheless, many basic uses to which the mentally handicapped child or adult uses arithmetic in his daily life.

The mentally handicapped have need for arithmetical concepts from the time before they can handle simple number problems through adulthood. Consequently, every classroom activity in which a number situation arises should be made use of to add to his meaningful experiences and to further his grasp of the concepts. Utilization should be made of whatever number situations arise in the life of the child to give him additional practice in understanding and manipulating numbers in the basic skills. His arithmetical needs include (1) the development, understanding, and use of an arithmetical vocabulary, (2) the development of number concepts and skills, (3) the development of the ability to apply number concepts, (4) the development of an understanding of various units of measurement, and (5) the development of an understanding of fractional parts.

THE DEVELOPMENT, UNDERSTANDING, AND USE OF AN ARITHMETICAL VOCABULARY

The child should acquire a working vocabulary of the arithmetical terms he will encounter in the everyday social and economic worlds. Since the whole program of the education of the mentally handicapped is based on the premise that getting along with his fellows socially and economically is the prime consideration in his education, this vocabulary must be limited to those terms used in daily living at his stage of development. Such a vocabulary would include:

(1) Terms relating to size, such as big, small, huge, and tiny.

(2) Terms relating to length and distance, such as inch, foot, yard, near, far, long, and short.

(3) Terms relating to other types of measurement, such as penny, nickel, dime, quarter, half dollar, dollar, dozen, ounce, quart, cup, and pound.

(4) Terms relating to amount, such as more, less, increase, decrease, some, none, apiece, double, twice, each, enough, both, many, pair, part, and half.

(5) Terms relating to location, such as up, down, above, below, right, left, under, over, at the beginning, at the end, and between.

(6) Terms relating to time, such as early, late, soon, on time, day, week, month, and year.

(7) Terms relating to comparisons, such as larger, smaller, longer, shorter, higher, lower, heavier, and lighter.

(8) Terms commonly used in commercial practice, such as bill, cost, rent, lease, buy, earn, sell, change, expense, spend, charge, price, worth, lay-away, time-payments, charge, and due.

In addition to the teaching of the meanings of these words and the related concepts, the commonly used abbreviations should also be included.

THE DEVELOPMENT OF NUMBER CONCEPTS AND SKILLS

Many of the arithmetic skills taught in the advanced grades of the regular school are beyond the comprehension and abilities of the mentally handicapped; much of this material is of little use to them in practical life situations. The use of and understanding of the *basic* arithmetical skills, however, are necessary in performing almost any number problem the individual might encounter. Consequently, the teacher of the mentally handicapped must make a definite place in the curriculum for the inclusion of basic number skills. This goal will enable the child to use these skills in those situations in which they are applicable. The basic skills in arithmetic should include:

Number concepts. The development of number concepts include learning concepts of quantity, such as the concepts of two, and so forth. These the child will learn in conjunction with the verbal name of the amount, and the association of three objects with the word "three." He is then taught to associate the concept and verbal name with the printed and finally the written number. In this way he will have an understanding of the quantity or amount in whatever form he may see or hear it.

Addition, subtraction, multiplication, and division skills. These skills are specific, mechanical skills that can be acquired by all mentally handicapped children to a greater or lesser degree. Again it must be emphasized that they must not be taught in isolation. To be meaningful and useful they must be fully understood by the child. He must know the *how* and the *why* of each process. The child progresses by developing the concept of more and of less; then, when the concept is understood, meaningful practice material should be introduced to facilitate its use. Finally, the materials should be presented in life-like situations.

THE DEVELOPMENT OF THE ABILITY TO APPLY NUMBER SKILLS

It is not enough that the child have good number concepts and that given a page of arithmetic computation (addition, subtraction, multiplication, and division examples) he can perform the correct procedure perfectly. He must be able to diagnose a problem, pick out the essentials, set the facts down in a manner in which they can be solved, and finally apply the correct procedure in finding a solution. This is part of the *why* in the use of number skills. Both the ability to perform the operation accurately and the ability to diagnose the problem correctly are necessary before it can be said that the individual is proficient in arithmetic.

THE DEVELOPMENT OF AN UNDERSTANDING OF VARIOUS UNITS OF MEASUREMENT

Understanding of units of measurement is a needed concept. In practice this includes mathematical vocabulary, the number skills, and the ability to apply them. It is necessary that a mentally handicapped child understand such relationships as minutes and hours, ounces and pounds, inches and feet, and cups and quarts. For the solution of certain types of problems merely an understanding of the relationships may be sufficient; for others the individual may need to use one or more of the fundamental arithmetic skills.

THE DEVELOPMENT OF AN UNDERSTANDING OF FRACTIONAL PARTS

An understanding and use of simple fractional parts, such as $\frac{1}{4}$, $\frac{1}{3}$, $\frac{1}{2}$, and $\frac{3}{4}$, is needed by mentally handicapped children in everyday living. How many is one-half dozen eggs? How much is one-fourth of a cup of flour? How long is one-third of a yard of cotton? While a few of the higher mentally handicapped group may be able to apply addition, subtraction, multiplication, and division facts to fractions, this need does not arise very often in the life of the mentally handicapped. Furthermore, there is no assurance that the mentally handicapped person who can divide one mixed number by another on a mechanical level either has the concept of what he is actually doing or knows how to apply this skill if the need were to arise.

PRINCIPLES OF TEACHING ARITHMETIC

To organize a developmental curriculum in arithmetic for mentally handicapped children, it is necessary (1) to understand the learning characteristics of mentally handicapped children in the development of arithmetical concepts, and (2) to evolve principles which take these characteristics into consideration. In the following, the principles of good teaching and the reasons for their formulation are given.

(1) *The concepts and skills that are introduced should be those which are within the child's ability to grasp and those which he will use.* The curriculum in the advanced elementary grades and secondary school includes such topics as discounting, use of negative and positive numbers, algebra, geometry, and trigonometry. These require too difficult and too advanced concepts for the mentally handicapped and should not be included as a part of their program.

(2) *The arithmetic program should teach the child to increase associations, relationships, and basic principles and concepts.* When teaching a mentally handicapped child addition, it is essential that he be taught specifically, through the use of meaningful objects and situa-

tions, what 2 + 2 means. If a mechanical method or memorization method of teaching 2 + 2 = 4 is used, the child may readily learn to respond with the correct answer. But, if a situation arises in class or in a life situation he will be unable to make use of it. 2 + 2 = 4 can be memorized, but if it has no meaning it is worthless learning.

(3) *Specific teaching methods for the elimination of counting on fingers, counting addition combinations, and other immature habits should be emphasized after the mentally handicapped children have matured sufficiently to require their use no longer.* Mentally handicapped children develop slowly intellectually and often have severe functional disabilities. Consequently "crutches" often need to be devised and many of the children may have need for the "crutches" and other immature methods for long periods of time. This emphasis may cause "crutches" to become so firmly established that the use of specific methods to insure their elimination is necessary.

Some methods of developing the child's ability to solve problems other than counting have been used. Carrison and Werner [16] recommend: (*a*) use configurations along with the teaching of number concepts. Instead of teaching the number 5 and associating it with five marks (/////) or five blocks, teach it as the recognition of domino type configuration (:·:) ; (*b*) use a peg board, marble board, or abacus.

(4) *Computation should be used in meaningful situations in order to aid in its later use in practical situations.* Instruction should be so adapted to make use of concrete, life-like, and socialized methods insofar as possible.

(5) *Recognition of and ability to read the words needed in understanding arithmetical concepts should be emphasized.* Since this is the area in which mentally handicapped children seem most deficient, it is of the utmost importance that this emphasis be made if they are to understand the meaning of words commonly used in number skills, measures, and arithmetical concepts. It is especially true if they are to have an understanding of what process is involved in the solution of problems in which the words appear.

[16] Carrison, Doris, and Heinz Werner, "Principles and Methods of Teaching Arithmetic to Mentally Retarded Children," *American Journal of Mental Deficiency*, 47 (January, 1943), pp. 309–317.

For example, in teaching the use of the ruler and linear measure, it is impossible for the child to make use of the concepts involved unless he can read and know the meaning of the terms "inch," "foot," "yard," and so forth. If he does not understand the meaning, confusion may occur, causing the child to interpret the word "foot" for the word "yard." If this were the case, the child's failure to know the meaning of the word would obviously cause him to make errors involving the use of these terms.

(6) *Teaching should be planned to improve the child's problem-reading and problem-understanding ability.* Numerous opportunities, accompanied by specific help in reading and interpreting problems and situations in which number skills are required, need to be provided to develop this ability.

Instead of giving the child repeated examples in addition, offer him situations and concrete problems in which addition is needed. $2 + 2 = 4$, $3 + 2 = 5$, $4 + 3 = 7$, and so forth, does not necessarily give the child an understanding of the process used. The use of an abacus, concrete objects, and actual situations will assist the process. A situation in which "3 boys and 2 girls each need a book, how many books are needed for the group?" or "John has 4¢ and Billy has 3¢, how much money do they have to spend?" is much more apt to teach the basic concepts.

(7) *Standards of achievement should be set at the child's level.* This is of importance for a number of reasons. First, the task must not be made too difficult or the child will tend to become disinterested, guess, and become careless in attempting to find a solution. Second, the task must not be made too easy because no challenge is there for the child, he already knows what to do and how to do it. Too simple a task will also promote disinterest and carelessness to the extent that the child will tend to make errors in processes which he knows how to perform perfectly. He will no longer see any "point" in attempting to perform the task satisfactorily. Third, a task at the child's level is one in which he is learning, will have to attend to what he is doing if he is to do it accurately and correctly, yet which will be within his level of ability. He will be conscious of learning, will have success, and his interest and consequent attention will be maintained. It is advisable to discour-

age carelessness or an incorrect solution of a problem that is within the child's ability. Habits of carefulness and neatness in all matters can be taught the same as any other habit.

8. *Emphasis should be given to accuracy, carefulness, and auto-criticism.* As an example, the case of Mary can be cited. Mary stated that the solution to a problem involving the subtraction of 5 from 9 was 3. Assuming that the concept and the ability to subtract had been established, she needed to be taught a method of checking. By teaching the method of adding the *difference* to the *subtrahend* which should result in the *minuend*, Mary would learn a method of checking her results. Another approach would be the actual division of a number of objects (9) into two groups (5 and a remainder of 4), thus showing her in a concrete situation the inaccuracy of her solution.

(9) *Additional emphasis should be placed on the multiplication and division skills and concepts.* Apparently more emphasis is usually placed on addition and subtraction than on multiplication and division, since mentally handicapped children do comparatively better on exercises involving addition and subtraction. This may be due to the fact that the concepts of addition and subtraction are easier to teach and are taught first, with the result that more practice is provided in their use. By giving additional time to building up the multiplication and division concepts and by showing their relationship to addition, mentally handicapped children will become more adequate in multiplication and division.

(10) *A definite effort should be made to develop the concepts of sequence and time.* This is essential in the making and keeping of appointments of various kinds, in knowing when bills are due and when they will be paid, the length of time it takes to accomplish a task, and so forth.

Instruction in time concepts can start on a simple level with the youngest group, such as time for school, time to eat, time to go home, and with the sequence of ordinary events, such as school time, recess, lunch, rest, and dismissal. When these time concepts have been learned, the children can be advanced to the actual telling of time, and the concepts of yesterday, today, tomorrow, last week, next week, months, and years.

(11) *A mastery of each fact, process, and skill should be insured before continuing to new ones.* This will facilitate the learning of new skills, since the child will have the necessary background upon which to build. It will also aid in promoting interest, attention, and success. Lack of interest is commonly the result of inability to comprehend the processes involved, something which will in turn lead to inattention. With success, interest and attention will usually follow. The child becomes interested and attends to those things in which he can and does succeed.

(12) *Practice should be used only where practice is needed, not as an easy method of teaching or as busy work.* After a child has obtained a concept and knows the use and application of a specific skill, it may be necessary to institute some practice to "short-cut" the process and reduce the amount of time needed to arrive at a solution. It is of the utmost importance, however, that the child realize the purpose of the practice and how it will help him, supplemented by situations in which the value of mastery of the material is demonstrated.

(13) *Repetition should be used freely and frequently.* The repetition should be in a variety of meaningful situations. In this way the child not only becomes adept at performing that particular manipulation; he also becomes more proficient in recognizing the content with which that skill is to be used. After the child has apparently mastered the skill, frequent review should be made to help him retain it.

(14) *Distributive rather than concentrated practice of skills for the implementation of knowledges and concepts should be used.* Where practice is used for "short-cutting," provide short periods of practice over a long period of time rather than pages and pages or hours and hours of practice over the period of a relatively few days.

An Arithmetic Program

The following program is divided into three developmental levels: (1) the development of quantitative concepts, (2) the systematic teaching of arithmetical skills in relation to their use, and (3) the development of efficient use of arithmetical skills. The program has been developed in recognition of the arithmetical needs of mentally handicapped children, and in relation to the achievement of the goals established for usable arithmetical concepts and skills.

THE DEVELOPMENT OF QUANTITATIVE CONCEPTS

The development of initial arithmetical and quantitative concepts takes place during the preschool and primary period. The children in these classes have chronological ages of three to six years in the preschool, and six to ten years in the primary classes. Their mental ages are usually two to four and one-half years in the preschool, and three to about six years in the primary classes.

At the initial stages of teaching quantitative concepts, particularly at the preschool level, all arithmetic is informal and incidental. Through daily activities, the children have need for and become acquainted with such mathematical concepts as now, soon, big, small, far, near, beside, next, up, down, under, above, and so forth. They are also becoming familiar with elementary number concepts and an awareness of the number names with corresponding quantities. This would be limited to the number 1 through about 3. No specific projects or activities are planned to emphasize these concepts, but the teacher who is aware of the needs of the children takes advantage of the many situations arising in their normal activities of play, story-telling, looking at pictures, painting, eating, and getting ready for rest periods.

The concepts of quantity, size, and position can be taught by making comparisons of the size of the children in the class, objects in the room, pictures, and buildings. The same methods can be used to introduce the concepts of tall and short. In the beginning the differentiations should be made between groups of very small and very large objects; later, finer discriminations can be developed.

Discrimination of quantity should also include an awareness of the parts constituting groups. Before a child can count, he can learn to choose the group with the smallest or largest number of objects. Working with small groups of objects is useful as an introduction to counting. Other counting activities to aid in number recognition are choosing one book, getting one chair, using one crayon, and getting one more block. These activities should be oral at this level.

Further counting can be introduced informally by the teacher through such activities as counting aloud during rhythms, while passing out materials and papers, and in games that lend themselves to its use. In this way the child becomes familiar with the number names and quantities through continuous repetition in many situations.

As the children mature and have grasped the initial quantitative concepts, more complex and advanced concepts are continuously presented.[17] The needs arising out of classroom activities at the "primary level" are counting, reading and writing numbers, and simple addition. These needs arise in such activities as the use of money, measuring, its occurrence in art and music, time, activities involving the use of concrete objects, and in the care of classroom pets and plants.

The mathematical situations lead to incidental but by no means accidental teaching. Many classroom situations arise in which numbers can be used legitimately, such as taking attendance, setting up the right number of chairs for visitors, and determining the number of bottles of milk needed. These activities should be taken from normal, meaningful activities of the children and not made counting activities as such. If a child is asked to count the number of children in the room for no apparent reason, he may just as well be asked to count pieces of straw, blocks, or any other objects.

To enrich the opportunities for providing experiences to meet the child's needs, the activity program is of utmost use to the alert teacher. In addition, it can be used as a method for introducing new basic concepts. Some of the advantages of the activity program are these: (1) concepts are presented in meaningful situations; (2) they provide opportunities to present concepts at various levels, thus caring for the needs of children at differing stages; (3) they promote interest in learning through interest in the related activities; and (4) concepts are not taught in isolation but in a context which is similar to the way they appear in life.

[17] A complete discussion of this program is found in the section "Quantitative Thinking" in Chapter 8.

THE SYSTEMATIC TEACHING OF ARITHMETICAL SKILLS

At the intermediate or preadolescent level, the development of basic arithmetical and quantitative concepts is continued as a preparation for the systematic teaching of arithmetical skills. The children at this level have chronological ages of about nine to thirteen years and mental ages of approximately six to nine years.

By the time a child is six to seven years of age mentally he can profit from and should be included in a systematic program of teaching arithmetic skills. With a mental age of seven to eight years, a child should be able to recognize, write, and relate symbols to 100, tell time, have a concept of the ordinal numbers, know all the addition and subtraction combinations not requiring carrying or borrowing, use inches, yards, feet, cents, and the calendar for names of the months, names of the days of the week, and the date, form groups of objects (as a basis for division and multiplication), and use the fraction $\frac{1}{2}$ correctly.

At mental ages of eight to nine years the children should learn to understand money values through one dollar (including ability to make change), and identify larger quantities, use the fractions $\frac{1}{3}$ and $\frac{1}{4}$, carry in addition, borrow in subtraction, and do simple multiplication and division.

The basic arithmetical skills need to be taught systematically. This does not mean, however, that they should be taught formally, and only through repetitive drill. The children should learn to recognize and understand relationships and then be able to apply them to concrete, meaningful situations.

During the time a child is in the intermediate class he should become familiar with the fundamental number processes and adept in their use. Occasionally it may be necessary to extend this systematic training to the secondary class if the child has been unable to grasp all the skills (such as understanding the meaning of numbers, reading and writing numbers, addition, subtraction, multiplication, division, and use of common fractions, simple decimal fractions, and denominate numbers), which he will need when he leaves school to take his place in the community.

Before computational work can start, the child must understand what numbers are and know their meaning. One of the earliest experiences a child has with numbers is learning to count. He can learn to count to 10 or to 100 by rote without actually knowing what the number names mean. He must, however, learn these names so that he will know the names when he deals with them in arithmetic situations. Consequently, this is usually the beginning of the more formal number work for most children.

Following rote counting, the child should be taught the ordinal number, that is, he should learn *which one* before he encounters *how many*. It is not necessary that the terms "ordinal number" and "cardinal number" be taught to the children, but they should be taught the terminology and relationship of *one, two, three,* and *first, second, third,* and so forth.

After a child has grasped the concept of the ordinal number — and this is often accompanied by counting — he has the necessary background against which to build an understanding of the cardinal number. It is upon the concept of the cardinal number that the four fundamental number processes are built.

The teaching of the four fundamental number processes (addition, subtraction, multiplication, and division) develops in the child an understanding of the processes of grouping and regrouping involved in each. Once a child understands these, it simplifies the understanding of the interrelationships involved and adds meaning to them.

All problems involving numbers can be solved by counting. When the numbers become large, however, counting becomes cumbersome and simplification is achieved by using the fundamental number processes. For example, in addition we can give a child two groups of objects (three blocks and two blocks) and he can *count* the total number of objects (five blocks); in subtraction we can give a child a group of objects (five blocks), have him separate two from the rest and then *count* how many are in the other group (three blocks); in multiplication we can give a child a number of groups of objects (four) with the same number of objects in each group (two blocks) and have him *count* how many objects we have (eight blocks); and in division we can give a child a group of objects (six blocks), have him separate the objects into equal groups (two blocks in each) and then *count* how many equal groups of objects there are (three).

The beginning number work should be done in this way to give the child early experience in grouping. This will, in turn, give him a basic understanding of the grouping involved in the basic number processes once he has passed the counting stage and is working with numbers or quantities that cannot be easily handled by counting.

In all the processes it should be remembered that the total quantity is always there. Addition is a process of putting two or more groups together; subtraction is a process of separating one group from another; multiplication is a process of putting two or more groups of the same size together; and division is a process of separating a group into two or more equal groups.

Thus, the fundamental number processes are seen to be interrelated. They all involve working with groups of numbers, either putting them together or taking them apart. As such interrelated processes, they should be taught together, with the children learning and understanding the relationship.

The teacher should provide specified times in classes at the intermediate level for the development of the fundamental number skills. During these times the teacher will probably find it necessary to supplement the activity-teaching situations with practice in the various skills so that all the children may become familiar with their use. Additional practice periods will also be necessary for the learning of fundamental number combinations for "short-cutting." This does not mean, however, that the special periods will merely consist of drill as such. To be of the greatest value the practice must be meaningful to the child. He must know why the practice is included, how it will help him, and what its values are. Experience preceding the practice can demonstrate the need as well as teach the child the basic principles underlying the processes. This may be followed by additional experiences designed to include situations in which the child will be given additional practice and learn their value. It should be remembered that the learning of number skills through practice is not an end in itself. It is the means to an end by saving the child time through short-cutting and improving his accuracy.

In conjunction with providing situations in which the various number skills are needed, the project method presents many opportunities to develop and improve the children's skills and concepts and gives the teacher a chance to emphasize those areas in which she feels the need is the greatest. Through these experiences the teacher will have ample opportunity to diagnose the weaknesses of the children in arithmetic and to provide adapted exercises in the arithmetic period which will produce systematic growth in the fundamental skills.

As the children become older and more advanced, the fundamental number processes remain the same but the problems become more difficult. They should be taught two-column addition, borrowing in subtraction, more advanced multiplication and division, the understanding and use of fractional parts and forms, and how to read, interpret, and solve problems using the number skills learned.

THE DEVELOPMENT OF EFFICIENT USE OF ARITHMETICAL SKILLS

The abilities of the various children at the oldest or secondary level are more diverse than at any other level because of the range in mental abilities. The one thing that they all have in common is that within the near future (usually within one to three years) they will be leaving school to take a place in the community. It becomes the problem of the teacher of this group to provide the opportunity to use all needed knowledge in community or future life situations so that their experiences may be of real value to them in their postschool social and economic adjustment. The areas of experience, such as homebuilding and occupational education described earlier in Chapter 10, offer numerous opportunities for the use of arithmetic concepts in practical situations.

The major emphasis of the work in the advanced level is on personal, social, and economic adjustment, or preparation for community adjustment. Thus, it will be in these areas of experience that the teacher will find arithmetical problems for use. Every opportunity should be given the child to practice his number skills and to use and expand his number knowledge in these areas, because they are the areas in which the need will arise. Such practice will familiarize him with their use in real-life situations.

In those schools in which a work-school program has been

developed, arithmetic should be of the type to meet the boys' and girls' vocational needs. Rather than the verbal or theoretical substitutes presented in the typical arithmetic text, problems the children are encountering in their work situations should be used. In school situations, the boys will have use for arithmetical concepts and skills in conjunction with their manual training, home mechanics, and in the study of occupations and vocations. Similarly, the girls will have need for them in cooking, sewing, homemaking, and in the study of occupations and vocations in their areas of interest. By including these skills as an integral part of this work, we are depending less upon the children's ability to transfer their knowledge and skills from school to their actual use, and are actually helping them to make the transfer by explaining the relationships and associations, and training their ability to make generalizations in the future.

DIAGNOSIS AND REMEDIATION

Many mentally handicapped children, especially those who have not had the opportunity to enter the special class at the primary level, have some arithmetical disability. It thus becomes the task of the special teacher to determine any deficiency that may exist and plan a program designed to correct it.

The administration of a good standardized test early in the year and an analysis of the results is an excellent method of determining which children are in need of supplemental work to bring their arithmetical skills up to their achievement level where they will be of maximum value. A necessary prerequisite for a remedial program is the knowledge or information which will enable the teacher to detect the symptoms of faulty learning in order to recognize the timeliness of the program. There are various symptoms by which the teacher can detect the existence of some sort of inadequacy in arithmetic. Some of them which may prove to be the most useful are:

(1) Relatively low score (as compared to reading) on standardized tests.

(2) Inability to work three or four examples of a type correctly.

(3) Continuous inaccuracy of work.

(4) Exceptionally slow rate of work for his ability level.

(5) Faulty methods of work. Counting, immature methods, roundabout methods, dawdling or repetition of work.

(6) Continuous guessing.

(7) Failure to improve with the practice given to the rest of the class.

(8) Excessive and unnecessary motor activity, disinterest, and inattention.

(9) Confusion of processes, using elements of several processes, and using incorrect elements.

(10) Inability to interpret simple tabular and graphic material or to set up his own materials in these forms.

(11) Inability to restate problems in his own words.

(12) Inability to apply knowledge, skills, and concepts to practical situations.

(13) Inadequacy of vocabulary, inability to express or understand the essentials due to lack of knowledge of the words used.

Summary

The few studies that have been made concerning the arithmetical concepts and abilities of mentally handicapped children indicate that the mentally handicapped have a number of specific difficulties. These difficulties should be considered in developing a curriculum involving the teaching of number concepts and mathematical usage. A curriculum making use of either an active, experiencing type of activity or one in which concreteness or realism of presentation is used is superior to a curriculum in which verbal description is used as a substitute for experience.

The arithmetic curriculum of the regular grades is designed, primarily, to provide the child with the necessary background to understand the skills and concepts taught at the next step. This is also a factor in the curriculum for mentally handicapped children. However, it does not take precedence over the teaching of those skills needed in everyday living. Of utmost importance is teaching them in such a way that the skills can later be used. Specifically, the objectives of teaching arithmetic to mentally handicapped children are:

(1) The development, understanding, and use of an arithmetical vocabulary.

(2) The development of number concepts and skills.

(3) The development of the ability to apply number skills.

(4) The development of an understanding of various units of measurement.

(5) The development of an understanding of fractional parts.

These objectives may be obtained by a program which is based on the following principles:

(1) The concepts and skills that are introduced should be those which are within the child's ability to grasp and those which he will use.

(2) The arithmetic program should teach the child to increase associations, relationships, and basic principles and concepts.

(3) Specific teaching methods for the elimination of counting on fingers, counting addition combinations, and other immature habits should be emphasized after the mentally handicapped children have matured sufficiently to require their use no longer.

(4) Computation should be used in meaningful situations in order to aid in its later use in practical situations.

(5) Recognition of an ability to read the words needed in understanding arithmetical concepts should be emphasized.

(6) Teaching should be planned to improve the child's problem-reading and problem-understanding ability.

(7) Standards of achievement should be set at the child's level.

(8) Emphasis should be given to accuracy, carefulness, and autocriticism.

(9) Additional emphasis should be placed on the multiplication and division skills and concepts.

(10) A definite effort should be made to develop the concepts of sequence and time.

(11) A mastery of each fact, process, and skill should be insured before continuing to new ones.

(12) Practice should be used only where practice is needed, not as an easy method of teaching or as busy work.

(13) Repetition should be used freely and frequently.

(14) Distributive rather than concentrated practice of skills for the implementation of knowledge and concepts should be used.

An arithmetic program for mentally handicapped children must be planned systematically and organized developmentally. It should be so organized to (1) develop quantitative concepts, (2) systematically teach arithmetical skills in relation to their use, and (3) develop efficient use of the skills in life situations.

REFERENCES

Adams, H. W. "The Mathematics Encountered in the General Reading of Newspapers and Periodicals." Unpublished Master's Thesis, Department of Education, University of Chicago, Chicago, 1924.

Baker, Harry J. *Introduction to Exceptional Children.* New York: The Macmillan Co., 1949.

Brueckner, Leo J., and Foster E. Grossnickle. *How to Make Arithmetic Meaningful.* Philadelphia: The John C. Winston Co., 1947.

Carrison, Doris, and Heinz Werner. "Principles and Methods of Teaching Arithmetic to Mentally Retarded Children," *American Journal of Mental Deficiency*, 47 (January, 1943), pp. 309–317.

Costello, Helen Marjorie. "The Responses of Mentally Retarded Children to Specialized Learning Experiences in Arithmetic." Doctor's Dissertation, University of Pennsylvania, Philadelphia, 1941.

Cruickshank, William M. "A Comparative Study of Psychological Factors Involved in the Responses of Mentally Retarded and Normal Boys to Problems in Arithmetic." Doctor's Dissertation, University of Michigan, Ann Arbor, 1946.

Gothberg, Laura C. "The Mentally Defective Child's Understanding of Time," *American Journal of Mental Deficiency*, 53 (January, 1949), pp. 441–455.

Henry, Nelson B. (Editor). *The Teaching of Arithmetic.* Fiftieth Yearbook of the National Society for the Study of Education. Part II. Chicago: The University of Chicago Press, 1951.

Ingram, Christine P. *Education of the Slow-Learning Child.* New York: World Book Co., 1935.

Wilson, G. M. "A Survey of the Social and Business Usage of Arithmetic." Teachers' College Contributions to Education, No. 100. New York: Teachers College, Columbia University, 1919.

Chapter 14

Teaching the Practical Arts

The Fine Arts

ART, whether in the form of music, drawing, or painting, is a means of expression. As a means of expression, it has no confining limits with reference to age, abilities, or capabilities and as such it becomes an integral part of our daily activities. The fine arts, correlated with the other subjects in the curriculum, render an incalculable service in clarifying ideas the children are attempting to visualize and express. Consequently, children should be given opportunities and encouragement to use the arts as a means of expression.

The generalizations given above are true for all children, but they are especially applicable in planning the curriculum for the mentally handicapped. The mentally handicapped tend to be weak in verbal understanding and verbal expression. Through the use of the arts, one more avenue of expression and understanding is opened to them. In this relation, Wallin [1] states that in the special class curriculum a great deal of emphasis should be placed on the motor forms of training. The arts then become an essential in the special class, although not to the exclusion of academic work.

[1] Wallin, J. E. W., *The Education of Handicapped Children.* Boston: Houghton Mifflin Co., 1924.

The arts, as with other specific areas of study, should not be taught merely for the sake of teaching music or drawing in its various forms or solely for the sake of introducing the children to the various forms of art and art materials. They should rather be taught and used in relation to other activities, making them both meaningful and pleasurable to the child. Gradually the child should develop an understanding of and an insight into their functions in the out-of-school world.

Young children are very individual in their actions. Consequently, a free environment, allowing for individual responses, must be provided. Utilization should be made of the natural activities of the children, such as rhythms, drawing, and finger painting. As the child grows and develops, he learns to express himself more surely and his activities become more expressive and meaningful. He is learning expression through the use of other than verbal methods.

The mentally handicapped child often has a mental and physical make-up that does not allow him to concentrate for long periods of time on a single interest. Allowances should be made for activity. However, if such activity is to be continued and is expected to result in desirable outcomes, it must give the child both pleasure and satisfaction. It is in the field of manual manipulations and art experiences that the mentally handicapped can usually find their greatest satisfactions. In this way they are aided in establishing constructive attitudes.

Arts and Crafts

It is commonly accepted that arts and crafts have a definite place in the education of the mentally handicapped. The teachers' understandings of the values and purposes of the arts in the curriculum vary a great deal. The principles upon which their programs are based also vary with the teachers' philosophies. As a result, the arts and crafts programs in the special classes have taken a number of different forms.

TYPES OF ARTS AND CRAFTS PROGRAMS

(1) Some teachers co-ordinate their arts and crafts closely with

the subject-matter areas. They teach essentially through projects, where the various skills are taught as the need for them arises. In this way the completed arts and crafts become functional. They are actually used in a situation in which the child has a realization of their need. They also help to increase the child's learning and understanding of the processes, materials, and end products. The art work does not become an end in itself. It is used as another means of expression by the children and as another means of conveying an idea by the teacher. Teachers advocating the usage of art in this manner allege that it aids in making concepts and ideas more meaningful to the child.

(2) Other teachers teach the arts and crafts as an end in themselves. This type of teaching is most apt to be found where a highly organized curriculum exists, i.e., where specific times of the day are set aside for reading, writing, arithmetic, social studies, music, and art. Skills in manipulating the various media are taught specifically. There is usually little or no consideration given to the interests of the children or to the relation of the current art work to the academic areas. A standardized curriculum, based upon the seasons, the supposed interests of all children of specific grade levels, and the abilities of children at specific chronological and mental ages is available. This, the teacher may accept in whole or in part. Thus the program is planned for relatively long periods of time. The teacher feels that the skills and appreciations expected of every adult will have been developed by following a logical sequence of art work throughout the child's school years.

(3) The third type of teacher is primarily interested in the end product. He judges the value of the arts and crafts program on the quality and quantity of articles produced. Emphasis is placed upon the ability to do a few things well. In this way products will be available for display in the room and for sale at the annual carnival or open house. Children are given little or no opportunity to experiment with materials and techniques as a method of learning; instead, they are taught specifically how to perform a limited number of skills. They are closely supervised to eliminate waste. This is continued until they become expert with the given material and technique and can actually perform the necessary operations quite

mechanically. The next phase is one of production. Few new skills or experiences are provided the child. He is expected and required to produce articles that are of no intrinsic value to him. As a result, however, quantities of articles, such as embroidery, knitting, weaving, and woodwork, are available for the annual sale to raise money to buy additional materials to be manufactured into more products during the next year for the following sale.

PRINCIPLES OF TEACHING ARTS AND CRAFTS

Unquestionably, the art program should be an integral part of the curriculum. To make it most useful and most valuable, it must be a part of the children's other school and living experiences. In deciding what arts and crafts to teach and how to teach them, the teacher should constantly be aware of the subsequent principles and should plan his activities in harmony with them.[2]

Techniques and skills should be taught in purposeful and functional situations. There are many opportunities for the children to construct things that are useful in their play activities and home situations. Use should be made of the children's interest in decorating the room, the doll house, the store, and the other projects being carried on. At the various levels the art activities may consist of different kinds of murals or group pictures depicting common activities and interests. These activities may be conceived by the group or by an individual. They may be pictures, drawn or painted by the children, of things they have enjoyed seeing or experiencing. Other purposeful activities may consist of constructing games, gifts, playthings, school equipment, models, and so forth.

Art should be used as a method of expression in correlation with other class activities. Every activity presents an infinite number of possibilities for correlation. Children enjoy illustrating stories and rhymes by drawing, clay modeling, or sand table construction. The illustrations, regardless of type, are used for clarification of the reading material and of concepts being presented. Drawings may

---

[2] The National Recreation Association, New York, has mimeographed a "Handicraft and Hobby Bibliography." It contains a compilation of books having practical value in the promotion of craft activities. This bibliography should prove to be of great value to special class teachers.

be developed into a sequence as a story-movie. The teacher must constantly be striving to improve the children's ability to choose illustrations that will be of value and of benefit to the children.

Opportunities for oral language and expression in connection with various types of handwork are almost unlimited. Discussion of plans and results should be made an integral part of the work. The children should be given an opportunity to talk about what they are going to make. Later they can discuss what they have made, how they made it, its values, and what uses may be made of it. The art activities and experiences acquaint the children with new materials, tools, and processes. Additions are thus made to their stock of ideas, meanings, and vocabulary. These can and should be used to enrich both their oral and written forms of expression.

Geography as such is not usually taken up in the special class. The children, however, do make a study of their immediate community and neighborhood. In connection with their stories and study of the community, typical surroundings may be constructed or presented through pictures. Thus visualization, manipulation, and construction are added to the more common verbalization and field trip methods of teaching. The children become more interested in what is read and discussed. The study of food, shelter, clothing, and sources of raw materials (all including geographical concepts) are enhanced through the use of manual art, visual materials, and creative activities.

There are few handwork activities that do not make use of the quantitative aspects of experience. When a child makes something with his hands, he is almost always using some form of measurement and is making comparisons of relative size and quantity. Frequently the child is not conscious of this. Concrete experience with actual quantities and spaces is necessary before the symbols that represent them have much meaning. Facility in the use of number and quantity concepts increase the child's ability to work with and construct art and craft projects. In handwork there are many opportunities to correlate symbols and number experiences in a meaningful way. The need for counting and measuring becomes obvious to the child when something he wants to make is dependent upon those abilities. Exactness and precision in the comparison of areas, quantities, volume, lines, and relative positions should be stressed.

The child should not be deprived of manipulative experiences because of his awkwardness and in-co-ordination. In many cases one may find the mentally handicapped child is clumsy and awkward. His desire to handle and manipulate materials and objects may lead to some destruction solely because of his in-co-ordination. He should, rather, be led through simple tasks to progressively more complicated ones. If deprived of such experiences his natural tendency to manipulate objects, to feel textures, and to experiment with materials may turn into unguided channels of destruction. Whether children learn to construct or destroy is largely dependent upon the satisfactions they have been helped to develop. When manual activity is rightly directed its inclusion as an integral part of the curriculum has an important effect upon training a child to enjoy the manipulation of materials and the construction of objects.

Eventually the development of manual dexterity and motor co-ordination will have two results. First, it will cultivate a desire to make useful things whose appropriate form and soundness of construction give them intrinsic beauty. As his skill grows the child desires accuracy and neatness in his work, and if he succeeds he is encouraged to continue his efforts to improve. Second, it should provide the child with the necessary initial training for his eventual occupational or vocational placement. The dexterities and co-ordinations developed in his early craft manipulations will help him to learn the skills and techniques of job requirements more easily. He will have a background of experience upon which he may more readily learn new motor requirements.

Arts and crafts should be used as a method to improve motor co-ordination. Art activities train the child to use his hands with certainty and precision. It should not be expected that these outcomes will develop in a week or in a month. They should be developed and evaluated over a number of years. Occasionally a child is kept at one type of handwork for a long period of time. This does very little for him once the initial learning process is over. For example, considerable learning may take place when a child weaves a first rug, but little learning occurs when the child makes a fifth rug of the same kind.

Through the activities of handwork the child is provided with an incentive to use his muscles and to improve his co-ordination. Watching his work grow and take shape creates a situation which increases his interest and attention. He is encouraged to continue to work for the improvement of his muscular control. Small accomplishments, for a child who has never succeeded, aid in the development of the confidence necessary to continue.

The choice of the project should originate with the child. The easiest and most effective way of promoting interest in the activity and motivating the child to do his best is to allow the child to originate his own activity. Even within a total class project there is considerable freedom for an individual child to select those activities that are meaningful and of interest to him. For example, in building a store for the classroom one child who is interested in lettering may print the signs and labels, another child who is interested in woodwork may help construct shelves and counters, while another less capable child who enjoys painting may aid in the painting of the finished articles.

The children should derive a personal satisfaction from a task well done. The children should be helped to develop an attitude of considering the appearance of things they have made. There is an important relationship between handwork and ownership. Through allowing and encouraging the child to make objects he can keep and use, his interest in better construction and design can be promoted. Through the construction of a well made and well designed article he becomes proud of his projects and derives a great deal of satisfaction from his endeavors. This is an important factor in the mental health of the child.

The arts and crafts program should be used to improve attitudes. Many opportunities are presented to improve the children's understanding and practice of co-operation, socialization, and sharing. The use of equipment, the helpful attitude of a fellow worker, the projects or pieces of work undertaken co-operatively, the care of tools, and the leaving of tools so that others can find and use them, all prepare the child for social living. These attitudes can be made real and vital to the child through emphasis of the many situations in which the co-operative use of materials and equipment occurs daily.

The attitude or ability of auto-criticism should result from well directed and conceived handwork. This ties in very closely with the personal satisfactions derived by a child as a result of his completed projects. He should be taught to evaluate his efforts in terms of his abilities and previous experiences. He should not be satisfied with the same quality of work from one project to the next. Improvement in skills and construction should be noted. He must also be encouraged to put forth his greatest efforts, to make each project his very best and to be satisfied with nothing less. This does not mean that perfection will be required. What is the best for one child may be a very poor piece of work for another.

Other attitudes to be stressed are a desire for some kind of orderliness or system and proper care of materials, tools, and equipment. The development of habits of economy are also by-products of manual work. These may be developed through the countless opportunities for measuring and cutting materials. Methods to conserve materials and construct things economically should be stressed. The drawing and use of patterns and the placing of patterns for the most advantageous use of materials before cutting is a method of eliminating impulsive and reckless waste of material.

The materials used in arts and crafts should be cheap and easy to handle. Apple boxes, orange crates, and cardboard cartons can be used for furniture and parts of structures such as the store, post office, or play house. Other things can be made from clay, paper, and similar materials. At the initial stages the child may enjoy just feeling the materials and manipulating them. At a later date, definite articles of interest may be constructed.

PRACTICAL ARTS

Every citizen needs to understand and become familiar with the basic industrial and home craft skills. Whether or not a person is actively engaged in industry, he is continually coming in contact with an increasingly industrial society. This does not mean that every child should be taught a specific skill or trade. For the mentally handicapped, the emphasis should be placed on a non-vocational-industrial type of industrial arts and home economics program. This will help him (1) to further develop the habits, attitudes, and knowledges that will be useful to him in his economic and vocational adjustment, (2) to learn to adjust to the industrial phases of modern society, and (3) to aid him in becoming a better home member.

The arts and crafts program acquaints the child with some of the common hand tools, materials, and attitudes necessary for co-operative group work, thus acting as the introductory phases of the practical arts program. The objectives of the arts and crafts program at the primary and intermediate levels lie in the areas which act as a foundation for industrial arts and home economics skills. Like the arts and crafts program, the practical arts are not taught with the thought of making the child proficient at any one of them. They too are taught as an introduction to the various areas and skills needed in the children's everyday living. Any or all of the industrial arts and home economics experiences may be provided to both the boys and the girls in the class.

Occasionally a child will display unusual abilities in a vocational area. He may have a great deal of aptitude for cooking, baking, upholstering, or cabinet-making. In cases of this type, the child should be encouraged and given opportunity to develop these skills to their utmost. Instead of going to all the classes with the rest of the children, he may go to special trades or vocational school classes part of the day and become a skilled craftsman by the time he leaves school.

INDUSTRIAL ARTS

The industrial arts classes should acquaint the children with the use of wood, metal, plastics, and other materials. The proper use and care of tools should be more highly emphasized than in the arts and crafts program. The children may also be given some instruction in operating simple machines.

The construction of a project should not consist solely of copying a pattern on material and then cutting it out. It should include elementary planning, constructing, and finishing. Where the child has an opportunity to select materials, tools, and designs, he is developing discriminative ability and learning the qualities and conservation of materials. In addition to teaching through the activities, additional learning situations should be provided through trips, visual materials, related readings, and discussions.

Specific instruction in industrial arts is almost entirely confined to the intermediate and secondary age groups. At the intermediate level the various skills are usually correlated within themselves as well as with the other class activities. A few generalizations and suggestions will be made concerning the industrial arts activities at the intermediate level before discussing the program at the secondary level.

The woodworking taught to the intermediate group should consist of simple projects selected by the children. Woods and finishes should be of a type easily worked with; this eliminates the hardwoods and complicated processes. Suitable materials in metal craft are tin can craft, simple wrought iron work, and possibly some sheet copper for the more capable children. Plastics is a relatively new craft that offers many possibilities. The tools needed are simple and materials handle in much the same way as wood. All these offer opportunities for the use of the saw, file, drill, vice, sandpaper, glue, plane, ruler, compass, and various finishing methods.

The simple home mechanics and repairs program should consist essentially of learning the proper use of common hand tools, such as the hammer, saw, plane, file, drill, screw-driver, and pliers. While many of the skills needed to do an acceptable job may not be developed at this level, the children are being introduced to the need for these skills and methods commonly used.

At the secondary or adolescent level, whether the special class is in a junior or senior high school or with the other special classes in a separate unit, the industrial arts program is usually somewhat apart from the experience units. While this is not actually the case in some classes, separate periods are usually designated for them.

The industrial arts program at the adolescent level is actually an extension of that at the intermediate or preadolescent level. However, relatively more time is usually devoted to it since the children will be leaving school to take their places in the community in a year or two. Again the program is not one designed to teach specific trades or skills but one designed to provide the children with the basic skills necessary for job placement in a number of areas and some skills that will aid the mentally handicapped to perform odd jobs around the house.

A number of shop areas will be discussed in this section. That does not mean any one or ones of these shops are specifically recommended. They are only mentioned and described to present some ideas of the experiences that may be provided and the shops that may prove to be of value.[3]

Woodwork. In working with wood, the emphasis should be on the selection of the correct tools for specific jobs, the care of tools, learning what types of woods are best suited for particular jobs, co-operation, and good work habits. High motivation is usually present when the child selects his own project, even though the teacher aids and counsels him in his choice. Specific instruction in the proper use of the plane, saw, hammer, chisel, drill, screwdriver, file, square, marking gauge, and sandpaper should be included. The construction of simple projects offers ample occasion to provide instruction in the use of tools.

Metal work. In working with metals stress should be placed on skills and attitudes, use of metals, and the tools designed for this type of work. Simple projects in sheet iron and wrought iron would be of the most value. Among the tools the child should become familiar with are the tin shears, ball peen hammer, hack saw, and drill. Simple soldering should be included as one of the skills taught. Projects should again be those of use to the children.

Home mechanics. The home mechanics program should be designed to provide the children with opportunities to become proficient with the tools and materials commonly used in making simple repairs of the house, home equipment, and household furnishings.

---

[3] The Department of Special Education of the Detroit Public Schools has mimeographed an "Organization of the Shop Program in Special Education." It includes the general organization, aims, courses of study, methods of instruction, and records, as well as the specific courses of study for the wood, metal, print, household mechanics, arts and crafts, foodhandling, personal service, and shoe repair shops.

Since stress is placed on maintenance and repair, no original projects would be constructed. Aside from the tools, the main equipment of the room should consist of faucets, electrical cords, plugs, appliances, and things of that type for the children to work on. Household equipment and furnishings not working properly, as well as a chair that is in need of repair, a table that needs refinishing, or a screen that needs reinforcing or new screening, should be brought to school by the children. There they can repair them under the supervision of the teacher. In this phase of work, it is advisable for the teacher to point out what repairs should not be attempted as well as teaching those that should be. For example, unskilled persons attempting to do additional house wiring may be creating a fire hazard and should be discouraged in this type of activity.

Other experiences. Other activities that might be included are auto mechanics, food handling and preparation in the cafeteria, and arts and crafts. In auto mechanics the emphasis would be placed on tire repairing, washing, and the general servicing of automobiles rather than the actual repairing of them.

The general shop. For the majority of the children, a general shop in which a number of activities can be carried on simultaneously or at different times meets their needs most fully. As the need arises, the instructor may direct activities in wood, metal, plastics, electricity, or plumbing. Such a shop is ideally suited for providing general information regarding the proper use of tools, equipment, skills, processes, and materials necessary in a number of areas.

At times the instructor may furnish information needed by the group through demonstrations and through contributions by experts from outside the school. The demonstration may be given to the class as a whole or to a group interested in a particular phase of the work. Films and slides may also play an important part in developing these knowledges, skills, and competencies. They not only make lectures and discussions more interesting; they also contribute substantially to the children's knowledge of materials and industrial products. Other types of visual aids, such as pictures, diagrams, drawings, and samples, should be used in profusion. Processes and principles can be clarified more easily in this way than by reading or explanation.

The most common method of teaching fundamental operations

should be through actual work with materials and through the construction of various kinds of projects. The children may learn the woodworking skills through the construction of toys, games, and pieces of furniture. General repairs, including metal, wood, soldering, and so forth, may be introduced by encouraging the children to bring appliances, furniture, screens, toys, and other broken objects from home to be worked on in class under the direction and supervision of the teacher. Much of the work thus becomes a home mechanics type of shop work supplemented by additional projects designed to improve specific skills in selected areas for specific children.

HOME ECONOMICS

The objectives of home economics instruction for the mentally handicapped are similar to those for normal children. Two things are of primary importance: (1) provision of opportunities for enriching child experiences and (2) guiding them in the interpretation of these so that happy, wholesome, useful members of society may result. This includes development of sound standards of living, an appreciation of the value of personal and social development, good judgment, and the power of critical and creative thought as applied to their immediate problems.

The children should be taught to see their personal home and family activities objectively, in relation to the general social environment in which they are now living. This can be done by giving the pupils an understanding and an appreciation of the functions, values, and ideals of normal family life in a changing society. The courses included in home economics should develop in the pupil a concept of homemaking as a function in which all members of the family must participate and co-operate.

To achieve these goals, the children must be provided with enough practice, under guidance, to enable them to acquire those skills which they need for carrying on effectively the activities of home and family life. A working knowledge of the procedures and opportunities necessary to participate in activities related to personal problems and home management are thus presented.

As with the industrial arts program, the home economics program starts with the intermediate or preadolescent group. Elementary experiences should be provided in sewing, cooking, clothing, needlework, and homemaking. These experiences will provide the child with the background to make maximum use of the more specific skills taught at the secondary or adolescent level.

For the preadolescent, sewing would call for learning basic sewing procedures (hand and machine) through experience with simple projects. Learning to care for clothes is probably even more important. Introduction to darning, repairing, patching, washing, starching, and ironing should be included. This should also be extended to hanging up clothes and cleaning and pressing. They are important not only from the appearance point of view but also for the additional wear and service the clothing will provide as a result of the care given them.

As previously indicated, much of the needlecraft work is coordinated with other phases of the arts and crafts program. Decorations of spatter painting, block printing, textile painting, and embroidery can be added to projects. Thus the articles become things of beauty to be used either by the child or for gifts. Many arts and crafts skills can and should be combined in the production of a finished piece of work. In this way these skills gain additional meaning for the child. In addition, those children interested in this type of work should be given an opportunity to learn additional needlecrafts such as knitting and crocheting. These should be taught as recreational or spare-time activities and not as activities on which a future vocation can be built. In the classroom, it gives the child something of interest and value to do during periods when he has finished his other work. This type of a recreational activity can then be easily carried into adult life.

Cooking at this level consists of familiarizing the child with the fundamental equipment, tools, and processes through extremely simple kitchen procedures. For most of these children many packaged foods, although more expensive, can be used to a much greater advantage than complicated cook book recipes. Canned soups, simple salads, complete macaroni and spaghetti dinner packages, canned meats and sea foods, biscuit mixes, packaged desserts such as puddings, gelatines, and cake mixes can be prepared with a minimum of technique. The basic cooking terms such as simmer, boil, bake, beat, and stir as well as procedures such as measuring, watching temperature, timing, and following simple directions, are encountered. Noon lunch programs and parties furnish incentives for carrying on these activities. Here it should be emphasized that the home economics experiences should not be for the girls alone but should also be included for the boys.

The home economics program for adolescents should consist of a study of foods, clothing, and home furnishings. These, as the various areas of industrial arts, are usually taught in specific laboratories. Ideally, they should be integrated into a general home arts program for the majority of the children.

Foods. The foods program should include the preparation and serving of foods, order and cleanliness in the kitchen, and experiences in buying and budgeting. It is somewhat doubtful that the mentally handicapped can comprehend the principles of proper nutrition and apply them. The best method might be to simply emphasize the need for fresh and cooked vegetables, meats, fruits, and various starches. The primary objective becomes one of developing the ability to plan, prepare, and serve simple meals. In the laboratory the class may co-operatively plan meals, determine the amount and kinds of foods, plan for the time required for preparation, and other necessary details. The students acquire experience in the preparation of individual foods, and finally are given the opportunity to prepare complete meals. Some supplementary experience in preserving foods may also be included, although this is less essential today, especially in urban areas, than it was a number of years ago.

Clothing. The primary clothing problem for most of the mentally handicapped is one of providing a supply of garments to insure adequate and proper dress. As a consequence, much of the time should be devoted to the care, alteration, and repair of garments. Practical methods for the care of clothing begin with daily habit training in the regular use of hangers, shoe trees, and hat boxes. The benefits derived from mending small tears, sewing on loose or missing buttons, and reinforcing worn spots should be emphasized. Repair techniques involving the use of darning, patching, reinforcing, and the use of commercial mending tapes should be included. Proper drying of wet garments, stain removal, and ironing and pressing techniques should be stressed. There is also a need to learn to alter garments to improve their fit and style, and to give additional wear. Altering the garment would include shortening, lengthening, and making minor style changes. Completely making over garments is too difficult a process for most of the mentally handicapped.

The clothing program should include experience in the construction of clothes. Making a garment includes choice of (1) pattern, which should include consideration of body build, purpose of the garment, and ease of construction, and (2) materials in which consideration must be given to cost, seasonability, durability, and ease of handling. Here the teacher can demonstrate the parts of the pattern according to use and place the pattern on the material in preparation for cutting. This experience is of value to the children in teaching them material conservation, matching material design, and how to lay a pattern on the material. In the construction of any article, additional experiences are provided in hand and machine sewing, embroidery for decoration, and evaluation of the completed article.

Home furnishings. The home furnishing program should include a number of phases not specifically included under foods and clothing. Consideration should be given to units in buying furniture, utensils, and applicances. Evaluating the objects in light of need, convenience, cost, and decorating should be included. Care of home furnishings and appliances should be emphasized.

General home arts. The best home economics program can be provided in a general home arts course. This course would include a home unit in which cooking, clothing, and home furnishing skills would be integrated in much the same manner that the industrial arts skills are integrated in the general shop. A home arts unit provides opportunities for numerous homemaking activities and practice in home living. It presents opportunities to learn cleaning, setting tables, giving parties, methods of general home care, washing dishes and clothes, ironing, cleaning, and bed making. These may be carried on simultaneously or at different times to meet the needs of the various children. At the same time, these separate activities should be integrated into the whole job of home care, thus aiding in their transfer to actual, out-of-school situations. Personal appearance should be stressed. Cleanliness, care of hair, nails, selection of make-up, care and selection of shoes are "musts" for the mentally handicapped adolescent.

SUMMARY

The fine arts, arts and crafts, and applied arts programs of the special classes are closely related and continuous throughout the child's school life. The general objectives of the fine arts program are (1) to give the children additional means of expression through such activities as drawing, painting, and music, and (2) to develop an appreciation and enjoyment of such things as music, pictures, and well designed and functional objects.

The arts and crafts and practical arts are very closely related. The arts and crafts program of the primary and preadolescent levels form the basis upon which the practical arts program at the same levels are built. Consequently, the general objectives for the arts and crafts and practical arts programs are the same, namely: (1) to develop an increased understanding of the industrial society in which we live; (2) to develop the basic habits, attitudes, and skills necessary for future economic and vocational adjustment; and (3) to develop better home membership.

SOURCES OF SUPPLIES AND EQUIPMENT

Most of the supplies and equipment used in the arts and crafts, industrial arts, and home economics programs can be obtained in local grocery, department, drug, paint, hardware, stationery supply, and book stores, lumber yards, and plumbing, automobile, and electrical supply houses. If the teacher explains her problem to these business men, they are usually very helpful in making suggestions about what products to use and how to use them. If one source of supply does not have the desired materials, they will often inquire of others in the community and locate it for the teacher. In addition, the following companies are sources for specialized supplies. The interested teacher may write to them for catalogues describing their complete line.

Ace Leather Company
5065 West 11th Street
Indianapolis, Indiana

American Art Clay Company
Indianapolis, Indiana

American Crayon Company
726–826 Hayes Avenue
Sandusky, Ohio

Bersted's Hobby-Craft, Inc.
Monmouth, Illinois

Carters Ink Company
11 W. Hubbard Street
Chicago, Illinois

Chicago Paper Company
811 S. Wells Street
Chicago, Illinois

Dennison Manufacturing Company
62 E. Randolph Street
Chicago, Illinois

Denver Fire Clay Company
Denver, Colorado

Easi-Bild Pattern Company
Pleasantville, New York

Eberhard Faber Pencil Company
20 N. Wacker Drive
Chicago, Illinois

Flexcraft Industries
1934 Webster Avenue
New York 57, New York

Metal Goods Corporation
5239 Brown Avenue
St. Louis 15, Missouri

Milton Bradley Company
811 S. Wabash Avenue
Chicago, Illinois

Plastic Supply Company
2901 N. Grand Boulevard
St. Louis 7, Missouri

Sanford Manufacturing Company
846 W. Congress Street
Chicago, Illinois

The Handicrafters
Waupaun, Wisconsin

FREE MATERIALS

Many manufacturers produce free materials that may prove to be of value to the teacher. The following are some of the corporations which have indicated that they supply free materials. To aid the teacher, *Practical Home Economics*, *The Grade Teacher*, and the *Instructor* provide a coupon service for obtaining many free teaching aids.

American Can Company
Home Economics Section, Department PH-1-48
230 Park Avenue
New York 17, New York

American Institute of Laundering
Joliet, Illinois

American Meat Institute
Chicago, Illinois

American Viscose Corporation
Box 864 G.P.O.
New York, New York

Armour and Company
Consumer Service Department
Chicago 9, Illinois

Botany Mills, Inc.
Passaic, New Jersey

Bristol-Myers Company
Educational Service Department
45 Rockefeller Plaza
New York 20, New York

Bureau of Educational Services
401 Broadway
New York 13, New York

Cannon Mills, Inc.
70 Worth Street
New York 13, New York

Carnation Company
Department 752-A
Milwaukee 2, Wisconsin

Casein Company of America
Division of Borden Company —
    Department No. GT-129
350 Madison Avenue
New York 17, New York

Cereal Institute, Inc.
135 S. LaSalle Street
Chicago 3, Illinois

Helena Rubenstein, Inc.
655 Fifth Avenue
New York 22, New York

Hoover Home Institute
The Hoover Company
North Canton, Ohio

Kellogg Company
Battle Creek, Michigan

Knox Gelatine
Department U-5
Johnstown, New York

Mrs. Stewart's Bluing
Minneapolis 3, Minnesota

National Association of Ice Industries
1706 L Street, N.W.
Washington, D.C.

National Canners Association
1739 H Street
Washington 6, D.C.

National Cotton Council
Box 76
Memphis 1, Tennessee

Rit Products Corporation
1401 W. Jackson Blvd.
Chicago 7, Illinois

Rubber Manufacturers Association, Inc.
Rubber Footwear Division
444 Madison Avenue
New York 22, New York

S. C. Johnson and Son, Inc.
Department PH-28
Racine, Wisconsin

Wheat Flour Institute
309 W. Jackson Blvd.
Chicago 6, Illinois

CHILDREN'S BOOKS

Many books on the community, vocations, and the home are on the market today. Single copies in the room library add a valuable source of reference on various areas being studied and discussed. The following are some of those that are available.

Baldwin, Myrtle C. *Johnny on the Spot.* Burlington, Vermont: University of Vermont, Waterman Building, 1945.

Butler, Frieden. *Wash Day With Mother.* Burlington, Vermont: University of Vermont, Waterman Building, 1945.

Carter, M. H. *Her Hobby is Mending.* Burlington, Vermont: University of Vermont, Waterman Building, 1945.

Carter, M. H., B. M. Thomas, and Marion Young. *Enemies of Clothing.* Burlington, Vermont: University of Vermont, Waterman Building, 1945.

Credle, Ellis. *Little Jeems Henry.* New York: Thomas Nelson & Sons, 1936.

Dale, Jane. *Meat, Flesh Foods From Farm, Range and Sea.* Poughkeepsie, New York: Artists and Writers Guild, 1939.

DeAngeli, Marguerite. *Copper Toed Boots.* New York: Doubleday & Company, Inc., 1938.

Donald, Thelma, Helene Nichols, Marion Young, and Mary Sullivan. *New Shoes! New Shoes!* Burlington, Vermont: University of Vermont, Waterman Building, 1947.

Field, Rachel. *Pocket Handkerchief Park.* New York: Doubleday, Doran, 1939.

Harris, Julia. *Visits Here and There.* Boston: Houghton Mifflin Company, 1930.

Hart, Mary, Marion Young, and Mary Sullivan. *Shoes Go to School.* Burlington, Vermont: University of Vermont, Waterman Building, 1946.

Harter, Helen. *Bread.* Chicago: Follett Publishing Company, 1936.

Harter, Helen, and Alta McIntire. *Food.* Chicago: Follett Publishing Company, 1936.

Kelikes, Alice V., and Others. *Household Workers.* (Picture Script Books.) New York: Harper & Brothers, 1941

Leaf, Munro, *Manners Can Be Fun.* New York: Frederick A. Stokes and Company, 1936.

Lindmand, Major J. *Snipp, Snapp, Snuer and the Red Shoes.* Chicago: Albert Whiteman & Company, 1932.

Marshall, Dean. *The Long White Month.* New York: E. P. Dutton & Co., Inc., 1942.

Marshall, Dean, and Kaleb Thesein. *A House for Elizabeth.* New York: E. P. Dutton & Co., Inc., 1941.

Montague, Audrey. *From Old to New.* Burlington, Vermont: University of Vermont, Waterman Building, 1947.

Murray, Gretchen. *Shoes for Sandy.* New York: Grosset and Dunlap, 1936.

McIntire, Alta. *Milk.* Chicago: Follett Publishing Company, 1936.

Newberry, Clare. *April's Kittens.* New York: Harper & Brothers, 1940.

Perry, Ida, and Gertrude Sapp. *Busy Betty.* Gainesville, Florida: Florida Curriculum Laboratory, 1945.

Perry, Ida. *Happy Helpers.* Gainesville, Florida: Florida Curriculum Laboratory, 1945.

Seredy, Kate. *Tree for Peter.* New York: The Viking Press, Inc., 1941.

Thomas, Eleanor. *Stories About Linda and Lee.* Boston: Ginn and Company, 1947.

Tillotson, W. R., E. Edie, K. Chamberlin, and Helene Nichols. (Revised by Young, Marion, and Mary Sullivan.) *Tales from the Salvage Can.* Burlington, Vermont: University of Vermont, Waterman Building, 1947.

Tippett, James S. *Busy Carpenters.* New York: World Book Company, 1929.

Turnbell, Agnes. *Elijah and the Fishbite.* New York: The Macmillan Company, 1940.

Van Stachum, Hilda. *The Cottage at Bonty Bay.* New York: The Viking Press, Inc., 1938.

References

Akin, B. U. "Care and Cleaning of Woolens," *Practical Home Economics,* 22 (October, 1945), p. 472.

Barry, A. G. "Underprivileged Girl: What the Homemaking Classes of San Jose Construction School Offer Her," *Practical Home Economics,* 13 (September, 1935), pp. 252–254.

Bell, Enid. *Tin Craft as a Hobby.* New York: Harper & Brothers, 1935.

Boehemer, Susan E., and Chris Groneman. *Making Things is Fun.* Austin, Texas: The Stick Company, 1947.

Cherry, Raymond. *General Plastics.* Bloomington, Illinois: McKnight and McKnight, 1941.

Cole, Natalie Robinson. *The Arts in the Classroom.* New York: John Day Co., Inc., 1940.

Coffman, S. V. "Homemaking Activities for Different Children," *Journal of Home Economics,* 23 (August, 1931), pp. 737–739.

Collins, A. T. "Home Arts in the Elementary School," *Teachers Outline,* 23 (November, 1939), pp. 42–43.

Crone, C. L. "Study of Home Economics in the Teaching of Handicapped Children," *Home Economics Journal,* 23 (August, 1931), pp. 732–735.

Detroit Public Schools. "Organization of the Shop Program in Special Education." File No. 3890, 1944.

Fleming, M. "Below Average Pupil Home Economics," *The School,* 30 (February, 1942), pp. 526–530.

Fryklund, Verne C., and Armand LaBerge, *General Shop Woodworking.* Bloomington, Illinois: McKnight and McKnight, 1946.

Hall, Ruth M., and Albert N. Hill. *Handicraft for Girls.* New York: Phillip Lippincott, 1941.

Hamilton, E. T. *Popular Crafts for Boys.* New York: Dodd, Mead & Co., 1935.

Handicraft and Hobby Bibliography. New York: National Recreation Association, New York.

Hughes, Dorothy. *Rhythmic Games and Dances.* New York: American Book Company, 1942.

Klenke, William W. *Things to Make and How to Make Them.* Peoria, Illinois: The Manual Arts Press, 1938.

Lemming, Joseph. *Fun With Boxes.* New York: Stokes, 1937.

Leeming, Joseph. *Fun With Paper.* New York: Stokes, 1939.

Leeming, Joseph. *Fun With Wood.* New York: Stokes, 1942.

Livingston, C. L. "Home Economics for Primary School Children," *Practical Home Economics,* 25 (December, 1947), p. 657.

Martens, E. H. "Home Economics for the Handicapped Pupil," *Practical Home Economics,* 16 (September, 1938), pp. 338–340.

Munyan, V. "Homemaking in an Elementary School," *Practical Home Economics,* 20 (July, 1942), pp. 252–255.

McLeisch, Minnie. *Beginnings: Teaching Art to Children.* New York: Studio Publications, 1941.

Newkirk, Louis V. *Integrated Handwork for Elementary Schools.* New York: Silver, Burdett & Co., 1940.

Newkirk, Louis V., and William H. Johnson. *Industrial Arts Program.* New York: The Macmillan Company, 1948.

Orata, P. T. "Education for Home and Family Living," *Journal of Home Economics,* 41 (January, 1949), pp. 5–7.

Schultz, Harold A., and J. Harlan Shores. *Art in the Elementary School*. University of Illinois Bulletin, 46, No. 16. Urbana, Illinois: Office of Publications, University of Illinois, 1948.

Sinclair, M. L. "Correlating Home Economics With the Life of a Girl," *The School*, 31 (June, 1943), pp. 916–919.

Tanner, Robin. *Children's Work in Blockprinting*. Peoria, Illinois: Manual Arts Press, 1938.

Wallin, J. E. W. *The Education of Handicapped Children*. Boston: Houghton Mifflin Company, 1924.

Chapter 15

Procedures Affecting Social Adjustment

ONE OF THE major goals of the education of mentally handicapped children is to effect adequate social adjustment. This adjustment does not imply conformity or strict obedience to authority, but the ability of the individual to adjust to situations independently of supervision and direction. It implies behavior that assists the individual in adjusting to situations with the least amount of tension, behavior that furthers the growth of the individual, and behavior which does not interfere with the lives of others.

While teachers find it more difficult to manage a special class than they do one which is composed of normal children, much can be done in the special classroom to promote behavior which is socially acceptable. For this reason many mentally handicapped children are referred to special classes because their behavior adjustment in the regular class is poor. As a matter of fact, students are frequently referred to special classes for reasons of behavior rather than because they lack adequate learning ability in the regular grades.

This chapter will give some suggestions for the management of behavior from the point of view of teacher-pupil relationships and mental hygiene, rather than from an administrative point of view.

PERSONALITY ADJUSTMENT

A number of studies have attempted to determine the personality characteristics of mentally handicapped children. In general, no one has found any specific personality characteristics among these children that are not found in normal ones. Their personality reactions, although they may be exaggerated because of the situation in which they have been placed, appear to be like other children's in similar situations. In a study of the personality of mentally handicapped boys and girls, Sarason[1] found indications of aggressiveness on the Thematic Apperception Test. He explained this aggression as a result of an unsatisfied desire for affection which resulted in frustration and aggression. Abel[2] found similar feelings of aggression among mentally deficient children, and even greater feelings of aggression among mentally deficient Negroes than among similar whites.

Lurie[3] found that incorrigibility and delinquency characterized subnormal children referred to a child guidance clinic. Very few of them were referred because of dull intelligence. Studies by Johnson,[4] and by Johnson and Kirk,[5] showed that mentally handicapped children in the regular grades are isolated and rejected by other children. The normal children rejected them, not because of poor learning ability, but because of unacceptable behavior such as fighting, misbehaving, swearing, showing off, bullying, cheating, and lack of ability to conform to group standards.

Throughout the preceding chapters it has been pointed out re-

[1] Sarason, Seymour B., "The Use of the Thematic Apperception Test with Mentally Deficient Children: I. A Study of High Grade Girls," *American Journal of Mental Deficiency*, 47 (April, 1943), pp. 414–442; "II. A Study of High Grade Boys," *American Journal of Mental Deficiency*, 48 (October, 1943), pp. 169–173.

[2] Abel, J. M., "Responses of Negro and White Morons to the Thematic Apperception Test," *American Journal of Mental Deficiency*, 49 (April, 1945), pp. 463–468.

[3] Lurie, L. A., "Conduct Disorders of Intellectually Subnormal Children," *American Journal of Psychiatry*, 91 (March, 1937), pp. 1025–1038.

[4] Johnson, G. O., "A Study of the Social Position of Mentally Handicapped Children in the Regular Grades," *American Journal of Mental Deficiency*, 55 (July, 1950), pp. 60–89.

[5] Johnson, G. O., and S. A. Kirk, "Are Mentally Handicapped Children Segregated in the Regular Grades?" *Journal of Exceptional Children*, 17 (December, 1950), pp. 65–68, 87–88.

peatedly that mentally handicapped children are not given the same opportunity in the schools as other children. They are allowed to fail, and have usually faced failure not only within their peer group, but in the eyes of their parents and teachers as well. This failure to achieve what is required of them has produced a discrepancy between their capacity to behave and the requirements of the environment. To adjust to failures or frustrating situations, these children have become aggressive, have withdrawn and regressed to more immature levels of behavior, or have compensated in one way or another. The behavior characteristics which these children show should not be considered a part of the mental handicap itself; they are rather a result of the situation in which the children have been placed.

Mentally handicapped children, like other children, have numerous fundamental needs. While the desire for security, or belongingness, is strong in all children, it is probably even stronger in mentally handicapped children because their security and belongingness have been challenged by failure in their social group. When a child is unable to cope with the program outlined for him by his society, he does not feel that he is an integral part of that social group. The experiment by Johnson,[6] indicating that in the earlier grades the mentally handicapped are rejected and isolated by regular children, presents some evidence that the desire for security and belongingness is thwarted in mentally handicapped children.

Another fundamental need of children is the feeling of accomplishment or adequacy. The personality grows in security and maturity when it is able to accomplish and find joy in accomplishment. Mentally handicapped children have been placed in situations in which they were unable to accomplish according to grade standards. Their parents have expected more of them than they could do, and their teachers have demanded more of them than they could produce. Their peer group has expected them to do as others do, and has looked down upon them when they did not achieve or conform. As a result, the desire for a feeling of adequacy through accomplishment has also been thwarted in mentally handicapped children.

[6] Johnson, *op. cit.*, pp. 60–89.

A good program for mentally handicapped children would be one that re-establishes feelings of security and adequacy and, above all, restores the child's self-respect. The program should encompass the essentials of a mental hygiene program which makes the individual feel an integral part of the group. To facilitate the growth of a strong personality, the special class should be so organized as to furnish the child with a feeling of security, belongingness, accomplishment and adequacy, as well as to satisfy other needs felt by him.

A class that places adequate emphasis on personality development must be organized in such a way that all phases of the class activities contribute to the personal development of the child. An adequate plan for such a class must include organization of the curriculum, the teacher-pupil relationship, and special programs. The following section attempts to emphasize the organization of the class along mental-hygiene principles.

SUGGESTIONS FOR FACILITATING ACCEPTABLE SOCIAL BEHAVIOR

Unfortunately there are no formulas for the universal management of all children. The best that can be done with the present knowledge of human behavior is to suggest various approaches to good mental-hygiene practices and rely upon the teacher to apply the principle that is best suited to a particular child in a particular situation.

In general, teachers desire the children in a classroom to follow certain routines, to adjust to the group without conflict, and to follow the teacher's suggestions and directions. To achieve those aims, it is necessary to motivate children to adjust to the classroom routines, to the social group, and to the learning situations.

Children conform or obey for a great number of reasons. Some of these reasons are:

(1) Children want to do the things that are right or that gain for them the approval of the people with whom they associate. They are willing to follow the suggestions of the teacher because by so doing they gain security through the teacher's approval of their acts.

(2) Some children who have been brought up to respect their elders and persons in authority obey commands or requests because of this feeling of respect. Respect is usually attained not as a result of fear of the adult, but because the child feels that the adult is fair.

(3) Experiments in psychology have shown that individuals behave in an acceptable manner to the extent that they receive rewards. A reward which a child accepts can be approval, praise, or material objects. The difficulty with giving children material objects in return for adequate behavior is that they will then expect material objects as a reward for all good behavior.

(4) Children sometimes obey because they fear punishment. This is not considered an adequate mental-hygiene method of obtaining obedience, since punishment is a negative approach rather than a positive one. For example, if a child says that seven and seven are fifteen, punishment tends to inhibit the response "fifteen" but does not teach the child the correct answer.

(5) Some children obey because they feel it is their duty to obey. The sense of duty to obey is attained when they have learned that the adult demands are reasonable and just and that obedience obtains intrinsic rewards and satisfactions. Consistency, honesty, and fairness with children tend to produce more adequate results.

CLASSROOM PRACTICES AFFECTING SOCIAL ADJUSTMENT

Good teaching involves good mental hygiene. An adequate educational program for the mentally handicapped encompasses within its own organization an adequate mental-hygiene program. The behavior of the children in a classroom is related to the educational program designed to meet their needs. The activities in the classroom, the attitude of the teacher toward the children, and the curriculum each have a bearing on the personality development and the behavior of the child in and out of the classroom. The following suggestions are made to help teachers in organizing an educational program in harmony with principles of mental hygiene.

Well-planned activities decrease unacceptable behavior. There is little time for misbehavior in a busy and interesting classroom. In general, the teacher should pursue a policy of carefully planned activities, since many discipline problems can be avoided by proper planning. To discourage tardiness in school, for example, the teacher should start the day's work with interesting activities, since doing something interesting at the beginning of the day motivates the child to want to arrive at school early.

Planning the work of the class beforehand, and with the children, tends to decrease disorderliness and disobedience. The program as a whole should be organized in such a way that the children are active in a learning situation at all times.

Self-direction should be encouraged. Although teachers are the leaders in the class, a democratic leader gives children opportunity to make rules and regulations for their own conduct, and encourages pupils to help plan their program and activities. Teachers should be willing to allow children to solve their own problems at their level of functioning, even though it involves allowing the children to make mistakes. Behavior of children is determined in part by the social approval of the group. When the group has defined its own rules of conduct, individual children are more apt to abide by these rules. This procedure gives the teacher an opportunity to remain as a friend and a counsellor, rather than as a policeman for rules he has made for the class. Examples of these procedures are given under "Classroom Group Procedures," page 334, and "The Wayne County Training School Experiment," pages 341–357.

Successful programs for children are based on the children's interests and experiences. The management of children in a classroom requires that the teacher organize the educational program around the children's interests and experiences. When outside experiences are lacking, it is the duty of the teacher to create opportunities for such experiences and to develop interest through these activities. It should be remembered that "interest" is learned and that children become interested in things which they can do successfully. Giving opportunities to the child to succeed in various activities will in turn develop motivation and interest on the part of the child.

Materials of instruction should be selected with care. Materials that are too simple or materials that are too difficult tend to produce inattention and disinterest in school work. Material presented to a mentally handicapped child should provide stimulation and should not continue for too long a period. As a rule, short and dynamic periods are more successful than long periods on any one activity. Dramatization of the material, intensity of presentation of material, and varying ways of presentation all aid attention and learning.

Instruction should begin with simple material. It is important that elementary and simple concepts and materials be presented to mentally handicapped children at the outset of any instructional unit so that instruction will remain at the child's level of understanding, and will assure success. Materials, language, directions, and statements should all be within the child's grasp at the outset so that disinterest in the task or activity will not result from lack of understanding or lack of successful accomplishment.

Familiar material aids instruction. At the beginning of any instructional unit the child should be presented with familiar material, since meaningful material is acquired more readily. Concentration, interest, and learning are accelerated when the child has familiar material with which to start.

Gradual introduction of new situations avoids misbehavior. Much inattention and misbehavior are caused by the introduction of new learning situations before a child is ready for them. All new situations should be introduced gradually so that inattention and disinterest are avoided.

It is advisable to avoid abstract materials and utilize concrete ones. Mentally handicapped children have difficulty in understanding such abstract generalizations as citizenship, thrift, and so forth. It is necessary that these abstract concepts be made concrete and meaningful. This may be accomplished through dramatization or visits to neighborhood projects.

Variety of methods and materials is recommended. The activities of a class should be changed frequently. Change of materials, methods, ideas, and activities tend to keep the interest and attention of the class alive. Learning is aided by the maintenance of such interest and attention. Repetition of learning materials in a variety of settings is necessary with mentally handicapped children to assure success and a feeling of accomplishment.

The routines of the class should be kept simple. Complicated procedures lend themselves to disobedience and disorderliness in the classroom. How the children should enter the classroom, where to sit, how to pass and collect papers, and other similar routines should be organized systematically and simply.

Out-of-class activities should be correlated with classroom activities. Great emphasis should be placed on activities in the classroom that are related to the out-of-school activities of the children. Interest, success, and integration of learning is maintained when school work is, so to speak, "brought home" to the children.

Instruction should be individualized. Attention to the learning and social problems of an individual child is a necessity in a class for mentally handicapped children. Classes for the mentally handicapped are reduced in size because of this necessity for individual attention. In such a class the teacher has a greater opportunity to "deal with the child instead of the act."

It should be recognized that all behavior, adequate or inadequate, is caused. Teachers too often emphasize the behavior, or misbehavior, of a child as the important factor. It is necessary to know the child and the cause of the problem before attempting any particular disciplinary treatment. It should be remembered that all behavior is adjustive behavior, and that whatever the child does is an attempt on his part to reduce tensions. Understanding the reason for his behavior or misbehavior aids in outlining adequate educational procedures.

Emphasis should be placed on successful accomplishments. Children, and especially the mentally handicapped, are motivated in an activity when they succeed in it and become disinterested when they are unsuccessful. Instructional materials, therefore, should always be of such a nature that success, social approval, and recognition are attained from accomplishment.

SUGGESTIONS FOR THE MANAGEMENT OF BEHAVIOR [7]

In a class for the mentally handicapped, instruction and management of children should always be positive. Rewards and encouragement are more effective for learning and adequate behavior than

[7] Results of experiments on the use of language with young children is reported by Johnson, M. W., "What We Say and How We Say It," *Childhood Education*, 14 (April, 1938), pp. 359–362.

punishment, scolding, or discouragement. Paying attention to desirable behavior is more effective than noticing misbehavior.

Teachers are required not only to control the behavior of children in a classroom, but to control behavior in such a way as to produce adequate learning and personality development. Good teachers are capable of managing the behavior of children by positive approaches, although they may not be able to analyze how it is done. The following are some suggestions of "Do's and Don'ts" that may be used profitably in a classroom.

Use positive rather than negative statements. Teachers who repeatedly use negative statements with children obtain poorer results than those who use positive language. "Close the door gently," is apt to secure less slamming of a door than "Don't slam the door." "Put your books away" is more effective than "Don't leave your books on the desk." Telling the child what to do focuses his attention on the correct act. Telling the child what you don't want him to do focuses his attention on the incorrect act. Since children tend to execute the act upon which their attention is focused, the teacher should always attempt, through positive statements, to focus the attention of the child on the thing he wants him to do.

Use encouraging rather than discouraging statements. Encouraging statements produce better results than discouraging statements. Commending a child for good behavior is more effective than only scolding him when he misbehaves or does not complete his work. If teachers can observe and approve correct acts, and disregard minor incorrect acts, the child will tend to behave more adequately. This principle is violated by many teachers, who disregard the child until he is misbehaving. thus focusing his attention on incorrect behavior. "You can do it" is more effective than "It is too hard." Statements should point to success rather than failure.

Use specific rather than general statements. Young children especially fail to comply when a general request is made and tend to obey when a specific request is made. The statement "Put on your clothes" is a general statement to a three- or four-year-old child and makes the task seem too complicated. More specific requests would be "Put on your stockings," "Now put on your dress," and so forth. In making requests of young children, tell them exactly what you want them to do, and how they should do it.

Use pleasant requests rather than scoldings. Many children respond to pleasant requests. If a child fails to pick up his materials before going to recess, a simple "Please pick up your materials" is more effective than a scolding.

Be consistent in requests. A child should know what is expected of him. If the teacher is inconsistent in his requests, misbehavior may result. Asking a child to finish his task one day and allowing him to leave other tasks unfinished might cause difficulty. Let the child know what is expected of him and maintain consistency in your requests.

Use substitute suggestions rather than negative commands. When a child is doing something you don't want him to do, it is more effective to suggest a substitute activity than to reprimand him with "Don't do that." If a child is taking a pencil from another child, suggest that he obtain a pencil from the desk. Asking him to stop annoying the other child does not tell him to do something. "This is no time for visiting" is a negative statement. Children cannot just stop doing something; they can, however, do something else.

Use unhurried directions rather than hurried commands. Statements such as "You can do it quickly" produce better results than "Hurry up, hurry up." Hurrying the child may tend to slow him up and at times to confuse him and produce dislike for the task.

Give the child a choice in activities. Offering a child a choice in activities tends to give the child a feeling of freedom, and practice in determining his own plans. "Would you like to paint or read?" is preferable to a command asking the child to read a book. A command represents domination to some children and may produce negativism.

Keep teacher "verbalism" to a minimum. Many teachers talk too much in a classroom because they feel that they must direct all the activities of all the children at all times. Continual direction by the teacher tends to force the children to disregard the teacher. When a teacher gives directions infrequently and at appropriate times, children will learn to listen and pay attention to the teacher. The loud or excitable voice of a teacher tends to produce confusion and noise in a classroom, whereas a calm voice and manner may help to obtain calmness from the children. A loud voice should be reserved for emergencies. A manner which suggests the expectation of the teacher that the children will use socially acceptable behavior in a classroom is more effective than the expectation that something will happen to disrupt the classroom.

Use manual guidance to aid verbal suggestion. Teachers are sometimes in doubt about using physical methods for securing compliance. In general, manual guidance can be effective with younger children, but it should not be used with adolescent children. The act itself is not as important as the spirit in which it is done. Taking the child by the hand and showing or leading him to the desired place may aid his initiating an activity. The statement "Would you like to sit down?" accompanied by a guiding hand on the shoulder is apt to produce greater results than the verbal statement alone. Manual guidance can be used effectively when accompanied by encouraging and kind statements.

Avoid issues with children. Teachers can save themselves much grief by avoiding issues with children concerning their conduct in class. It is more advisable to discuss the misconduct of the child in private, thus avoiding the danger of forfeiting the respect of the class for the child, or the class for the teacher. It is well to handle difficult children individually outside of the class without calling class attention to their misbehavior. Waiting until a stubborn child has calmed down before discussing his problem with him avoids an issue and is more effective.

Avoid making threats. In many instances threats are not carried out by the teacher. Thus children tend to disregard threats, which encourages misbehavior and hostility. If the teacher makes threats and attempts to carry them out, he will be forcing issues with children.

Avoid anger in the presence of children. When a teacher becomes angry at children in the classroom, it is well for him to do nothing in that state. Punishment, scolding, or reprimands administered in anger are seldom good mental hygiene.

Isolate hyperactive children when necessary. Some children are overstimulated by activity and the presence of other children. In these cases it is advisable to isolate the child from the group, not as punishment, but to decrease the environmental stimulation that is causing hyperexcitability. In these cases the child should be helped to understand why he is being isolated.

Stimulate shy and withdrawn children. Many children in special classes have become withdrawn because of continual failure in school and in social contacts. It is the duty of a special-class teacher to provide a stimulating environment for these children so that they will react more overtly to the environment and to the other children. Giving them opportunities for success in a social situation, having them do things in class that would attract other children to them, and praising or encouraging them for small evidence of socialization are some of the techniques that are used.

CLASSROOM GROUP PROCEDURES

In addition to giving individual attention to each child in a classroom, there are various effective group procedures for the development of personality, for releasing tensions, and for evoking maturity and responsibility. Many of these procedures have been practiced by teachers as a part of allowing the children to plan the program; others are modifications of group therapy procedures used by psychologists, sociologists, and psychiatrists for removing anxieties, decreasing delinquent tendencies, or decreasing behavior problems. Although the teacher of the mentally handicapped must view the children as individuals, he must deal with them as members of a group structure. It is thus necessary that group procedures be used for the purpose of understanding the children, and for assisting their emotional adjustment.

Examples of various group procedures are given below. These consist of (1) planning programs with children, (2) structural self-government periods, and (3) the use of sociodrama.

Planning programs with children. The most common form of group procedure used by teachers of the mentally handicapped is the conventional discussion and planning which ordinarily accompanies the execution of a unit of experience. In this plan the teacher aids the children in evolving a unit of experience based on the children's interest. The classroom discussion reveals the interest and background of the children, gives them a part in the total planning, and motivates them to carry out that which they have helped to formulate.

Many experiences and activities in a classroom lend themselves to group discussion and decision. One teacher, for example, took the class to a restaurant to give them experience in ordering, eating, and conforming to restaurant procedures. When leaving, several children took away sugar cubes and a few spoons. The next day several other children informed the teacher of the thefts. The teacher gave the children a verbal spanking and informed them that if that is how they would behave, she would not repeat the excursion again. The children would have profited more from the experience had the teacher taken advantage of the misbehavior by utilizing it as a basis for discussion. By raising questions concerning the consequences of such actions on the individual and the group, and allowing the children to derive insights concerning their behavior, much more could have been accomplished. The excursion to the restaurant should have been repeated and discussed until all of the children were able to enter and leave without taking any of the restaurant's property.

Self-government class organizations. The most successful self-government activities in a classroom are those that are kept simple and at the children's level of comprehension. Organizations such as a court, a legislative organization, or a city government are too formal and complex for mentally handicapped children.

A simple organization might consist of devoting one or two afternoons each week to a program of improving the classroom. A rotating chairman elected by the class each month is sufficient to constitute an administrative organization. A secretary to keep the minutes each week, with the help of the teacher, is usually advisable. Such an organization in a class can discuss the improvement of the physical appearance of the class, receive complaints from the children, discuss problems of the children, make rules for the class, plan dramatizations, parties, trips, or activities on special occasions, such as Halloween, Christmas, and so forth. The teacher plays a definite role as counsellor, devoting special periods with the chairman or with some members of the class to aid them in organizing suggestions for the meetings.

Sociodrama. One teacher of the mentally handicapped reported considerable success with sociodrama as a method of developing social concepts in mentally handicapped youngsters. An illustration of this personalized approach is presented below.

The following skit [8] developed out of a discussion concerning what time a girl should get in and how much she should tell her family. This skit had been recorded and played back to the students. The following has been transcribed from the recording.

TEACHER: (*First period in the morning*) This afternoon, the sixth period, we are going to have another skit and see if you can answer some of these questions yourselves. Now this is what has happened. The girl in this skit, we'll call her Mary, has not been dating. Since she is only fifteen her folks think that she is not old enough. She has left her home tonight to go to the show with her girl friends. At the show she meets a nice fellow whom she has liked for quite a while. It is only nine o'clock when the show gets out. Her parents do not expect her home before ten. The boy has a car and he asks her to go for a ride. He promises that he will have her home by that time. They have a nice time and get home about 10:15 P.M. The mother and father are both up reading. They are not too worried but ask the girl where she has been. Now, that is where we will start this afternoon. We'll have a boy take the part of Mr. Brown, one girl to take the part of Mrs. Brown, and one to take the part of Mary.

STUDENT: Who will take the part of the boy?

TEACHER: Well, he won't be heard. Now you can think and talk about this the rest of the day, because I don't know who will take each part yet.

TEACHER: (*Sixth period*) All right, we are ready for the skit now. Do you remember the situation? (*Brief review*) All right, D, you take the part of the father, you can be reading at the table; and K, you be the girl. Now you go outside the door and we'll call you when we are ready. L, you be the mother. You are also at the able reading. All set?

---

[8] This sociodrama was contributed by Ivan Garrison, Director of Special Education, Jacksonville Public Schools, Jacksonville, Illinois.

L: What if she tells a lie?

TEACHER: We'll see if she does.

L: That's the way girls are.

TEACHER: Let's start. O.K., now remember that you two are Mr. and Mrs. Brown and your daughter's name is Mary. (*To class*) Tell Mary to come in now.

MR. B: It's about time you were coming in.

MRS. B: Where have you been?

MARY: You know that I went to the show.

MR. B: Yes, but where did you go after the show?

MARY: I went riding.

MR. B: Who with?

MARY: Kenny.

MR. B: Kenny who?

MARY: (*To teacher*) What is his other name?

TEACHER: Oh, just give him a last name.

MARY: Kenny Jones.

MR. B: Where did you go?

MARY: Oh, just riding.

MRS. B: Are you sure?

MARY: Yes, I am sure.

MR. B: How old is he?

MARY: Twenty.

MR. B: (*To Mrs. B.*) Don't you think that he is too old for her to be running around with?

MRS. B: Yes, I do. I thought you were going to the show with the girls.

MARY: I did.

MRS. B: Well, where did you meet this boy?

MARY: At the show.

MRS. B: Is this the first time you have known him?

MARY: No, I have known him a long time, and he's a nice boy.

MRS. B: How do I know that he is nice?

MR. B: Well, what are we going to do to her?

MRS. B: I don't know, she isn't supposed to date and she didn't get home when I told her to.

MR. B: Mary, you go on to bed, and we'll decide what your punishment shall be and tell you tomorrow.

TEACHER: Now, let's everyone get in on this discussion whether you took part or not. How did they handle the situation?

BOB: They did better than we have before.

TEACHER: I think so too, but let's go back and play it over and see if this is the way you would have acted if you had been the parents of the girl. (*The recording is played over and left on for the discussion.*) How about when the girl first came in?

JOAN: Well, they shouldn't have both jumped on her at once.

LILLY: But she was late and had been riding.

KEN: Yes, but you didn't know that yet.

SUSY: The girl didn't answer her parents very nice.

KITTY: (*Took girl's part*) Well, she didn't lie the way L said that she would.

MRS. B: If we had been in bed sleeping she wouldn't have had to lie or tell us where she had been.

MR. B: We would have found out next day and that might have been worse for her.

TEACHER: Why?

MR. B: Well, parents usually find out those things.

TEACHER: Let's remember the time. She was just fifteen minutes late.

JOAN: They shouldn't have made such a fuss about that. A girl should try and be home when they tell her to but that is not very late. The thing they should have punished her for is dating.

TEACHER: You think she should have been punished?

LILLY: She should have been spanked.

TEACHER: Spanked?

LILLY: Yes, I was. The first time they found out I sure remember.

TEACHER: You think this girl should have been spanked just because you were?

SUSY: No, I think they should have done like Mr. B. said. Send the girl to bed and talk it over, then tell her tomorrow.

TEACHER: Should there have been any talk then as to whether she was old enough to date?

LILLY: I don't think she is old enough.

BOB: What about you, Lilly? When did you start?

LILLY: Oh, 14, 13, 12 ——

BOB: See!

JOAN: I think the girl and her mother should talk it over; maybe she is.

TEACHER: Should the girl have gone out with the boy even though she knew him?

MR. B: No. He was too old for her and the parents didn't know him.

BOB: He should have taken her home and asked the old man.

KITTY: What if the parents didn't think she should go with him because they didn't know whether he was a nice boy or not? Then she wouldn't have got to go.

BOB: She should have brought him home anyway.

LILLY: He might be a nice boy in her home and not when he's away.

TEACHER: Well, how are the parents going to tell?

KEN: They may know his folks or maybe he had gone out with some other girl and they can ask her.

JOAN: Mr. G. (*Teacher*) — say a boy comes from a home where the mother chases other men and say his father drinks all the time, that's no reason why the boy is going to be like that, is it?

TEACHER: Perhaps not, but if you were a parent wouldn't you think about those things?

MR. B: If he's seen all that, he's apt to be that way.

TEACHER: Shall we say that the parent is just going to have to take a chance either way? The boy may act nice around the girl's home but not when they are away from home, and he may come from a bad home and still be a nice boy.

CLASS: Yes.

LILLY: A girl can change a bad boy if she handles it right.

TEACHER: We hope that we can help people to act better than the way they are raised. Our penitentiaries would probably be much fuller than they are if we couldn't. Perhaps the parents should see as much of the boy as possible before letting the girl go out with him and then take a chance. Of course it's up to the boy to keep his reputation as good as possible. Now let's see if we can wind the discussion up. Are we all agreed that the boy should have brought the girl home and asked the parents if the girl could go riding and if they said no, visited with the family for a while?

CLASS: (*Mostly*) Yes.

TEACHER: Isn't it possible that this could be the very thing that would prove to the folks that she is old enough to date? That is, if she brings the fellows home that she would like to date and lets the parents meet them? That shows that she is respecting them and is acting as they would want her to. Then if they decide that she is old enough, they could talk it over together and decide what rules they would make about dating.

SUSY: Rules?

TEACHER: Sure, as to how late she could stay out, and what night that she could go out, where she could go, and how they wanted to handle it as to whom she could go out with. Now what about the punishment?

JOAN: I think they should skip the whole thing. She wasn't very late and maybe after they talk it over, they could tell her whether she could go out or not. I don't think that she should be punished.

TEACHER: (*After considerable discussion*) Maybe Joan has the answer here. Let's remember that this was her first date. Perhaps they would punish her another time for being late, and maybe they should punish her another time for going out with a boy without asking their consent, but this is the first time, the first date; so, they would in their talking tell the girl why it is necessary that she be home on time. They would tell her they would want to know whom she is out with and where she is going. Parents probably have the right to tell her whom she can go with until she gets a lot older than she is. They probably have the right to decide whether a boy is too old for a girl or not. Now, after they make some of these rules together, then if the girl breaks a rule she probably should be punished, but I believe that I feel like Joan. I believe that I would let the girl off with a talking to and try and decide from her actions whether she is old enough to date or not. I believe that we had better stop here. I have left the recorder on for discussion, so we'll rewind it and play it back for you.

This skit, or sociodrama, is presented as an example of how such learning experiences can contribute to group morale in a classroom and further acceptable attitudes and social skills. When a student reports what has happened to himself or to one of his friends and it is believed that there is a possibility of a lesson to be learned, it is used as a situation for a skit. Sometimes the situation grows out of what is read in a newspaper or out of a discussion on some controversial question. Many of the skits are concerned with boy-and-girl problems and the way these problems are dealt with at home. Some deal with how to apply for a job or what to do in certain social situations.

It would be impossible to determine how much these dramatizations have contributed to the total adjustment and improvement that some special class pupils have made. One teacher reports:

There has been an improvement in the total personality picture of nearly every child. One boy had only one answer to give to every teacher request the first few months of school. He would say, "I ain't going to do it." By the end of the year this was changed. Another pupil, a girl, reported that some boys wanted to take her to a nightclub in a near-by city. She stated that she was going to go until all at once she remembered a skit we had about a girl going out with strange boys. I have just received a letter from a boy who has moved to a city in another state. The boy states that he had just been hired as a car washer in a filling station and reports that he knew how to apply for the job as a result of his experience in a sociodrama on applying for a job.

The Wayne County Training School Experiment in Self-Determination [9]

In the summer of 1935 the Wayne County Training School launched a new and radical program in cottage management for higher-grade mentally defective, socially maladjusted boys. This program, including a system of self-determination and democratiza-

---

[9] The material on the Wayne County Training School Experiment on self-determination has been derived from several sources. In 1935 Samuel A. Kirk, who was then mental hygienist at that institution, was charged by the medical superintendent, Dr. Robert H. Haskell, with the activation, organization, and management of an experimental cottage. Although he subsequently left the institution, he had the opportunity to revisit it in 1942, after the experiment had been under way for seven years. There he read all of the records, and conferred with the superintendent and others. Additional information has been obtained through correspondence with Dr. Haskell and from the published articles of Dr. Newell C. Kephart, who continued and extended the experiment for a number of years.

tion of cottage management, has now functioned successfully for a period of fifteen years.

It is very difficult to evaluate a program of social rehabilitation by objective means. A subjective evaluation of this program, however, indicated that it is a practical demonstration of the influence of democracy on character development. The following report will include a description of (1) the Wayne County Training School, (2) how the self-determining cottage started, (3) the rules of the cottage, (4) how morale was maintained, (5) incidents of misbehavior, (6) examples of adjustment under group autonomy, and (7) the influence of the experiment on institutional management.

THE WAYNE COUNTY TRAINING SCHOOL [10]

The Wayne County Training School, located at Northville, Michigan, has now become recognized as one of the outstanding institutions in the United States for the rehabilitation of higher-grade mentally defective problem children. It was established in 1926 for the purpose of caring for, educating, and rehabilitating children who show signs of social maladjustment and who are low in intelligence. It was believed that this group of children should not be admitted to a traditional institution for the mentally deficient but that they should be trained in an institution whose prime purpose is rehabilitation. Lower-grade mentally deficient children, usually falling in the uneducable or custodial group, are not knowingly admitted into this institution.

The institution consists of about 700 boys and girls who are housed in cottages, holding from thirty-five to fifty children each. In these cottages are found children of the same sex and of approximately the same age level.

The management of cottages of that size requires a certain degree of routinization of living. The administrators of the institution allow as much freedom as possible to the children, but this freedom, in a large group, does not resemble the freedom a child would have in his own home and in the determination of his own conduct. As

[10] Haskell, Robert H., "An Organization for the Training of Higher Grade Mental Defectives," *The American Association for the Study of the Feebleminded,* Proceedings, 37 (May, 1932), pp. 252–270.

part of the training program the children are required to do much of the work in the cottage, such as serving meals, making beds, and keeping the cottage clean. The cottage parent usually assigns some task to each child.

HOW THE SELF-DETERMINING COTTAGE STARTED

In the spring of 1935 a new cottage was completed. This cottage was approximately one-half mile from the main group of buildings on an institutional farm. It was an ideal place to start a new project in cottage management and in rehabilitation of mentally handicapped adolescents. This program was activated during the summer of 1935.

The philosophy and points of view which determined the organization of the self-determining cottage were as follows:

(1) Most self-governing organizations are adult-controlled and usually too complicated for mentally handicapped children. It was decided that no self-governing organization would be outlined by the administration, but that the method of self-government would be allowed to evolve as the boys themselves met their problems. It was felt that by allowing the boys to evolve their own method of organization and government, the rules and regulations would be kept within the mentality and needs of the boys themselves.

(2) It was anticipated that starting a self-governing cottage with a large heterogeneous group would very likely be slow and cumbersome. Consequently, it was decided that a group of only twelve boys would be admitted initially to the cottage and that sufficient time would be given them to organize the cottage on a self-government basis. It was felt that gradually new boys would be admitted, one or two at a time, and that those boys already established would indoctrinate the new ones in the customs and mores of the cottage. Social conformity and responsibility would then be produced through the influence exerted by the larger group on the smaller group, instead of by the house parent in charge. Group autonomy would be developed gradually as the boys learned socially approved forms of conduct.

(3) A cottage father and mother would be appointed to the cottage, not to manage the cottage but to cook for the boys, to fur-

nish guidance and suggestions, and to keep records of the progress of the cottage.

(4) The boys would be informed that they were then responsible for their own conduct and for that of the cottage and that it was up to them to establish their own rules of conduct and cottage management. It was decided that they would be allowed to make mistakes if those mistakes did not conflict with the management of the rest of the institution or would not be detrimental to the outside community. A part of their education was to learn by being allowed to make mistakes.

(5) The supervision of the cottage was not assigned to the general supervisor of all cottages but to the mental hygienist of the institution. This mental hygienist was given complete responsibility for the cottage organization, for the determination of policy, and for the selection of the original boys. The cottage father and mother were responsible directly to the mental hygienist of the institution.

(6) The general rules of the institution for cottage organization did not apply to this experimental cottage.

Before any boys were admitted to the cottage, a number of them who had made a fair adjustment to the institution were interviewed by the mental hygienist. They were informed that they were being considered for admission to the cottage and that the boys selected would be those who did not require supervision by an adult, but who could manage their own affairs. All of the boys appeared to be eager for this opportunity. After interviewing a number of boys, the mental hygienist selected twelve of them for transferral to the cottage.

On the first day the boys were quite confused. They had been in attendance at other cottages and had learned the rules of those cottages. They were now placed in a situation in which those rules did not apply. For example, smoking was not allowed in the institution. They asked if they could smoke in their new home. They wondered what time they should go to bed. They wanted to know if they could go to town to a show without an attendant. They wondered who should sweep the floor and who should wash the dishes. To all of these questions the cottage father was instructed to say "I don't know; I don't make the rules." After several days of such confusion with conflicting opinion among the boys, they insisted on being told what they could do and what they could not do. The cottage father suggested to them, after some frustration on their part, that they send a few boys to the office of the mental hygienist and inquire about the rules and regulations. When they came to the mental hygienist with these questions he also informed them that he did not know what they could or could not do. He reminded them that they had previously informed him that they knew enough to run the cottage. The boys explained that they did know how to run the cottage but that some of the other boys thought differently. It was then suggested to them that they hold a meeting that evening and decide on what they could or could not do.

The meeting that evening was very serious. They elected a chairman and a secretary and decided on some of the issues. First they assigned a cottage task to everyone. Next they decided that since many of them were over sixteen years of age they should be allowed to smoke. They also decided to go to the show in town without supervision.

Space will not permit a description of the evolution of all of these rules, but an example should be mentioned. The rule on smoking, for instance, violated the institution rule, and the boys decided to send a letter to the superintendent asking him for permission to smoke. They received permission from the superintendent, provided they also obtained permission from their parents. When this issue was settled, the boys smoked in the cottage, on the playground, and took cigarettes with them to their occupational assignments. They gave themselves complete freedom in smoking at any time and at any place. This practice, however, did not last long. First, all the boys who were assigned to occupational classes in the institution found other boys asking them for cigarettes. Second, a written complaint came in from an attendant at another cottage saying that these boys had given other boys cigarettes. At the next meeting of the Council, as they now called it, this complaint was read and discussed. The boys then voted that they could smoke but that no boy was allowed to take cigarettes with him to the institution proper. All cigarettes were then turned in to the cottage parents for safekeeping while the boys were in school.

Restricting smoking to the cottage or cottage grounds was not the end of smoking difficulties. Some boys who had assigned themselves the tasks of keeping the cottage clean, complained that "butts" were thrown on the floor by other boys immediately after cleaning. One morning the chairman of the group came to breakfast after the boys had finished. Oatmeal was the main dish. The chairman had added his sugar and cream and was ready to start eating when the boy waiting on the table reached over his shoulder to put some toast on his plate. The waiter had a cigarette in his mouth. This cigarette with abundant ashes slipped out of the smoker's mouth and landed in the cream and the oatmeal. A new serving of oatmeal came forward quickly. But there was no more cream. The chairman had to eat his breakfast with plain Holstein milk. He did not like it a bit, and the more he talked about it the more determined he was that this sort of carelessness had gone too far. A special meeting was called for that noon, various complaints about carelessness in smoking aired, and further restrictions on time and place of smoking in the cottage imposed. Hence, the rules for smoking were finally evolved: (1) requiring permission to smoke from the parents, and (2) limiting smoking to the playground and the recreation room of the cottage.

The same pattern was noted with many other activities which were discovered in their newly found freedom. Initially, complete freedom of action was taken. As the boys discovered that this freedom caused complaints and difficulties, they imposed limitations on their own activities.

The method of admitting new boys was determined at a council meeting with the mental hygienist. A list of three to five eligible boys was sent to the cottage periodically by the mental hygienist. From this list the boys elected one or two every time they wished to admit other boys. Their selection was based on various factors; namely, their knowledge of the boy, whether or not they liked him, what they needed him for, and how they thought he would fit into the cottage group. At one time, for example, they admitted a boy because they wished to strengthen their baseball team; they selected the boy because he was a good baseball player.

After the cottage was organized and was functioning, it was found that some of the boys violated some of the rules. Their names were brought before the Council meeting. At the outset the boys were quite severe in the punishment that was meted out. For smoking on the institution grounds they took all the privileges away from one boy for three weeks. He was not allowed to leave the cottage even to go to the playground for that length of time. After good behavior for two weeks, however, he asked that his privileges be reinstated and was granted the request.

THE RULES OF THE COTTAGE

The rules and regulations of the "Homestead Cottage" (as it was named by its charter members) were posted on the bulletin board. Most of these rules were established by the boys during the first six months of the cottage organization. Each of these regulations evolved, like the smoking regulation, after the boys had felt a need for it, and usually after problems had arisen or mistakes been made. After a number of years of operation, the following regulations were found posted on the bulletin board:

(1) Any boy who wishes to smoke must receive permission from home.
(2) Smoking must be confined to the Club Room and the grounds near the cottage.
(3) No boy is to carry cigarettes to the institution grounds.
(4) No boy is to smoke until his work is done.
(5) Boys going to and from work are not to go by way of the teachers' residence, unless with an attendant. Boys going to and from church on Sunday may use the walk alongside the teachers' residence.
(6) No one should use the sewing machine except the clothes room boy.
(7) Every boy should see that the bowls in the lavatory are clean after using them.
(8) Any boy wanting to go to bed before the usual time may do so.
(9) No boy should smoke going to and from work nor on the way to and from shows.
(10) One boy at each table serves and clears away the dishes.
(11) All money should be handed to the advisor and not carried or kept in lockers or chests.

(12) Boys should not wear each other's clothes unless permission is received from the owner.

(13) Hard shoes are not to be worn in the cottage unless on special occasions or with orders from the clinic.

(14) When a boy loses his privileges, he gives up the right to leave the immediate vicinity of the cottage.

(15) Boys may go to a show in Plymouth or Northville twice a month.

(16) No more than five or less than three boys may go to the show at one time.

(17) A list of those going to a show should be handed to the advisor so that he will know where the boys are in case they receive a visitor or are needed for some purpose.

It should be noted that the above are written rules. There are many unwritten rules that have become customs of the cottage. For example, every boy takes care of his own bed. This was done in other cottages and was carried over as a matter of fact. The rules listed above are rules that usually did not apply to the other cottages and were, therefore, deviations from their previous training. Most of the rules, habits of cleanliness, and so forth that were taken for granted were not listed as rules of the cottage.

HOW MORALE WAS MAINTAINED

During the first three months of the existence of the cottage the morale was high. The boys were very proud of their achievements and of their newly found freedom and responsibility. They carried out many projects, such as making a baseball diamond, clearing out the yard, and organizing the cottage for comfortable living. They had many visitors during these earlier months and were always proud to explain the functioning of their cottage.

Soon, however, the novelty of the cottage began to wear off, and some of the boys needed new techniques to keep up the morale of the cottage. Consequently, new ideas had to be suggested to keep morale at a high pitch. Some of these are:

(1) During the fall it was suggested to them that the teachers and others in the institution wanted to know what the boys were doing in the new cottage. To meet this demand the boys held an open house during a council meeting and invited the teachers, attendants,

social workers, and others in the institution. For two weeks they wrote up the minutes of their council meetings, what they did and how they did it. That evening they conducted a council meeting, then reported on their various activities. The open house technique in which the boys reported their activities to the institution personnel proved to be a morale builder.

(2) Most of the boys did not attend the academic school but were assigned to vocational jobs. They wanted some instruction at the cottage in the evening. To achieve this, they asked for one teacher to help them do handwork, one for academic work, and one to teach them how to play cards and other games. Here we find the interesting phenomenon of the boys selecting their own teachers for specific reasons.

(3) Activities and projects tended to produce group unity. Many of these were carried out throughout the years. For example, during the summer of 1942 each boy had a victory garden.

(4) Incidents of misbehavior and incidents which brought dishonor to the group aided group morale. In all societies a decrease of morale and group unity occurs until a crisis again brings about unity; note the reactions of the American people before and after Pearl Harbor. The same happened at the Homestead Cottage. Group unity and morale fluctuated. At times when morale decreased and some boys did something which brought dishonor upon the cottage, unity was again re-established.

(5) Competitive games with the neighboring public schools and with the other cottages were also means of unifying the group.

(6) In 1942 the organization of the cottage was changed by establishing guides, leaders, and probation periods for newcomers. In addition certain rituals, such as those practiced in fraternities, were introduced. It was believed that these rituals, carried out when boys were promoted from one bracket to another, would focus the attention on character development. In addition to these rituals, various robes for the different groups were worn at the council meeting. This seemed to keep the meeting at a more serious level. The practice of formalizing the meetings, which was a reversal of the original philosophy of the cottage, did not last long. It was found to be an adult-imposed formality and was soon abolished.

INCIDENTS OF MISBEHAVIOR

It would not be truthful to state that by giving the boys responsibility for their own conduct the whole problem of misbehavior was solved. Many incidents of misbehavior occurred at this cottage, but these incidents were minor and not as frequent as incidents in cottages that were under strict adult supervision.

When reading of all the incidents of misbehavior that happened in this cottage during the first seven years of operation, one is impressed by the lack of serious offenses. This emphasizes that adolescent boys could be given much responsibility for their own conduct. Typical examples of these incidents are:

> Three boys picked strawberries from a neighboring farm.
> One boy gave cigarettes to a boy in another cottage.
> Several boys were found walking on the girls' side of the institution.
> Money was stolen from one boy's chest.
> Two boys were reported as being late for work.
> Boys continued to leave the cottage and go to the girls' side.
> Three boys were voted out of the cottage during the year for violating rules.
> One boy read in the morning instead of doing his work.
> Boys were fighting.
> Several boys wore other boys' clothes without permission.
> One boy's bicycle broken. No one admitted using it.

It will be seen from these incidents that they are very minor and are of the type which occur even in college dormitories. The punishment given was a reprimand at the council meeting or the restriction of privileges.

The experiment has functioned for fifteen years without the occurrence of any major incident which would warrant closing the cottage. It should be remembered that during all this time many boys left the cottage without supervision and went to the neighboring town to attend a show. Only once during this period did a group of boys become boisterous in the town or at the show to an extent which would warrant withdrawal of their privileges by the other boys.

With the exception of a few minor incidents, such as stealing strawberries from a neighboring farmer, there have been no major incidents leading to community disapproval of these boys. Ample opportunity to create damage was offered since there were many hours in which no adult was at the cottage to watch the boys.

On one occasion a number of the boys went with boys from another cottage to the Scout Cabin of the Institution, where they broke the windows. For this incident, and because a large proportion of the boys were involved, the Superintendent took away the privileges of the cottage. During this period the boys were supervised by an attendant, could not smoke, and could not go to shows unsupervised. They were allowed to hold meetings and discuss their plight. After several weeks the Superintendent granted their request that privileges be restored.

EXAMPLES OF ADJUSTMENT UNDER GROUP AUTONOMY

The effect of self-determination within a group must be measured mainly by its effect on the adjustment of the individual. The boys in this cottage had had varying adjustment records in the other cottages. Some were obedient and conforming under adult supervision. Others were not so conforming. A few incidents involving different boys will give some indication of the differences among the boys and their modes of adjustment to a peer group instead of to adult authority.

Joe was voted upon by the original twelve boys as a suitable member of the group. At the Council meeting following his admission to the cottage, he was given the responsibility of cleaning the main room of the cottage. Since this room was used by visitors, the boys desired that it be clean at all times. Joe had the reputation of being an expert housekeeper in his former cottage.

After a week the "inspector" reported that the main room was not kept in good condition. Joe was surprised at this accusation. He insisted that the room was kept clean and asked the boys not to withdraw his assignment, since in the past he had obtained recognition for his work in sweeping and mopping floors. The following week the inspector again reported that the room was not kept clean and recommended that Joe be dismissed from this responsibility. Again Joe pleaded to keep his assignment. He did not agree that the room was unkempt. At this meeting the chairman asked the cottage parent to assist in the inspection of the room. The house parent confirmed the inspector's report that Joe seemed unable to keep the room clean. At this point Joe came to the mental hygienist with tears in his eyes. He was fearful that he would lose his responsibility and could not understand why his work was always praised in other cottages and unsatisfactory in this one.

An analysis of the situation showed that Joe was able to clean a room as long as an attendant was present to direct his movements. When he was left alone without supervision, he was unable to carry out the assignment, even though he wished to do so. An arrangement was made whereby the cottage parent would inspect the room and point out to Joe where he forgot to clean. Joe accepted the responsibility of asking the cottage parent to assist him by inspecting his work daily. After three weeks of this routine Joe was able to clean and inspect his own room to the satisfaction of the boys.

The case of Joe exemplifies the difficulties involved in learning a simple task. Although Joe had cleaned floors under supervision for two years previous his admission to the Homestead Cottage, he was unable to carry out the task without supervision. He actually failed in his task until he learned, through partial supervision and then no supervision, to clean floors. The social approval of the group was the motivating factor in driving him to learn to do a task independently of adult suggestions and supervision.

Kephart states:

By far the most potent disciplinary force with these boys is group disapproval. The selection of new members by the group itself results in strong ties between the boys which make social approval an unusually strong motive with them. Group disapproval is expressed formally when an offender stands before the group and is publicly accused; but it is often expressed also in an informal way when, without suggestion or definite planning, the group merely withdraws from an individual and leaves him socially isolated.

Illustrative of this type of discipline is the incident of John, who worked in the cottage kitchen and who went for a walk one morning and did not return in time to prepare the noon meal. The boys came in at noon and found that there was no food. There was, of course, a great deal of concern and much condemnation of John. When the food finally came, the boys were thoroughly angry. The result was that without any discussion or planning, for the rest of the day no one spoke to John; he was not invited to participate in any activity, and when he came up to a group who were engaged in something, it melted away and left him alone. Since this incident, John has never taken an unauthorized vacation from the kitchen.[11]

Kephart describes the adjustment of Alfred:

Alfred was committed to the Wayne County Training School in 1933 at the age of twelve, because of behavior difficulties in school and because he was unable to adjust in boarding homes. His initial adjustment at the training school was not good. He was described as argumentative, quarrelsome, mischievous, bullying, overactive, and sullen. He resented authority and correction. His difficulties included fighting, picking on smaller and duller children, refusal to do cottage work, defiance of attendants when disciplined, truancy from the institution, and extreme profanity. He was unable to adjust to the routine of the institution or to any cottage in which he was placed. A rather extended program of psychotherapy proved unsuccessful, and attempts to interest the child or to capture his imagination failed. All attempts to adjust this child to the training school were unsuccessful.

In November of 1936, as a last resort, this boy was transferred to the Homestead Cottage, as an experiment. The experimental nature of the project was presented to the boys of the cottage and they were asked if they would not accept him provisionally in order that we might see whether he could become adjusted in such a situation. This they agreed to do, and Alfred was accordingly sent to the cottage.

His initial reaction was similar to his reaction in previous cottage placements. He was given punishment by the boys for failure to do his cottage work, for smoking unlawfully, and for refusing to get up in the morning. His reaction to this was that the boys were "picking on him." He became sullen and defied the boys to make him serve his punishment. He soon saw, however, that such behavior did not cause any excitement in this cottage, but that he was only brought up again in meeting for these actions and given further punishment. No one was interested in forcing him; the group was content merely to express their disapproval and to take the outcome for granted. Thus his defiance did not gain for him any marked attention. In several long talks with him the supervisor adopted the same

[11] Kephart, Newell C., "Group Autonomy in a Children's Institution," *Mental Hygiene*, 22 (October, 1938), p. 587.

attitude; the desirability of conformity was pointed out to him without any
attempt at forcing him to conform. Group ostracism was slow in producing its usual effect. The boys were puzzled by his solitary failure to respond, but their morale was sufficiently well grounded not to be affected
by it.

Early in April Alfred began to strike up a closer individual acquaintanceship with another boy in the cottage, Mike. This acquaintanceship was
originally colored by a fiction of belligerency. Mike's daily chore was the
cleaning of a certain room, and when his job was done, he would make a
great show of keeping everyone out of the cleaned room. Alfred began
coming into this room as soon as Mike had finished, and inevitably a
"rough-house" would result, although each boy was very careful not to
hurt the other. This gave Alfred a chance to try out social contacts, and at
the same time permitted him ostensibly to preserve his old pose of nonconformity, since on the surface he appeared to be disturbing Mike, whereas
actually for both boys the fighting was nothing but a game. This activity,
because it was noisy and showy, always drew a crowd, and gradually other
boys were enlisted on one side or the other of the jangle. Thus Alfred was
drawn into acceptable prominence in a group situation that brought with
it the satisfaction of group acceptance and the realization of the fun that
may be had only when one is co-operating with a group.

From this Alfred progressed to an interest in the activities undertaken
by the cottage as a group. At first he was interested only in the rougher
games, in which he could still, in his own mind, keep up a pretense of nonconformity. Gradually, however, he became interested in all the activities
of the group.

Alfred now began to bid for popularity with the group. He became one
of the most co-operative boys in the cottage and was willing to help any
one at any time. The boys responded to this by accepting him. He became one of the most popular boys in the cottage and finally was elected
chairman of the group. In this office he has handled the affairs of the cottage very well and has been an enthusiastic leader in all cottage activities.
Our last report from Alfred was the remark, "Now I see how much
trouble I caused when I was bad because, as chairman, I see how much
trouble the other boys cause me when they are bad."

It is our opinion that such a result could not have been achieved in this
case in a cottage operated in the usual way. We feel that it was achieved
through showing the boy that nonconformity does not bring extra attention, but merely isolation from the group. In the usual cottage situation
something must be done specifically about each misbehavior of which the

cottage administration chooses to make an issue, and the punishment must be carried out; otherwise the attendant cannot "save his face." This sets the boy off as opposing the attendant and thus the institution in general, and too often the boy carries the group with him. In the Homestead, the problem is the group's problem, not the supervisor's; thus the boy opposes the group, not the supervisor. This can result only in group disapproval of misbehavior. Furthermore, the boy is allowed to bridge the gap between nonconformity and conformity in his own way, and thus can do so in such a manner that he does not have to admit his defeat in the process, but can maintain his self-respect in his own eyes throughout.[12]

THE INFLUENCE OF THE EXPERIMENT ON INSTITUTIONAL MANAGEMENT

After one year of successful operation of the Homestead Cottage, another cottage in the institution was converted into a self-determining cottage. This cottage, named the "Elks," was to be identical in operation to the Homestead Cottage with the exception of the privileges of attending movies in a neighboring town without an attendant.

After the Elks cottage had been in operation for one year there appeared to be marked differences between the Homestead and the Elks Cottages. Kephart states:

The Homestead was a going concern whereas the Elks group was rather markedly a failure; the Homestead ran their affairs with virtually no interference from adults, whereas the Elks group frequently needed the intervention of the staff in an autocratic way to prevent complete disorganization; the Homestead group was acknowledged to be the best group in the institution, whereas the Elks group was among the most troublesome.[13]

To discover the basic differences in these cottages, Kephart [14] studied the composition of the groups and found, through sociometric techniques, that the factor of "homogeneity" was greater in the Homestead Cottage than in the Elks Cottage. The Homestead

[12] *Ibid.*, pp. 588–590.
[13] Kephart, Newell C., "A Method of Heightening Social Adjustment in an Institutional Group," *The American Journal of Orthopsychiatry*, 8, No. 4 (October, 1938), p. 711.
[14] *Ibid.*, pp. 710–716.

Cottage group was more closely knit, whereas the Elks Cottage did not consist of a socially integrated or unified group.

To remedy this situation, Kephart selected a subgroup from the Elks Cottage and formed them, through activities, into a unit. Gradually other members entered into the activities. Five months later, a repetition of the sociometric technique showed progress toward greater homogeneity in the Elks Cottage.

Kephart's findings of lack of homogeneity in the Elks Cottage are not surprising. The Homestead Cottage was organized with a small group, the primary purpose of which was to form a homogeneous group that would gradually absorb new members as they were admitted. The Elks Cottage was begun as a complete unit with a relatively large number of boys. The heterogeneity of the group and its size were not conducive to forming a self-determining and unified group.

Kephart's study has demonstrated that homogeneity in a large group can be established by organizing a small unified subgroup as a nucleus which could, through its activities, draw in the other members of the total group. Teachers may find this method of inestimable value when faced with the problem of unifying a large group.

From these initial experiences the philosophy of the Homestead Cottage spread to one after another of the cottages in the institution. In 1950 the superintendent wrote:

It is my feeling, after years of observation of this project, that it has gradually become less and less conspicuous as the basic philosophy of its operation has spread throughout all of the various groups within the institution — both boys and girls.

I think you might be interested in part of a report made by Mr. Rossettie concerning our children's activities this past Hallowe'en.

"I am calling special attention to our Hallowe'en celebrations this year because I feel that they were particularly outstanding, not only according to standards which might be peculiar to children's institutions, but because they would compare very favorably to the standards we might find in the average community. Actually, our children had a variety of parties, particularly tailored to best meet the needs of each individual group.

"Our older children, with the exception of Cottages D, 2, and 8, participated in parties in which both boys and girls took part. At these mixed parties, which were held at the Children's Community Center, the Elks Lodge, and the Homestead, the main attraction probably was the square dancing.

"One of the things that impressed me most was the freedom with which our children were able to mix while at the same time maintaining a constraint and control which only a short time ago we would have considered beyond their ability to demonstrate.

"The one factor, which is borne most strongly upon my consciousness, is the realization that the accomplishments demonstrated can be attributed only to the excellent quality of leadership which is being furnished to our children by the cottage workers. I would say that this high quality leadership is far from anything new, but can be traced back to its real beginning when self-determination was first successfully introduced on June 17, 1935[15] (the date of the activation of the Homestead Cottage).

Summary

Throughout the book the social adjustment of mentally handicapped children has been repeatedly cited as a major aim in the education of children with mental handicaps.

The personality characteristics of mentally handicapped children do not differ basically from the personality characteristics of normal children. The differences found are invariably the result of frustrations resulting from failure to meet the requirements of school and society. Feelings of security, belongingness, and accomplishment have been thwarted as a result of the child's inability to cope with the standard requirements of his environment.

The classroom teacher is faced with the problem of organizing an educational environment which will harmonize with the child's abilities and disabilities and which will develop security through belongingness and adequacy through success and achievement.

Some of the methods that have been successful in the management of these children are:

(1) Organizing teaching procedures in harmony with good mental-hygiene principles.

[15] Quoted from letter of Robert H. Haskell, M.D., Medical Superintendent, Wayne County Training School, Northville, Michigan, to Samuel A. Kirk, December 11, 1950.

(2) Focusing the child's attention through positive suggestions and a positive classroom atmosphere on acceptable social behavior.

(3) Allowing children to plan activities within their range of interests and abilities.

(4) Using such techniques as sociodrama for the purpose of developing insights in practical life situations.

(5) Organizing self-determining activities to give children practice in the independent management of their affairs.

REFERENCES

Abel, J. M. "Responses of Negro and White Morons to the Thematic Apperception Test," *American Journal of Mental Deficiency*, 49 (April, 1945), pp. 463–468.

Axline, Virginia M. *Play Therapy*. Boston: Houghton Mifflin Company, 1947.

Baker, Harry J. *Introduction to Exceptional Children*. New York: The Macmillan Company, 1945.

Carroll, Herbert A. *Mental Hygiene*. New York: Prentice-Hall, Inc., 1948.

Garrison, Karl C. *The Psychology of Exceptional Children*. New York: The Ronald Press Company, 1950.

Haskell, Robert H. "An Organization for the Training of Higher Grade Mental Defectives," *The American Association for the Study of the Feebleminded*, Proceedings, 37 (May, 1932), pp. 252–270.

Johnson, G. Orville. "A Study of the Social Position of Mentally-Handicapped Children in the Regular Grades," *American Journal of Mental Deficiency*, 55 (July, 1950), pp. 60–89.

Johnson, G. Orville, and Samuel A. Kirk. "Are Mentally-Handicapped Children Segregated in the Regular Grades?" *Journal of Exceptional Children*, 17 (December, 1950), 65–68, 87–88.

Johnson, Marguerite W. "What We Say and How We Say It," *Childhood Education*, 14 (April, 1938), pp. 359–362.

Kephart, Newell C. "Group Autonomy in a Children's Institution," *Mental Hygiene*, 22 (October, 1938), pp. 585–590.

Kephart, Newell C. "A Method of Heightening Social Adjustment in an Institutional Group," *The American Journal of Orthopsychiatry*, 8, No. 4 (October, 1938), pp. 710–716.

Lurie, L. A. "Conduct Disorders of Intellectually Subnormal Children," *American Journal of Psychiatry*, 91 (March, 1937), pp. 1025–1038.

Lurie, L. A., Sol Levy, and Florence M. Rosenthal. "The Defective Delinquent," *American Journal of Orthopsychiatry*, 14 (January, 1944), pp. 95–103.

Rivlin, Harry N. *Educating for Adjustment*. New York: Appleton-Century-Crofts, Inc., 1936.

Sarason, Seymour B. "The Use of the Thematic Apperception Test with Mentally Deficient Children: I. A Study of High Grade Girls," *American Journal of Mental Deficiency*, 47 (April, 1943), pp. 414–442. "II. A Study of High Grade Boys," *American Journal of Mental Deficiency*, 48 (October, 1943), pp. 169–173.

Shaffer, Lawrence F. *The Psychology of Adjustment*. Boston: Houghton Mifflin Company, 1936.

Selected Annotated Bibliography*

THE LITERATURE on mental deficiency or mental retardation is scattered in numerous medical, psychological, sociological, and educational journals, and to have access to it a research worker or a teacher must of necessity be near a very excellent and complete library. For that reason a compilation of *selected* books, pamphlets, and articles in the field of the education of the mentally retarded has been made.

The references in this bibliography are confined primarily to educational articles or to articles which have a direct application to educational procedures. Purely medical or psychological literature has not been included.

No pretense is made that every educational article has been included, or even that what has been included is the best choice. Undoubtedly many worth-while articles have been overlooked.

Section I

BOOKS

There is a great scarcity of books dealing with the problem of the mentally handicapped. Many of the books listed below are already

* This is a revision of Kirk, Samuel A., and Robert L. Erdman, *Education of the Mentally Handicapped — Selected Annotated Bibliography*. University of Illinois Bulletin, 46, No. 14 (September, 1948). The present authors are indebted to Mr. Erdman for assistance in the preparation of the revision.

out of print but can be obtained from libraries. Much of the material needed by teachers and research workers is found in pamphlets and magazine articles.

ABEL, THEODORA M., and KINDER, ELAINE. *The Subnormal Adolescent Girl.* New York: Columbia University Press, 1942. 186 pp.

Discusses the problems that confront subnormal girls in their homes, at school, in industry, in institutions, and in the community.

AMOSS, HARRY, and DELAPORTE, HELEN L. *Training Handicapped Children.* Toronto, Canada: The Ryerson Press, 1933. 328 pp.

Describes the organization of classes for mental and physical deviates in Ontario, Canada. Includes a discussion of an adapted curriculum, and the problems of organization and administration.

BENDA, CLEMENS E. *Mongolism and Cretinism.* New York: Grune & Stratton, 1946. 310 pp.

A comprehensive review of the facts concerning mongolism and cretinism based on research studies.

BERRY, RICHARD J. A., and GORDON, R. C. *The Mental Defective, A Problem in Social Inefficiency.* New York: McGraw-Hill Book Company, 1931. 146 pp.

Mental deficiency is viewed from its physiological and social aspects.

BURT, CYRIL. *The Subnormal Mind.* New York: Oxford University Press, 1935. 368 pp.

A report of lectures given at the University of London. Discusses the diagnosis and problems of mental deficiency, backwardness, delinquency, and the neuroses. Examples of tests and questionnaires are included.

DAVIES, STANLEY P. *Social Control of the Mentally Deficient.* New York: Thomas Y. Crowell Company, 1930. 389 pp.

Discusses mental deficiency from a social rather than a clinical point of view, with particular reference to the responsibility of society. Problems of segregation, sterilization, and care in institutions are fully discussed. Discusses the functions, activities, and achievements of institutions caring for mental defectives, and the education of the children and parents.

DAVIS, GUY PRATT. *What Shall the Public Schools Do for the Feeble-Minded?* Cambridge, Mass.: Harvard University Press, 1927. 225 pp.

> Describes the major objectives of the education of mentally deficient children and analyzes the instructional program for them in terms of sense training, manual training, physical training, occupational training, academic training, and mental hygiene. Outlines a plan for the organization of the education of mental defectives on state-wide basis, including centers for both rural and urban communities.

DESCŒUDRES, ALICE. *The Education of Mentally Defective Children.* (Translated from the second French edition by Ernest F. Row.) Boston: D. C. Heath & Co., 313 pp.

> Discusses the history, organization, and methods of diagnosis of the mentally defective in Europe. Devotes most of the book to the analysis of learning difficulties and the instructional techniques which are employed for the education of the mentally defective. Describes games for the teaching of reading, writing, and arithmetic; and includes methods for other aspects of the curriculum such as handwork, art, projects, physical training, and training the senses and attention.

DOLL, EDGAR A., PHELPS, WINTHROP M., and MELCHER, RUTH T. *Mental Deficiency Due to Birth Injuries.* New York: The Macmillan Company, 1932. 289 pp.

> A report of an investigation of the frequency and characteristics of birth injured children at Vineland institution. Emphasizes birth injury as a greater cause of mental deficiency than has been admitted.

DUNCAN, JOHN. *The Education of the Ordinary Child.* New York: Ronald Press Company, 1943. 237 pp.

> A description of a systematically developed curriculum for the education of mentally handicapped children in a residential institution in England. The curriculum is based on the theory of G and S factors of intelligence (Professor Spearman). The instructional procedure is systematically developed for the various aspects of the curriculum. Achievement results of such a curriculum are also included.

FEATHERSTONE, WILLIAM B. *The Curriculum of the Special Class.* New York: Teachers College, Columbia University, 1932. 157 pp.

> A report of a doctor's dissertation including a critique of traditional

methods of teaching in special classes for retarded children. The author condemns "the subject-matter-set-out-to-be-learned policy" and urges that teachers of special classes follow the Dewey philosophy in the education of the slow learners.

FEATHERSTONE, WILLIAM B. *Teaching the Slow Learner* (Revised Edition). New York: Bureau of Publications; Teachers College, Columbia University, 1951. 118 pp.

A brief and concise pamphlet covering the entire area of teaching the slow learner. Such topics as how to locate him, how to organize for teaching, how to guide his activities, how to teach the fundamental processes, and how to help the slow learner (not the mentally deficient) with his personal problems, are discussed.

GESELL, ARNOLD. *The Retarded Child: How to Help Him.* Bloomington, Ill.: Public School Publishing Company, 1925. 100 pp.

Offers practical suggestions for an individual program involving various activities, including handicraft, and vocational work for mentally deficient children.

HOLLINGWORTH, LETA S. *The Psychology of Subnormal Children.* New York: The Macmillan Company, 1920. 288 pp.

Offers teachers of mentally handicapped children a basic knowledge of the physical and psychological characteristics of deficient children.

INGRAM, CHRISTINE P. *Education of the Slow-Learning Child.* Yonkers: World Book Company, 1935. 419 pp.

Describes the characteristics of the mentally retarded and their physical, social, and mental traits at each age level. Discusses the objectives and organization of a special class. Emphasizes the unit method of instruction and offers examples of effective units of work.

INSKEEP, ANNIE D. *Teaching Dull and Retarded Children.* New York: The Macmillan Company, 1926. 455 pp.

Describes a modified traditional curriculum for the education of mentally handicapped and dull children. Includes discussions of methods of teaching reading, language, spelling, arithmetic, and other usual subjects of the curriculum, with some attention also to games and projects for the education of the handicapped.

ITARD, JEAN-MARC-GASPARD. *The Wild Boy of Aveyron.* Translated by George and Muriel Humphrey. New York: Appleton-Century-Crofts, Inc., 1932. 104 pp.

> An English translation of the historical work of Dr. Itard (1801) in his attempt to educate a wild boy found in the woods who had been diagnosed as an idiot. The book discusses in detail the instructional program employed in sense and intellectual training over a period of five years.

KIRK, SAMUEL A. *Teaching Reading to Slow-Learning Children.* Boston: Houghton Mifflin Company, 1940. 225 pp.

> Discusses the characteristics of mentally handicapped children, their achievement in reading, and a method of teaching reading to slow learners. Includes a discussion of readiness, initial stages in learning, increasing efficiency in reading, and remedial procedures.

PENROSE, LIONEL S. *The Biology of Mental Defect.* New York: Grune & Stratton, 1949. 285 pp.

> A discussion of the relationship between genetics and mental defect.

SARASON, SEYMOUR. *Psychological Problems in Mental Deficiency.* New York: Harper and Brothers, 1949. 366 pp.

> A critical review of the literature on the psychological aspects of mental deficiency. Discusses criteria for mental deficiency, problems in classification, diagnosis of brain injury, problems in test interpretation, garden-variety mental deficiency, cultural factors in the etiology of garden-variety deficiency, cerebral palsy, projective techniques, psychotherapy, and other forms of mental deficiency.

STRAUSS, ALFRED A., and LEHTINEN, LAURA E. *Psychopathology and Education of the Brain-Injured Child.* New York: Grune & Stratton, 1947. 270 pp.

> A review of the neurological and psychological methods of diagnosis of brain-injured children and a description of the special instructional procedures employed with such children.

TREDGOLD, ALFRED F. *Mental Deficiency.* New York: William Wood and Company, 1937. 535 pp.

> A medical treatise on mental deficiency. Describes in detail the diagnosis and treatment of various types of mental deficiency.

WALLIN, J. E. WALLACE. *Children With Mental and Physical Handicaps*. New York: Prentice-Hall, Inc., 1949. 549 pp.

Discusses definitions, psychological concepts, and theories of mental defectiveness. Also presents the various classificatory schema that can be used in classifying mental deficients.

WALLIN, J. E. W. *The Education of Handicapped Children*. Boston: Houghton Mifflin Company, 1924. 394 pp.

Discusses the history and care of handicapped children in general and presents the theories of mental deficiency and differential education. Describes instructional procedures with the mentally handicapped, as well as curricula and objectives of special classes. Discusses the consequences of feeble-mindedness. The appendix includes a classification of the mentally deficient.

WHIPPLE, HELEN D. *Making Citizens of the Mentally Limited*. Bloomington, Ill.: Public School Publishing Company, 1927. 374 pp.

Advocates meeting the needs of special class pupils so that they may make adequate postschool adjustments.

Section II

CHARACTERISTICS, SELECTION, AND PLACEMENT

How to find children who have mental handicaps, how to differentiate them from reading disabilities and emotional problems, and what provisions to make for them are some of the tasks facing workers in this field. The following publications deal primarily with the problems of diagnosis, selection, and placement.

ABEL, THEODORA M., and HUMPHREYS, EDWARD J. "Institutional Biographies of Unstable Subnormal Girls," *American Journal of Mental Deficiency*, 46 (April, 1942), 514–18.

Discusses the cases of the behavior of six high-grade, borderline, and dull-normal patients in an institution and the problems of organization for the care of these mentally defective, unstable girls.

ALLEN, MARK K., "A Comparison Between Test Scores on the Original and the Revised Stanford-Binet Intelligence Scales Administered to a Group of Retarded and Mentally Deficient Subjects," *American Journal of Mental Deficiency*, 46 (April, 1942), 501–07.

A comparative study of test scores on the original and revised Stanford-Binet of retarded and mentally deficient subjects in which it was found that differences in I.Q. on the two scales were significant.

ARTHUR, GRACE. "Some Factors Contributing to Errors in the Diagnosis of Feeblemindedness," *American Journal of Mental Deficiency*, 54 (April, 1950), 495–501.

Discussion of physical handicaps, brain-injury, early illness in childhood, delayed speech, and academic disabilities as possible factors that contribute to incorrect diagnosis of mental deficiency.

ARTHUR, GRACE. "The Relative Difficulty of Various Tests for Sixty Feeble-minded Individuals," *Journal of Clinical Psychology*, 6 (July, 1950), 276–79.

Found that the group showed little difference in their verbal and nonverbal abilities as measured on the Grace-Arthur Performance Scale, Form I.

BAKER, HARRY J. *Characteristic Differences in Bright and Dull Pupils*. Bloomington, Ill.: Public School Publishing Company, 1927. 118 pp.

A summary of mental and educational characteristics and methods of teaching dull and bright children. The data was obtained from a questionnaire submitted to 500 teachers in Detroit.

BIJOU, SIDNEY. "A Genetic Study of the Diagnostic Significance of Psychometric Patterns," *American Journal of Mental Deficiency*, 47 (October, 1942), 171–77.

A study in which it was found that the adjustment of a group of mentally retarded boys, who had a high performance quotient and good arithmetic achievement, was better than the other group who had a low performance quotient and was poor in arithmetic achievement relative to their Binet score.

BIJOU, SIDNEY W. "The Psychometric Pattern Approach as an Aid to Clinical Analysis — A Review," *American Journal of Mental Deficiency*, 46 (January, 1942), 354–62.

A discussion of the literature on test patterns and their implications for clinical analysis of mental deficiency.

BOND, ELDEN A. "A Method of Selecting Subnormal Children for a Vocational School," *Journal of Juvenile Research*, 21 (July, 1937), 188–92.

> Describes the methods used in a city school system for the assignment of retarded children to vocational schools.

BRILLE, MOSHE. *A Comparative Study of the Performance of Adjusted and Maladjusted Mentally Deficient Boys on Twenty-two Tests and Scales.* New York: New York University, 1935. 146 pp.

> A study was carried on at the New Jersey State Colony for feeble-minded males, New Lisbon, New Jersey. The performance of two equated groups was compared on twenty-two tests and scales, of both verbal and non-verbal character. Intelligence, social adjustment, and various behavior patterns were considered.

BROWN, ANDREW W. *The Unevenness of the Abilities of Dull and of Bright Children.* New York: Teachers College, Columbia University, 1926. 112 pp.

> Compares dull and bright boys in abstract, mechanical, and non-verbal ability. Finds that the dull do not show greater unevenness in the development of abilities than do the bright.

CASSEL, ROBERT H. "Relation of Design Reproduction to the Etiology of Mental Deficiency," *Journal of Consulting Psychology*, 13 (December, 1949), 421–28.

> Twenty-five endogenous and twenty-five exogenous male mentally deficient subjects were given the Ellis Visual Design test. The exogenous group was inferior to the endogenous group in design reproduction.

CRUICKSHANK, WILLIAM M., and QUALTERE, THOMAS J. "The Use of Intelligence Tests with Children of Retarded Mental Development: I. Comparison of the 1916 and 1937 Revision of the Stanford-Binet Intelligence Scales," *American Journal of Mental Deficiency*, 54 (January, 1950), 361–81.

> Two tests were administered to one hundred mentally retarded children. It was found that there was a statistically significant difference between the two scales. It was also suggested that the same qualities of the mentally retarded were not being measured.

CRUICKSHANK, WILLIAM M., and QUALTERE, THOMAS J. "The Use of Intelligence Tests with Children of Retarded Mental Development: II. Clinical Considerations," *American Journal of Mental Deficiency*, 54 (January, 1950), 370–81.

Discusses the clinical considerations involved in testing limits, and in interpreting hard and easy items on the Stanford-Binet scale.

CUTTS, RICHARD A., and SLOAN, WILLIAM. "Test Patterns of Adjusted Defectives on the Wechsler-Bellevue Test," *American Journal of Mental Deficiency*, 50 (July, 1945), 98–101.

Found that the Wechsler-Bellevue could not be used as a satisfactory instrument to distinguish between institutionalized defectives who are adjusted and maladjusted.

DOLL, EDGAR A. "Etiology of Mental Deficiency," *Training School Bulletin*, 41 (November, 1944), 129–37.

A discussion of the causes of mental deficiency, with a differentiation between the exogenous and endogenous types.

EARL, C. J. C. "The Affective-Instinctive Psychology of Imbecile Children," *British Journal of Medical Psychology*, 15 (February, 1936, Part 4), 266–78.

Reports differences between mentally-defective and normal children in "affective-instinctive energy," attention, interest, and physical, intellectual, and social maturity.

FRAZEUR, HELEN A., and HOAKLEY, Z. PAULINE. "Significance of Psychological Test Results of Exogenous and Endogenous Children," *American Journal of Mental Deficiency*, 51 (January, 1947), 384–88.

A study that compared the scores of exogenous and endogenous children on the Arthur Point Scale and found no statistically significant difference between the two.

GESELL, ARNOLD. *Exceptional Children and Public-School Policy*. New Haven: Yale University Press, 1921. 66 pp.

Reports a survey of the intelligence of elementary school children in New Haven. Recommends school provisions for exceptional children and a policy of state support.

GLANVILLE, A. D. "Psychometric Patterns in Industrial School Boys," *Delaware State Medical Journal*, 9 (April, 1937), 91–94.

Language retardation is shown to be an important cause of delinquency among industrial school boys.

GRAHAM, RAY. "Handbook and Manual for the Qualified Psychological Examiner," *The Illinois Plan for Special Education of Exceptional Children*, Supplement to Circular Series B, No. 12. Springfield, Illinois: Superintendent of Public Instruction, 1949. 64 pp.

States the procedure in determining the eligibility and placement of mentally handicapped children in special education classes in the state of Illinois.

HACKBUSCH, FLORENTINE. "Responsibility of the American Association on Mental Deficiency for Developing Uniform Psychological Practices in Schools for Mental Defectives," *American Journal of Mental Deficiency*, 45 (October, 1940), 233–37.

Reports a survey of the practices of 100 state and private institutions in psychological service.

HAMLEY, H. R., and OTHERS. *Education of Backward Children and Juvenile Delinquency in England and Wales.* London: Institute of Education, University of London, 1936. 104 pp.

A symposium by several British authors. Part I of the report describes the characteristics of backward and dull children, causes of backwardness, and the education of backward children. Part II considers psychological aspects of juvenile delinquency and surveys the problem. A description of the characteristics of mentally retarded children, the causes of retardation, and educational provisions for such children.

HAMLIN, ROY. "Test Pattern of High Grade Mentally Defective Girls," *Proceedings and Addresses of the Sixty-second Annual Session of the American Association on Mental Deficiency*, 43, No. 1 (1938), 161–65.

Studied the relation between test-score patterns of defective girls and adjustment on parole.

HERSHFIELD, ALEXANDER S. "The Mentally Handicapped Child," *Illinois Medical Journal*, 77 (April, 1940), 369–71.

> Recommends a working-colony type of organization for mental defectives in Illinois. Includes a description of known characteristics and a prognosis for such children.

HOAKLEY, Z. PAULINE, and FRAZEUR, HELEN A. "Significance of Psychological Test Results of Exogenous and Endogenous Children," *American Journal of Mental Deficiency*, 50 (October, 1945), 263–71.

> Found significant differences in the perceptual field between the responses of brain-crippled mentally defective and familial mentally defective children on the items of the Binet.

HOLLINGWORTH, LETA S. *Special Talents and Defects*. New York: The Macmillan Company, 1923. 216 pp.

> Describes the procedures and principles in the diagnosis of talents and defects in children and relates these abilities and disabilities to school subjects.

ISRAELITE, JUDITH. "A Comparison of the Difficulty of Items for Intellectually Normal Children and Mental Defectives on the Goodenough Drawing Test," *American Journal of Orthopsychiatry*, 6 (October, 1936), 494–503.

> An analysis of the Goodenough drawing-a-man test. The results for mental defectives and normal children were different in certain fundamental characteristics.

JOHNSON, G. ORVILLE. "A Study of the Social Position of Mentally Handicapped Children in the Regular Grades," *American Journal of Mental Deficiency*, 55 (July, 1950), 60–89.

> An experimental study which found that mentally handicapped children in a regular classroom were more isolated and rejected than normal children.

JOHNSON, G. ORVILLE, and KIRK, SAMUEL A. "Are Mentally-Handicapped Children Segregated in the Regular Grades?" *Journal of Exceptional Children*, 17 (December, 1950), 65–67, 87–88.

> A sociometric study of the status of mentally handicapped children in

traditional and progressive schools. It was found that normal children in progressive schools as well as in traditional schools tend to isolate and reject the mentally handicapped.

JOLLES, ISAAC. "The Diagnostic Implications of Rorschach's Test
in Case Studies of Mental Defectives," *Genetic Psychology Monographs*, No. 36 (1947), 89–198.

Concludes that "mental deficiency of the familial and undifferentiated
types is a symptom of a personality disorder...."

KANNER, LEO. "A Miniature Textbook of Feeblemindedness,"
Child Care Monographs, No. 1. New York: Child Care Publications, 1949. 31 pp.

A discussion of the etiology and characteristics of the feeble-minded.
Prefers using "determiners of mental deficiency, rather than cause."

KELLY, ELIZABETH, and STEVENS, HARVEY A. "Special Education
for the Mentally Handicapped," *National Society for the Study of
Education*, Forty-ninth Yearbook, Part II, 1950, 237–53.

A discussion of classification, discovery, and characteristics of the
mentally handicapped. Also discusses educational provisions for
them.

KENNEDY-FRASER, DAVID. *Education of the Backward Child*. London: University of London Press, 1932. 254 pp.

A psychologist in Scotland reports his views on diagnosis, definitions,
and etiological factors in mental retardation. He discusses the practical problems faced by teachers of such children.

LANE, ELIZABETH B., and KINDER, ELAINE F. "Relativism in the
Thinking of Subnormal Subjects as Measured by Certain of
Piaget's Tests," *Pedagogical Seminary and Journal of Genetic Psy-
chology*, 54 (March, 1939), 107–18.

Summarizes data obtained from the use of the Piaget technique with
Letchworth Village children. It was found that with a rise in mental
age there was an improvement in performance.

LAYCOCK, SAMUEL R., and CLARK, STANLEY. "The Comparative
Performance of a Group of Old-Dull and Young-Bright Children
on Some Items of the Revised Stanford-Binet Scale of Intelli-

gence, Form L," *Journal of Educational Psychology*, 33 (January, 1942), 1–12.

Found that no statistically significant difference existed between the two groups.

MARTINSON, BETTY, and STRAUSS, ALFRED A. "A Method of Clinical Evaluation of the Responses to the Stanford-Binet Intelligence Test," *American Journal of Mental Deficiency*, 46 (July, 1941), 72–83.

Made qualitative and quantitative analyses of responses of normal and mentally defective children to certain levels on the Stanford-Binet test. Found that each group of children displayed a characteristic pattern of successes and failures. An outline based on the analyses is suggested for the clinical evaluation of the test responses.

MARTINSON, BETTY, and STRAUSS, ALFRED A. "Education and Treatment of an Imbecile Boy of the Exogenous Type," *American Journal of Mental Deficiency*, 45 (October, 1940), 274–80.

A case study of a brain-injured child. Authors believe that children with brain injuries require educational treatment different from that given to mental defectives of endogenous origin.

Massachusetts Department of Education and Department of Mental Diseases. *Regulations for Determining the Number of Children Three Years Retarded in Mental Development*. Boston, 1931. 79 pp.

Describes the State regulations concerning the selection of children for examination and the type of tests given. A list of available clinical services to school districts is included.

McCANDLESS, BOYD, and STRAUSS, ALFRED. "Objective Criteria Diagnostic of Deviant Personality: An Exploratory Study," *American Journal of Mental Deficiency*, 47 (April, 1943), 445–49.

A study in which no criteria for the diagnosis of a deviant personality were found between accident proneness, ratings of supervisor, and scores on the Kent Rosanoff word list.

MERRILL, MAUDE A. "On the Relation of Intelligence to Achievement in the Case of Mentally Retarded Children," *Comparative*

Psychological Monograph, 2, Serial No. 10. Baltimore: Williams & Wilkins Company, 1924. 100 pp.

This study showed that "there are characteristic differences in mental traits between normal and retarded children of the same mental level, but that 'capacity for learning' in the two groups is not significantly different at any given level."

NASH, A. M. "Classified Standards Are Upheld by Pattern Children," *Training School Bulletin*, 41 (October, 1944), 11–23.

A discussion of the methods and techniques used in categorizing children at the Vineland Training School.

NEMZEK, CLAUDE L. "Academic Progress of Subnormal Pupils," *School and Society*, 50 (December 16, 1939), 806–08.

Describes the results of objective tests in determining the academic progress of mentally retarded children in special classes.

ODELL, CHARLES W. *Provisions for Mentally Atypical Pupils*. Urbana, Ill.: University of Illinois. (Bureau of Educational Research, College of Education, Bulletin No. 59), 1931. 73 pp.

Describes the provisions for mentally superior and inferior pupils in the State of Illinois.

PARKYN, G. W. "Clinical Significance of I.Q.'s on the Revised Stanford-Binet Scale," *Journal of Educational Psychology*, 36 (February, 1945), 114–18.

Discusses the changes in interpretation of scores on the 1937 revision of the Stanford-Binet. The author believes that the same classification can be made with the 1937 scales as was made with the 1916 scale for children whose I.Q.'s are under 80.

ROBERTS, A. DUDLEY. "Intelligence and Performance Test Patterns Among Older Mental Defectives," *American Journal of Mental Deficiency*, 49 (January, 1945), 300–03.

A comparative study of the Stanford-Binet L, Arthur Performance Scale, and Wechsler-Bellevue Intelligence Scale. Found that the Grace-Arthur Performance Scale was not as satisfactory as the Stanford-Binet and Wechsler-Bellevue Intelligence Test for older mentally retarded subjects.

SARASON, ESTHER K., and SARASON, SEYMOUR B. "A Problem in Diagnosing Feeblemindedness," *Journal of Abnormal and Social Psychology*, 40 (July, 1945), 323–29.

Discusses the diagnosis of mental deficiency by the use of psychological examinations, personality organization, test analysis, and the influence of environmental factors.

SLOAN, WILLIAM, and CUTTS, RICHARD A. "Test Patterns of Defective Delinquents on the Wechsler-Bellevue Test," *American Journal of Mental Deficiency*, 50 (July, 1945), 95–97.

A study that found the test pattern for a group of mentally defective delinquents was similar to that for adolescent psychopaths on the Wechsler-Bellevue Intelligence Scale.

STARR, ANNA SPIESMAN. "The Significance of Qualifying Factors in the Diagnosis of Borderline Mentality," *Training School Bulletin*, 34 (October, 1937), 113–18.

Emphasizes the potentialities shown by borderline cases of mental retardation and their achievement in school.

STRAUSS, A. A., and KEPHART, NEWELL C. "Behavior Differences in Mentally Retarded Children Measured by a New Behavior Rating Scale," *American Journal of Psychiatry*, 96 (March, 1940), 1117–24.

It is possible to differentiate between two groups of mentally retarded children, one of which shows brain damage, by the behavior rating scale.

SYMPOSIUM. "Segregation Versus Non-Segregation of Exceptional Children," *Journal of Exceptional Children*, 12 (May, 1946), 235–40.

Views on segregation and non-segregation of exceptional children expressed by members on a panel at the Twenty-second Annual Meeting of the International Council for Exceptional Children. The conclusion reached was that "it would seem right, therefore, that, with our knowledge of modern educational methods, a more scientific treatment than segregation be afforded all children within the school."

SYMPOSIUM. HACKBUSCH, FLORENTINE. "When Should the General Social Agency or the School Refer the Mentally Defective

Client to an Agency Specializing in Work with Defectives?" *American Journal of Mental Deficiency*, 45 (October, 1940), 296–303; ENGEL, ANNA M. "When Should the School Refer the Mental Defective to the Specialized Agency or Institution?" *Ibid.*, 304–09; BROWN, CECIL H. "When Should the General Social Agency Refer the Mental Defective to the Specialized Agency or Institution?" *Ibid.*, 310–15.

> A discussion on the communities' responsibility for care of mental defectives in relation to that of the institution.

THOMPSON, WILLIAM H., and EDWARDS, FRANCES M. "The Reliability of Teachers' Reports about Subnormal Children Sent to the Child Study Bureau," *Proceedings and Addresses of the Sixty-second Annual Session of the American Association on Mental Deficiency*, 43, No. 2 (1938), 98–104.

> The teachers' reports on referring children for special classes are found to be very valuable and reliable information.

WALKER, MARGARET. *A Study of High School Failures.* Philadelphia: Temple University, 1935. 114 pp.

> Reports a study showing that 44 per cent of children who failed in high school subjects were retarded in intelligence. Eleven per cent of those with below-average scores on intelligence tests did not fail.

WALLIN, J. E. WALLACE, and HULTSCH, CATHARINE. "The Pathognomonic Significance of Psychometric Patterns," *American Journal of Mental Deficiency*, 48 (January, 1944), 269–77.

> A study that illustrates the need for caution in using a psychometric pattern as a guide to diagnosis of personal and social maladjustment of children.

WEXBERG, ERWIN. "Testing Methods for the Differential Diagnosis of Mental Deficiency in Case of Arrested Brain Tumor," *American Journal of Mental Deficiency*, 46 (July, 1941), 39–45.

> Found that the Stanford-Binet was of greater diagnostic value than the Weigl, Vigotsky, and Goldstein performance tests.

WILSON, FRANK T. *Learning of Bright and Dull Children.* New York: Teachers College, Columbia University (Teachers College Contributions to Education, No. 292), 1928. 56 pp.

> Compared four groups of children of different levels of mentality on

different learning tasks. Concludes that where the motor factor in learning is predominant, chronological age has some effect. In purely intellectual activities Binet ratings correlated with learning ability.

WOODY, CLIFFORD. "An Analysis of Differences in the Learning of Bright and Dull Children," *University of Michigan School of Education Bulletin*, 8 (December, 1936), 37–39.

An analysis of differences in the learning of bright and dull children reveals that learning ability differs in degree rather than in kind.

Section III

PHILOSOPHY, ORGANIZATION, AND ADMINISTRATION

The publications included in this section deal with the attempts of authors to formulate an adequate educational philosophy for the mentally handicapped, with procedures in organizing programs and classes, and with problems in administration. Such articles usually include other aspects of the program such as curricula.

ADE, LESTER K. *Meeting the Needs of the Mentally Retarded*, Bulletin No. 420. Harrisburg· Pennsylvania State Department of Public Instruction, 1939. 168 pp.

A state department publication giving the philosophy of special education, the practical considerations for the establishment of special classes, and the curricula for special classes. Bibliographical references, forms, and equipment needed are included in the appendix.

ALLEN, AMY A. *Let Us Look at Slow-Learning Children.* Columbus, Ohio: State Department of Education, 1949. 54 pp.

Describes philosophy of program for Special Education in the state of Ohio.

ANDERSON, META L. "The Meaning of Education for the Mentally Retarded," *American Journal of Mental Deficiency*, 46 (July, 1941), 6–16.

Points out defects in present programs for dull children and suggests new types of schools for the low-intelligence groups.

BAKER, HARRY J. "Administration of Special Education," *Review of Educational Research*, 14 (June, 1944), 209–16.

Discusses teacher training, special class statistics, costs and finances.

and vocational guidance and placement in relation to the administration of special education.

BERRY, CHARLES SCOTT. "Helping the Mentally Retarded Child," *Nation's Schools*, 13 (May, 1934), 27–32.

Describes the organization of services for mentally retarded children in the public schools including special classes, modified special classes, and individual programs.

BERRY, CHARLES SCOTT. "Public School Education of Mentally Retarded Children," *Proceedings and Addresses of the Sixtieth Annual Session of the American Association on Mental Deficiency*, 41 (1936), 111–30.

Describes the objectives and provisions for the education of mentally retarded children in the public schools.

BERRY, CHARLES SCOTT. "General Problems of Philosophy and Administration in the Education of Exceptional Children," *Review of Educational Research*, 11 (June, 1941), 253–60.

A bibliography of titles published since 1935 summarizing the literature on philosophy, administration, national and state programs, and city and rural programs.

BOSSHART, JOHN H. *The Classroom Teacher Can Help the Handicapped Child*. School Bulletin No. 12. Trenton: State of New Jersey, Department of Education, 1947. 62 pp.

Describes philosophy of program for Special Education in New Jersey.

BYRNE, MAY E. "Program of Education for Mentally Retarded Children in a Public School System," *Proceedings and Addresses of the Sixty-second Annual Session of the American Association on Mental Deficiency*, 43, No. 2 (1938), 116–22.

Describes the activity program used in Minneapolis with special class children.

Connecticut Special Education Association. *History of Special Education for Mentally Deficient Children in Connecticut*. New Haven: Columbia Printing Company, 1936. 125 pp.

Includes the activities of the Connecticut Special Education Association, a history of the work in Connecticut, and the organization of special classes.

DOLL, EDGAR A. "Foster Care for Mental Defectives," *Training School Bulletin*, 36 (February, 1940), 193–205.

It is recommended that hostels or colony houses be established to act as adjustment centers between institutional care and home care in the provision for mental defectives.

DOYLE, FRANCIS W. *Questions on the Education of Mentally Retarded Minors in California.* Sacramento: California State Department of Education, 19, No. 1 (January, 1950). 47 pp.

Describes philosophy of program for special education in the state of California.

EDGAR, J. W. *Special Education for Exceptional Children in Texas.* Austin: The Division of Special Education, Texas Education Agency. Reprint, 1950. 136 pp.

Describes philosophy of program for Special Education in Texas.

ENGLISH, COLIN. *Developing a Program for Education of Exceptional Children in Florida.* Bulletin No. 55. Tallahassee: State Department of Education, 1948. 136 pp.

Describes philosophy of program for Special Education in the State of Florida.

FEATHERSTONE, WILLIAM B. *The Curriculum of the Special Class.* New York: Teachers College, Columbia University, 1932. 157 pp.

A report of a doctor's dissertation including a critique of traditional methods of teaching in special classes for retarded children. The author condemns "the subject-matter-set-out-to-be-learned policy" and urges that teachers of special classes follow the Dewey philosophy in the education of the slow learners.

GRAHAM, RAY. "The Educable Mentally Handicapped," *The Illinois Plan for Special Education of Exceptional Children*, Circular Series B, No. 12. Springfield, Illinois: Superintendent of Public Instruction, 1945. 45 pp.

Presents the general philosophy with respect to the handicapped, the Illinois Plan, organization of classes, steps to be followed by districts in organizing these classes, and problems of teacher supply and training.

GRAHAM, RAY, and ENGEL, ANNA M. "Administering the Special Services for Exceptional Children," *National Society for the Study of Education*, Forty-ninth Yearbook, Part II, 1950, 18–36.

Discussion of objectives, principles of administration, and organization of special education at the state and local level.

GRUENER, JENNETTE R. *Feebleminded Children as a Massachusetts Problem.* Boston: Massachusetts Child Council (41 Mount Vernon Street), 1941. 64 pp.

Presents to the general public a description of the problems involved in the community adjustment of the mentally deficient and the community's responsibility to this group.

HANNA, AGNES K. "Some Observations on Extramural Care of Mentally Deficient Children," *Proceedings and Addresses of the Sixty-second Annual Session of the American Association on Mental Deficiency*, 43, No. 1 (1938), 115–21.

Reviews state and federal legislation dealing with mentally defective children.

HECK, ARCH O. "General Problems of Philosophy and Administration in the Education of Exceptional Children," *Review of Educational Research*, 14 (June, 1944), 201–08.

A discussion of financing special education, organization of classes, prevention, curriculum development, employment, and so forth as problems of philosophy and administration of exceptional children.

HILDRETH, G. H. "Educational Provisions for Slow-Learning Pupils," *Educational Administration and Supervision*, 25 (October, 1939), 491–512.

Reports a survey of public school provisions for slow-learning children.

HEDGE, OLIVER. *A Program of Education for Exceptional Children in Oklahoma.* Oklahoma City, Oklahoma: Bulletin, S. E. No. 1, State Board of Education, 1949. 69 pp.

Describes philosophy of program for Special Education in Oklahoma.

HUNGERFORD, RICHARD H. "Philosophy of Occupational Education," *Reprints from Occupational Education.* Publication of the

Association for New York City Teachers of Special Education (224 E. 28th Street, New York 16, New York), 1948. 46 pp.

Describes philosophy of program for special education in New York City schools.

HUNGERFORD, RICHARD H. "A Practical Program of Training and Service for the High Grade Defective and Borderline Group," *American Journal of Mental Deficiency*, 48 (April, 1944), 414–16.

Outlines community and school services available to high-grade defectives and borderline cases.

HUNGERFORD, RICHARD H., and ROSENZWEIG, LOUIS E. "The Mentally Retarded," *Journal of Exceptional Children*, 10 (May, 1944), 210–13.

Discusses the advantages of training retarded children so that they may contribute to society. Emphasizes long-term preparation based on the qualitative study of each individual's potentialities.

INGRAM, CHRISTINE P. "Opportunity for the Slow-Learning Child," *Educational Method*, 17 (May, 1938), 409–16.

Stresses the responsibility of the school in making provisions for older mentally handicapped children beyond the age of 16.

KELLY, ELIZABETH M. "Organization of Special Classes to Fit the Needs of Different Ability Groupings," *American Journal of Mental Deficiency*, 48 (July, 1943), 80–86.

Describes a plan for the organization of special classes for the mentally handicapped. Discusses the curriculum, teacher preparation, and integration with the school system.

KUNZIG, ROBERT W. *Public School Education of Atypical Children.* Washington: U.S. Government Printing Office (Bulletin, No. 10), 1931. 160 pp.

Reports the provisions made for special education in cities of 100,000 population or more and includes statistics and descriptions of organizational and administrative procedures.

LANDELL, CATHERINE. "Why Ignore the Problem of the Subnormal Child?" *American School Board Journal*, 91 (August, 1935), 24–25.

Recommends that school administrators organize special classes for mentally handicapped children in public schools so that their children will obtain better educational opportunities.

MARTENS, ELISE H. *Organization for Exceptional Children Within State Departments of Education.* Washington: U.S. Government Printing Office (Pamphlet No. 42), 1933. 35 pp.

A survey of the provisions made in state departments of education for the organization and supervision of the education of exceptional children.

MARTENS, ELISE H. *State Legislation for Education of Exceptional Children.* Washington: U.S. Government Printing Office (Bulletin No. 2), 1949. 61 pp.

A summary and discussion of the state legislation for the education of exceptional children in the United States.

MARTENS, ELISE H. *Statistics of Special Schools and Classes for Exceptional Children, 1947–48.* Federal Security Agency. United States Office of Education, Biennial Survey of Education in the United States — 1946–48. Chapter 5. 82 pp.

Data showing the number, grade level, and type of exceptional children enrolled in special schools and public school classes; number of public and residential schools; number of teachers in special schools and classes; and so forth.

Massachusetts Department of Education. *Manual for Special Classes.* Boston, 1931. 79 pp.

A pamphlet prepared by the special class teachers in Massachusetts. Discusses the organization, administration, and curriculum content of special classes for retarded children and gives the state regulations for the establishment of such classes.

Mental Deficiency Committee. *Report of the Joint Committee of the Board of Education and Board of Control.* London: His Majesty's Stationery Office, 4 Parts, 1929.

A report of the Committee on Mental Deficiency in England. Discusses legislation, present administrative arrangements, and provisions for mentally defective and retarded children. Gives recommendations for policies, standards, and educational procedures.

PUTNAM, REX. *Special Education — Your Questions Answered.* Salem, Oregon: Superintendent of Public Instruction, 1949. 27 pp.

Describes philosophy of program for Special Education in the state of Oregon.

SLICHTER, BETTY. "Rural Training Units," *The School* (Elementary Edition), 34 (October, 1945), 137–39.

A description of training for subnormal children in special classes in rural areas in Ontario, Canada.

SMERLING, FRANK A. "What the Schools as Constituted at Present Can Do for the Low Ability Pupil," *High Points in the Work of the High Schools of the City of New York*, 18 (June, 1936), 35–38.

Recommends that the administrative structure of high schools be revised so that it will be better adapted to the 20 per cent of the children at the lower levels in intelligence. Changes in policies of promotions and retardations for the physically and mentally handicapped are recommended.

SPOHN, A. L. "Curriculum Provision for Slow Pupils," *North Central Association Quarterly*, 12 (January, 1938), 331–33.

Presents data from a survey by the North Central Association to determine the provisions for slow-learners in the high school.

TENNY, JOHN W. "Adjustment of Special Class Pupils to Regular Classes," *Journal of Exceptional Children*, 10 (March, 1944), 139–45.

A plan which enables the regular school program to be adjusted to meet the needs and the abilities of handicapped children.

White House Conference. *Committee on Physically and Mentally Handicapped. The Handicapped Child.* White House Conference Report. New York: The Century Company, 1933. 452 pp.

A report of the Committee on the physically and mentally handicapped and their considerations of physical, social, and educational problems involved in working with the handicapped child.

WILCOX, CATHERINE J. "The Work with Retarded Children in the State of Virginia," *Proceedings and Addresses of the Sixty-*

second *Annual Session of the American Association on Mental Deficiency*, 43, No. 1 (1938), 128–36.

> Summarizes the data on the care and placement of mentally deficient
> children in the State of Virginia.

WILLIAMS, HAROLD A., and STEVENS, HARVEY A. *A Public School
Program for Retarded Children.* Madison, Wis.: Dept. of Public
Instruction, 1947. 39 pp.

> Reviews the philosophy, practices, and organization of special classes
> for mentally handicapped children in the State of Wisconsin.

WINTERBOURN, RALPH. "Educating Backward Children in New
Zealand," *New Zealand Council for Educational Research*, Educa-
tional Research Series No. 20. Wellington, New Zealand: New
Zealand Council for Educational Research, 1944. 392 pp.

> Summarizes the provisions made for the mentally retarded in New
> Zealand.

WITTY, PAUL. "Special Class Curricula for the Retarded," *Illinois
Teacher*, 24 (January, 1936), 132–34, 158.

> Summarizes the studies on the education of the mentally handicapped
> and recommends a child-centered curriculum. The curriculum of the
> Montefiore Special School in Chicago is evaluated in terms of the
> activity preferences of the students enrolled.

Section IV

CURRICULUM AND INSTRUCTION

Publications on the general curriculum have been classified into
three groups — (1) Preschool Programs, (2) General and Elementary Programs, and (3) Secondary School Programs.

Preschool Programs

CURTIS, ETHEL LOUISE. "Building Toward Readiness in Mentally
Deficient Children," *American Journal of Mental Deficiency*, 48
(October, 1943), 183–87.

> Reports a program for the development of the language, reasoning,

quantitative thinking, auditory and visual memory, and discrimination of mentally deficient children.

ETZ, ELIZABETH. "Pre-Academic Activities to Challenge the Mentally Deficient Child from Five to Eight Years of Mental Age," *American Journal of Mental Deficiency*, 48 (October, 1943), 179–82.

Classifies activities into order of difficulty for young mentally retarded children. Relates these to academic and crafts readiness.

FERNALD, W. E. "Sense Training for Low Grade Children," *Training School Bulletin*, 41 (January, 1945), 170–74.

Describes Dr. Fernald's techniques of sense training for low-grade defectives.

KIRK, SAMUEL A. "A Project for Pre-School Mentally Handicapped Children," *American Journal of Mental Deficiency*, 54 (January, 1950), 305–10.

Describes an experimental pre-school for young mentally handicapped children. The problem is to determine the effects of a maximum educational program on the subsequent social and mental development of the children when education is offered during the formative years.

KIRK, SAMUEL A., and STEVENS, IRENE. "A Pre-Academic Curriculum for Slow-Learning Children," *American Journal of Mental Deficiency*, 47 (April, 1943), 396–405.

Describes a systematic program of readiness activities designed to train psychological functions.

MELCHER, RUTH T. "Developmental Progress in Young Mentally Handicapped Children Who Receive Prolonged Pre-Academic Training," *American Journal of Mental Deficiency*, 45 (October, 1940), 265–73.

Reports the readiness factors in young mentally retarded children and the benefits derived from a pre-academic program.

PATTERSON, R. MELCHER, and CURTIS, ETHEL LOUISE. "Observing the Learning Difficulties in a Pre-Reading Situation for Higher Grade Mental Defectives," *American Journal of Mental Deficiency*, 49 (October, 1944), 165–70.

A study of the important instructional elements in preparing higher grade mental defectives for academic work.

PATTERSON, R. MELCHER. "Organization of a Residence Unit for Pre-Academic Training of Mentally Deficient Children," *American Journal of Mental Deficiency*, 48 (October, 1943), 174–78.

Reports a project of a cottage-school unit at the Wayne County Training School in Michigan for preschool mentally handicapped children.

PATTERSON, R. MELCHER, and CURTIS, ETHEL LOUISE. "Observing For Learning Difficulties in a Pre-Reading Situation for High Grade Mental Defectives," *American Journal of Mental Deficiency*, 49 (October, 1944), 165–70.

Presents methods that can be used to locate problems in the pre-reading situation.

WIENER, BLUMA B. "A Preacademic Program for Slow-Learning Children," *Supplementary Educational Monographs*, No. 69, University of Chicago Press, 1949, 177–81.

Description of a plan for training slow-learning children at the primary level.

WIENER, B. B. "Classroom Observations for Learning Difficulties of High-Grade Mentally Defective Children with Mental Ages Below Six Years," *American Journal of Mental Deficiency*, 50 (April, 1946), 495–502.

Reports the observations a teacher can make on learning problems of young mentally retarded children.

General and Elementary Programs

ATHENS, IDA. "The Activity Program for Mental Defectives," *Ohio Schools*, 14 (April, 1936), 124–57.

Describes an activity program which integrates various aspects of the curriculum and which emphasizes social adjustment and character building.

BEAMAN, FLORENCE N. "Progressive Education for the Mentally Retarded Child," *Proceedings and Addresses of the Sixty-second Annual Session of the American Association on Mental Deficiency*, 43, No. 2 (1938), 86–90.

Recommends that classes for the mentally handicapped become more progressive, and tells how these changes can be made.

BEER, ETHEL S. "Special Training for Subnormal Children," *Journal of Abnormal and Social Psychology*, 32 (October-December, 1937), 382–91.

Describes the program for mentally handicapped children at the Montgomery School in Newark, New Jersey.

BYRNE, M. E. "Curriculum Planning for Exceptional Children," *Journal of Exceptional Children*, 12 (May, 1946), 231–34.

Discusses curriculum planning for exceptional children and implementation of the curriculum with help from the central office force.

CORRE, MARY P. "An Adjusted Curriculum for the Dull-Normal Pupil," *Occupations*, 17 (October, 1938), 34–39.

A report of a survey of curriculum programs in ten cities for the dull-normal child.

Course of Study in Special Education for Retarded Children. Minneapolis, Minn.: Public Schools, 1933. 262 pp.

A course of study for retarded children in Minneapolis. Describes units of activity for kindergarten, pre-primary, and intermediate grades.

GRILL, HELEN A. "Teaching Slow-Learning Children," *Social Education*, 3 (March, 1939), 169–72.

Methods in teaching social studies to slow children of elementary school age are discussed.

HANKINS, RUTH. "Principles of Teaching Exceptional Children in the Elementary Schools," *Child Research Clinic Series*, 3, No. 1. Langhorne, Pennsylvania: Child Research Clinic, Woods Schools, 1939. 24 pp.

Reports cases and illustrations and gives thirty principles of good educational practice with exceptional children.

HOLMES, MOSSIE D. *Handbook of Suggestions and Course of Study for Subnormal Children.* Mountain Lake Park, Md.: National Publishing Company, 1926. 110 pp.

A description of the course of study used in Youngstown, Ohio, with suggestions for teaching the various subjects.

LANE, DAVID J. "Facing the Problems in Teaching the Slow Pupils," *High Points in the Work of the Schools of New York City*, 27 (October, 1945), 41–46.

> Recommends that effort as well as scholastic attainment should be the basis for promotion for slow learners.

LYNCH, KATHERINE D. "Enrichment of the Program for Subnormal Children," *Journal of Exceptional Children*, 5 (December, 1938), 49–53.

> Describes the types of activities in which mentally handicapped children can engage for more effective learning.

MARTENS, ELISE H. *Curriculum Adjustments for the Mentally Retarded.* Washington: U.S. Government Printing Office (Bulletin, No. 2), 1950. 100 pp.

> A U.S. Office of Education bulletin describing the principles, curriculum, and instructional organization for mentally handicapped children.

MARTENS, ELISE H. *Group Activities for Mentally Retarded Children — A Symposium.* Washington: U.S. Government Printing Office (Bulletin, No. 7), 1933. 146 pp.

> Describes units of activities and projects contributed by successful teachers of the mentally handicapped.

McCANDLESS, ESTHER. "A Study of Educative Methods Used in the Treatment of the Feeble-Minded," *Training School Bulletin*, 41 (April, 1944), 22–29.

> Describes activities for training the feeble-minded to eliminate faulty habits and to prepare for useful work.

ORTLEB, RUTH. "The Needs of the Dull-Normal Elementary School Child," *School and Society*, 1 (October 7, 1939), 453–61.

> Describes the traits of dull-normal children and their problems. Gives fourteen suggestions for effective teaching.

RHODES, GLADYS L. "The Nonacademic Part of Our Program for the Mentally Retarded: II. How to Meet the Needs of the Child," *Journal of Exceptional Children*, 9 (February, 1943), 145–48, 154; "III. Desirable Features," *ibid.*, (March, 1943), 180–83.

> In addition to academic work the aspects of the curriculum which are

emphasized in special classes are visual education, music, art, recreation, social studies, and science. Lists kindness, sympathy, understanding, tolerance, unselfishness, honesty, and friendliness as characteristics which should be developed in mentally retarded children.

SCHECK, R. R. "The Use of Experience Units in Teaching Mentally Deficient Boys," *American Journal of Mental Deficiency*, 45 (October, 1940), 97–103.

Discusses the use of experience units in an institution for the mentally deficient.

The Boston Way. Boston Special Class Teachers. Boston: Geo. T. Angell School, 1928. 127 pp.

Outlines extensively the educational experiences offered to children of subnormal intelligence. Includes sense training, health training, academic work, hand work, and social relations.

WYGANT, ALICE. *A Guide Book for the Slow Learner's Teacher.* Honolulu: Department of Public Instruction, Office of Supervising Principles, 1947. 109 pp.

Describes a curriculum for slow-learning children and includes aims, goals, and developmental teaching procedures for the various aspects of the curriculum.

Secondary School Programs

CURTIS, FRANCIS D. "Specific Suggestion for Teaching Dull-Normal Pupils," *School Review*, 44 (September, 1936), 525–32.

Presents twenty-four principles for teaching dull-normal pupils in high school.

FEMIANI, W. "Mentally Retarded Go to High School," *High Points*, 27 (November, 1945), 23–32.

Describes a curriculum for mentally retarded high school children.

HILL, ARTHUR S. "Special Education in the Secondary Schools," *Journal of Exceptional Children*, 18 (April, 1947), 193–97, 220.

Lists criteria used in the development of special education in the secondary schools in Des Moines, Iowa.

MECKER, H. H. "An Experiment in the Adjustment of Retarded

Upper-Grade Pupils," *National Elementary Principal*, 15 (April, 1936), 162–65.

Describes a prevocational program for retarded high school children of low intelligence.

MONES, LEON. "Cleveland Junior High Develops Courses for Binet (Low I.Q.) Pupils," *Clearing House*, 14 (April, 1940), 451–57.

Describes an experimental junior high school project and curriculum for mentally retarded adolescents.

MORSE, GRANT D. "A Differentiated Program for Duller High School Pupils," *Journal of Experimental Education*, 10 (September, 1941), 38–40.

Presents the results of a study made to determine the extent of the problem and the educational needs of dull pupils in certain communities in New York State. Includes recommendations.

N.E.A. Research Division. "High School Methods with Slow Learners," *Research Bulletin of the National Education Association*, 21, No. 3. Washington: Research Division of the National Education Association, 1943, 59–88.

A survey of the needs and practices of a thousand junior and senior high schools in their provisions for pupils of low intelligence. Discusses and describes current practices.

PORTENIER, LILLIAN G. *Pupils of Low Mentality in High School.* New York: Teachers College, Columbia University, 1933. 109 pp.

Reports findings that there is a tendency for children of lower I.Q.'s to be admitted to high school. Discusses the problems now associated with this group in the secondary schools.

ROGERS, WILLIAM C. "An Experimental Curriculum for Retarded Pupils," "Enriching the Curriculum for the Elementary School Child," *Eighteenth Yearbook of the Department of Elementary School Principals*. Bulletin of the Department of Elementary School Principals, 18, No. 6. Washington: Department of Elementary School Principals of the National Education Association, 1939, 532–37.

Describes an experimental program in Philadelphia for mentally and educationally retarded pupils who are twelve years of age or older and who have spent six years in school. An educational center with a nontraditional program at the junior high school level is described.

STEWART, RUTH AXFORD. "Dedicated to the Low I.Q.," *English Journal*, 24 (March, 1935), 204–07.

Discusses a modified English course for children with low intelligence in a high school.

WIGHT, M. A. "Teaching the Older Slow Learner," *Journal of Exceptional Children*, 12 (November, 1945), 42–46, 56.

Describes a unit on sound as an example of a method of producing effective learning situations in children of low intelligence.

Section V

SPECIAL ASPECTS OF INSTRUCTION

Publications in this section deal primarily with instructional procedures in (1) arithmetic, (2) practical arts, (3) music, (4) physical education, and (5) reading. There appear to be very few publications in other fields of instruction.

Arithmetic

CARRISON, DORIS, and WERNER, HEINZ. "Principles and Methods of Teaching Arithmetic to Mentally Retarded Children," *American Journal of Mental Deficiency*, 47 (January, 1943), 309–17.

Describes results of teaching arithmetic to mentally retarded children at the Wayne County Training School in Michigan, and the methods of teaching and measuring results.

COSTELLO, HELEN M. *The Responses of Mentally Retarded Children to Specialized Learning Experiences in Arithmetic*. Philadelphia: University of Pennsylvania. Doctoral Dissertation, 1941. 115 pp.

An experiment in which three general methods were used in teaching arithmetic to the mentally retarded. The three general methods were (1) socialization — the active — experiencing type of endeavor, (2) sensorization — devoted to concreteness or realism of presentation,

(3) verbalization — the method of substitute experience (and conventionally the method in most general use).

CRUICKSHANK, WILLIAM M. "Arithmetic Work Habits of Mentally Retarded Boys," *American Journal of Mental Deficiency*, 52 (April, 1948), 318–30.

In an analysis of the work habits of mentally retarded boys in arithmetic it was found that the work habits of the mentally retarded are usually poorer than those of normal children.

CRUICKSHANK, WILLIAM M. "Arithmetic Vocabulary of Mentally Retarded Boys," *Journal of Exceptional Children*, 13 (December, 1946), 65–69, 91.

A report of a research study which found that mentally retarded boys were inferior in their ability to define, or use in context, terms that are associated with arithmetic processes.

GOTHBERG, LAURA. "The Mentally Defective Child's Understanding of Time," *American Journal of Mental Deficiency*, 53 (January, 1949), 441–55.

A study in which the mental defective's understanding of time was measured; age relationships, periods of time, duration, clock time, sequence, and historical time were the factors studied.

LEHTINEN, LAURA E., and STRAUSS, ALFRED A. "Arithmetic Fundamentals for the Brain-Crippled Child," *American Journal of Mental Deficiency*, 49 (October, 1944), 149–54.

Describes successful special methods of teaching arithmetic to brain-injured children.

McALLISTER, CHARLES I., *et al.* "Arithmetic Skill Sequences," *Occupational Education*, Association for New York City Teachers of Special Education, 6, No. 5 (February, 1949). 23 pp.

A plan for the development of arithmetical skills in mentally handicapped children in New York City.

WERNER, H., and STRAUSS, A. A. "Problems and Methods of Functional Analysis in Mentally Deficient Children," *Journal of Abnormal and Social Psychology*, 34 (January, 1939), 37–62.

Describes different patterns of arithmetic disabilities found in the mentally retarded.

Practical Arts

BUDLONG, BERNICE. "Meeting the Needs of the Underprivileged Girl," *Practical Home Economics*, 12 (September, 1935), 251–52.

A plan which enables junior high school underprivileged girls who are not able to take the traditional school program to study home economics.

HALL, HERBERT J., and KNOX, MERTICE B. *Handicrafts for the Handicapped*. New York: Dodd Mead and Company, 1928. 181 pp.

Discusses techniques and processes in teaching basketry, chair seating, netting, weaving, bookbinding, cement working, pottery making, and light blacksmithing.

KOENIG, FRANCIS G. "Implications in the Use of Puppetry with Handicapped Children," *Journal of Exceptional Children*, 17 (January, 1951), 111–12, 117.

A discussion of the use of puppets as a means of self-expression for handicapped children.

MARTENS, ELISE H. "Home Economics for the Handicapped Pupil," *Practical Home Economics*, 16 (September, 1938), 338–40.

The school curriculum should include home economics for the retarded child. A correlation should be made with experiences outside of school.

MCELWEE, EDNA WILLIS. "The Constructive Ability of 150 Subnormal Children," *Journal of Juvenile Research*, 19 (January, 1935), 25–26.

With the use of a jigsaw puzzle the author compared mentally retarded children of the same mental age who differed in chronological age. Success was dependent on chronological age.

METZNER, ALICE B. *Organization of the Shop Program in Special Education*, Detroit, Michigan Board of Education, Detroit Public Schools. (Mimeographed) 1944. 158 pp.

Description of the philosophy and organization of shop classes for pupils in special education in the Detroit Public Schools.

PATTERSON, R. MELCHER, and LEIGHTNER, MARY. "A Comparative Study of Spontaneous Paintings of Normal and Mentally Deficient Children of the Same Mental Age," *American Journal of Mental Deficiency*, 48 (April, 1944), 345–53.

Concludes that mentally deficient children respond longer to sensory stimuli and are more satisfied with a simple technique than are normal children.

SPOERL, DOROTHY TILDEN. "The Drawing Ability of Mentally Retarded Children," *Pedagogical Seminary and Journal of Genetic Psychology*, 57 (December, 1940), 259–77.

Compared the drawing ability of retarded and normal children and found that retarded children were slightly superior.

STEIN, MARGARET. "Art as a Means of Expression for the Mentally Retarded," *Journal of Exceptional Children*, 4 (March, 1938), 141.

Suggests that art in the classroom be used so that the mentally retarded child will have an adequate means of expressing himself.

VAUGHN, CHARLES L., and HOOSE, ELIZABETH S. "Special Abilities in a Mentally Deficient Boy," *Proceedings and Addresses of the Sixtieth Annual Session of the American Association on Mental Deficiency*, 41 (1936), 197–207.

Report of guidance to a mentally handicapped Negro boy who was gifted in drawing and painting.

Music

BOWERS, MABEL. "Music as a Means of Increasing Responsiveness in Young Mental Defectives," *Journal of Exceptional Children*, 3 (February, 1937), 95–96.

Suggests that music can be used as a valuable aid in the emotional development of mental defectives.

NAMENY, GRACE W. "Inaugurating a Music Education Program for Mentally Retarded," *Journal of Exceptional Children*, 15 (February, 1949), 134–38, 160.

Presents a plan for providing music experiences for mentally retarded children from six through adolescence.

PRATHER, V. A. "Teaching Instrumental Music to Mentally Deficient Boys," *American Journal of Mental Deficiency*, 51 (January, 1947), 467–76.

Describes attitudes and techniques needed to teach instrumental music to mentally deficient children and indicates the socializing effects of music.

ROTH, GERTRUDE HELEN. "Music for the Mentally Retarded," *Journal of Exceptional Children*, 11 (October, 1944), 12–15.

Presents the thesis that music and rhythmic expression are enjoyed by the mentally retarded, and considers the effect of music on socialization.

WILDER, H. HUNTER, and STOWELL, GERALDINE. "Instruction in Band Music to Mentally Deficient Children," *Proceedings and Addresses of the Fifty-ninth Annual Session of the American Association on Mental Deficiency*, 40 (1935), 415–22.

Describes adaptability tests used to select mentally deficient children for a band and discusses the adaptation of instruction to the players.

WILLIAMS, LAUREL. "Singing Games in Opportunity Classes," *The School* (Elementary Edition), 32 (May, 1944), 806–07, 811.

Proposes singing games and rhythmic activities as a method of socializing and giving security to mentally retarded children.

Physical Education

DAYTON, N. A. "Height, Weight, and Intelligence Relationships in 31,939 Retarded Children Examined by Fifteen Massachusetts Traveling School Clinics, 1921–1932," *Proceedings and Addresses of the Sixty-first Annual Session of the American Association on Mental Deficiency*, 42, No. 2 (1937), 84–100.

A study of the relations of height, weight, and intelligence in normal, retarded, and mentally defective children.

FLORY, CHARLES D. "Physical Growth of Mentally Deficient Boys," *Society for Research in Child Development Monographs*, 2, No. 6. Washington: National Research Council, 1936. 120 pp.

Reports a study of the anthropometric measurements, X-ray photographs, medical diagnoses, and case histories of 800 patients in institutions.

HORNE, BETTY, and PHILEO, CHARLOTTE C. "A Comparative Study of the Spontaneous Play Activities of Normal and Mentally Defective Children," *Pedagogical Seminary and Journal of Genetic Psychology*, 61 (September, 1942), 33–46.

> Mentally defective children choose less constructive play materials than do normals.

SCHLOTTER, BERTHA, and SVENDSEN, MARGARET. *An Experiment in Recreation with the Mentally Retarded.* Chicago: Behavior Research Fund, 1933. 75 pp.

> Reports an extensive project of the play abilities, activities, and interests of various mental and chronological levels of mentally deficient children in an institution.

STAFFORD, GEORGE T. *Sports for the Handicapped.* New York: Prentice-Hall, Inc., 1947. 334 pp.

> Discusses the philosophy, organization, and types of sports program that can be used with physically handicapped children. Describes adaptations of games to varying types of handicapping conditions.

STECHER, WILLIAM A. *Physical Training Lessons for Backward Classes*, Philadelphia: John Joseph McVey, 1923. 38 pp.

> Exercises and games for the mentally retarded.

VALENTINER, HARRIETT L. "The Comparative Fatigability of Normal and Mentally Deficient Children," *Journal of Abnormal and Social Psychology*, 36 (January, 1941), 51–61.

> Comparison of fatigability in normal and mentally deficient children of the same age.

Reading

ANNON, FRED A., and COCHRAN, MILDRED G. "The School Failure Learns to Read," *Journal of Exceptional Children*, 12 (December, 1945), 66–72, 90.

> Summarizes the individual progress of a group of adolescent boys of low intelligence and discusses the principles of teaching.

BIJOU, SIDNEY W., and WERNER, HEINZ. "Vocabulary Analysis

in Mentally Deficient Children," *American Journal of Mental Deficiency*, 48 (April, 1944), 364–66.

> Reports a study of the range and quality of the vocabulary of brain-injured and non-brain-injured mentally deficient children. Finds that the brain-injured are superior.

BLAIR, GLENN M. "Techniques and Adjustments for Slow Learners in Junior and Senior High Schools, with Special Reference to Reading," *Supplementary Educational Monographs*, No. 69, University of Chicago Press, 1949, 186–91.

> Discusses techniques and methods in reading that can be used with slow learners in junior and senior high schools.

BURT, CYRIL, and LEWIS, R. B. "Teaching Backward Readers," *British Journal of Educational Psychology*, 16 (November 18, 1946), 116–32.

> Reports the results of experiments on the relative merits of the phonic, kinesthetic, alphabet, and mixed methods of teaching reading to dull normals. Concludes that best method is visual.

COLEMAN, MARION. "Remedial Reading for Special Groups," *Proceedings and Addresses of the Sixty-second Annual Session of the American Association on Mental Deficiency*, 43, No. 2 (1938), 123–27.

> Reports the procedures in diagnosing children and suggests appropriate remedial instruction.

DAVIDSON, HELEN P. "An Experimental Study of Bright, Average, and Dull Children at the Four-Year Mental Level," *Genetic Psychology Monographs*, 9, Nos. 3 and 4 (1931), 119–289.

> A comparative study of dull, average, and bright children with mental ages of four, in their ability to learn to read. Experiment showed great individual differences, but in general younger and brighter children learned faster than older dull children.

EWERHARDT, PAUL J. "Reading Difficulties in Subnormal Children," *Proceedings and Addresses of the Sixty-second Annual Session of the American Association on Mental Deficiency*, 43, No. 1 (1938), 188–93.

> Classifies the types of reading difficulties found among subnormal children and recommends appropriate remedial instruction.

FARSON, MABEL R. "A Program for Low Ability Children in the Regular Grade," *American Journal of Mental Deficiency*, 50 (July, 1945), 107–14.

> Discusses the adaptation of reading materials to the maturity level of backward children.

FEMIANI, WINIFRED, HARNETT, MARY E., JACKSON, FLORENCE, MAY, BARBARA, and POLLARD, IRENE. "Skill Sequences in Language Arts," *Occupational Education*, Association for New York City Teachers of Special Education, 6, No. 4 (January, 1949). 23 pp.

> A plan for the development of language arts with mentally handicapped children in New York City.

GATES, ARTHUR I. "The Reading Program for Dull-Normal Pupils," *The Role of Research in Educational Progress*. Official Report of the American Educational Research Association. Washington: American Educational Research Association of the National Education Association, 1937, 224–28.

> Describes a reading program for dull children in an experimental public school in New York.

GROELLE, MARVIN, C. "Techniques and Adjustments for Slow Learners with Special Reference to Reading," *Supplementary Educational Monographs*, No. 69. University of Chicago Press, 1949, 182–86.

> Gives practical suggestions that can be used when working in reading with slow-learning children.

HEGGE, THORLEIF G. "Results of Remedial Reading at the Middle Moron Level," *Journal of Juvenile Research*, 19 (July, 1935), 128–34.

> Reports a three-year reading training program with a mentally retarded child of foreign background.

HEGGE, THORLEIF G. "The Problem of Reading Deficiency in the Mentally Handicapped," *Journal of Exceptional Children*, 4 (March, 1938), 121–25.

> Summarizes the need for a remedial program in the Wayne County Training School at Northville (Detroit), Michigan.

HEGGE, THORLEIF G. "Special Reading Disability with Particular Reference to the Mentally Deficient," *Proceedings and Addresses of the Fifty-eighth Annual Session of American Association on Mental Deficiency*, 39 (1934), 297–343.

> A report of the reading progress made by a group of high grade mentally deficient children who were considered to be special reading problems.

HEGGE, THORLEIF, and VOELKER, PAUL. "Social Guidance and Reading Materials for Adolescent Mentally Retarded and Non-Academic Pupils," *Journal of Exceptional Children*, 16 (May, 1950), 225–28.

> Discussion of reading materials and how they can be used in social guidance with adolescent mentally retarded children.

HEGGE, T. G., KIRK, S. A., and KIRK, W. D. *Remedial Reading Drills.* Ann Arbor, Mich.: Geo. Wahr, Publisher, 1936. 58 pp.

> A systematic phonetic book of exercises used to teach mentally-retarded children with severe reading disabilities.

HEYERDAHL, TORDIS M. "A Library Program for the Feeble-Minded," *American Journal of Mental Deficiency*, 47 (January, 1943), 318–25.

> Describes the function of a library program in an institution for the feeble-minded. Offers a list of books of proved interest to the children in the school.

KELLY, ELIZABETH M. "The Improvement of Reading in Special Classes for Mentally Retarded Children," *Training School Bulletin*, 31 (February, 1935), 186–91.

> Gives results of achievement tests on sixteen hundred subnormal school-age children. Concludes that the lower the mental age, the higher the percentage of non-reading.

KIRK, SAMUEL A. "A Reading Program for Mentally Retarded Children," *Journal of Exceptional Children*, 6 (November, 1939), 49–54, 71.

> Discusses a reading program for various age levels of mentally retarded children.

KIRK, SAMUEL A. "Characteristics of Slow Learners and Needed Adjustments in Reading," *Supplementary Educational Monographs*, No. 69. University of Chicago Press, 1949. 172–76.

> Discussion of characteristics of slow learners and basic principles to follow in promoting growth through reading for them.

KIRK, SAMUEL A. "Nature of the Adjustments in Teaching to Meet the Needs of Bright and Dull Pupils: The Slow or Mentally Retarded Learner," *Supplementary Educational Monographs*. The University of Chicago, No. 52 (October, 1941), 272–78.

> Outlines the learning characteristics of the slow learner and the adaptations in teaching which should be made to conform to these characteristics.

KIRK, SAMUEL A. *Teaching Reading to Slow-Learning Children*. Boston: Houghton Mifflin Company, 1940. 225 pp.

> Discusses the characteristics of mentally handicapped children, their achievement in reading, and a method of teaching reading to slow learners. Includes a discussion of readiness, initial instruction in learning, increasing efficiency in reading, and remedial procedures.

KIRK, SAMUEL A. "The Effects of Remedial Reading on the Educational Progress and Personality Adjustment of High-Grade Mentally Deficient Problem Children: Ten Case Studies," *The Journal of Juvenile Research*, 18 (July, 1934), 140–62.

> Describes the personality and social adjustment of ten cases following successful remedial reading instruction.

KIRK, SAMUEL A. "The Influence of Manual Tracing on the Learning of Simple Words in the Case of Subnormal Boys," *The Journal of Educational Psychology*, 24 (October, 1933), 525–35.

> Describes an experiment on the efficiency of the kinesthetic method and finds that tracing words assists subnormal boys in recalling them later.

"Library Books Best Liked by Retarded Children," *Reading and the School Library*, 3 (January, 1937), 100.

> Lists books that are liked best by adolescents of low mentality.

MacINTYRE, E. MILDRED. "Teaching of Reading to Mentally

Defective Children," *Proceedings and Addresses of the Sixty-first Annual Session of the American Association on Mental Deficiency,* 42, No. 2 (1937), 59–67.

> Describes procedures in teaching reading to children of low intelligence.

MARTINSON, BETTY. "Post Training Progress of Mentally Handicapped Children Given Intensive Remedial Reading Lessons," *American Journal of Mental Deficiency,* 45 (January, 1941), 408–12.

> Reports the progress of the mentally retarded in reading after they had completed intensive remedial instruction in an institution.

MEIER, C. "Effect of Prizes in Increasing the Word Learning of Subnormal Children," *Training School Bulletin,* 32 (December, 1935), 146–57.

> Describes several types of incentives used in teaching words to subnormal children with I.Q.'s of 33 to 70. Concludes that extrinsic types of stimulation are beneficial.

ROTHENBERG, JULIUS G. "English Errors of Slow Learners," *English Journal,* 32 (December, 1943), 551–56.

> Studies the causes of illiteracy, including dialect, anomalous and unphonetic spelling, slovenly speech, a poor sense of discrimination, a misguided English-conscience, inflectional errors, and omissions and additions.

SEARS, RICHARD. "Characteristics and Trainability of a Case of Special Reading Disability at the Moron Level," *Journal of Juvenile Research,* 19 (July, 1935), 135–45.

> A thorough study of a moron boy with a reading disability. Evaluates the results of special training and suggests certain limits of trainability.

STOCK, EARL K. "Factors in Reading Readiness for the Mentally Retarded," *Journal of Exceptional Children,* 6 (May, 1940), 296–99, 306.

> Emphasizes the need for an adequate readiness program when working with mentally retarded children.

VAUGHN, CHARLES L., and HUBBS, LORENA. "Teaching Reading Vocabulary to Lower Grade Morons," *Proceedings and Addresses of the Sixty-first Annual Session of the American Association on Mental Deficiency*, 42, No. 2 (1937), 68–76.

Reports the results of special help in reading in a class of mentally retarded teen-age boys. Discusses the results of repetition.

WALCOTT, FRED G. "New Methods and Objectives in Teaching Dull-Normal Pupils to Read," *School Review*, 44 (May, 1936), 348–61.

Reports the results of a special program with high school pupils in comprehension and in rate of reading. Recommends earlier segregation and remedial instruction for this group.

Section VI

SOCIAL AND VOCATIONAL ADJUSTMENT OF THE MENTALLY HANDICAPPED

The ultimate goal of the education of the mentally handicapped is to develop personal, social, and vocational characteristics which will facilitate their social adequacy and industrial competency. The following publications are concerned with this phase of the education of the mentally handicapped.

ABEL, T. M. "A Study of a Group of Subnormal Girls Successfully Adjusted in Industry and Community," *American Journal of Mental Deficiency*, 45 (January, 1940), 66–72.

A study conducted to determine the success of a group of subnormal girls in industry and the factors making for this success.

ABEL, THEODORA M. "Work Adjustments of Adolescent Subnormal Girls," *Industrial Conflict*. Edited by George W. Hartmann and Theodore Newcomb. First Yearbook of the Society for the Psychological Study of Social Issues, an Affiliate of the American Psychological Association. New York: Cordon Co., Inc., 1940, 131–41.

Sheltered shops or long-term apprenticeships are recommended for girls who need more care and supervision than can be found in business.

ABEL, THEODORA M., and KINDER, ELAINE. *The Subnormal Adolescent Girl*. New York: Columbia University Press, 1942. 186 pp.

Discusses the problems that confront subnormal girls in their homes, at school, in industry, in institutions, and in the community.

ALLEN, ARDA TALBOY. "Cogs in the Occupational Wheel." *Occupations*, 20 (October, 1941), 15–18.

A plea is made for more vocational guidance for high school dull-normals. Bibliography lists books describing unskilled and semi-skilled jobs.

ARMSTRONG, CLAIRETTE. "Some Mental and Social Inadequates," *Journal of Abnormal and Social Psychology*, 30 (October-December, 1935), 371–83.

Because of a survey in New York City showing that three-fourths of the mental defectives in ungraded classes were found to have foreign parents, the author suggests that a law be enacted admitting only immigrants who can meet the mental ability standards of the general population.

BALLER, WARREN ROBERT. "A Study of the Behavior Records of Adults Who, When They Were in School, Were Judged to Be Dull in Mental Ability," *Pedagogical Seminary and Journal of Genetic Psychology*, 55 (December, 1939), 365–79.

An analysis of conduct records and adjustment difficulties of dull adults.

BALLER, WARREN ROBERT. "A Study of the Present Social Status of a Group of Adults, Who, When They Were in Elementary Schools, Were Classified as Mentally Deficient," *Genetic Psychology Monographs*, 18, No. 3 (1936), 165–244.

A study comparing a group of special class pupils with a group of normal adults showed that the special group was found to be economically, socially, and vocationally inferior.

BEAMAN, FLORENCE N. "The Intangibles of Special Education," *Journal of Exceptional Children*, 9 (May, 1943), 231–35, 246.

Poor adjustment to our cultural standards was found to be a greater cause of failure of retarded children after leaving school than incompetence in basic skills.

BERRY, RICHARD J. A., and GORDON, R. G. *The Mental Defective. A Problem in Social Inefficiency.* New York: McGraw-Hill Book Company, 1931. 146 pp.

Mental deficiency is viewed from its physiological and social aspects.

BIJOU, SIDNEY, AINSWORTH, MILDRED, and STOCKEY, MERREL. "The Social Adjustment of Mentally Retarded Girls Paroled from the Wayne County Training School," *American Journal of Mental Deficiency*, 47 (October, 1943), 422–28.

A study in which a rating scale was constructed to evaluate the social adjustment of a group of girls paroled from the Wayne County Training School. On the basis of the rating scale it was found that approximately 70 per cent of all the girls were making good adjustments.

BRADWAY, KATHERINE P. "Paternal Occupational Intelligence and Mental Deficiency," *Journal of Applied Psychology*, 19 (October, 1935), 527–42.

A study made in the New Jersey Training School for Backward Children showed that there was a negative correlation between intelligence quotient and paternal occupational status.

CARPENTER, MARY S. *A Study of the Occupations of 207 Subnormal Girls After Leaving School.* Ann Arbor, Mich.: School of Education, University of Michigan, 1925. 40 pp.

An analysis of the occupations of girls that had been enrolled in the special classes of the Detroit city schools.

CHANNING, ALICE. *Employment of Mentally Deficient Boys and Girls.* Washington: U.S. Government Printing Office, 1932. 107 pp.

A study of the various types of work, continuity of employment, wages, and success of 949 mentally handicapped children formerly enrolled in special classes in a number of large cities.

DE PROSPO, CHRIS J., and HUNGERFORD, RICHARD H. "A Complete Social Program for the Mentally Retarded," *American Journal of Mental Deficiency*, 51 (July, 1946), 115–22.

Describes a program of occupational guidance for the mentally retarded.

DIMICHAEL, SALVATORE. *Vocational Rehabilitation of the Mentally Retarded.* Washington, U.S. Government Printing Office (Rehabilitation Service Series No. 123), 1950. 184 pp.

A discussion of the medical, psychological, educational, and sociological aspects of mental deficiency and their implications for vocational rehabilitation of the mentally retarded.

DOLL, EDGAR A., and LONGWELL, S. GERALDINE. "Social Competence of the Feeble-Minded under Extra-Institutional Care," *Psychiatric Quarterly*, 11 (July, 1937), 450–64.

It is suggested that communities develop supervised programs for the noninstitutionalized feeble-minded.

DOLL, EDGAR A., and McKAY, B. ELIZABETH. "The Social Competence of Special Class Children," *Journal of Educational Research*, 31 (October, 1937), 90–106.

In determining the difference between dull-normal and feeble-minded children in special classes for the mentally retarded, the Vineland Social Maturity Scale was used to supplement other data.

DOOLEY, WILLIAM H. "Vocational Training for the Nonacademic Pupil in the Academic High School," *High Points in the Work of High Schools of New York City*, 23 (June, 1941), 37–45.

An improved plan for academic and vocational training of dull-normal pupils in high school.

DUNLOP, FLORENCE S. *Subsequent Careers of Non-Academic Boys.* Doctor's dissertation at Columbia University. Ottawa, Canada: National Printers Limited, 1935. 93 pp.

From this study of 257 boys who had left the Boys' Vocational School in Ottawa it was found that the non-academic boy has a definite place in the community.

FARSON, MABLE R. "Education of the Handicapped Child for Social Competency," *Journal of Exceptional Children*, 6 (January, 1940), 138–44, 150.

Programs which develop self-reliance and self-respect for the subnormal child help prevent common frustrations and inferiorities.

FINLAYSON, ALICE B. "Social and Economic Background of Retarded Children," *Journal of Education Sociology*, 15 (September, 1941), 38–45.

> Inferior social and economic status were found to be contributing factors in the retardation and delinquency of Negro children.

HUMPHREYS, EDWARD J., WATTS, GEORGE W. T., and BOLDT, WALDEMAR H. "An Investigation into the Case Records of One Thousand High Grade Mentally or Developmentally Defective Children," *Proceedings and Addresses of the Sixty-first Annual Session of the American Association on Mental Deficiency*, 42, No. 2 (1937), 9–46.

> Case records of feeble-minded individuals in a state institution are analyzed for physical, mental, educational, economic, and social factors.

HUNGERFORD, RICHARD H. "Guidance and the Classroom Teacher," *Occupational Education*, 3 (November, 1945), 29–31.

> An article explaining the role of the guidance counselor and his relation to the classroom teacher. The guidance program needs the cooperation of the two. Guidance is a part of the teaching process.

HUNGERFORD, RICHARD H. "The Detroit Plan for the Occupational Education of the Mentally Retarded," *American Journal of Mental Deficiency*, 46 (July, 1941), 102–08.

> The plan for occupational education in the special classes in Detroit.

JEWELL, ALICE A. "A Follow-Up Study of 190 Mentally Deficient Children Excluded Because of Low Mentality from the Public Schools of the District of Columbia, Divisions I–IX, September, 1929, to February 1, 1940," *American Journal of Mental Deficiency*, 45 (January, 1941), 413–20.

> Suggests that a competent field worker help parents in training and adjusting the mentally deficient child in the home.

KATZ, G. HENRY. "Re-Educational Therapy," *Nervous Child*, 2 (October, 1942), 37–43.

> Advises that early boarding school placement is less frustrating to feeble-minded children than regular homes and schools.

KEATOR, MAUD. "Industrial Supervision of Mentally Inferior

Youths," *Proceedings and Addresses of the Sixtieth Annual Session of the American Association on Mental Deficiency*, 41 (1936), 89–95.

The city commission in Hartford, Connecticut, helps mentally inferior boys and girls find jobs.

KENNEDY, RUBY JO. *The Social Adjustment of Morons in a Connecticut City.* Governor's Commission to Study the Human Resources of the State of Connecticut, in collaboration with the Carnegie Institute of Washington. Mansfield-Southbury Training Schools, Social Service Department, State Office Building, Hartford, Connecticut, 1948. 120 pp.

A comparative study between morons and nonmorons with respect to their social characteristics and behavior. The comparison included five areas: parental family background, marital adjustment, economic adjustment, anti-social behavior, and social participation.

KEPHART, NEWELL C., and AINSWORTH, MILDRED. "A Preliminary Report of Community Adjustment of Parolees of the Wayne County Training School," *Proceedings and Addresses of the Sixty-second Annual Session of the American Association on Mental Deficiency*, 43, No. 1 (1938), 161–66.

Compared the community adjustment of two groups of mentally handicapped boys who were formerly in an institution. It was found that those boys who were paroled from the institution made a better community adjustment than those that left by means other than parole.

KINDER, ELAINE F., CHASE, ANNETTE, and BUCK, ELIZABETH W. "Data Secured During a Follow-Up Study of Girls Discharged from Supervised Parole from Letchworth Village," *American Journal of Mental Deficiency*, 14 (April, 1941), 572–78.

Describes the adjustment levels reached by ten groups of mentally deficient paroled cases.

KINGSLEY, L. V., and HYDE, R. W. "The Health and Occupational Adequacy of the Mentally Deficient," *Journal of Abnormal and Social Psychology*, 29 (January, 1945), 37–47.

From a study of 600 selectees rejected by the Army for failure to meet the mental and literacy standards it was found that they were making a satisfactory community adjustment.

LURIE, L. A. "Conduct Disorders of Intellectually Subnormal Children," *American Journal of Psychiatry*, 91 (March, 1937), 1025–38.

A study of the problems of subnormal children and their relationship to the intelligence level.

MARTENS, ELISE H., *et al.* "Educational Provisions for Mentally Deficient Adolescents: A Symposium," *American Journal of Mental Deficiency*, 47 (July, 1942), 79–95.

A discussion of a problem that has resulted from present labor shortages and the advisability of work experience as a part of school training.

MARTENS, ELISE H. "Occupational Preparation for Mentally Handicapped Children," *Proceedings and Addresses of the Sixty-first Annual Session of the American Association on Mental Deficiency*, 42, No. 2 (1937), 157–65.

Special class children should be prepared for service jobs in industry because of the paucity of unskilled and semi-skilled jobs.

MARTIN, M. FRANCES. "Personality Development and Social Adjustment of Mentally Retarded Children," *American Journal of Mental Deficiency*, 46 (July, 1941), 94–101.

A discussion of the personality development and social adjustment of mentally retarded children in Los Angeles.

MICHAL-SMITH, A. "A Study of the Personal Characteristics Desirable for the Vocational Success of the Mentally Deficient," *American Journal of Mental Deficiency*, 5 (July, 1950), 139–43.

A study to determine the success to be expected of feeble-minded individuals in each of eight types of jobs falling within four broad occupational areas: manual, machine-operation, repetitive, and social (*i.e.*, jobs involving contact with public). Also, an attempt was made to determine the importance of fifteen personal characteristics in the success of those with low intelligence who are employed. Data for the study was obtained from industry and the institutions.

MILL, H. F. "Training for Social Competency," *Training School Bulletin*, 43 (October, 1946), 121–24.

Discusses the social development of two mentally retarded adults in society.

MURPHY, M. "The Social Adjustment of the Exceptional Child of Borderline Mentality," *Journal of Consulting Psychology*, 2 (December, 1938), 169–75.

The problems met by ten mentally backward children in making social adjustments.

NEHAM, SARAH. "Mental Hygiene Implications in Occupational Education," *Occupational Education*, 4 (November, 1946), 25–35.

The author stresses the value of occupational guidance as a source of good mental hygiene. Every child has the desire to be in harmony with a society to which he can prove a real asset. Occupational guidance for the mentally retarded is a means of satisfying this desire.

NEUBER, M. A., and SNYDER, W. U. "Evaluating a Special Class in Terms of Personality Development," *Journal of Exceptional Children*, 13 (February, 1947), 135–40.

Describes an experiment to determine the value of a special class. Eight children were selected for study in an experiment group. At the end of the experiment one boy had increased 14 points in I.Q.; others had decreased up to 9 points in I.Q. All the children increased in social skills. It was concluded that while the improvement was greater for some children than for others the general tendency is quite favorable.

RHODES, GLADYS L. "The Non-Academic Part of Our Program for the Mentally Retarded," *Journal of Exceptional Children*, 9 (January, 1943), 107–20.

Describes the vocational and prevocational instruction in a class for the mentally handicapped.

SHIMBERG, M. E., and REICHENBERG, W. "The Success and Failure of Subnormal Children in the Community," *Mental Hygiene*, 17 (July, 1933), 451–65.

Found that it is possible to predict the conditions under which subnormal children will make a satisfactory adjustment in the community.

STOGDILL, RALPH M. "Some Behavior Adjustment Techniques in Use with Mentally Retarded Children," *Journal of Exceptional Children*, 5 (November, 1938), 25–30, 45.

Explains the therapy used in working with behavior problem children at the Wayne County Training School in Michigan.

SULLIVAN, LYNN C. "Occupational Guidance for the High-Grade Mental Defective," *Journal of Exceptional Children*, 9 (October, 1942), 3–6.

Emphasizes that it is necessary to have a survey of jobs available in a community before specific types of vocational training should be presented.

UNGER, EDNA W., and PURR, EMILY T. *Minimum Mental Age Levels of Accomplishment.* Albany, N.Y.: The University of the State of New York, 1931. 108 pp.

A survey of 2,649 employed girls of low-grade intelligence to determine the relationship between mental levels and employment.

WALKER, HELEN M., and SHAUFFLER, MARY C. *The Social Adjustment of the Feeble-Minded: A Group Thesis Study.* Cleveland, Ohio: Western Reserve University Press, 1930. 220 pp.

It was found through a study of 898 feeble-minded children known to Cleveland social agencies that emotional factors, training, and environmental conditions, rather than the mental level, are what make for success and failure of the feeble-minded.

WHIPPLE, HELEN D. *Making Citizens of the Mentally Limited.* Bloomington, Ill.: Public School Publishing Company, 1927. 374 pp.

Advocates meeting the needs of special class pupils so that they may make adequate postschool adjustments.

WOOLEY, HELEN T., and HART, HORNELL. *Feeble-Minded Ex-School Children.* Cincinnati, Ohio: The Helen S. Trounstine Foundation, 1921. 264 pp.

A follow-up study of vocations of children who have been in special classes of Cincinnati. The importance of early school careers is emphasized.

YEPSEN, L. Y. "Mentally Deficient Probationer and Parolee," *Training School Bulletin*, 41 (December, 1944), 150–56.

A guide for social workers in guidance of the mentally deficient.

Section VII

MISCELLANEOUS

A group of publications dealing primarily with experimental or observational data, not readily classified into any one area.

ABEL, THEODORA M. "Moral Judgments among Subnormals," *Journal of Abnormal and Social Psychology*, 36 (July, 1941), 378–92.

> Subnormal adolescent girls were studied by the Piaget technique to determine their moral judgments.

ABEL, THEODORA M., and SILL, JANE B. "The Perceiving and Thinking of Normal and Subnormal Adolescents and Children on a Simple Drawing Task," *Pedagogical Seminary and Journal of Genetic Psychology*, 54 (June, 1939), 391–402.

> On a simple drawing task of dividing squares on paper into smaller squares it was found that normal and dull subjects showed characteristic differences in quantity and quality.

BENNETT, ANNETTE. *A Comparative Study of Subnormal Children in the Elementary Grades.* New York: Teachers College, Columbia University, 1932, 81 pp.

> Compared subnormal children in special classes with similar children in the regular grades. Finds little difference in results of instruction and some difference in characteristics.

BRILLE, MOSHE. "Measuring Institutional Adjustment of Mentally Deficient Boys," *Journal of Applied Psychology*, 20 (December, 1936), 736–47.

> Found that the Vineland Adjustment Score card differentiated between adjusted and maladjusted institutional boys.

BUSS, OTTO E. "Educating the Submerged," *California Journal of Secondary Education*, 20 (March, 1945), 158–59.

> Explains the gains made by subnormal children in the ungraded class when assignments and instruction were designed to meet their needs.

CARROLL, HERBERT A. *Generalization of Bright and Dull Children.*

New York: Teachers College, Columbia University, Teachers College Contributions to Education, No. 439, 1930. 54 pp.

> A comparative study of bright and dull children in spelling methods used. Concludes that intelligence is correlated with generalization in spelling.

CHARNEY, HATTIE, and BERKEN, RUTH. "A Year of Nature Study in Our City," *Curriculum Bulletin* No. 10, Publication No. 11. New York: Division of Elementary Schools, Board of Education of the City of New York, 1940. 72 pp.

> Activities used in connection with teaching natural science to slow-learning children.

CUTTS, NORMA E. "The Mentally Handicapped," *Review of Educational Research*, 11 (June, 1941), 261–76.

> A review of recent research in the field of mental retardation.

ELLIS, W. J. "State Program for the Care of the Mentally Deficient: Changes in Conception of Care," *Training School Bulletin*, 44 (March, 1947), 211–13.

> Discusses the changes in the care of the mentally deficient in state institutions.

FLETCHER, BASIL A. "The Backward Child and the Teacher," *Understanding the Child*, 6 (October, 1937), 18–22, 32.

> A discussion of causes of backwardness from the physical, intellectual, and emotional viewpoint.

FOURACRE, MAURICE H. "Improving the Relationship between the Community and the Class for the Mentally Retarded," *Journal of Exceptional Children*, 12 (January, 1946), 108–12, 121.

> Presents methods by which parents, teachers, and the public can be informed of the progress of children in special classes.

FRANDSEN, ARDEN W. "Mechanical Ability of Morons," *Journal of Applied Psychology*, 19 (August, 1935), 371–78.

> From a study of one hundred moron boys who were inferior in mechanical ability it was concluded that above a certain mental level there was little correlation between mechanical ability and intelligence.

FRIED, RUDOLPH S. "Ten Years of Relaxation and Self-Direction at Bailey Hall and a Description of New Methods in Training of Children," *American Journal of Mental Deficiency*, 45 (January, 1941), 459–63.

Emphasizes the need of conserving the nervous energy of mentally deficient children so that they may be taught effectively.

HECK, ARCH O. *Special Schools and Classes in Cities of 10,000 Population and More in the United States.* Washington: U.S. Government Printing Office (Bulletin No. 7), 1930. 33 pp.

A statistical tabulation of the facilities existing in city school systems for the different types of exceptional children.

HECKER, ARTHUR O. "Low Intelligence: An Investigation of 501 Consecutive Admissions to Polk State School," *Proceedings and Addresses of the Sixty-first Annual Session of the American Association on Mental Deficiency*, 42, No. 2 (1937), 181–90.

A summary of data relating to age of admission, social and mental status, heredity, etiology, and physical defects of the population in a state school for mental defectives.

KEPHART, NEWELL C. "Notes on Social Group Structure in an Institution for Retarded Children," *Sociometry*, 2 (April, 1939), 95–98.

A cottage plan at the Wayne County Training School in Michigan is arranged to give the child greater social competency and thus try to eliminate antisocial and self-centered activities.

KIRK, SAMUEL A. "An Evaluation of the Study by Bernardine G. Schmidt entitled 'Change in Personal, Social, and Intellectual Behavior of Children Originally Classified as Feeble-minded,'" *Psychological Bulletin*, 40 (July, 1948), 321–33.

Studied the records of the Bureau of Child Study in Chicago and found that the Schmidt claims of changes in I.Q. were not confirmed. Discrepancies in data and errors in statistics were also found.

LONGWELL, S. GERALDINE. "Influence of Muscle Training on Birth-Injured Mentally Deficient Children," *Pedagogical Seminary and Journal of Genetic Psychology*, 46 (June, 1935), 349–70.

Discusses results obtained in giving therapy for motor handicaps due to birth injuries to ten mentally deficient children as compared to those obtained from ten control cases not treated. It was found that the treated group gained 25 per cent in motor control; the non-treated group, 15 per cent.

MARTENS, ELISE H. *Opportunities for Preparation of Teachers of Exceptional Children.* Chicago: National Society for Crippled Children and Adults, Inc., 1949. 99 pp.

A survey of opportunities available for those who wish to teach exceptional children. Specifies institutions that provide training in the field and brief resumé of courses offered at each.

MARTENS, ELISE H. *Parents' Problems with Exceptional Children.* Washington: U.S. Government Printing Office (Bulletin No. 14), 1932. 72 pp.

A pamphlet designed to aid the parent in the treatment and training of exceptional children.

MAY, BARBARA. "Appraising and Reporting the Progress of Mentally Retarded Children," *Journal of Exceptional Children,* 12 (February, 1946), 141–46.

An evaluation of methods used in New York City to show pupil progress.

McGEHEE, WILLIAM. "A Study of Retarded Children in the Elementary School," *Contribution to Education,* No. 246. Nashville, Tenn.: George Peabody College for Teachers, 1939. 128 pp.

Discusses the status of mentally retarded children in the elementary grades.

McKAY, B. ELIZABETH. "A Study of I.Q. Changes in a Group of Girls Paroled from a State School for Mental Defectives," *American Journal of Mental Deficiency,* 46 (April, 1942), 496–500.

It was found that in 80 per cent of the cases of fifty high-grade defective girls working at domestic labor, a change of 11.5 points took place in the intelligence quotients. Comparable changes were not noted in an institutional group.

MOORE, THOMAS V. "Standards in Training Teachers of Backward Children," *Catholic Educational Review*, 36 (November, 1938), 525–29.

A curriculum designed to prepare teachers for work with subnormal children.

PERTSCH, F. FREDERICK. *A Comparative Study of the Progress of Subnormal Pupils in the Grades and in Special Classes.* New York: Teachers College, Columbia University Doctor's Dissertation, 1936. 101 pp.

Compares a special class group of children with group of similar mentality in the regular grades. Finds little advantage in segregation.

RAVEN, J. C., and WAITE, A. "Experiments on Physically and Mentally Defective Children with Perceptual Tests," *British Journal of Medical Psychology*, 18 (March, 1939), 40–43.

Results of experiments on physically and mentally defective children with perceptual tests show that the physically handicapped score normal while the mentally defective children score below normal.

Russell Sage Foundation. *Backward Children.* New York: Sage Foundation (Bulletin No. 57), 1923. 4 pp.

A selected bibliography on the nature and education of atypical children, primarily the mentally subnormal.

PRITCHARD, MARIAM. *The Mechanical Ability of Subnormal Boys.* New York: Teachers College, Columbia University (Doctor's dissertation abstract), 1936. 73 pp.

It was found that the correlation between mechanical tests scores and intelligence quotients is very slight. Emphasizes the need of giving training to the pupil of low intelligence who possesses a great deal of mechanical ability.

SCHLEIER, LOUIS M. *Problems in the Training of Certain Special-Class Teachers.* New York: Teachers College, Columbia University, 1931. 138 pp.

Reports existing state laws concerning the qualifications of teachers of mentally and physically handicapped children and courses offered in colleges for such teachers. Gives statistics for all states.

SCHMIDT, BERNARDINE. "Changes in Personal, Social, and Intellectual Behavior of Children Originally Classified as Feeble-minded," *Psychological Monographs*, 60, No. 5, 1946. 144 pp.

Evaluated the achievement and growth of 254 mentally deficient children during a period of eight years. Found sensational changes in I.Q. and in tests of personality and social maturity.

STEVENS, G. D. "Suggested Criteria for the Selection of Items for a Cumulative Case Study Record for the Mentally Retarded," *Journal of Educational Research*, 39 (November, 1945), 201–09.

The author suggests criteria for selection of items for a cumulative case study and gives a review of the literature in this field.

TALLMAN, FRANK F. "The School Adjustment of the Mentally Retarded," *American Journal of Mental Deficiency*, 45 (October, 1940), 238–42.

Procedures used in the treatment of behavior problems by the conference method.

WALLIN, JOHN E. *Studies of Mental Defects and Handicaps.* Oxford, Ohio: Miami University (Miami University Bulletin, Series 22, No. 5, January, 1924). 177 pp.

A group of reprints of articles concerning problems of diagnosis, psychology, causation, treatment, education, and allied subjects in their relation to mental handicaps.

WARD, LEWIS B. "Motor Conflicts and Transfer of Training in High Grade Mental Defectives," *Proceedings and Addresses of the Sixtieth Annual Session of the American Association on Mental Deficiency*, 41, No. 2 (1936), 50–59.

An attempt to determine the amount of bilateral transfer of training in maze learning of twenty-four mentally defective subjects who were divided into three groups on the basis of handedness.

WERNER, HEINZ. "Development of Visuo-Motor Performance on the Marble-Board Test in Mentally Retarded Children," *Journal of Genetic Psychology*, 64 (June, 1944), 269–79.

The implications of the marble-board test in its uses with mentally retarded children.

OTHER BIBLIOGRAPHIES

MARTENS, ELISE H. "An Annotated Bibliography on the Education and Psychology of Exceptional Children," Washington: U.S. Office of Education (Pamphlet No. 23), July, 1931. 48 pp.

An annotated bibliography up to 1931 for all types of exceptional children including the mentally handicapped.

MARTENS, ELISE H. "Annotated Bibliography on the Education and Psychology of Exceptional Children," Washington: U.S. Office of Education (Pamphlet No. 71), 1937. 42 pp.

An annotated bibliography up to 1937 for all types of exceptional children including the mentally handicapped.

(Supplements to Pamphlet No. 71 are issued from time to time by the U.S. Office of Education, Washington, D.C.)

"Selected References from the Literature on Exceptional Children," *Elementary School Journal*. (In the May issues since 1936.)

Author Index
to
Selected Annotated Bibliography

Index

A and B factor, 21
Abel, J. M., adjustment, 358; personality, 324
Absurdities, auditory, 168–169; use, 168
Acceptance, 122
Achievement, academic, 179; arithmetic, 277, 287; relation to behavior, 330
Achievement tests, 48–50; items used, 49
Activity program, 205; advantages, 291
Adams, F., 275
Adams, H. W., 281, 299
Addition, 293
Ade, L. K., 130
Adjustment, definition, 323; of morons, 5; postschool, 227; school's responsibility, 243; social, 232, 327; to personal environment, 189–190; to physical environment, 187–188; to school, 121, 211; to social environment, 188; under group autonomy, 351–355; value of preschool program, 136; vocational factors, 231–232
Administration, attitudes, 121; secondary schools, 200–202
Adult education, 233
Akin, B. U., 320
Alexander, W. P., 96
Alexander Performance Tests, referred to, 97, 100
Amentia, primary, 16; secondary, 16
Anger, teachers', 333
Appearance, 160
Arithmetic, 92; abilities as compared to normal, 278–279; achievement, 277, 287; application to real-life situations, 296; basic skills, 279;

curriculum needed, 278; development of concepts, 283–284, 290–291; development of skills, 282–284; disabilities, 279–280; fractional parts, 285; in a unit of experience, 195, 295; intermediate class, 184, 292; needs, 281–283; number recognition, 167; practice, 289, 294; primary class, 164–165, 290; principles of teaching, 285–290; quantitative thinking, 167; secondary class, 295–296; skills applied, 284; teaching methods, 280; teaching skills, 292–295; time concepts, 280; units of measurement, 284; use of classroom activities; vocabulary, 165, 279, 282–283
Art, 99; correlation with other subjects, 90–91
Arthur Point Scale of Performance Tests, 44
Arts and crafts, as an end in themselves, 302; as an introduction to practical arts, 308; choice of project, 306; co-ordination with other subjects, 302; emphasis on end product, 302–303; improvement of attitudes, 306–307; materials, 307; method of expression, 303; principles of teaching, 303–307; to improve motor co-ordination, 305–306; types of programs, 301–303; value, 305–306
Attention, training, 88–89
Attitudes, 174–175; development, 188, 307; improvement using arts and crafts, 306–307; of administrators, 121; toward reading, 270; training, 119

Muscular training, 76, 173
Music, 195
Myerson, A., 27

Nathan, J. M., 228, 250
Nativist, 29, 71
N.E.A. Research Division, 200
Nebraska Test of Learning Aptitude for Young Deaf Children, 44
Needlecraft, 313
Newkirk, L. V., 321
New York City, occupational education, 103; rehabilitation program, 237–238; special classes, 123
Number, concepts, 283–284, 290; recognition, 166; skills, 284
Nutrition, 159

Object-assembly type test, 44
Objectives, education, 115, 116–121; primary class, 157–158; social adequacy, 119
Occupational adequacy, 118–119; adjustment, 104; competence, 10; status, 101; training, 118–119
Occupational education, 101–105, 114, 207–208; areas developed, 103–104; correlation with subject matter, 105; objectives, 102
Occupations, 228; boys, 229–230; girls, 229–230
Offerman, E. M., 35
Olson, W. C., 61–62, 64
Ontario School Ability Test, 44
Oral, reading, 267; use of description, 163
Orata, P. T., 321
Ordinal numbers, 299
Orthophrenic School, 78
Oseretsky Test, 55
Otis Quick-Scoring Mental Ability Tests, 47–48

Parent education, preschool class, 151–152; primary class, 160–161
Parent cooperation, 127
Parent-teacher meetings, 161
Paris schools, 41, 75
Patterson, R. M., 137, 154, 176–177

Pediatricians, referrals to preschool, 137
Pennsylvania Training School, 75
Perception, disturbances, 107; training, 110
Performance intelligence tests, 43–44
Perry, H. A., 20, 35
Perseveration, 107, 111
Personal adequacy, 120
Personal environment, 189–190
Personal guidance, 218–220
Personal history, 38
Personality, characteristics, 324; tests, 51–53
Phenylpyruvic amentia, 28
Philosophy, democratic, 116
Phonics, 266–267
Physical, environment, 187–188; health, 142–143, 208–209; training, 89–90
Physiological disturbances, 6
Physiological method, 75–76
Pictures, use of, 163
Placement, job, 245; school practices, 135
Positive vs. negative statements, 331
Postschool youth, adjustment, 227; chronological age, 129; follow-up, 248; further training, 247; job placement, 246–247
Postschool program, need, 226; school's position, 244; school-work-experience, 245–246
Potts, J. H., 239
Power tests, achievement, 49; intelligence, 45
Practical arts, 308
Prereading activities, 259
Preschool children, chronological age, 137; clinical education, 152–153; diagnosis, 138–139; emotional health, 141–142; imagination and creative expression, 145–147; intellectual development, 149–151; motor development, 148–149; parent education, 151–152; physical health, 142–143; selection, 137–138; self-help, 143–144; social development, 147–148